Simon Episcopius' Doctrine of Original Sin

american
university
studies

Series VII
Theology and Religion

Vol. 240

PETER LANG
New York • Washington, D.C./Baltimore • Bern
Frankfurt am Main • Berlin • Brussels • Vienna • Oxford

Mark A. Ellis

Simon Episcopius' Doctrine of Original Sin

PETER LANG
New York • Washington, D.C./Baltimore • Bern
Frankfurt am Main • Berlin • Brussels • Vienna • Oxford

Library of Congress Cataloging-in-Publication Data

Ellis, Mark A.
Simon Episcopius' doctrine of original sin / Mark A. Ellis.
p. cm. — (American university studies. VII, Theology and religion; v. 240)
Includes bibliographical references (p.   ) and index.
1. Sin, Original—History of doctrines. 2. Episcopius, Simon, 1583–1643.
3. Arminius, Jacobus, 1560–1609. I. Title. II. American university studies.
Series VII, Theology and religion; v. 240.
BT720.E37   233'.14'092—dc22   2005024265
ISBN 978-0-8204-8109-8
ISSN 0740-0446

Bibliographic information published by **Die Deutsche Bibliothek**.
Die Deutsche Bibliothek lists this publication in the "Deutsche
Nationalbibliografie"; detailed bibliographic data is available
on the Internet at http://dnb.ddb.de/.

The paper in this book meets the guidelines for permanence and durability
of the Committee on Production Guidelines for Book Longevity
of the Council of Library Resources.

Dedicated to
Brian G. Armstrong:
a gentleman, scholar and friend

Table of Contents

ACKNOWLEDGMENTS ix

LIST OF ABBREVIATIONS xi

INTRODUCTION 1

The Problem 1

Thesis 4

Method 5

Episcopius in Contemporary Scholarship 6

Arminianism and Reformed Scholasticism 7

Conclusion 13

**CHAPTER 1. ARMINIUS AND EPISCOPIUS IN
HISTORICAL CONTEXT** 25

Precursory Trends and Events: Dutch Religion, Culture and
Politics 25

The Arminian Phase of the Controversy 30

Episcopius' Life and Work 32

Summary, Observations and Conclusions 40

CHAPTER 2. ARMINIUS' DOCTRINE OF ORIGINAL SIN 63

Adam as Created in the Image of God 64

The Fall of Adam 68

Arminius' Doctrine of Grace 79

Conclusion 85

CHAPTER 3. EPISCOPIUS ON ORIGINAL SIN UP TO 1621... 101

    Comparison of Arminius' and Episcopius' Public
    Disputations 102

    Comparison of Arminius' and Episcopius' Private
    Disputations 111

    The *Confessio Remonstrantium* 121

    Parallels Between Episcopius and the Greek Fathers.................... 128

    Summary 129

**CHAPTER 4. ORIGINAL SIN IN THE *INSTITUTES
THEOLOGICÆ*** 149

    Episcopius' First Explication of Original Sin 150

    The Creation of Adam.. 153

    Sin and Redemption 157

    Conclusion.. 166

SUMMARY AND CONCLUSIONS 177

    Summary of Arminius' Doctrine of Original Sin 178

    The Development of Episcopius' Doctrine of Original Sin 179

    Episcopius As Heir of Arminius' Theology................................ 182

    A Comparison of Theological Methods.. 183

BIBLIOGRAPHY 187

INDEX 213

Acknowledgments

I am grateful for the opportunity to acknowledge those who contributed in various ways to the writing of this monograph. First and foremost was the faculty of Dallas Theological Seminary, especially Drs. Zane Hodges, Lanier Burns, and my dissertation supervisor, Stephen Spencer. Aside from the seminary faculty, Dr. Brian Armstrong made himself available to discuss the evolution of Reformed theology. He and his wife Carol very graciously received me into their home so that I could have extended conversations with Dr. Armstrong.

This monograph required extensive use of original sources obtained through the assistance of Bob and Emily De Graaf and Ton Bolland of the Netherlands, and David McLoughlin of the United States. Gilbert Vanblarcum, Ronny Saevering and the staff of the *Fundashon pa Planifikashon di Ydioma*, Bob Vermeulen, Constantine Maria Marijs and Penny Van Waegeningh assisted in translating Episcopius' writings. Vanessa Toré and the Chamber of Commerce of Curaçao facilitated travel to the island and locating translators.

I prepared this monograph for publication while my wife Diane and I were on furlough from missionary service in Brazil. We were immensely grateful to Dr. David Dockery and Union University for providing stateside housing during that time, and especially appreciative of the warm hospitality of Todd Bradey and Suzanne Mosley in Student Ministries and the collegiality of Dr. George Guthrie and the other fine members of the Biblical Studies department.

Finally, I am thankful to Dr. Heidi Burns and Peter Lang Publishing for their willingness to accept this project.

Mark A. Ellis
Jackson, TN
June, 2005

Abbreviations

CR	*Corpus Reformatorum*
Conf. Rem.	*Confessio Remonstrantium*
Disp. Priv.	"Disputationes Privatæ," in *Opera Theologica* (Arminius)
Disp. Pub.	"Disputationes Publicæ," in *Opera Theologica* (Arminius)
DTT	*Disputationes Theologicas Tripartites*
IT	*Institutiones Theologicæ*, in *Opera Theologica* (Episcopius)
OT	*Opera Theologica* (Arminius)
OTE	*Opera Theologica* (Episcopius)
OTPA	*Opera Theologica, Pars Altera* (Episcopius)
OVO	*Oratio De Vita et Obitu Reverendi et Clarissimi Viri D. Iacobi Arminii*
Priv. Disp.	Private Disputation(s), in *Works of Arminius* (Nichols)
Pub. Disp.	Public Disputation(s) in *Works of Arminius* (Nichols)
WA	*Works of Arminius* (Nichols)
WrA	*Writings of Arminius* (Nichols and Bagnalls)

Introduction

The Problem

This monograph compares the theology of original sin of Jacobus Arminius (1560–1609) and that of his pupil and successor, Simon Episcopius (1583–1643) for the purpose of measuring changes in content and method. Just as scholars have debated the fidelity of Calvinists to the theology of John Calvin (1509–64),[1] others have raised the same question concerning Arminians and the theology of Arminius. Several scholarly works have already established that such divergences did occur. MacCulloch contrasted Arminius with his immediate followers.[2] Tyacke examined the relation between Arminius and the English Arminians of seventeenth-century England.[3] Nuttall considered Arminianism in America, and Meeuwsen compared Arminius with Methodism as a whole.[4] While these studies treated developments outside the original Remonstrant[5] movement, Hicks demonstrated fundamental changes between Arminius' theology and that of the Remonstrant leader Philip van Limborch (1633–1712). Van Limborch was a Remonstrant preacher, professor of theology and author of an important systematic theology written nearly a century after Arminius' death.[6] Although many have presumed that later Arminians/Remonstrants differed from Arminius, Hicks was one of the first to demonstrate such distinctions through an extensive comparison of Arminius and van Limborch, based on their theology of grace.

The original movement's emphasis on liberty of conscience and religious toleration, in opposition to Calvinist creedalism, left it open to divergent developments to the point that it is difficult to define "Arminianism." Carl Bangs, one of the foremost twentieth-century scholars of Arminianism, offered three suggestions. "Arminianism" can refer to (1) the theology that originated with the founder of the movement, Jacobus Arminius, (2) any protest against Calvinism, or (3) any "rallying point for dissent under the banner of toleration."[7] Bangs concluded that the lack of careful distinction among researchers has resulted in confused thinking and discussions about the subject. Two extremes complicate its definition even further. On the one hand are those who use the term pejoratively, lumping it together with Pelagianism,[8] Semi-Pelagianism[9] or Socinianism,[10] appellatives which Calvinists have employed as synonyms for Arminianism from the beginning of the controversy.[11] On the other are large numbers of groups that consider themselves Arminian because of their opposition to unconditional predestination and/or perseverance.[12]

Hicks enriched his study by documenting three common opinions regarding the relationship between Arminius and those are consciously within the Arminian theological tradition.[13] The first includes those who equate Arminius with the theology of later Arminians, believing their theologies are fundamentally identical. This includes non-Arminians who assume both Arminius and his followers were Pelagian, Semi-Pelagian or Socinian. Second, under "logical entailment," Hicks identified those who "recognize some important differences between Arminianism and Remonstrantism, but argue that there is a logical connection between the two."[14] Arminius may have been a Reformed theologian, but he initiated ideas that led the Remonstrants to "unorthodox" conclusions. Hicks offered Charles Hodge as an example of those who place the Remonstrants in this category.[15] A. H. Haentjens, a Remonstrant theologian and historian, though not concurring that Remonstrant "conclusions" were unorthodox, would have agreed that the Remonstrants worked out the logical conclusions of Arminius' theology. He went even further, however, and identified Simon Episcopius as the principle source for these developments. He believed that "(i)n Episcopius is Arminius tot volle ontwilleling gekomen," and "dat de consequenties van Arminius' opvatting ook wetenschappelijk konden worden aanvaard."[16] Hicks' final category included those who have posited a "radical distinction" between Arminius and the Remonstrants.[17] He included himself here, and wrote, "the theology of Arminius is that of the Reformers while that of Limborch belongs to the Semi-Pelagianism of Tridentine Catholicism or even the Pelagian tendencies of Socinianism."[18] He concluded that, unlike his successors, Arminius was a Reformed theologian. Hicks was not the first to attempt to restore Arminius to the ranks of Reformed Orthodoxy.[19] Certainly, Arminius viewed himself as a Reformed pastor within a reformation tradition that was wider than Calvin and polymorphic on the doctrine of predestination.[20]

There are, however, problems with his analysis. First is his use of the term "Remonstrant" as if it referred to a unified theological position. While the *Remonstrantsche Broederschap* was not formally organized until after the national Synod of Dort (1618–1619),[21] many who took part in the Remonstrant protest had not been converted by Arminius away from Calvinism. Rather, they reflected a strong pre-Calvinist reformed movement of various theological sources (such as Philip Melanchthon [1497–1560] and Heinrich Bullinger [1504–75]) for whom Arminius served as a rallying point.[22] From the beginning the Remonstrants were marked by the Dutch spirit of toleration[23] and theological divergence.[24] One may raise a second challenge to Hicks' conclusion that the Remonstrants were "radically distinct" by comparing Arminius' declarations with the Remonstrance of 1610 on perseverance and eternal security. Although Arminius never publically repudiated perseverance, his discussions in "Declaration of Sentiments"[25] and his defense of the hypothetical possibility of falling from grace in "Examination of Perkins' Pamphlet"[26] demonstrate that it was no great leap to move from Arminius' hesitations in 1609 to Remonstrant denials in 1610. The Remonstrant denial of perseverance and eternal security, made just one year after Arminius' death, was at least a logical entailment of Arminius' theology, and not a radical distinction.

Finally, one may question Hicks' attribution of the change between Arminius and the Remonstrants to the Enlightenment. Hicks thought that these differences were not the result of some "logical framework inherent in Arminius' system," but "the principles and spirit of the Enlightenment impinging upon Arminius' original thinking."[27] While René Descartes (1596–1650) and Benedict Spinoza (1632–77), the progenitors of the Enlightenment, were friends with important Remonstrant leaders[28] and may have influenced van Limborch and Jean Le Clerc (1657–1736),[29] they were too late to have affected early Remonstrant theologians such as Johannes Wtenbogaert (1557–1644), Nicholas Grevinchoven (d. 1632) and most importantly, Simon Episcopius.[30] Without question, the Enlightenment occurred too late to have precipitated such an alteration between Arminius and Episcopius. This monograph will attempt to show that differences between Arminius and the later Episcopius can be more attributed both to changes in theological method and other more personal influences.

Several factors indicate Episcopius as an important, if not better, basis of comparison for measuring change in Arminian theology. Not only did he teach in Arminius' place at the University of Leiden, lead the Remonstrants at the Synod of Dort and singularly guarantee the survival of the movement, we may rightly regard him as the theological genius behind Arminianism. He developed and systematized ideas which Arminius was tentatively exploring before his death and then perpetuated his theology by founding the Remonstrant seminary and teaching the next generation of pastors and teachers.[31] Both friends and foes considered him the legitimate heir and champion of Arminius' theology. Most importantly, this book will demonstrate that many of the changes evident in later Remonstrant theologues had their origin in Episcopius, not in the Enlightenment. Finally, a tantalizing question regarding Episcopius' importance comes from the journals of John Wesley, perhaps the single most important promulgator of Arminian theology. While Wesley did not read Arminius until later in life, his journal recorded that he came across Episcopius' *Opera Theologica* while a student at Oxford and was so captivated by it that he read it through. I leave to Wesleyan scholars to determine the degree to which Wesley was Arminian or "Episcopian."

Thesis

The thesis of this monograph is that there are significant differences between Arminius and later Arminians which originated under the theological leadership of Simon Episcopius. These differences, however, are the result of Episcopius' legitimate developments of Arminius' theology and method. Hicks assumed a serious disjunction between Arminius and Episcopius, but as it was not his purpose, he did not support this assertion in his dissertation.[32] The purpose of this monograph is to test this hypothesis. We will see that at first there were broad parallels between Arminius and the early Episcopius, that the theology he taught at Leiden was a continuation and development of Arminius' thought and theological method. He borrowed theological terms, constructs, outlines and even illustrations from Arminius. However, even at this early stage we can detect Episcopius going beyond Arminius in both his methods and conclusions.

These developments expanded as Episcopius grew older and more secure in both his thought and status. His theology became increasingly independent of Arminius. I argue that Episcopius was a legitimate heir of Arminius' theology, no less a disciple of Arminius than Theodore Beza (1519–1605) was of Calvin.[33] His conclusions were sometimes unique and many times went beyond his teacher, but not because he rejected Arminius. Rather, these changes can be attributed to two factors: the working out of the ramifications of Arminius' theology and method, joined with the opportunity to do so once he was free from confessional restraints.

Method

I defend the thesis through a comparison of Arminius' and Episcopius' ideas of original sin and its attendant doctrines. Along with predestination and grace, Arminius' enemies were convinced he had also defected from an "orthodox" understanding of original sin. Both Pelagius and Augustine included original sin as an integral part of their discussions concerning grace, predestination and free will, and many Calvinists considered anything less than Augustine's ideas on original sin as necessarily leading to Pelagianism. Both Arminius and Episcopius responded to Calvin and Beza's writings on original sin, because they believed Genevan predestination necessarily implied that God was the author of sin, a conclusion which Beza's supralapsarian schema seemed to confirm. Finally, like many evangelicals today, Calvinists in Arminius' day considered original sin as a "benchmark" of orthodoxy. Thus, it is neither an irrelevant nor an insignificant object for study. Western theologians since Augustine have discussed the concept of original sin as part of a larger network of ideas. These include Adam's pre-fallen state, the causes, events and actors involved in the fall, its effects, and how the fall necessitates grace. Arminius and Episcopius followed these same lines of discussion and inclusion of these ideas helps develop comparisons between their theologies.

The monograph is divided into five chapters. Chapter 1 traces the origins of the Arminian conflict in the Netherlands, Arminius' involvement and the development of Episcopius as both Arminius' successor and leader of the Remonstrants. Chapter 2 is an exposition of Arminius' thought on original sin and its attendant doctrines, with comparisons with John Calvin and Franciscus Junius (†1602). I have included Junius because he was responsible for the development of scholasticism at the University at Leiden and was a pioneer in prolegomena and theological method.[34] Chapters 3 and 4 analyze Episcopius' thought on original sin. Chapter three presents his early views as expressed in his public and private disputations while at the University of Leiden (1612–1618),[35] and in the Remonstrant confession,[36] with special reference to corresponding sections in Arminius' writings. Chapter 4 is most important for the monograph, for it presents Episcopius' mature thought on the subject. The source for this information is his lectures at the

Remonstrant Seminary (1628–1642).[37] It is here we will observe his greatest deviation from Arminius and must answer the questions raised by Hicks concerning how Episcopius' thought relates to that of his master. Because Episcopius was both a prolific and consistent theologian, it will be possible to synthesize and contrast clear descriptions of what he believed during each period. We will also be able to identify the degree to which he maintained Arminius' theology, and see close correlations with the theology of early Greek theologians. The monograph concludes with a summary of the relation between Arminius' and Episcopius' theologies.

Episcopius in Contemporary Scholarship

The initial barrier to studying Episcopius is the difficulty of obtaining primary sources. Although two smaller works were translated into English in the seventeenth century, there are no modern editions of his books, and the originals are scarce.[38]

Regarding secondary analyses, the most important is Haentjens' doctoral monograph, *Simon Episcopius als Apologeet van het Remonstrantisme in zijn leven en werken geschestst*. Although biographical, it included substantial analysis of Episcopius' theology from a sympathetic perspective. It is also an essential source of information on Episcopius' life and work, drawing from Episcopius' many letters that are either unavailable outside the Netherlands or have since been lost.

John Platt provides the most extended contemporary treatment of Episcopius' theology and relationship to Arminius.[39] Platt's treatment of the Remonstrants is positive and fair. He documented Jacobus Triglandius' (1583–1654) misrepresentations of Episcopius' thought, criticized the Synod's substitution of Remonstrant statements with Pelagian verbiage and detailed Episcopius' interactions with the irascible Festus Hommius.[40] He also described the quandry that confronted the Remonstrants. If they denied knowing God apart from special revelation, the Contra-Remonstrants accused them of Socinianism. If they affirmed the contrary, they were Pelagian.[41] Episcopius first appears in Platt's analysis when the latter noted parallels between their disputations. Platt also provides an extended analysis of both Episcopius' earlier and later thoughts on the ability of human reason to perceive God, and suggestions for sources he may have used in forming his opinions.[42]

Arminianism and
Reformed Scholasticism

An important part of this monograph is that both Arminius and Episcopius represent not just a change in theological content but also in theological method, namely, they represent a centuries-old struggle between scholasticism and humanism. The definitions of each movement and their relationship to one another have been a source of discussion among interested scholars. To what degree were they distinguishable movements, and when considering Reformed theologians of the late sixteenth and seventeenth centuries, can we divide them into "two tight camps, one scholastic and the other marked by humanism"?[43] This confusion has led some modern scholars to deny that scholasticism and humanism were antithetical at all, a modern disavowal that would have surprised Luther, Melanchthon[44] and Calvin. Certainly it was clear to Episcopius that his method of doing theology contrasted with the scholastic theology of his opponents, a distinction to which he would appeal repeatedly throughout his theological works. Although a brief history of these two movements runs the risk of overgeneralization, some information is necessary to appreciate the importance of theological method when examining Episcopius' theology.

The Origins of Scholasticism

Scholasticism as a method of teaching and doing Christian theology developed in European universities at the end of the eleventh century, but its origins predated these developments. The content of Christian scholastic theology arose out of a synthesis of three sources: the philosophy of neo-Platonism, the theology of Augustine and the efforts of Boethius (c. 470–524)[45] to preserve the classical heritage of Aristotle and Plato.[46] Marenbon demonstrated that numerous perennial questions in Christian theology, such as the perception of God as the unmoved mover, the question of future contingents, foreknowledge and free will, the nature of the human soul, the interplay between the intellect and the will, and whether necessity can be reconciled with free will, originated from Platonic or Aristotelian philosophy.[47] Initially the scholastic task was merely explanatory. Anselm of Canterbury (1033–1109), the founder of medieval scholasticism, described the role of philosophy as "faith seeking understanding" (*fides quaerens intellectum*). He used classical philosophy not to expand theology but explain what his Augustinian faith had already dictated. By the fourteenth-century, however, scholastics were asking whether logic could not also function deductively in order to enlarge theology beyond Scripture. While Richard of St. Victor (1121–1173) and Peter of Aureoli (1280–1322) had affirmed the traditional position, Gregory of Rimini (c. 1300–1358) pressed for the latter.[48] Brown summarized Gregory's opinion: "The theologian in his proper role sees that these truths demanded by intellectual reflection on the faith must be assented to with the same force of assent as the truths found in Sacred Scripture and that they must be admitted as unhesitatingly as the principles or premises found formally in Scripture itself."[49] We may see the results of this approach in Peter of Ailly's (1350–1420) speculations on divine omnipotence. He concluded that, although God cannot deceive by his ordinary power (*potentia ordinata*), he could deceive by right of his absolute power (*potentia absoluta*).[50]

The Resurgence of Humanism

While scholasticism dominated the intellectual life of western Christianity, an alternative approach to learning which emphasized the liberal arts and rhetoric, as opposed to philosophy and dialectics, survived the fall of the Roman empire in schools located in northern and central Italy.[51] In the late thirteenth and early fourteenth centuries, these schools produced scholars who turned their attentions to classical writers, especially Ovid, Cicero and Virgil.[52] They also revived the arts of rhetoric: the *ars dictaminis*, the art of writing well, and *ars arengandi*, the ability to argue well.[53] These men were not drawn from any one tradition, for as Kristeller explained, "Renaissance humanism as such was not Christian or pagan, Catholic or Protestant, scientific or unscientific, Platonist or Aristotelian, Stoic or Epicurean, optimistic or pessimistic, active or contemplative, although it is easy to find these attitudes, and for many others, a certain number of humanists who favored them. What they all have in common is something else: a scholarly, literary and educational ideal based on the study of classical antiquity."[54]

Three general tendencies of humanists scholars become important when we consider the influence of humanism on Arminian theology. The first is the exegetical method that resulted from their study of the classics. While scholastics worked from compendiums and textual glosses in Latin, the humanist heritage was a revival of the study of classical texts in their original languages, Latin, Greek and Hebrew. Their goal of understanding the text, as opposed to concerns for correct theology, led them to develop what would become the historical, grammatical, contextual method of interpretation of Calvin. Humanist hermeneutics was a decided rejection of the *grammatica speculativa*, "founded on theoretical distinction between various 'modes of signification,' which in turn depended on the Aristotelian scheme of four causes. The humanists shifted to a common sense and semantic approach, however, which rejected the artificialities of scholastic analysis…. In general, humanist grammar represented a shift from the formal and structural approach of the scholastic 'modalists' to a more semantic, historical and relativist conception."[55] This "common sense approach" insisted that a scholar did not need the artificial logic of Aristotelian categories or syllogisms in order to understand the text. It required just the native ability to think clearly ("natural reasoning" or common sense), and a good dictionary. Melanchthon and Calvin were famous for their skill in humanist hermeneutic.[56]

A second characteristic of humanists was their high estimation of the dignity of man. Kristeller commented, "We cannot escape the impression that after the beginnings of Renaissance humanism, the emphasis on man and his dignity becomes more persistent, more exclusive and ultimately more systematic than it had even been during the preceding centuries and even during classical antiquity."[57] Humanists used the word *humanitas* to summarize the marks of human dignity, chief of which was science of living well. The possessor of *humanitas* was not a sedentary and isolated philosopher, but an active participant in life. This led humanists to make strong declarations of human freedom and dignity and affirmations of practical aspects of learning.[58] Both were hallmarks of Arminius' and Episcopius' theology.

A third development concerns the relationship between humanism and scholastic philosophy. There was no intrinsic contradiction between scholasticism and humanism, between their methods of dialectics and rhetoric. Aristotle himself was something of a champion of the rhetorical arts.[59] Nevertheless, there is more than enough evidence that humanists, especially those of northern Europe, despised traditional scholastics for their inelegant Latin, their quiddities and curiosities, and their excessive distinctions and divisions.[60]

Reformed Scholasticism in Contemporary Scholarship

How the scholastic system of teaching and doing theology, so criticized and rejected by the early reformers, made its way back into the Reformation has been the subject of extended debate.[61] Two broad positions have emerged. On the one hand are those who find significant change between Calvin and Beza et al., and attribute these changes to the reestablishment of scholasticism and Aristotelian logic as a method of teaching and doing theology.[62] There is often implied criticism in this attribution. Armstrong, representative of this position, suggested a four-part description of this reapproachment:

> (1) Primarily, it will have reference to that theological approach which asserts religious truth on the basis of deductive ratiocination from given assumptions or principles. This provides a logically coherent and defensible system of belief, which generally takes the form of syllogistic reasoning. It seems invariably based upon an Aristotelian philosophical commitment and so related to medieval scholasticism. (2) The term will refer to the employment of reason in religious matters, to that reason has at least equal standing with faith in theology. (3) It will comprehend the sentiment that the scriptural record contains a unified, rationally comprehensible account. It may be used as a measuring stick to determine one's orthodoxy. (4) It will include a pronounced interest in metaphysical matters, and abstract, speculative thought, particularly with reference to the doctrine of God. The distinctive Protestant position is made to rest on a speculative formulation of the will of God.[63]

Similar conclusions regarding the philosophical impact of scholasticism upon Dutch Reformed theology were drawn by the Dutch Reformed scholar B. J. van der Walt. Van der Walt made a close examination of the "philosophical impurities" and "alien, unscriptural philosophical influences" in the *Synopsis Purioris Theologiae* (*SPT*),[64] a summary of Dortian theology which served as the textbook for Reformed pastors in the Netherlands until the end of the seventeenth century.[65] He concluded,

> I trust that it is also clear that such a theology cannot do justice to the Word of God. There are many examples of how the writers of the *SPT* play at ventriloquism with Biblical texts in order to justify their philosophical viewpoints....The *SPT* therefore does not succeed in being pure—that is, if one should use pure in the sense of being in accordance with the Word of God. The theology of the *SPT* is not radically biblical, because the philosophy underlying it is not pure. A scripturally bound philosophy is able to reveal many unbiblical points of departure in the theological system of the *SPT*.[66]

The *Synopsis Purioris Theologiae* is germain to our discussions, because its authors (the theological faculty at Leiden) were in direct debate with Episcopius.[67]

Richard Muller has led the movement to blunt such criticisms and reestablish Reformed orthodox scholasticism both as a legitimate development of Calvin's theology and as a means of doing theology.[68] Muller defends the Reformed scholasticism as an important advance in teaching theology. He defines scholasticism as "the formal theology of the systems and doctrinal compendia developed out of the classroom experience of the academies and universities," "a methodological approach to theological system which achieves precision of definition through the analysis of doctrinal loci in terms of scripture, previous definition (the tradition), and contemporary debate. Even when organized synthetically, such systems tend to concentrate on the analysis of particulars and for the sake of their educational and polemical goal seek to establish minute distinctions and precise determinations of doctrine."[69] Muller gave two reasons for this reapproachment by the Reformed, the demands of teaching efficiently in an academic setting and thwarting the scholastic attacks of the Roman Catholic theologians.[70]

John Bray charted a middle course between Armstrong and Muller in his analysis of Calvin and Beza's doctrine of predestination.[71] While Stephen Spencer wrote approvingly of Bray's milder, more "nuanced" conclusions,[72] those who agree with Armstrong's criticisms could point to Bray's definitive agreement with and augmentation of Armstrong's paradigm.[73] Bray concluded that Beza met five of the six scholastic tendencies Bray enumerated, including the return to Aristotelianism and the use of speculative and rationalist methods.[74]

We can verify that Dutch Reformed Scholastics were sensitive to Remonstrant accusations of excessive speculation, innovation, "bogging down" on small points and minutiae from Voetius' defense against such criticisms.[75] From the beginning of the Arminian crisis until recently, Arminius was viewed as a theologian in revolt against Reformed scholasticism in favor of a return to the earlier humanist methods of Melanchthon, Calvin, and especially Desiderius Erasmus (c. 1466–1536).[76] Certainly Arminius viewed himself in this same way. Although he was very adept at operating within the norms of the scholastic environment at Leiden, there is clear evidence that he was attempting to sway his students toward the more biblical and less philosophical method of theology of John Calvin.[77]

Muller has challenged this perspective.[78] He extensively examined Arminius' theology and concluded he was a scholastic par excellance. Even before Muller, John Platt arrived at similar conclusions through an examination of the origins of Arminius' arguments for the existence of God.[79] He thought he found them in Conrad Vorstius, though not without significant and intelligent dialogue with Aquinas.[80] He, too, commented on Arminius' scholastic abilities. He concluded that in Arminius "the use of scholastic arguments for the existence of God has reached a high level of sophistication within Dutch reformed circles for such a discussion to be encouraged among his students by a professor of theology."[81]

Muller is certainly correct that it is futile to argue Arminius was not a representative of Reformed scholasticism.[82] Arminius' opponents never questioned his scholastic or academic skills. His abilities as student and scholar elicited an invitation from Johannes Jacobus Grynaeus (1540–1617) to teach at Berne and led to his appointment to the faculty at Leiden. Like Beza, he could be scholastic in his method of presenting theology in the academy and humanist in his preaching.[83] Concerning his use of logic, like many Reformed theologians of his time, he was a noted Ramist.[84] His commitment to Ramism resulted in his leaving the academy at Geneva, because in spite of Beza's efforts to institutionalize Aristotelianism,[85] Arminius gave private lessons in Ramist logic. Still, he consistently used Aristotelian causality in his disputations and incorporated other theological insights from medieval thinkers into the content of his lectures. His "Conference with Junius" and "Examination of Perkin's Pamphlet" demonstrate his skill in the use of the syllogism and the identification of logical errors as classified by Aristotle.[86] But we still must ask whether there is a basis for the assertion that Arminius was moving away from the rationalist tendencies of Reformed scholastics such as Junius.

Questions of method become even more important when we consider Episcopius. While Episcopius was a creative, original thinker and communicator, his earlier writings show marked dependence upon Arminius in method and content. He adopted Arminius' scholastic approach and used his arguments and illustrations. However, even at this early stage we will see Episcopius moving even further from scholastic methods than Arminius. Episcopius was not just turning from dialectical forms and methods of teaching and doing theology. He deliberately and decisively rejected them in order to return to an earlier, rhetorical method more closely aligned with Erasmus and Calvin. Returning to the three general tendencies of humanist scholars which were listed above, we find them well represented throughout Episcopius' works. We will see that he built his theology on exegesis and repudiated theological speculations, even those of Arminius. He emphasized the dignity of fallen humans, and insisted on theology as an entirely practical science. There is no lack of criticism of the scholastic method and theology of his opponents. This is not to deny that, just as we find occasional indications of scholastic method in the humanist rhetoric of Calvin,[87] Episcopius occasionally used scholastic methods, but normally only when refuting the scholastic argumentation of the Dortian Reformed. Especially in his later writings, he employed a combination of intense analysis of biblical texts with a humanist confidence in his ability to reason, joined with a powerful mastery of verbal images and illustrations. Reason, exegesis and illustration are Episcopius' methodological troika.

Conclusion

Just as modern scholars have raised questions concerning the relationship between the thought of Calvin and later Calvinists, such doubts have also surfaced with respect to Arminius and the Arminians. While others have shown differences exist between Arminius and later generations, the thesis of this monograph is that many of these changes have their origin in the first generation of Remonstrants, specifically in Simon Episcopius. Largely overlooked by modern scholarship, Episcopius was a central figure in the development, if not the survival, of the Arminian tradition. The thesis of this monograph is that we can discern two stages in Episcopius' theology. We can observe the first stage in his disputations as professor of theology at Leiden and in the *Confessio Remonstrantium*. In this early period, although he maintained much of the theology and methodology he received from Arminius, we can already note modifications in content and method. We will see early deviations from Arminius' theology, but we will also be able to understand how these resulted from Episcopius' application of Arminius' own theological conclusions and methods. As he grew older, he continued to develop his theology along the trajectory established by Arminius. Even though Episcopius went far beyond Arminius' conclusions, we will see how the latter's mature theology was the logical entailment of the former's thought.

Notes

[1] The question concerning the relationship between Calvin and later Reformed theologians has come to be referred to as "Calvin against the Calvinists," a name taken from an article by Basil Hall (Basil Hall, "Calvin Against the Calvinists," in *John Calvin: A Collection of Distinguished Essays*, ed. Gervase Duffield (Grand Rapids: Eerdmans, 1966), 19–37). The question of differences between Calvin and later "Calvinists" arose early in Reformed theology through the Amyraldian debate among the French Reformed. See Brian G. Armstrong, *Calvinism and the Amyraut Heresy* (Madison: University of Wisconsin Press, 1969) and F. P. van Stam, *The Controversy over the Theology of Saumur, 1635–1650: Disrupting Debates Among the Huguenots in Complicated Circumstances* (Amsterdam: APA-Holland University Press, 1988), 54–56 and 426–38. Armstrong's analysis has become pivotal to the question, especially concerning changes introduced into Calvin's theology through the development of Reformed scholasticism. R. T. Kendall also provoked a particularly strong response from the Reformed community in R. T. Kendall, *Calvin and English Calvinism to 1649* (Oxford: Oxford University Press, 1979), which contrasted faith and assurance in Calvin and English Puritans. The strongest and most persistent defender of continuity between Calvin and the Calvinists has been Richard Muller. See Richard A. Muller, "Calvin and the 'Calvinists': Assessing Continuities and Discontinuities Between Reformation and Orthodoxy," *Calvin Theological Journal* 30 (1995): 345–75, for a summary analysis of the history of the discussion; see idem, *Christ and the Decree: Christology and Predestination in Reformed Theology from Calvin to Perkins* (Durham, N.C.: Labyrinth Press, 1986), 1–9, for comparisons between the theologies of various Reformed thinkers.

[2] Diarmaid MacCulloch, "Arminius and the Arminians," *History Today* 39 (1989): 27–34.

[3] Nicholas Tyacke, *Anti-Calvinists: The Rise of English Arminianism, c. 1590–1640* (Oxford: Clarendon Press, 1987).

[4] Geoffry F. Nuttall, "The Influence of Arminianism on American Theology," in *Man's Faith and Freedom: The Theological Influence of Jacobus Arminius*, ed. Gerald O. McCulloh (New York: Abingdon Press, 1962), 46–63; James Meeuwsen, "Original Arminianism and Methodistic Arminianism Compared," *Reformed Review* 14 (1960): 21–36. For other comparisons between Arminius and the later Arminians, see Gordon S. Wakefield, "Arminianism in the Seventeenth and Eighteenth Centuries," *London Quarterly and Holborn Review* 185, 6th ser., no. 29 (1960): 253–258; Howard Slaatte, *The Arminian Arm of Theology: The Theologies of John Fletcher, first Methodist theologian, and his precursor, James Arminius* (Washington DC: University Press of America, 1977), and Craig A.

Blaising, "John Wesley's Doctrine of Original Sin," (Ph.D. diss., Dallas Theological Seminary, 1979).

5   The term "Remonstrant" originated in an appeal (a "remonstrance") which presented the five articles of Arminianism to the representatives of Holland and West Friesland in 1610 and asked for protection for assenting ministers. The Calvinist party, led by Petrus Plancius (1553–1622) and Franciscus Gomarus (1563–1641), promptly filed a "contra-remonstrance," or opposing petition. Hence the names "Arminian" vs. "Gomarist," and "Remonstrant" vs. "Contra-Remonstrant." Chapter 1 of this dissertation presents more concerning the controversy and a definition of the five articles.

6   John Mark Hicks, "The Theology of Grace in the Thought of Jacobus Arminius and Philip van Limborch: A Study in the Development of Seventeenth-Century Dutch Arminianism," (Ph.D. diss., Westminster Theological Seminary, 1985).

7   Carl O. Bangs, "Arminius and Reformed Theology," (Ph.D. diss., University of Chicago, 1958) 249. In addition, "simply on the basis of their being liberal, rationalist or 'enlightened,' many other theological trends have been labeled Arminian" (Thomas C. O'Brien, "Arminianism," in *Encyclopedic Dictionary of Religion*).

8   "A heresy in the theology of grace, which was formulated and spread within the ancient Church by the monk Pelagius (early fifth century)…and combated by St. Augustine and his disciples. Pelagianism rejects the doctrine of original sin, overlooks the pressure of concupiscence and the nature of suffering and death as consequences of sin. It conceives of human freedom as complete autonomy which by itself can and must observe the law of God, thus denying the necessity of grace for natural and salutory observance of the moral law" (Karl Rahner and Herbert Vorgrimler, "Pelagianism," in *Concise Theological Dictionary*). See also excellent introductory articles by R. Lorenz, "Pelagius und Pelagianismus," in *Die Religion in Geschichte und Gegenward: Handwörterbuch für Theologie und Religionswissenschaft*, 3d ed.; Bruce L. Shelley, "Pelagianism," in *Evangelical Dictionary of Theology*; Robert L. Wilken, "Pelagius," in *Encyclopedia of Religion*; and A. Hamman, "Pelagianismus," in *Lexikon Für Theologie und Kirche*, 2d ed..

9   "A crude and heretical attempt (from the end of the fifth century) by certain Gallic theologians (Vincent of Lerins, Faustus of Riez, etc.), to reconcile the orthodox (Augustinian) doctrine of grace with Pelagianism. It was condemned by the decrees of Orange (Ceasarius of Arles) in 529. Semi-Pelagianism divides salvation between God and man in a primitive synergism; man begins his salvation by his own unaided powers; God then responds to this independent 'good will' by granting the grace to complete the work of salvation. Its adherents rightly emphasize against St. Augustine the real universality of God's salvific will" (Karl Rahner and Herbert Vorgrimler, "Semi-Pelagianism," in *Concise Theological Dictionary*). Domingo Bañez coined the term in the sixteenth century to refer to the doctrines of Jesuit Luis de Molina (1535–1600) in the controversy between Dominicans and Jesuits over grace and free will, which paralleled discussions among Protestants. The term entered Protestant theology through inclusion in the Lutheran Formula of Concord (1580). See also excellent introductory articles by Richard Kyle, "Semi-Pelagianism," in *Evangelical Dictionary of Theology*, and G. May, "Semipelagianismus," in *Lexikon Für Theologie und Kirche*, 2d ed.

10 Socinianism, a movement named for founder Lælius Socinus (1525–62) and his nephew Faustus (1539–1604), rejected the doctrine of the trinity and considered Jesus Christ as a mere man, divine by office rather than by nature. Although the Socinii were Italian, Raków, Poland became the center for Socinianism, with some 300 affiliated congregations. Benrath (Gustav Adolph Benrath, "Sozinianismus," in *Evangelischen*

Kirchenlexikon) is especially helpful, not only because of his explanation of the anti-trinitarianism of the movement, but also concerning Socinian thought on theological and exegetical method and the subject of divine foreknowledge vs. future contingents, which allowed the Contra-Remonstrants to slander the Remonstrants as Socinians.

[11] For early accusations of Semi-Pelagianism, see the anonymous *Een Kort en Waerachtich Verhael / wat voor een grouwelijck ghevoelen dat de Arminianen / Vortianen / ofte nieuwe Arrianen / Pelagianen / Socinianen / Samosatinianen ghesocht hebben in de Gehereformeerde kercke in te voeren / en in kort heir teghen gestelt het ghevoelen der Ghereformeerde kerche* (N.p.: "Ghedruckt buyten Romen," n.d.), and Gratianus Civilis Anglus (pseud.), *Remonstrantium in Belgio Semi-Pelagianismus in Pietate Ordinum Hollandiæ ac West Frisiæ defensus per Hugonem Grotious, eorundum Ordinum fisci advocatum* (Basle: n.p., 1616). R. L. Dabney provides a more recent example of this linking of Pelagianism and Arminianism. He wrote, "The essential idea and argument of the Arminian is, that God could not punish man justly for unbelief, unless He conferred on him both natural and moral ability to believe or not. So here we have, by a different track, the old conclusion of Semi-Pelagianism" (Robert Louis Dabney, *Syllabus and Notes of the Course of Systematic and Polemic Theology*, 4th ed. [Richmond, VA: Presbyterian Committee of Publication, 1890], 581). We will consider the validity of this characterization in chapters two and three.

[12] Examples would include many members of Baptist denominations, most Methodists and almost all evangelical Pentecostal and Charismatic movements. See Robert Letham, "Arminianism," in *Encyclopedia of the Reformed Faith*.

[13] Ibid., 13–9.

[14] Ibid., 15. The examples Hicks gave for this category still point in the direction of Pelagianism and Socinianism

[15] Ibid., 16.

[16] Anton Hendrik Haentjens, *Simon Episcopius als Apologeet van het Remonstrantisme in zijn leven en werken geschestst* (Leiden: A. H. Adriani, 1899), iv.

[17] Hicks, "Theology of Grace in Jacobus Arminius," 17–29. Note again the confusion in linking "Pelagianism" with Socinianism.

[18] Ibid., 24.

[19] F. Stuart Clark, "The Theology of Arminius," *London Quarterly and Holborn Review* 185, 6th ser., no. 29 (1960): 254. See also Slaatte, *The Arminian Arm of Theology*, 23, 304, and Gerrit Jan Hoenderdaal, "Arminius, Jacobus/Arminianismus," in *Theologisch Realenzyklopädie*. For an extensive defense of this idea, see Carl O. Bangs, "Arminius As A Reformed Theologian," in *The Heritage of John Calvin: Heritage Hall Lectures, 1960–70*, ed. John H. Bratt (Grand Rapids: Eerdmans, 1973).

[20] We may add a fourth category composed of those who call themselves Arminians but really are eclectics incorporating several theological strands into their systems. This includes those who hold the sinner either initiates the salvation process (true Semi-Pelagians) or has the ability to respond to the gospel without the enabling of the Holy Spirit (true Pelagians). Both Arminius and the first Remonstrants rejected these ideas.

[21] For twentieth century histories of the Remonstrant movement see G. J. Heering, "Het Godsdienstig Beginsel," in *De Remonstranten Gedenkboek bij het 300-jarig bestaan der Remonstrantsche Broederschap*, ed. G. J. Heering (Leiden: A. W. Sijthoof's Uitgevers, 1619); Hendr. C. Diferee, *Drie Eeuwen Kerkgeschiedenis* (Amsterdam: N. V. Van Holkema & Warendorf's Uitgevers-Mij, 1930); and Gerrit J. Hoenderdaal and P. M. Luca, eds.,

Staat in de vrijheid: de geschiedenis van de remonstranten (Zutphen: De Walburg Pres, 1982). I will cite older historical sources below.

22 See Godfrey's discussion of Arminian controversy as a a conflict between "those sometimes called 'the national Reformed' and the strict Calvinists" (Godfrey, "Calvin and Calvinism in the Netherlands," 99). For an extended treatment of a Reformed "campaign of uniformity" in the Netherlands, see Jelsma, *Frontiers of the Reformation*, 110–32. For an early 20th century Remonstrant perspective on the growth of Calvinism in the Netherlands as a supplanting native Arminianism, see G. J. Heering, "Het Godsdienstig Beginsel," in *De Remonstranten Gedenkboek bij het 300-jarig bestaan der Remonstrantsche Broederschap*, ed. G. J. Heering (Leiden: A. W. Sijthoof's Uitgevers, 1919).

23 One of the many marks which Dutch Humanism left on the Netherlands was a spirit of toleration unlike anywhere else in Europe. Dresden wrote, "as for tolerance, it scarcely existed even in the sixteenth century. That it existed at all was admittedly due to humanist and Erasmian ideas" (S. Dresden, *Humanism in the Renaissance* [London: Weidenfeld & Nicolson, 1968], 231). For an extended examination of humanism as the primary promoter of religious toleration in the sixteenth century, with special focus on Erasmus, see Henry Kamen, *The Rise of Toleration* (New York: McGraw-Hill, 1967), 24–29, 86–110. For the relation between humanism and toleration in the Netherlands, see F. H. Waterbolk, "Humanisme en de Tolerantie-Gedachte," in *Opstand en pacificatie in de Lage Landen. Bijdrage tot de studie van de pacificatie van Gent* (Ghent: Snoeck-Ducaju/Nijgh & Van Ditmar, 1976). The noted Dutch humanist Dirk Volkerszoon Coornhert (1522–90) was singularly important regarding this, especially in opposition to Beza's call for the persecution and execution of heretics (Théodore de Bèze, *De hæreticis a ciuili magistratu puniendis libellus, aduersus Martini Bellii farraginem, & nouorum academicorum sectam* [Minerva (Geneva), Unveränderter Nachdruck: Oliua Roberti Stephani, 1554]; cf. Dieryck Volkertszoon Coornhert, *À l'aurore des libertés modernes: Synode sur la liberté de conscience (1582)* [Paris: Éditions du Cerf, 1979]). For scholarly examinations of Coornhert as a proponent of religious liberty and toleration, see Carl Lorentzen, "Dieryck Volkertszoon Coornhert: der Vorläufer der Remonstranten: ein Vorkämpfter der Gewissensfreiheit: Versuch einer Biographie," (Ph.D. diss., University of Jena, 1886); H. Bonger, "De motiviering van de godsdienstvrijheid bij Dirck Volckertszoon Coornhert," (Van Loghum Slaterus, 1954); Bruno Becker, *Sébastien Castellion et Thierry Coornhert* (Amsterdam: Hertzberger, 1968); item, *Dirck Volckertszoon Coornhert: dwars maar recht* (Zutphen: De Walburg Pers, 1989); Gerrit Voogt, *Constraint on Trial: Dirck Volckertsz Coornhert and Religious Freedom* (Kirksville, MO: Truman State University Press, 2000).

24 This is why Hick's quotation of H. Y. Groenewegen is suspect (Hicks, "Theology of Grace in Jacobus Arminius," 17). Groenewegen's comments were not representative of Remonstrants from Episcopius' or Van Limborch's period, but from his own (1919).

25 James Arminius, "A Declaration of the Sentiments of Arminius on Predestination, Divine Providence, The Freedom of the Will, the Grace of God, the Divinity of the Son of God, and the Justification of Man Before God," in *The Works of James Arminius*, trans. James Nichols, London ed. (London: Longman, Hurst, Rees, Orme, Brown and Green, 1825; reprint, Grand Rapids: Baker, 1986).

26 James Arminius, "Friendly Conference of James Arminius, The Illustrious Doctor of Sacred Theology, With Mr. Francis Junius, About Predestination," in *The Works of James Arminius*, trans. William Nichols, London ed. (London: Thomas Baker, 1875; reprint, Grand Rapids: Baker, 1986), 474–83.

27 Hicks, "Theology of Grace in Jacobus Arminius," 21.

28 "Stephan Curcellæus (1586–1659) was ein Freund von Descartes und führte die Cartesianische Methode in sine Theologie ein" (Hoenderdaal, "Arminius, Jacobus / Arminianismus," in *Theologisch Realenzyklopädie*. Regarding this, see also Rosalie L. Colie, *Light and Enlightenment* (New York: Cambridge University Press, 1957); and Lambertus Jacobus Van Holk, "From Arminius to Arminianism in Dutch Theology," in *Man's Faith and Freedom: The Theological Influence of Jacobus Arminius*, ed. Gerald O. McCulloh (New York: Abingdon Press, 1962), 38–39. Consider also van Limborch's ties with John Locke (1632–1704). Locke wrote *Epistola de Tolerantia* in the winter of 1685–86, probably just after the revocation of the Edict of Nantes (October 18, 1685), and dedicated it to van Limborch (John Locke, *A letter Concerning Toleration*, ed. William Popple [London: Awnsham Churchill, 1690]; John Locke, *Epistola De Tolerantia. A letter on Toleration*, ed. Raymond Klibansky, trans. J. W. Gough, with an introduction and notes [Oxford: Clarendon Press, 1968]). Locke was a close friend with the Remonstrant pastor and theologian, and corresponded with him often. See John Locke, *Lettres Inédites de John Locke à Ses Amis Nicolas Thoynard, Philippe van Limborch et Edward Clarke*, ed. Henri Ollion and T. J. de Boer (La Haye: M. Nijhoff, 1912).

29 Ibid., 20–21. Hicks noted how these influences affected not only the Remonstrants, but Reformed theologians as well.

30 The Remonstrants played an important part in the introduction of Cartesian philosophy into the Netherlands. See David Oog, *Europe in the Seventeenth Century* (London: Adam and Charles Black, 1948), 416.

31 Although van Limborch was too young to have studied under Episcopius at the seminary, Episcopius was his uncle and we have numerous indications of his admiration. Van Limborch wrote the definitive biography, and was responsible for publishing Episcopius' sermons and letters.

32 Hicks, "Theology of Grace in Jacobus Arminius," 13–15.

33 The question of the relation of Theodore Beza's theology (1519–1605) to Calvin's is closely (if not centrally) allied with the "Calvin against the Calvinists" debate mentioned in footnote 1. A large body of scholarly studies supports the idea that Beza significantly changed Calvin's theology through greater emphasis upon scholastic method, Aristotelian logic and speculative theology, resulting in a supralapsarianism that departed from Calvin. As early as 1862, William Cunningham detailed four areas in which Beza deviated from Calvin (William Cunningham, *The Reformers and the Theology of the Reformation*, ed. James Buchanan and James Bannerman [Edinburgh: T. and T. Clark, 1862], 345–391), including original sin. Scholars filling out this thesis are Edward A. Dowey, *The Knowledge of God in Calvin's Theology* (New York: Columbia University Press, 1952), 218; Karl Barth, *The Doctrine of God*, trans. Geoffry W. Bromiley, vol. 2/2 (Edinburgh: T. & T. Clark, 1957), 335–40; Ernst Bizer, *Frühorthodoxie und Rationalismus*, vol. 71 (Zürich: EVZ-Verlag, 1963), 5–15; François Laplanche, *Orthodoxie et prédication: l'oeuvre d'Amyraut et la querelle de la grâce universelle* (Paris: Presses Universitaires de France, 1965), 25; John W. Beardslee, ed., *Reformed dogmatics: J. Wollebius, G. Voetius and F. Turretin* (New York: Oxford University Press, 1965), 19–20; Basil Hall, "The Calvin Legend," in *John Calvin*, ed. Gervase E. Duffield and F. L. Battles, Courtney studies in Reformation Theology, no. 1 (Appleford: Sutton Courtney Publishing, 1966), 1–18; item, "Calvin Against the Calvinists," 19–37; Johannes Dantine, "Die Prädestinationslehre bei Calvin und Beza," (Ph.D. diss., Göttingen University, 1965); idem, "Les Tabelles Sur la Doctrine de la Prédestination par Théodore de Bèze," *Revue de Théologie et de Philosophie* 15 (1966): 81–

96; idem, "Das christologische Problem in rahmen der Prädestinationslehre von Theodor Beza," *Zietschrift fur Kirchengeschichte* 78 (1966): 375–77; Walter Kickel, *Vernunft und Offenbarung bei Theodor Beza. Zum Problem der Verhältnisses von Theologie, Philosophie und Staat* (Neukirchen-Vluyn: Neukirchener Verlag, 1967); Armstrong, *Calvinism and the Amyraut Heresy,* 37–42, 136–7, 198–9; David Curtis Steinmetz, *Reformers in the Wings* (Grand Rapids: Baker, 1981), 162–71; Carl O. Bangs, *Arminius: A Study in the Dutch Reformation,* 2d ed. (Grand Rapids: Francis Asbury Press, 1985), 64–80 and Michæl Jinkins, "Theodore Beza: Continuity and Regression in the Reformed Tradition," *Evangelical Quarterly* 64 (1992): 131–154. Robert Letham challenged this thesis (Robert Letham, "Theodore Beza: A Reassessment," *Scottish Journal of Theology* 40 [1987] 25–40) and it appears that he structured his article as a refutation of Cunningham. See also Muller, "Calvin and the 'Calvinists'," 345–59. Two other authors who are notable for their careful analysis and cautious conclusions are Jill Raitt (*The Colloquy of Montbéliard: Religion and Politics in the Sixteenth Century* [New York: Oxford University Press, 1993]; idem, *The Eucharistic Theology of Theodore Beza: Development of the Reformed Doctrine* [Chambersburg, PA: American Academy of Religion, 1972]) and John S. Bray (*Theodore Beza's Doctrine of Predestination,* vol. no. 12 [Nieuwkoop: De Graaf, 1975]). Both identify changes in Beza's theology and method, but deny the rationalistic scholastic tendencies proposed by his harsher critics. Although Arminius did not contrast Calvin and Beza concerning supralapsarianism (Arminius, "Conference with Junius," 3:22, 28–36), his criticisms were consistently aimed at Beza (James Arminius, "Dr. James Arminius' Modest Examination of a Pamphlet, Which That Very Learned Divine Dr. William Perkins, Published Some Years Ago, On The Mode and Order of Predestination, and On the Amplitude of Divine Grace," in *The Works of James Arminius,* trans. William Nichols, London ed. [London: Thomas Baker, 1875; reprint, Grand Rapids: Baker, 1986], passim). Holtrop's summary seems sound: "Current discussions center on how to interpret Beza's scholastic tendencies. Walter Kickel (with E. Bizer and H. Heppe) has exaggerated the discontinuities between Calvin and Beza, while Richard Muller (with Ian McPhee) has underscored the continuities. Brian Armstrong and John Bray tend toward the former, and Jill Raitt and Tadataka Maruyama toward the latter" (Philip C. Holtrop, "Beza, Theodore (1519–1605)," in *Encyclopedia of the Reformed Faith*).

34 Junius was highly respected in Reformed theological circles and instrumental in introducing the scholastic method at Leiden. For information on Junius' life, see his autobiography, Franciscus Junius, "Franciscii Junii Vita," in *Opuscula Theologica Selecta,* ed. Abr. Kuyperus (Amsterdam: Fredericum Muller Cum Soc. et Joannem Hermannum Kruyt, 1882). Most of his more contemporary biographies are from the nineteenth century (Alfred Davaine, *François du Jon (Junius) pasteur et professeur en théologie, 1545–1602; étude historique* [Paris,: Imprimé par C. Noblet, 1882]; Johannes Reitsma, "Franciscus Junius: een Levensbeeld Uit den Eersten tijd der kerkhervorming," [Ph.D. thesis, Hoogeschool te Groningen, 1864]; Fr W. Cuno, *Franciscus Junius der Ältere, Professor der Theologie und Pastor (1545–1602): sein Leben und Wirken, seine Schriften und Briefe* [Amsterdam: Scheffer, 1891]). For his role in the development of the Reformed scholasticism, see Donald Sinnema, "*Antoine de Chandieu's Call For A Scholastic Reformed Theology (1580),*" (n.p.) manuscript; and Richard A. Muller, *God, Creation, and Providence in the Thought of Jacob Arminius: Sources and Directions of Scholastic Protestantism in the Era of Early Orthodoxy* (Grand Rapids: Baker, 1991).

35 His public disputations were published as Simon Episcopius, "Disputationes Theologicæ, Publicè olim in Academia Leydensi habitæ," in *Disputationes Theologiæ Tripartæ* (Amsterdam: Ioannem Blæv, 1644); His private disputations were published as idem,

"Disputationum Theologicarum, à M. Simone Episcopio in Academia Leydensi privatim olim habitarum, Collegium Primum," in *Disputationes Theologiæ Tripartæ* (Amsterdam: Ioannem Blæv, 1644); and idem, "Disputationum Theologicarum, à M. Simone Episcopio in Academia Leydensi privatim olim habitarum, Collegium Secundum," in *Disputationes Theologiæ Tripartæ* (Amsterdam: Ioannem Blæv, 1644).

36 Simon Episcopius, *Confessio, sive, Declaratio, Sententiæ Pastorum, qui in Foederato Belgio Remonstrantes Vocantur, Super Præcipuis Articulis Religionis Christianæ* (Harderwijk: Theodorum Danielis, 1622).

37 Simon Episcopius, *Institutiones Theologicæ, Privatis Lectionibus Amstelodami Traditæ*, in *Opera Theologica* (Amsterdam: Ioannis Blæv, 1650).

38 Simon Episcopius, *The Confession or Declaration of the Ministers or Pastors which in the United Provinces are called Remonstrants, Concerning The Chief Points of Christian Religion* (London: Francis Smith, 1676); idem, *The Popish Labyrinth: Wherein is made manifest, that the papists are entangled in the Fundamental Article of their Faith, that the Church cannot Erre*, trans. "J. K." (London: Ratcliff and Thomson for Francis Smith, 1673). The *Confession* is an important declaration of Remonstrant beliefs at the time of the Synod of Dort.

39 Platt, *Reformed Thought and Scholasticism*.

40 Ibid., 171–72, 181, respectively. Regarding Hommius, Platt wrote, "there can be no doubt that Hommius' version misquoted Episcopius. Furthermore, there must be the strongest suspicion that Hommius was fully aware of this" (Ibid., 215). Regarding the absence of Pelagian or Socinian theology among the Remonstrants, see W. Robert Godfrey, "Calvin and Calvinism in the Netherlands," in *John Calvin, His Influence in the Western world*, ed. W. Stanford Reid and Paul Woolley (Grand Rapids, Zondervan, 1982), 104–05.

41 Platt, *Reformed Thought and Scholasticism*, 111–12

42 Ibid., 161; 196–201, 212–238.

43 The phrase is from Bray, *Beza's Doctrine of Predestination*, 10. The following discussion of the definition of Reformed scholasticism draws heavily from Bray's analysis.

44 While it has become common to appeal to Melanchthon in order to defend the reintroduction of scholasticism into Protestant theology, this opinion has been seriously questioned by Paul Schwarzenau, in *Der Wandel im theologischen Ansatz bei Melanchthon von 1525–1535* (Gütersloh, C. Bertelsmann, 1956). See also Robert Scharlemann, *Aquinas and Gerhard: Theological Controversy and Construction in Medieval and Protestant Scholaticism* (New Haven: Yale University Press, 1964), 22–28.

45 For centuries, Boethius was the only source for Aristotle's treatises on logic (the *Organon*, the *Posterior Analytics*, and *On Interpretation*) and for Porphyry's *Eisagoge*, a Greek introduction to Aristotle's logic. About AD 520, he used Aristotelian categories to compose four short defenses of the Trinity and the nature of Christ. He was also the author of the celebrated *De Consolatione Philosophiæ*, a largely Neoplatonic work which affirmed the existence of a "highest good" which controls and orders the universe. Fortune and misfortune are subordinate to Providence, and though man has free will, this poses no difficulty for divine order and foreknowledge. For an examination of Boethius' importance to the development of medieval philosophy, see John Marenbon, *Early Medieval Philosophy* (London and New York: Routledge, 1988), 27–48.

46 S. J. Curtis, *A Short History of Western Philosophy in the Middle Ages* (London: MacDonald and Co., 1950), 13–21; Michæl Haren, *Medieval Thought: The Western Intellectual Tradition from Antiquity to the Thirteenth Century* (New York: St. Martin's Press, 1985),

38–59; Gerard J. P. O'Daly, *Augustine's Philosophy of Mind* (Berkeley and Los Angeles: University of California Press, 1987), 1–6; Dominick A. Iorio, *The Aristotelians of Renaissance Italy: A Philosophical Exposition* (Lewiston: E. Mellen Press, 1991), 1–21; *Oxford Dictionary of Philosophy*, s.v. "Scholasticism."

47   Concerning the dominance of Aristotelian logic in Catholic theology from AD 480 to 1350 see Marenbon., *Early Medieval Philosophy*, 6–8, 20–26, 28–30, 36–38, 76–77, 80–83, etc.; idem, *Later Medieval Philosophy* (London and New York: Loutledge and Kegan Paul, 1987), *passim*; Haren, *Medieval thought: The Western Intellectual Tradition from Antiquity to the Thirteenth Century*, 83–118.

48   Stephen F. Brown, "Peter of Candia's Hundred-Year 'History' of the Theologian's Role," in *Medieval Philosophy & Theology*, ed. Norman Kretzmann et al. (Notre Dame: University of Notre Dame Press, 1991), 162–170.

49   Ibid., 170.

50   Peter of Ailly, *Peter of Ailly and the Harvest of Fourteenth-Century Philosophy*, ed. Leonard A. Kennedy (Queenston/Lewiston: Edwin Mellen Press, 1986), 133.

51   G. R. Evans, *Old Arts and New Theology: The Beginnings of Theology as an Academic Discipline* (Oxford: Clarendon Press, 1980), 10. The interpretation of Renaissance humanism has also been the subject of scholarly debate. Bouwsma indicated the beginnings of this debate in 1959, and provided a thorough bibliography up to that point (William James Bouwsma, *The Interpretation of Renaissance Humanism* [Washington: Service Center for Teachers of History, 1959]). He was followed by the more comprehensive research of Kristeller (Paul Oskar Kristeller, *Renaissance Thought: The Classic, Scholastic and Humanist Strains* [New York: Harper and Row], 1961), who cast doubt upon traditional associations between the Renaissance and humanism and conflict between humanists and scholastics. A modern synthesis by Kelly suggests the original understanding of humanism as a source for the Renaissance is still appropriate, with corrections suggested by Kristeller (Donald R. Kelly, *Renaissance Humanism*, ed. Michæl Roth [Boston: Twayne Publishers, 1991]). See also Albert Rabil, *Renaissance Humanism: Foundations, Forms, and Legacy* (Philadelphia: University of Pennsylvania Press, 1988).

52   Charles B. Schmitt, Quentin Skinner, and Eckhard Kessler, *The Cambridge History of Renaissance Philosophy* (Cambridge: Cambridge University Press, 1988), 127.

53   Kristeller, *Renaissance Thought: The Classic, Scholastic and Humanist Strains*, 91

54   Ibid., 39.

55   Kelly, *Renaissance Humanism*, 77.

56   See especially Richard C. Gamble, "Exposition and Method in Calvin," *Westminster Theological Journal* 49 (1987): 153–65; and also Arvin Vos, "As the Philosopher Says: Thomas Aquinas and the Classical Heritage," in *Christianity and the Classics: The Acceptance of a Heritage*, ed. Wendy E. Helleman, Christian Studies Today (Lanham, MD: University Press of America, 1990), 111–12.

57   Kristeller, *Renaissance Thought: The Classic, Scholastic and Humanist Strains*, 170.

58   For Italian humanist affirmations of the dignity of man and human freedom, see H. A. Enno Van Gelder, *The Two Reformations in the 16th Century: A Study of the Religious Aspects and Consequences of Renaissance and Humanism* (The Hague: M. Nijhoff, 1961), 21–30.

59   Aristotle, *The "Art" of Rhetoric* (Cambridge, MA: Harvard University Press, 1994).

60   Kelly, *Renaissance Humanism*, 8, 36–39; Geoffrey Dipple, "Humanists, Reformers and Anabaptists on Scholasticism and the Deterioration of the Church," *The Mennonite*

Quarterly Review 68 (1994): 461–48; Craig W. D'Alton, "The Trojan War of 1518: Melodrama, Politics and the Rise of Humanism," *Sixteenth Century Journal* 28 (1997), 732–737, Charles G. Nauert, Jr., "The Clash of Humanists and Scholastics: An Approach to Pre-Reformation Controversies" in *Sixteenth Century Journal* 4 (April 1973): 1–18, idem "Humanism as Method: Roots of Conflict with the Scholastics" in *Sixteenth Century Journal* 29 (summer 1998): 427–38, Alan Perreiah, "Humanist Critiques of Scholastic Dialectic," in *Sixteenth Century Journal* 13 (fall 1982): 3–22, Erika Rummel, "Et cum theologo bella poeta gerit: The Conflict between Humanists and Scholastics Revisited," in *Sixteenth Century Journal* 23 (winter 1992): 713–26, Warren W. Wooden, "Anti-Scholastic Satire in Sir Thomas More's Utopia," *Sixteenth Century Journal* 7 (1977): 29–45. We cannot, however, equate this rejection of scholasticism with an outright rejection of Aristotle. This was Kristeller's corrective to earlier perspectives on the conflict between humanism and scholasticism. Plato and Aristotle were pinnacle examples of Greek texts which attracted the attention of the humanists and brought them into contact with classical logic and philosophy. This resulted in humanists who were worldview was Platonic or Aristotelian, but whose methods were humanist. See Kristeller, *Renaissance Thought: The Classic, Scholastic and Humanist Strains*, 100–05.

[61] "It is significant to note that the scholastic method, which had primarily been a medieval Roman Catholic approach to theological study, began to penetrate Protestantism in the wake of both Luther and Calvin" (John Platt, *Reformed Thought and Scholasticism*, 17.

[62] Modern scholars have debated who should receive the most credit for the reintroduction of scholastic method into Reformed theology. For example, Collinson attributes the greater part to Zanchi and Vermigli (Patrick Collinson, "England and International Calvinism, 1558–1640," in *International Calvinism, 1541–1715*, ed. Menna Prestwich (Oxford: Clarendon Press, 1985), 197–223), while Boughton specifically denies this role to Zanchi and Vermigli and awards the palm to Beza (Lynne Courter Boughton, "Supralapsarianism and the Role of Metaphysics in Sixteenth-Century Reformed Theology," *Westminster Theological Journal* 48 [1986]: 63–96).

[63] Armstrong, *Calvinism and the Amyraut Heresy*, 32.

[64] Johannes Polyander et al., *Synopsis Purioris Theologiæ, disputationibus quinquaginta duabus comprehensa* (Leiden: Ex Officinâ Elzeviriana, 1625).

[65] Barend Johannes Van der Walt, "The Synopsis Purioris Theologiæ—Is It Really So Pure? Philosophical Impurities in the Post-Dortian Theology," in *Our Reformational tradition: a rich heritage and lasting vocation* (Potchefstroom: Potchefstroom University for Christian Higher Education, 1984), 378–423. This article is a summary a Van der Walt's extensive two volume analysis, *Natuurlike Teologie, met besondere aandag aan di visie daarop by Thomas van Aquino, Johannes Calvyn en die "Synopsis Purioris Theologiæ,"* 2 vols. (Franeker: Wever, 1974). He focuses especially on the influence of Thomas Aquinas.

[66] Van der Walt, "Synopsis Purioris Theologiæ," 423.

[67] For a discussion of the importance of the *Synopsis Purioris* in Dutch Reformed theological education, see G. P Van Itterzon, *Het Gereformeerd Leerboek der 17de Eeuw: "Synopsis Purioris Theologiæ"* (The Hague: M. Nijhoff, 1931).

[68] See Richard Muller's criticisms of Armstrong's paradigm (Muller, *Christ and the Decree*, 196–97), followed by Martin I. Klauber (*Between Reformed Scholasticism and Pan-Protestantism: Jean Alphonse Turretin and the Enlightened Orthodoxy at the Academy of Geneva* [Selingsgrove: Susquehanna University Press, 1994], 17–25; and Stephen R. Spencer ("Reformed Scholasticism in Medieval Perspective: Thomas Aquinas and Francois Turrettini on the Incarnation," [Ph.D. diss., Michigan State University, 1988] 5–9). For a

summary of Muller's central role in this movement, see Douglas F. Kelly, "A Rehabilitation of Scholasticism? A Review Article of Richard Muller's *Post-Reformation Reformed Dogmatics*, vol. 1, *Prolegomena to Theology*," *Scottish Bulletin of Evangelical Theology* 6 (1988): 112–22; and Klauber, *Reformed Scholasticism and Pan-Protestantism*, 17–25.

69 Muller, *Christ and the Decree*, 11–12.

70 Muller, *God, Creation, and Providence*, 3–4. The parties involved in this discussion generally fall into the same ones involved in the "Calvin against the Calvinists" and the "Calvin vs. Beza" debate. Consequently, see footnotes 1 and 24 above for literature associated with this discussion.

71 However, Armstrong wrote in the cover of my copy of Bray, "The material here is all worth my blessing, if not my prose."

72 Bray, *Beza's Doctrine of Predestination*, 142–43, cf. Spencer, "Reformed Scholasticism," 3.

73 Bray, *Beza's Doctrine of Predestination*, 12–17.

74 Ibid., 119–31, 139–41.

75 Gisbert Voetius, "Selectæ Disputationes Theologicæ," in *Reformed Dogmatics*, ed. John W. Beardslee III (Grand Rapids: Eerdmans, 1977), 268, 278.

76 Hicks wrote that Arminianism can trace its beginning to the spirit of Erasmus ("Theology of Grace in Jacobus Arminius," 21), an opinion with which the Remonstrants would strongly agree. Hoenderdaal called Erasmus "Een van de bronnen van het resmonstrantisme" (Gerrit J. Hoenderdaal, "Begin en beginsel," in *Staat in de vijheid: de geschiedenis van de remonstranten*, ed. Gerrit J. Hoenderdaal and P. M. Luca [Zutphen: De Walburg Pers, 1982], 9).

77 On October 8, 1603, Arminius observed his first student-led disputation. It treated original sin, no less. He commented at the time that the presenter, Gilbert Jacchæus, depended too much on logic and too little on Scripture, and afterward he encouraged his colleagues to abandon "the cumbrous mass of scholastic assertions" for "the earlier and more masculine method of study" of the Scriptures (Caspar Brandt, *The Life of James Arminius*, trans. John Guthrie [Nashville: E. Stevenson & F.A. Owen, Agents for the Methodist Episcopal Church South, 1857], 191–92). We can identify the author of this "earlier and more masculine method" from Arminius' statement concerning Calvin: "Sed post Scripturæ lectionem, quam vehementer inculco, & magis quam quisquam alius, quod tota Academia testabitur, etiam conscientia meorum collegarum, ad Calvini Commentarios legendos adhortor, quem laudibus majoribus extollo.... Dico enim incomparabilem esse in interpretatione Scripturarum, & majores faciendos ipsius commentarios quam quidquid Patrum Bibliotheca nobit tradit" (Jacobus Arminius to Sebastian Egbert, 3 May, 1607, Christiaan Hartsoeker and Philippus van Limborch, eds., *Præstantium ac eruditorum virorum epistolæ ecclesiasticæ et theologicæ* [Amsterdam: Henricum Wetstenium, 1660], 236–37).

78 Richard A. Muller, "Arminius and the Scholastic Tradition," *Calvin Theological Journal* 24 (1989): 263–77; *Muller, God, Creation, and Providence in the Thought of Jacob Arminius*; idem, "The Priority of the Intellect in the Soteriology of Jacob Arminius," *Westminster Theological Journal* 55 (1993): 55–72.

79 Platt, *Reformed Thought and Scholasticism*, 148–161.

80 Ibid., 149–58. However, Gerrit Hoenderdaal disputes this attribution. See Hoenderdaal, "Arminius en Episcopius," 212

81 Platt, *Reformed Thought and Scholasticism*, 155. See also page 157.

82 Muller, *God, Creation, and Providence in the Thought of Jacob Arminius*, ix–x.

83   I.e., he was a gifted and interesting rhetorician, and his sermons were practically oriented.

84   For an introduction to Pierre Ramus, see Walter J. Ong, *Ramus: Method, and the Decay of Dialogue: From the Art of Discourse to the Art of Reason* (Cambridge, MA: Harvard University Press, 1958).

85   Calvin inaugurated the scholastic method at Geneva, but permitted the use of Aristotle, though only in physics (S. Fowler, "Faith and Reason in the Period of the Reformation," in *Our Reformational Tradition: A Rich Heritage and Lasting Vocation* (Potchefstroom: Potchefstroom University for Christian Higher Education, 1984), 80–81). Beza instituted studies in Aristotelian logic and brought in the noted Italian Aristotelians Zanchi and Vermigli. See Bray, *Beza's Doctrine of Predestination*, 121–23.

86   Arminius, "Conference with Junius;" idem, "Examination of Perkins' Pamphlet."

87   Spencer cites 28 examples of scholastic terms and concepts in the 1521 pages of Calvin's *Institutes*, the vast majority being references to Aristotelian causality (Spencer, "Reformed Scholasticism," Appendix). Bray, however, advised caution when he wrote "one must hasten to add that Calvin's use of this fourfold schema of causation does not make him a scholastic. His goal was not to solve the philosophical problems of determinism, nor was he concerned about producing a philosophical theology" (Bray, *Beza's Doctrine of Predestination*, 52). [10,346]

CHAPTER ONE

Arminius and Episcopius in Historical Context

As stated in the Introduction, to treat the Arminian controversy as though it were an isolated event in the development of Reformed theology would be to reduce the conflict to a mere heresy trial and misunderstand both its development under the guidance of Jacobus Arminius and its continuation under the leadership of Simon Episcopius. This chapter identifies the religious, cultural and political trends that led to the Arminian controversy. It then provides a brief introduction to Arminius' and Episcopius' lives and labors, demonstrates how these trends influenced the Remonstrant controversy, and establishes the closeness of the personal ties between master and student. This will prepare a foundation for the comparison of their respective theologies.

Precursory Trends and Events: Dutch Religion, Culture and Politics

Two centuries of religious, social and political processes came together in the sixteenth century to facilitate the rise and remarkable progress of the Reformation in the Netherlands and foment the Arminian controversy. These included a heightened spiritual awareness because of various renewal movements, the impact of Dutch humanists on Dutch intellectual life, a singular culture of toleration, religious pluralism, and a political system unique to the Low Countries.[1]

Dutch spirituality was the fruit of a long history of religious renewal movements that focused on personal piety in the Christian life.[2] The Waldensee refugees in the thirteenth and fourteenth centuries,[3] the Brethren of the Common Life[4] and pietist preachers such as Ruysbroec and Hinne Rode[5] all contributed to this. Extensive lay leadership in both Catholic and Reformation churches also brought these movements into the general population.[6] Lay involvement included teaching and preaching, as indicated by the imposition of the death penalty by Charles V on anyone who taught the Bible or even discussed the interpretation of Scripture without the approval of the seminaries.[7] The Dutch boasted "even fishermen who dwelt in the huts of Friesland could read and write and discuss how the Bible should be understood."[8]

Second, Desiderius Erasmus and the other northern humanists had intellectually prepared the Dutch for the Reformation. These humanists called for ecclesiastical reforms prior to Luther, and were beginning to supplant scholastic approaches to the Scriptures mediated through glosses and compendia with exegetical studies.[9] Perhaps of even greater consequence, they were responsible for developing a mentality of openness and toleration among the Dutch unlike anywhere else in Europe. Dresden wrote, "as for tolerance, it scarcely existed even in the sixteenth century. That it existed at all was admittedly due to humanist and Erasmian ideas."[10]

Third, Dutch toleration resulted in a religiously pluralistic society, a principal factor precipitating the theological aspects of the Arminian controversy.[11] The Dutch were willing to accept religious alternatives to standard Romanist religion so long as they did not threaten societal unity.[12] By the time Calvinism gained a presence in the Netherlands in the 1560s, the Dutch were forty years into the Reformation.[13] Although Lutheranism never captured Dutch society as did Calvinism, this was not because of a rejection of Lutheran ideas but because of a lack of national unifying leadership.[14] Even more noteworthy were the Anabaptists. While their practices and beliefs were strange to the general population, their willingness to die for their faith powerfully affected those who witnessed the "Mennists" being "led to the butcher block,"[15] and opened the door for Reformed advancement.

Religious pluralism extended to the theology and practice of the Dutch Reformed.[16] The Reformed movement in the Netherlands developed along national and linguistic lines. While Calvin's influence was strongest in the French-speaking southern provinces,[17] Philip Melanchthon and Heinrich Bullinger guided the thinking of the Reformed in the Germanic northern provinces.[18] Melanchthon originally agreed with Luther regarding unconditional predestination, but he developed a view that allowed for freedom of the will and human cooperation in salvation.[19] Melanchthon's theology found an able advocate in one of his students, Nicholas Hemmingius (1513-1600), a Danish Lutheran and professor of theology at Copenhagen.[20] Hemmingius in turn taught Johannes Holmannus (1523–1586), one of the first professors of theology at the University of Leiden when it opened in 1575. Enrolled among the students of that first class was Jacobus Arminius, of Holland.[21]

Heinrich Bullinger had an even deeper impact among the Reformed than Melanchthon. Overshadowed by Calvin in contemporary Reformed studies,[22] he shaped the theological development in the Netherlands through his *Decades*, or as the Dutch called it, the *Huisboek* (or *Huysboec*).[23] During the initial phases of the Dutch Reformed movement, the *Huisboek* exercized greater influence than its counterpart,[24] Calvin's *Institutes*.[25] Bullinger taught a form of predestination that contrasted with Calvin and reconciled with that of Melanchthon,[26] affirming that Christ's redemptive work was available to all mankind upon the condition of faith.[27] Nor were Bullinger's differences with Calvin over predestination limited to the printed page. Calvin's persecution of Jerome Bolsec (d. 1584) over predestination elicited a sharp letter from Bullinger in which he criticized both Calvin's theology and conduct, and created a temporary breach in their relationship.[28]

Three factors allowed Genevan religious theory to overtake other Reformed models in the northern provinces: the arrival of Calvinist books,[29] Dutch exposure to Calvinism either in exile or at the Academy in Geneva and the influx of French Reformed refugees fleeing from persecution in the southern provinces and France.[30] These refugees radicalized Calvinist attitudes in the northern provinces.[31] Furthermore, Walloon refugees took advantage of disorganization in the north to hold an "official" synod outside the Netherlands (at Emden),[32] adopting the Belgic and French Confessions and instituting a Calvinist church order.[33] This adoption created what Godfrey called "tensions between those sometimes called 'the national Reformed' and the strict Calvinists."[34]

Finally, the political realities of the Netherlands in the sixteenth century were fundamental to the growth of Dutch Calvinism and the development of the Remonstrant controversy. The question of state control over Reformed churches fueled the Arminian conflict as much as predestination. Ironically, the road to Reformed predominance began with Charles V's institution of the Inquisition in the Netherlands. While the Dutch were willing to tolerate the inquisition out of loyalty to the emperor,[35] this ended with the accession of Charles' son, Philip II.[36] Raised in Spain and viewed as a foreign oppressor, he declared himself ready to depopulate the Netherlands if necessary to restore the Catholic religion. Even the nobility was not immune to attack and their ancient privileges no longer protected them from summary arrests, torture, death and confiscation for the mere suspicion of Reformation sympathies.[37] These provocations welded Catholics, Lutherans and Calvinists together into what Wakefield termed "a glorious national resistance to Catholic Spain."[38]

Of the original three leaders of the revolt, only William the Silent survived to lead the Dutch armies. William had three goals in mind: (1) the restoration of ancient rights and privileges of the provinces and the nobility, along with a cessation of religious persecution, (2) the prevention of a Protestant crusade which would alienate the Catholic nobility,[39] and (3) the maintenance of Reformed participation in the war, his most dependable source of military support.[40] Calvinists earned distinction as true defenders of the *patria* and a crucial component to the survival of the young republic, especially after southern nobles made peace with Philip.[41] When the remaining seven provinces bound themselves together by the Union of Utrecht (1579), delegates granted the Reformed church legal recognition in Holland and Zeeland and agreed that each province was also free to do the same. These political realities explain how a movement representing ten percent of the population could become the predominant religion in a Catholic country.[42] The Reformed did not, however, obtain a religious monopoly. Following William's lead, church membership was not compulsory, and while the non-Reformed Christians could not meet publically, they maintained the right to meet in their homes.

The interaction between church and government had always been a critical aspect for the Reformed.[43] Zwingli in Zurich, the Huguenots in France and Calvin in Geneva all depended on political and military factors for their success (or failure). Motivated in part by a rash of excommunications (*febris excommunicatoris*) following efforts to impose Calvin's system of church discipline in Heidelberg, Thomas Erastus (1524–1583) protested what he viewed as mistreatment of private citizens.[44] Although he did not address many of the aspects of church/state relations that existed in the Netherlands, his name came to be associated with those who urged state supremacy over the church.[45]

The Netherlands were "Erastian" long before Erastus. The Union of Utrecht maintained for the government the right to approve or deny syndic meetings, and the final word on the calling or removal of pastors.[46] Such claims incensed Calvinists during the predestination controversy. They could not meet to deal with the Arminian threat, nor could they remove non-Calvinist Reformed pastors from their ministries,[47] as when the magistrates in

Amsterdam protected Arminius from criticisms by Peter Plancius (1552–1622) in 1592.[48] Especially significant was the provision that any decision by the States–General[49] that affected all the provinces had to be unanimous, including the calling of a national synod. These rights of state, not Arminian interference, kept the Calvinists from holding a national synod until 1618.

A final political factor was the alliances between these Reformed factions and the two most powerful leaders of the Netherlands.[50] The assassination of William the Silent (1584) created a crisis in that the Union of Utrecht did not specify who would replace him as head of state. The resulting struggle pitted the nation's leading military leader, William's son, Maurice of Nassau, against its leading diplomat, Johannes Oldenbarnevelt.[51] Although Maurice was the "stadholder" (vice-regent) of various provinces and seemed the natural choice, Oldenbarnevelt prevailed through his political skills.[52] Tensions grew as Oldenbarnevelt thwarted Maurice's efforts to be crowned king, and by concluding a peace treaty with Spain.[53] Maurice opposed the settlement because he viewed a successful war with Spain as a means of gaining the Dutch monarchy.

Each man also attracted sectors within the Reformed church.[54] Oldenbarnevelt represented the ancient system of provincial autonomy and the aristocratic oligarchy to which Wtenbogært and Arminius were linked by blood and marriage, respectively.[55] Oldenbarnevelt also agreed with them regarding predestination.[56] Furthermore, he alienated the Calvinists by frustrating their attempts at independence, forestalling the calling of provincial and national synods and by his willingness to permit a revision of the Belgic Confession and the Heidelberg Catechism. Although Maurice was theologically confused,[57] he sided with the Calvinists because of their loyalty to his father, friendship with his Calvinist troops and the realization that the Calvinists could further his political purposes. Maurice resolved both his conflict with Oldenbarnevelt and the Calvinists' struggle with the Arminians by overthrowing the government, installing Calvinist officials who could control the calling of a national synod and engineering what Oog called the "judicial murder" of Oldenbarnevelt.[58]

In sum, the Arminian controversy was not a debate between the Reformed and "heretics" who had grown up in their midst. Rather, this conflict reflected social, political, religious and ethnic factors which originated before the Reformation. The Dutch Reformation built upon a strong base of Catholic and humanist renewal movements, accompanied by a spirit of toleration and assisted by specific political realities. National characteristics of Erasmian toleration and Erastian ecclesiology brought earlier Dutch reformers into direct conflict with the theological and political purposes of Calvinist refugees. In the end, its resolution depended far more upon the force of arms and political maneuvering than the effectiveness of Scripture, reason and conscience.

The Arminian Phase of the Controversy

Although Arminius did not originate the ideas which provoked the Remonstrant controversy, he became a rallying point for those who disagreed with Calvin and Beza's theories of predestination.[59] While questions exist whether Arminius ever held to Beza's supralapsarianism, there can be no doubt that the strength of his opposition to Genevan predestinarianism made him the leader of like-minded people.[60]

Even though Arminius' father died near the time of his birth in 1559 or 1560,[61] his family's connections and his intelligence provided him with a series of sponsors who provided excellent education and continuous advancement in his studies. For a time he lived at Marburg, a center for Melanchthon's theology. He was under the care of Rudolphus Snellius, a mathematician who had rejected Aristotelian logic for the new methods of Petrus Ramus (1515–1572). In 1575, he enrolled as part of the first class at the University of Leiden.[62] Upon graduation in 1581, he studied at the Academy in Geneva under the direction of Beza. Arminius admired Beza, but clashed with the Spanish Aristotelian Petrus Galesius over Ramism and in 1583 he transferred to Basel to study under Grynæus. After a year, he returned to Geneva to complete his studies without further incident. When he arrived in Amsterdam in the fall of 1587, he was able to present a positive letter of recommendation from Beza.

In 1587, the Reformed church had been in Amsterdam for nine years, and Arminius was its first Dutch pastor. However well he served as pastor, his sermons on Romans 7 and 9 caused Plancius[63] to question Arminius' orthodoxy.[64] The dispute over Romans 7 took on Erastian overtones when the burgomasters and their deputies resolved it with stern warnings to guard ministerial collegiality and refrain from introducing new theology. The consistory resolved the conflict over Romans 9 without political interference. Arminius argued that the Belgic Confession did not specify whether the decree of election was to bestow faith or save those who believed.

Remarkably, this view of conditional predestination satisfied Calvinist objections. The rest of his pastorate was pacific and when he left for the university of Leiden he received two letters of recommendation from the other pastors which emphasized his soundness of doctrine and the "virtuous tenor of his life."[65]

Arminius wrote his most extensive refutations of unconditional predestination during his pastorate.[66] The first took the form of a *disputatio* with Franciscus Junius, then professor of theology at Leiden.[67] Arminius attacked all three forms of unconditional predestination: the supralapsarianism of Calvin and Beza, the infralapsarianism of Thomas Aquinas and the sublapsarianism of Augustine.[68] The second, Arminius' refutation of William Perkins' defense of supralapsarianism[69] provides his clearest and most detailed statements on grace, predestination and perseverance. From these we gather Arminius' reservations about Calvinist theology. First, he defended the goodness and mercy of God. He was convinced that, in spite of denials to the contrary and appeals to Aristotelian causality, supralapsarianism made God the author of sin.[70] Second, he stressed the importance of faith and holiness in the Christian life and feared that some elements of Calvinist theology undermined morality. Arminius resolved both through conditional election. He wrote to Perkins, "You assert that divine election is the rule of giving or withholding faith. Therefore election does not pertain to believers, but faith rather pertains to the elect, or is from the gift of election. You will allow me to deny this, and to ask for the proof, while I plead the cause of those whose sentiment you oppose. Election is made in Christ. But no one is in Christ, except he is a believer. Therefore no one is elected in Christ, unless he is a believer."[71]

The opportunity for Arminius to teach at Leiden opened in 1602 when two theology professors, Lucas Trelcatius (b. 1542) and Franciscus Junius, died from plague. Wtenbogært nominated Arminius for the position,[72] and the curators of the university were anxious to attract the gifted and intelligent Dutchman as the first Hollander to teach there. Franciscus Gomarus (1563–1641) performed Arminius' doctoral examination and granted the first doctorate from the university. This cleared the way for Arminius to teach.[73] While Arminius' admittance provoked the Calvinist community throughout the Netherlands, the professors maintained peace between themselves for almost two years. This ended on October 31, 1604, when Gomarus attacked Arminius in a public disputation on predestination. Arminius' response was immediate, but kept private until after his death.[74]

This assault marked the beginning of a campaign against Arminius and his students, prompting him to defend his opinions on three occasions.[75] In spite of intervention by public authorities, hostilities escalated to the point that the central government summoned Arminius and Gomarus to give depositions on their beliefs. The resulting "Declaration of Sentiments" represents Arminius' mature thought, forcefully stated.[76] Although the meeting resolved nothing, Oldenbarnevelt continued to call government-supervised conferences which he hoped would alleviate the conflict. Arminius' health had been poor for some time, and he could hardly participate in the conference on August 13, 1609. Finally, on October 9, he succumbed to an illness that his friends attributed to the burden of defending himself and his doctrine, but his enemies to the avenging wrath of God.[77] As his opponents feared, Arminius had exercised a wide influence. In 1619, as the effects of the Synod of Dort reverberated throughout the United Provinces, more than 200 pastors chose expulsion from their ministries rather than give up Arminius' theology.[78]

Episcopius' Life and Work

One such individual was Arminius' former student and then professor at Leiden, Simon Bisschop, better known by the latinized form of his name, Simon Episcopius.[79] Episcopius was born to a tailor in Amsterdam on January 8, 1583. He was one of the youngest of ten children, of whom three survived to adulthood. His parents had embraced the Reformed faith early, and their family had strong ties with Arminius. All three sons advanced beyond their parents in wealth and social position. The oldest, Jan, was a prominent merchant and the leader of the group that protected Arminius from Plancius' attacks in 1593.[80] The next, Rembert (or "Rem," 1571–1625), would become the leading Remonstrant layman in Amsterdam and corresponded regularly with Arminius. From childhood, Simon demonstrated a keen intellect, and his brother Rem and a city councilman provided for his early education.[81] At Arminius' insistence, his parents permitted his adoption as an *alumnus* of the city of Amsterdam so that he could attend the University of Leiden (1600 to 1606). While there, he lost both parents to plague, his father in 1602 and his mother in 1603. He received his master's degree on February 27, 1606,[82] and then dedicated himself to the disputations and lectures of the three theology professors: Gomarus, Trelcatius and Arminius. He was present when the conflict over predestination erupted between Arminius and Gomarus.[83]

Several incidents indicate the depth of the relation between teacher and pupil. Hæntjens found numerous unpublished letters in the *Biblioteque te Amsterdam* from Episcopius to Rembert; he mentioned Arminius in almost every letter.[84] In his only extant letter to Arminius, he addressed him as "my father,"[85] and as their friendship grew, Episcopius sometimes accompanied Arminius in his travels.[86] His association with Arminius was strong enough that Calvinists blocked his return to minister at Amsterdam.[87] We may conjecture that the orphaned Episcopius found a surrogate father in Arminius, and Arminius' own experiences of losing his family in the Spanish massacre of the inhabitants of Oudewater would have made him sympathetic for his gifted student.

In 1609, Episcopius went to Franeker to study Hebrew.[88] Arminius had warned Episcopius not to debate while there,[89] a warning repeated by Henry Antonides, a professor at Franeker and sympathetic to both Arminius and his theology.[90] In spite of these admonitions, Episcopius succumbed to calls by other students to dispute with the theologian Sibrandus Lubbertus over Romans 7. This was an essential passage for any disciple of Jacobus Arminius. Although he won the debate, he made a life-long enemy.[91] Later, he received a letter from Adrian Borrius, who wrote that Arminius, "nostra lux quam Deus faciat diu lucere in nostro hemisphærio," was dying.[92] Although Episcopius traveled to Leiden and spent long hours by Arminius' side, others convinced him that Arminius would recover and he returned to Franeker. Arminius died shortly thereafter.[93]

When Episcopius returned to Amsterdam in May of 1610, his opponents were waiting. They excluded him from the Lord's Supper on the contrivance that he had not presented his testimonials when expected,[94] and then attempted to block his call as pastor to Blijswick.[95] However, his status continued to grow among the Arminians. In 1610, Wtenbogært wrote and forty-three ministers (including Episcopius) signed a remonstrance asking the States of Holland for protection from Calvinist persecution with respect to five points of faith.[96] The Gomarists, led by Plancius, filed a counter-petition,[97] and the government called a conference to resolve their differences. Wtenbogært invited Episcopius to participate as one of the seven Remonstrant representatives. The Calvinist historian Le Vassor wrote that, though he spoke just once, "he defended the Remonstrants on this occasion to a miracle."[98] Otherwise, Episcopius was also a successful pastor, and a rivalry was developing among Arminian Reformed churches for his services. He cut short his pastoral ministry on February 15, 1612, when the curators of the University of Leiden extended an invitation to serve as professor of theology.[99]

Episcopius' Seminary Ministry and Participation at Dort

Like most incoming professors, Episcopius began his teaching ministry with an inaugural address, and then delivered his first lecture on February 28, 1612 over Romans 1:16.[100] In his exegetical classes he first taught on Revelation 2–3,[101] then 1 John,[102] and concluded with the Gospel of Matthew.[103] He commented on Romans 8–11[104] and wrote an introduction and explanation of the epistles of the New Testament.[105] Episcopius taught systematic theology in both public and private disputations.[106]

The same types of conflicts Arminius had endured marked Episcopius' seminary experience. Students disrupted his inaugural address, Walloon pastors prohibited their young men from attending his lectures[107] and others accused him of Socinianism.[108] Just as Arminius had his Gomarus, Episcopius found his opponent in Johannes Polyander (1568–1646). The relationship began amicably but soured quickly. Polyander felt threatened by Episcopius,[109] and Episcopius viewed him as easily swayed by others, quick-tempered,[110] of questionable mental abilities[111] and more motivated by envy than concern for theological purity.[112] Episcopius also made himself vulnerable by meeting with hostile parties who distorted his words and denounced him from pulpits in Amsterdam.[113] It became impossible for Episcopius to appear on the streets of Amsterdam without verbal and physical assaulted.[114] Nor were his experiences unique. Remonstrant homes were sacked, their wives molested, and their meeting places destroyed while Calvinist pastors and burgomasters, schouts (sheriffs) and soldiers either encouraged their attackers or stood by and did nothing.[115]

Although it was obvious that only a national synod would resolve the crisis, Oldenbarnevelt continued to forestall. Maurice ended these delays by effecting a coup d'etat, arresting Oldenbarnevelt and installing a Contra-Remonstrant government. Episcopius recognized the ramifications for a future national synod[116] and despaired of a national synod resulting in peace and mutual toleration.[117] Wtenbogært, particularly vulnerable because of his political activities, shared his sentiments. When the Remonstrants agreed it was no longer safe for him to remain in the United Provinces, he fled the country on August 30, 1618 and the leadership of the Remonstrants fell to Episcopius.

The Gomarists called for a national synod in short order. The Synod of Dort has become a hallowed touchstone for Calvinists,[118] and an object of derision for many who are not. It is clear that the Contra-Remonstrants engineered a synod guaranteed to fulfill their purposes.[119] The Remonstrants had hoped for an open debate, but it was obvious that their participation was a "farce."[120] The Contra-Remonstrants demanded absolute subjection from the Remonstrants, limited their participation to the presentation of their views and prohibited criticisms of Contra-Remonstrant positions, especially reprobation. The Remonstrants defied the orders of the president, denied the synod's legitimacy and demanded the right of free debate. The Contra-Remonstrants were also careful from which regions they invited delegates from outside the United Provinces. Even then, theological differences among them threatened the overarching purposes for the synod, the appearance of a united Reformed front against the Arminians.

We may view the synod from two perspectives. Some would have no difficulty condemning the synod as a "kangaroo court," if measured by principles of American democratic idealism and fairness. The president of the synod, Johannes Bogarman, was a professed enemy of the Arminians. He was responsible for the publication in the United Provinces of a treatise by Beza which called for the execution of religious heretics, and Bogerman had the Arminians in mind when he did so.[121] The first secretary of the synod was Festus Hommius, whom Harrison called "one of the cleverest manipulators of the Anti-Arminian machine."[122] The common criticism of Dortian Calvinists, that the Remonstrants were "uncooperative," sounds like censuring someone for not lying still at their own crucifixion.[123] On the other hand, it is not difficult to feel sympathy for the Contra-Remonstrants. From their perspective, they were defending the purity of the Gospel against Semi-Pelagian, Pelagian and Socinian heresies promulagated by insincere men who were masters at hiding behind the skirts of bureaucratic dupes. Although this cannot justify their harsh treatment of the Remonstrants, it explains why they acted as they did.

The history of the synod is too Byzantine to consider here. John Hales compared the synod to a clock—not much movement on the face, but tremendous activity behind it.[124] Given Episcopius' participation and the impact of the Synod upon his life and ministry, we need at least to consider his participation at the Synod.[125] At first, the States of Holland and West-Friesland appointed Episcopius as a delegate to the synod. Nevertheless, while he was traveling to Dort, the synod convened for the first time on November seventeenth and one of its first acts was to change Episcopius' status to a cited person.[126] This was equal to removing a person from a panel of judges at a trial, and putting them among the accused. Convinced the synod would result in their condemnation, the Remonstrants met in Rotterdam on December 2, 1618, to decide whether to acquiesce or defend their faith. They chose to defend and elected Episcopius as their spokesman. He sprang to the attack in his opening speech on December 7, 1618, during the twenty-third session of the Synod.[127] The hour and a half oration gave the Remonstrant version of the conflict and accused the Contra-Remonstrants of lying, slander and persecution. This speech impressed many of the foreign delegates, horrified the Contra-Remonstrants and spread throughout the Netherlands and beyond.[128] By it, he initiated a war between himself and Bogerman, a conflict that continued until the president unilaterally expelled the Remonstrants from the Synod.[129] The rest of the delegates did not take his eruption seriously and were shocked when the Remonstrants stood up and walked out.

Unable to recall the Remonstrants without embarrassment, the delegates set about both to disprove the Remonstrant sentiments and to defend their own. Both tasks proved difficult. Not having any Remonstrants to interrogate, they chose to judge them from their writings.[130] Neither was there total agreement among the delegates. Gomarus and Johannes Maccovious (1578–1644) found few that were sympathetic to their supralapsarian views.[131] Gomarus was astounded and angered when Matthias Martinus and the delegation from Bremen defended the Remonstrants on the extent of the atonement and the relationship of Christ to the decree of election. Several shouting matches ensued between the ancient Martinus and Gomarus, until the British delegation convinced the old German to put his differences aside for the sake of the appearance of unity.[132] Perhaps the knowledge that the same differences of opinion existed among the British delegation helped Martinus to acquiesce.[133] In spite of these difficulties, the synod condemned the Remonstrant opinions on April 24, 1619, and canonized their own.

The civil authorities sentenced the Remonstrants on May 6, 1519, remanded them to the Hague on June thirtieth and demanded their submission to the Canons of Dort on July third.[134] When the Remonstrants refused, the government confiscated their property and transported them out of the country on July 5, 1619.[135] The Remonstrants reunited within a month, made plans for the future and one of their first acts was to form a new fellowship of believers, the Remonstrant Brotherhood.

The Solidification of Episcopius' Leadership
Among the Remonstrants

By his performance at the synod Episcopius won the respect of his peers, and along with Wtenbogært and Grevinchoven they elected him to the "foreign directorship" of the Brotherhood.[136] Unable to participate in the daily affairs of the Remonstrant Brotherhood within the country, his ministry was mostly one of encouraging pastors still in the United Provinces to stand firm.[137] This became especially important when the Remonstrants came under intense persecution, after they were wrongly associated with an attempt on Maurice's life. It was a time of great discouragement.[138]

Of greater importance was his written ministry. At the same meetings in which the Remonstrants elected him to the directorship, they commissioned him to write their account of the Synod.[139] They also asked him to write a confession in order to refute accusations of Socinianism and Pelagianism, and to encourage the Arminians who were still in the United Provinces.[140] Episcopius completed the *Confessio Remonstrantes* in Latin by February 6, 1620, the Remonstrants discussed and approved it on the seventh, and Wtenbogært and Episcopius had translated it into Dutch by the ninth.[141]

During his exile, Episcopius wrote very little against the Contra-Remonstrants in the Netherlands. He wrote a denial of the spiritual legitimacy of the Calvinist practice of exiling their enemies and a refutation of accusations of Socinianism by a former Remonstrant pastor.[142] Most of his works were the result of interactions outside the United Provinces. Three letters and a small pamphlet, unrelated to the Remonstrant controversy, were the fruits of his conversations with Jesuit priest.[143] He directed the remainder against Reformed theologians in France, John Cameron (1579–1625), the forerunner of Moise Amyraut (1596–1664), and Jacob Capellus, one of Cameron's disciples.[144] The ensuing debate produced three more treatises against what would become Amyraldian Calvinism,[145] and he wrote to a friend that he hoped to be free of "strijdigh schrijven en weerschrijven."[146]

Episcopius' exile lasted seven years, from July 1619 until July 1626. Relief came through Maurice's death and the ascension of his half-brother Henry, a Remonstrant sympathizer. The Remonstrants began calling for Episcopius' return to the Netherlands,[147] and he arrived in Rotterdam on July 25, 1626.

Episcopius' Later Ministry

For the remaining nineteen years of his life, Episcopius divided his time between leading the Remonstrant Brotherhood, defending their theology and preparing their pastors by opening and teaching in the Remonstrant Seminary.

Episcopius as Director of the Remonstrant Brotherhood

When Episcopius returned to the Netherlands, Grevinchoven resolved any possible leadership conflicts by declaring him the leader of the cause. At first, he shared the practical management of the movement,[148] but by the fall of 1628, the leadership rested with him alone. He also shared in pastoral responsibilities. He returned to Amsterdam in 1629 to build up a small Remonstrant community in this center of Dutch Calvinism, purchased property for a new meeting hall and divided his time between preaching there and at Rotterdam. Episcopius used his writing skills for pastoral concerns by producing the baptismal and communion formularies for the Brotherhood.[149] In the midst of all this, he found time to marry the widow of Remonstrant pastor Henricus Niellius, Maria Jans. Presser, on December 8, 1630.

Episcopius as Apologete for the Remonstrant Faith

Episcopius wrote most of his polemic works from this later period in answer to two sources of opposition: the theological faculty at Leiden and a Reformed pastor of growing reputation, Jacobus Triglandius.[150]

The Leiden theologians took five years to write their rejoinder to the *Confessio Remonstrantes*.[151] One of them, Antonius Walæus, followed this with the publication of twenty-four theses attacking the Remonstrants on election, reprobation, predestination, free will, and the perseverance of the saints.[152] Episcopius responded first to Walæus,[153] and then to the *Censura*.[154] He was surprised at the continued accusations of Socinianism, because the *Confessio* was orthodox concerning the trinity and the satisfaction of Christ's death.[155] The faculty published two more attacks at the conclusion of the 1620s,[156] eliciting a final response from Episcopius.[157] Accusations and denials of Socinianism and Pelagianism comprise a large part of this material.

Episcopius' interactions with Triglandius were more bitter. Triglandius had written against the Arminians,[158] but his attacks on Remonstrant pastor Eduardus Poppius especially provoked Episcopius.[159] Poppius, well known for his gentleness and passivity, was imprisoned died in prison after Calvinists incarcerated him. Triglandius and Episcopius wrote against one another,[160] culminating with Episcopius' *Der War-Religie ofte de verwarde, valsche en redenloose Religie Jacobi Triglandii.*[161] He regretted both the sharpness of the book and its title.[162] The last attack from a faculty member at Leiden came from Abraham van der Heyden, the first of a new generation of Contra-Remonstrants. His analysis of the Remonstrant catechism appeared in 1641,[163] and although Episcopius answered it, it was published post-humously.[164] Episcopius' final work was a rejoinder against an anonymous accusation of Arianism and Socinianism.[165]

Episcopius and the Remonstrant Seminary

Perhaps Episcopius' most lasting contribution to the Remonstrant movement was founding the Remonstrant Seminary in 1632. Episcopius began holding classes in his living room with seven students on October 28, 1634.[166] He eventually taught both Stephanus Curcellæus, and his nephew, Philip van Limborch, who would become future theologians of the Remonstrant movement.[167] In spite of the complaints of Calvinist pastors[168] and the election of a new city council,[169] the government was increasingly tolerant.[170] Episcopius devoted himself to the seminary so much that Grotius worried he was getting out of touch with theological developments outside the Netherlands.[171]

We encounter Episcopius' mature theology in his lectures from this period, the *Institutiones Theologicæ, privatis lectionibus Amstelodami traditæ,*[172] and *Responsio ad Quæstiones Theologicas sexaginta quatuor, ipsi a discipulis in privatio disputationem collegio Amstelodami propositas.*[173]

Episcopius' Death

Episcopius' frequent travels precipitated his death. A violent storm overtook him and his wife while they were on their way to Rotterdam in August 1640. They arrived too late to enter the city, and he contracted a fever that permanently damaged his health. He suffered similar circumstances in February 1643, and declined until at last he died on April 4. He was buried four days later in the Western Church beside his wife.[174] Although many came to his funeral, the most poignant presence was that of Johannes Wtenbogært. Van Limborch recorded that when his attendants helped the old man into the room where the body was laid out, Wtenbogært approached it and placing his hands upon Episcopius' head, cried out "O caput, quanta sapientia in te recondita fuit!"[175] He had buried Arminius; he would bury Episcopius as well.

Summary, Observations and Conclusions

First, this chapter provided a socio-historical background for the Arminian controversy and for Episcopius' life and ministry. Several factors that gave rise to the Reformation in the Netherlands also provided for the development of the Arminian controversy. The Reformation flourished because of the religious preparation of the Dutch people by means of various spiritual renewal movements, the rise of northern humanism and a resulting ambient of religious toleration, and the political realities of the Netherlands in the sixteenth century. These factors in turn produced a polymorphic Reformed church differentiated by ethnicity and theological leadership. While these factors allowed the Reformed church to become the predominate religion of the Low Countries, they also frustrated those who desired a Genevan-styled ecclesiology. Because of both political and religious divisions, Gomarist and Arminian parties brought the United Provinces to the brink of civil war in their struggle for control of the United Provinces. The military resolution of this political crisis provided for the denouement of the religious as well.

Second, we considered the lives of Arminius and Episcopius. We established that a close relationship existed between them, and noted their many parallel experiences. We may also observe marked differences. One of the most noticeable is their leadership style. During Arminius' life, he maintained a clear division of roles between his capacity as the theological leader of the movement and Wtenbogært's political and organizational activities. Because of Arminius' death and Wtenbogært's decision not to lead the Remonstrants at the Synod of Dort, Episcopius inherited both responsibilities. He brought the Remonstrants through a Weberian transition from charismatic to bureaucratic leadership. He took over the defense of the Arminian faith, first at Dort, and then by his unrelenting output of polemical and apologetic writings throughout his life. The Remonstrants recognized this leadership, and turned to him for the writing of the *Confessio*, their catechism and formularies. They entrusted him with founding the Remonstrant seminary and training the next generation of Remonstrant pastors. While Arminius gave life to the movement, it was Episcopius fought for and guaranteed its survival.

We may also observe differences in their ministerial orientation. While Arminius invested fifteen years in pastoral ministry before becoming a professor and continued to preach in Leiden even after his call to the university, Episcopius was a professor waiting for a call, and gave up preaching as soon as he began to teach. Although his pastoral inclinations grew with his leadership in the Remonstrant Brotherhood, he was primarily a theologian. Finally, we may observe significant differences in their personalities. Arminius was cautious. He guarded his words and protected himself behind Erastian interplay between church and state. He avoided conflict as much as possible, sometimes taking advantage of the "near-misses" in his opponents' representations in order to protect himself from criticism. Episcopius was the opposite. As a student, he delighted in debate. He provoked conflict at Dort. He was incessant in his defense of Arminianism, showing no tolerance for what he perceived as the ignorance, prejudice or prevarications of his opponents. However, like Arminius, he tired of the battle, and in the end, he dedicated himself to training and equipping a future generation of Remonstrant pastors.

Notes

[1] Carter Lindberg, *The European Reformations* (Oxford: Blackwell Publishers, 1996), 299–300. For a modern history of the Netherlands, with detailed analysis of the Reformation period, see Pieter Geyl, *Geschiedenis van de Nederlandse Stam*, 6 vols. (Amsterdam: Wereldbibliotheek, 1961–62). Two older but still respected and often cited introductions to this period of history in the Netherlands are John Lothrop Motley, *The Rise of the Dutch Republic: A History*, 3 vols. (New York: Harper & Bros., 1856), and Petrus Johannes Blok, *Geschiedenis van het Nederlandsche Volk*, 6 vols. (Groningen: J. B. Wolters, 1892). Perhaps the best introductions to the history of the Dutch Reformation dates from the seventeenth century, Geerært Brandt and Johannes Brandt, *Historie der Reformatie en Andere Kerkelyke Geschiedenissen in en Ontrent de Nederlanden*, 2d ed., 4 vols. (Amsterdam: Jan Rieuwertsz. Hendrik and Dirk Boom, 1677–1704), available in English as Geerært Brandt, *The History of the Reformation and other Ecclesiastical Transactions In and About the Low-countries: From the Beginning of the Eighth Century, Down to the Famous Synod of Dort, Inclusive: faithfully translated from the original Low-Dutch*, 4 vols. (London: Printed by T. Wood for T. Childe, 1720). The Reformation in the Netherlands has been the subject of numerous monographs and books. For general introductions to the history of the Reformation in the Netherlands, see Johannes Reitsma, *Geschiedenis Van de Hervorming en De Hervormde Kerk der Nederlanden*, 4th ed. (Utrecht: Kemink & Zoon, 1933); Willem Nijenhuis, *Ecclesia Reformata: Studies on the Reformation*, 2 vols. (Leiden: Brill, 1972); Geoffrey Parker, *The Dutch Revolt* (Ithaca, NY: Cornell University Press, 1977) and Alastair C. Duke, *Reformation and Revolt in the Low Countries* (London: Hambledon Press, 1990).

[2] John Thomas McNeill, *The History and Character of Calvinism* (New York: Oxford University Press, 1954), 225; Gerrit J. Hoenderdaal, "The Life and Thought of Jacobus Arminius," *Religion in Life* 29 (1960): 544–45; Alistair C. Duke, "Salvation by Coercion: the Controversy Surrounding the 'Inquisition' in the Low Countries on the Eve of the Revolt," in *Reformation Principle and Practice: Essays in Honour of Arthur Geoffrey Dickens*, ed. Peter Newman Brooks (London: Scholar's Press, 1980), 141–142; W. Robert Godfrey, "Calvin and Calvinism in the Netherlands," in *John Calvin, His Influence in the Western World*, ed. W. Stanford Reid and Paul Woolley (Grand Rapids, Zondervan, 1982), 96.

[3] Reitsma, *Geschiedenis*, 17–18; Brandt, *History of the Reformation*, 1:3–11.

[4] Reitsma, *Geschiedenis*, 29–55, but especially Albert Hyma, *The Christian Renaissance: a history of the "Devotio moderna."* 2d ed. (Hamden, CT: Archon Books, 1965) and idem, *The Life of Desiderius Erasmus* (Assen: Van Gorcum, 1972).

[5] Reitsma, *Geschiedenis*, 22–25.

[6] Diedrich Hinrich Kromminga, *The Christian Reformed Tradition: From the Reformation till the Present* (Grand Rapids: Wm. B. Eerdmans, 1943), 7; Alistair C. Duke, "The

Netherlands," in *The Early Reformation in Europe* (Cambridge: Cambridge University Press, 1992), 148–49. For the importance of lay leadership in Amsterdam, see Carl O. Bangs, "Arminius As A Reformed Theologian," in *The Heritage of John Calvin: Heritage Hall Lectures, 1960–70*, ed. John H. Bratt (Grand Rapids: Eerdmans, 1973), 210–211.

[7] The penalty for anyone who confessed to having done so was unmitigated death. Those who repented either died by the sword (in the case of men) or by being buried alive (if the offender were female). Those who did not recant were burned alive (Lindberg, *The European Reformations*, 303).

[8] Peter Y. De Jong, "Rise of the Reformed Churches in the Netherlands," in *Crisis in the Reformed Churches: Essays in the Commemoration of the Great Synod of Dort, 1618–1619*, ed. Peter Y. De Jong (Grand Rapids: Reformed Fellowship, 1968), 6.

[9] "Christian humanism had influential advocates in the grammar schools, among the jurists and among the leading clergy…. The growing popularity of Erasmus' *Enchiridion* provided yet another indicator of the way opinion among the intellectual elite had changed. The founding in 1517 of the Trilingual College at Louvain seemed to offer tangible proof that the philological approach to the text of the Scriptures, recommended by Erasmus and others, was finally gaining acceptance" (Duke, "The Netherlands," 142–43). For the importance of the humanist movement in the Netherlands with respect to the Reformation, see Wiebe Bergsma, "The Low Countries," in *The Reformation in National Context*, ed. Robert W. Scribner, Roy Porter, and Mikuláš Teich (Cambridge: Cambridge University Press, 1994), 69–70; Duke, "The Netherlands," 142–44; De Jong, "Rise of the Reformed Churches in the Netherlands," 15; Nijenhuis, *Ecclesia Reformata: Studies on the Reformation*, 134–35; Jozef Ijsewijn, "Humanism in the Low Countries," in *Renaissance Humanism: Foundations, Forms, and Legacy*, ed. Albert Rabil (Philadelphia: University of Pennsylvania Press, 1988) and Diarmaid MacCulloch, "Arminius and the Arminians," *History Today* 39 (1989): 31–32.

[10] S. Dresden, *Humanism in the Renaissance* (London: Weidenfeld & Nicolson, 1968), 231. For an extended examination of humanism as the primary promoter of religious toleration in the sixteenth century, with special focus on Erasmus, see Henry Kamen, *The Rise of Toleration* (New York: McGraw–Hill, 1967), 24–29, 86–110. For the relation between humanism and toleration in the Netherlands, see F. H. Waterbolk, "Humanisme en de Tolerantie-Gedachte," in *Opstand en pacificatie in de Lage Landen. Bijdrage tot de studie van de pacificatie van Gent* (Ghent: Snoeck-Ducaju/Nijgh & Van Ditmar, 1976). The noted Dutch humanist Dirk Volkerszoon Coornhert (1522–90) was singularly important regarding this, especially in opposition to Beza's call for the persecution and execution of heretics (Théodore de Bèze, *De hæreticis a ciuili magistratu puniendis libellus, aduersus Martini Bellii farraginem, & nouorum academicorum sectam* [Minerva (Geneva), Unveränderter Nachdruck: Oliua Roberti Stephani, 1554]; cf. Dieryck Volkertszoon Coornhert, *À l'aurore des libertés modernes: Synode sur la liberté de conscience (1582)* [Paris: Éditions du Cerf, 1979]). For scholarly examinations of Coornhert as a proponent of religious liberty and toleration, see Carl Lorentzen, "Dieryck Volkertszoon Coornhert: der Vorläufer der Remonstranten: ein Vorkämpfter der Gewissensfreiheit: Versuch einer Biographie," (Ph.D. diss., University of Jena, 1886); H. Bonger, "De motiviering van de godsdienstvrijheid bij Dirck Volckertszoon Coornhert," (Van Loghum Slaterus, 1954); H. idem, *Dirck Volckertszoon Coornhert: dwars maar recht* (Zutphen: De Walburg Pers, 1989); Bruno Becker, *Sébastien Castellion et Thierry Coornhert* (Amsterdam: Hertzberger, 1968);

Gerrit Voogt, *Constraint on Trial: Dirck Volckertsz Coornhert and Religious Freedom* (Kirksville, MO: Truman State University Press, 2000).

11 Bergsma, "The Low Countries," 67–70.

12 Auke Jelsma, *Frontiers of the Reformation: Dissidence and Orthodoxy in Sixteenth-Century Europe* (Aldershot, England: Ashgate, 1998), 116–17.

13 McNeill, *The History and Character of Calvinism*, 257.

14 See a letter from a rural Reformed pastor in which he complained that in the "quite populous" village of Aarlanderveen there were a "huge number" of Lutherans and only eleven members of the Reformed church (Johannes Lydius to Franciscus Junius, May 3, 1602, in Alastair C. Duke, Gillian Lewis, and Andrew Pettegree, *Calvinism in Europe, 1540–1610: A Collection of Documents* (Manchester: Manchester University Press, 1992), 195–96).

15 Lindberg, *The European Reformations*, 208. For information on the Mennonite presence in the Netherlands, see J. J. Westerbeek van Eerten, *Anabaptisme en Calvinisme: Tafereelen uit de Vaderlandsche Kerkgeschiedenis der 16e eeuw, 1531–1568* (Kampen: J. H. Kok, 1905); Alistair C. Duke, "The Ambivalent Face of Calvinism in the Netherlands, 1561–1618," in *International Calvinism, 1541–1715*, ed. Menna Prestwich (Oxford: Clarendon Press, 1985), 114–16. For an early Anabaptist martyriology, see Thieleman J. van Braght, *Het Bloedig Tooneel, of Martelærs Spiegel der Doops-gesinde of Weerloose Christenen: Versamelt uyt verscheyde geloofweerdige chronijken, memorien, en getuygenissen*, 2nd ed., 2 vols. (Amsterdam: H. Sweerts, J. ten Hoorn, J. Bouman, and D. van den Dalen, 1685), available in English as idem, *The Bloody Theater, or, Martyrs' Mirror*, 17th ed. (Scottdale, PA: Herald Press, 1951). Regarding Dutch society's mixed reactions to the persecution of the Mennonites see Duke, "Salvation by Coercion," 142–43.

16 Concerning doctrinal diversity among the Dutch Reformed before the National Synod of Dort, see especially L. Knappert, *Het Ontstaan en de Vestiging van het Protestantisme in de Nederlanden* (Utrecht: A. Oosthoek, 1924), 237–59. See also Bangs, "Arminius As A Reformed Theologian," 212–14; Nijenhuis, *Ecclesia Reformata: Studies on the Reformation*, 164–182; and Willem Nijenhuis, "Variants within Dutch Calvinism in the Sixteenth Century," *The Low Countries History Yearbook* 12 (1979). For disagreements between the Reformed delegates at the Synod of Dort, see W. Robert Godfrey, "Tensions within International Calvinism: the Debate on the Atonement at the Synod of Dort, 1618–1619," (Ph.D. diss., Stanford University, 1974).

17 Bergsma, "The Low Countries," 75. Calvin sent Pierre Brully, his first emissary to the Netherlands, to Tournai and Valenciennes in 1544. His quick martyrdom precluded significant results.

18 For discussions of the importance of Melanchthon and Bullinger in guiding the Reformation in the northern provinces, see Antonius Johannes van't Hooft, "De Theologie van Heinrich Bullinger in Betrekking tot de Nederlandsche Reformatie," (Ph.D. thesis, Rijksuniversiteit te Leiden, 1888); F. Pijper, "Geestelijke Stroomingen in Nederland Vóór de Opkomst van het Remonstrantisme," in *De Remonstranten Gedenkboek bij het 300-jarig betstaan der Remonstrantsche Broederschap*, ed. G. J. Heering (Leiden: A. W. Sijthoff's Uitgevers, 1919), 50–51; Duke, "The Ambivalent Face of Calvinism," 118–22. However, see also Winkelmen regarding pre-Arminian sentiments among Dutch Catholics which may have prepared the way for Melanchthon, Bullinger and ultimately Arminius (P. H. Winkelman, *Remonstranten en Katholieken in de eeuw van Hugo de Groot* (Nijmegen: Uitgeverij de Koepel, 1945), 75–83.

19 For a description of Melanchthon's original agreement with Luther regarding predestination and free will, and eventual rejection, see Philip Schaff, *The Creeds of Christendom, with a History and Critical Notes*, 6th ed., (New York: Harper & Brothers, 1919), 3:259–71.

20 For Hemmingius' theological works, see Nicolas Hemmingius, *Tractatus* (Copenhagen: Munksgaard, 1591).

21 Arminius specifically cited Melanchthon and Hemmingius in the defense of conditional predestination. See James Arminius, "A Declaration of the Sentiments of Arminius on Predestination, Divine Providence, The Freedom of the Will, the Grace of God, the Divinity of the Son of God, and the Justification of Man Before God," in *The Works of James Arminius*, trans. James Nichols, London ed. (London: Longman, Hurst, Rees, Orme, Brown and Green, 1825; reprint, Grand Rapids: Baker, 1986), 1:642–43.

22 Fritz Büsser, *Wurzeln der Reformation in Zürich: zum 500 Geburtstag des Reformators Huldrych Zwingli* (Leiden: E.J. Brill, 1985), 170. See also McNeill, *The History and Character of Calvinism*, 66–72; W. Stanford Reid and Paul Woolley, eds., *John Calvin, His influence in the Western world*, Contemporary Evangelical Perspectives (Grand Rapids: Zondervan, 1982), 40–41.

23 Henry Bullinger, *The Decades of Henry Bullinger*, ed. Thomas Harding, trans. "H. I." (Cambridge: The University Press, 1849). First published in Latin as Heinrich Bullinger, *Sermonum decades quinque, de potissimis Christianæ religionis capitibus in tres tomos digestæ* (Zurich: In officina Christoph. Froshoveri, 1552), published in Dutch as idem, *Hvysboec \ Viif Decades* (Emden: n.p., 1563). For an analysis of the *Huisboek*, see Walter Hollweg, *Heinrich Bullingers Hausbuch: eine Untersuchung über die Anfänge der Reformierten Predigtliteratur* (Neukirchen: Krs. Moers, 1956). For support of distinctions between Bullinger and Calvin, see J. Wayne Baker, *Heinrich Bullinger and the Covenant: The Other Reformed Tradition* (Athens, OH: Ohio University Press, 1980); for a defense of unity between Calvin and Bullinger and a response to Baker, see Cornelis P. Venema, *Heinrich Bullinger and the Doctrine of Predestination: Author of "the Other Reformed Tradition"?* (Grand Rapids: Baker Academic, 2002).

24 Godfrey, "Calvin and Calvinism in the Netherlands," 98; see also G. Oorthuys, *Anastasius' "Wechwyser," Bullingers "Huysboeck" en Calvyns "Institutie" vergeleken in hun leer van God en mensch* (Leiden: Brill, 1919); Büsser, *Wurzeln der Reformation in Zürich*, 172–74. Some have denied any differences between Bullinger and Calvin on predestination on the basis of the *Consensus Tigurinis*, which he developed in conjunction with Calvin (De Jong, "Rise of the Reformed Churches in the Netherlands," 19; Louis Praamsma, "The Background of the Arminian Controversy (1586–1618)," in *Crisis in the Reformed Churches: Essays in Commemoration of the Great Synod of Dort, 1618–1619*, ed. Peter Y. De Jong [Grand Rapids: Reformed Fellowship, 1968], 22–38). However, it was not *Consensus Tigurinis* but the *Hausbuch* that influenced the Netherlands, which he wrote before Calvin's influence. Bergsma offered support for Bullinger's priority in the Netherlands from a letter dated 1586 in which Reformed pastor Johannes van der Mijle recommended the *Hausbuch* for the theological instruction of his congregation (Bergsma, "The Low Countries," 73). In spite of Calvin's collaboration, the *Consensus Tigurinis* was nearly rejected by French Reformed at La Rochelle (Blanke and Leuschner, *Heinrich Bullinger*, 266).

25 "Das Werk erschein in den Jahren 1549 bis 1551 und umfaßlich nicht 60, sondern nur 50 Predigten, in denen Bullinger sine theologischen Erkenntniss verarbeitet hatte, die er in seinem schweren Amt als Antistes Zürcher Kirche hat sammeln können. Sie sind ein

würdiges Gegenstuck zur «Institutio» von Johannes Calvin" (Fritz Blanke and Immanuel Leuschner, *Heinrich Bullinger: Vater der Reformierten Kirche* [Zürich: Theologischer Verlag, 1990], 184).

26 For a summary of Bullinger on predestination in the *Decades*, see Blanke and Leuschner, *Heinrich Bullinger*, 190–96. We may also note the absence of predestination in Bullinger's popular essay, "The Old Faith" (Heinrich Bullinger, *Der alt gloub das der Christen gloub von anfang der wält gewart habe der recht waar alt und ungezwyflet gloub sye klare bewysung* [Zürich: Christoffel Froschouer, 1539]). For an analysis of the theological content of this essay, consult E. A. Downey, "Comments on One of Heinrich Bullinger's Most Distinctive Treatises," in *Calvin: Erbe und Auftrag: Festschrift für Wilhelm Heinrich Neuser zum 65. Geburtstag*, ed. W. van 't Spijker and Wilhelm H. Neuser (Kampen: J. H. Kok, 1991). Although Bullinger seemed to anticipate Arminius' views on predestination when he wrote "God the Father hath ordained that...whosoever doth believe in the only-begotten Son of God, shall be made partaker of Christ his righteousness" (Bullinger, *Decades*, 110), elsewhere his opinions appear infralapsarian.

27 Bullinger, *Decades*, 53, 69, 76 ("...a full pardon of all sins is promised to all men"), 110–12 ("The eternal and unchangeable will of God is, that he will give eternal life unto the world. But he will give the life through Christ"), 129, 133, 136, 165 ("Moreover, it is not for the sins of a few men, of one or two ages...but the sins of all men, of all ages, the whole multitude of sins").

28 Bullinger wrote that many were displeased with what Calvin had written in the *Institutes* about predestination, and others had drawn the same conclusions from it as Bolsec has drawn from Zwingli's book on Providence. Schaff added that this affair caused a temporary alienation between Calvin and Bullinger which was not overcome until ten years later when Bullinger decidedly embraced Calvin's perspective, though without any emphasis on reprobation (Philip Schaff, *History of the Christian Church*, vol. 8 [New York: 1910], 3:618). For a summary of the conflict between Calvin and Bolsec, and Bolsec's defense by some Genevans and other Reformed leaders, see R. M. Kingdon, "Popular Reactions to the Debate between Bolsec and Calvin," in *Calvin: Erbe und Auftrag: Festschrift für Wilhelm Heinrich Neuser zum 65. Geburtstag*, ed. W. van 't Spijker and Wilhelm H. Neuser (Kampen: J. H. Kok, 1991), 138–145. For more on differences between Bullinger and Calvin with respect to predestination, consult Ulrich Gäbler, *Huldrych Zwingli: His Life and Work*, trans. Ruth C. L. Gritsch (Philadelphia: Fortress Press, 1986), 158.

29 For the importance of Calvin's letters, books and pamphlets in supplanting Lutheranism, see W. Stanford Reid, "The Transmission of Sixteenth Century Calvinism," in *John Calvin, His Influence in the Western World*, ed. W. Stanford Reid and Paul Woolley, Contemporary Evangelical Perspectives (Grand Rapids: Zondervan, 1982), 50.

30 Gerald Cerny, *Theology, Politics, and Letters at the Crossroads of European Civilization: Jacques Basnage and the Baylean Huguenot Refugees in the Dutch Republic* (Dordrecht: M. Nijhoff, 1987), 54–57; cf. D. F. Poujol, *Histoire et Influence des Églises Wallonnes dans les Pays-Bas* (Paris: Fischbacher, 1902); Frank Le Cornu, *Origine des Eglises réformées wallonnes des Pays-Bas: étude historique* (Utrecht: J. van Boekhoven, n.d.); Lindberg, *The European Reformations*, 306. However, see Bangs on Albert Hardenberg, pastor of the Reformed church at Emden (Carl O. Bangs, "Arminius and the Reformation," *Church History* 30 (1961): 158–59. The identification of these "three avenues" by which Calvinism influenced the Netherlands is De Jong's (De Jong, "Rise of the Reformed

Churches in the Netherlands," 9). F. L. Rutgers has written a detailed account of the growth of Calvin's predominance in the Netherlands, with excerpts of numerous rare documents (F. L. Rutgers, *Calvijns Invloed Op de Reformatie in de Nederlanden, Voor Zooveel Die Door Hemzelven is Uitgeoefend*, 2d ed. [Leiden: D. Donner, 1899]).

[31] "The Reformed Church in the north had a large number of clergy who were exiles from the south and whose Calvinism was reinforced by their fierce longing for a lost home. For them, any attack on the faith for which so many had fought and died was an act of political treachery as well as blasphemy" (MacCulloch, "Arminius and the Arminians," 30).

[32] "The Walloon church promoted the establishment of the Dutch Reformed Church, and thus became esteemed as the 'mother church.' Meeting in Emden in East-Friesland in joint session with the Synod of the Walloon Church between October 4–14, 1517, the newly constituted Dutch Reformed Church adopted the Walloon Confession of Faith" (Cerny, *Theology, Politics, and Letters*, 55). For the importance of the time that Reformed refugees spent at Emden, see Andrew Pettegree, *Emden and the Dutch Revolt: Exile and Development of Reformed Protestantism* (Oxford: Oxford University Press, 1992).

[33] Godfrey, "Calvin and Calvinism in the Netherlands," 100–101. Regarding the importance of the Belgic Confession, see Cerny, *Theology, politics, and letters*, 54. Regarding the organization of Calvinist churches in the Netherlands, see F. R. J. Knetsch, "Church Ordinances and Regulations of the Dutch Synods 'Under the Cross' (1563–1566) Compared With The French (1559–1663)," in *Humanism and Reform: The Church in Europe, England, and Scotland, 1400–1643: Essays in Honour of James K. Cameron*, ed. James Kirk, Studies in church history. Subsidia; 8 (Oxford: Published for the Ecclesiastical History Society by Basil Blackwell, 1991) and Richard Fitzsimmons, "Building a Reformed ministry in Holland, 1572–1583," in *The Reformation of the Parishes: The Ministry and the Reformation in Town and Country*, ed. Andrew Pettegree (Manchester: Manchester University Press, 1993).

[34] Godfrey, "Calvin and Calvinism in the Netherlands," 99. For an extended treatment of a Reformed "campaign of uniformity" in the Netherlands, see Jelsma, *Frontiers of the Reformation*, 110–32. For the Remonstrant perspective from the previous century on the growth of Calvinism in the Netherlands as a supplanting native Arminianism, see G. J. Heering, "Het Godsdienstig Beginsel," in *De Remonstranten Gedenkboek bij het 300-jarig bestaan der Remonstrantsche Broederschap*, ed. G. J. Heering (Leiden: A. W. Sijthoof's Uitgevers, 1619).

[35] Lindberg, *The European Reformations*, 299–301,

[36] Aside from Motley's colorful description both of Philip and the political events surrounding the Dutch revolt against Philip (Motley, *The Rise of the Dutch Republic*), see two modern biographies, Peter Pierson, *Phillip II of Spain* (New York: Transatlantic Arts, 1975) and Geoffrey Parker, *Philip II*, 3d ed. (Chicago: Open Court, 1995).

[37] Although the number of martyrs in the Netherlands is debated, there were 3,000 confirmed deaths in the first three months of the reign of terror instituted by the Spanish general Alva, which eventually claimed 18,000 lives over three years. Scholarly estimates of the total number of deaths before 1609 range as high as 100,000 (Arthur C. Cochrane, *Reformed Confessions of the 16th Century* (Philadelphia: Westminster Press, 1966), 185; De Jong, "Rise of the Reformed Churches in the Netherlands," 20). For a brief but thorough summary of the inquisition in the Netherlands, consult Duke, "Salvation by Coercion," *passim*.

[38] Gordon S. Wakefield, "Arminianism in the Seventeenth and Eighteenth Centuries," *London Quarterly and Holborn Review* 185, 6th ser., no. 29 (1960): 254.

[39] For an extended discussion of the evolution of William's relationship with Calvinist leadership, see Jelsma, *Frontiers of the Reformation*, 112–16.

[40] Godfrey, "Calvin and Calvinism in the Netherlands," 102. Regarding William the Silent's efforts to keep the revolt from becoming a Calvinist movement, and his concerns for religious inclusiveness, see especially Kamen, *The Rise of Toleration*, 145–50, but also Nijenhuis, *Ecclesia Reformata: Studies on the Reformation*, 171–172; Godfrey, "Calvin and Calvinism in the Netherlands," 102; Bergsma, "The Low Countries," 21, and Lindberg, *The European Reformations*, 307 . William's mentality was shared by Marcus Pérez, leader of the Marrano Calvinists; see Alistair C. Duke, "A Footnote to 'Marrano Calvinism' and the Troubles of 1566–1567 In The Netherlands," *Bibliotheque d'humanisme et Renaissance* 30 (1968).

[41] De Jong, "Rise of the Reformed Churches in the Netherlands," 10, 15. For a good summary of the provincial relationships in the Netherlands, see David Oog, *Europe in the Seventeenth Century* (London: Adam and Charles Black, 1948), 408–13.

[42] For population studies indicating the small proportion of the Reformed in the Netherlands, see Duke, "The Netherlands," 130, 132; and Bergsma, "The Low Countries," 74–75.

[43] Oog, *Europe in the Seventeenth Century*, 86–87.

[44] Carl O. Bangs, "All the Best Bishoprics and Deaneries: The Enigma of Arminian Politics," *Church History* 42 (1973): 8. Bangs provided an extensive analysis of Erastianism in the Netherlands.

[45] Regarding Erastus' personal relationships with Bullinger and Beza, see Blanke and Leuschner, *Heinrich Bullinger*, 242–49.

[46] The Netherlands were not alone in this. Zwingli and Bullinger both accepted some form of Erastianism in which the magistrates had a voice in the affairs of the consistory. See Bangs, "Arminius and the Reformation," 159.

[47] Godfrey, "Calvin and Calvinism in the Netherlands," 103–04; Oog, *Europe in the Seventeenth Century* .

[48] Carl O. Bangs, "Dutch Theology, Trade and War: 1590–1610," *Church History* 39 (1970): 471.

[49] "The States-General which met at the Hague was really an assembly of ambassadors from sovereign states. The deputies were elected for three or six years and were convoked by the Council of State; they were not free agents but merely the mouthpieces of their constituents. In other words, each state could, by its dissent, exercise what might, in effect, be a *liberum veto*, and it was only by a series of accidents that the Dutch did not share the fate of the Pole. At first the whole assembly discussed questions of foreign policy, but after the execution of Barnevelt in 1619 Maurice of Nassau interested himself in this department and gradually the Orange family came to influence the direction of foreign affairs" (Oog, *Europe in the Seventeenth Century*, 410).

[50] Godfrey, "Tensions within International Calvinism," 102–03.

[51] Oog described Oldenbarnevelt as "the great and patriotic Advocate of Holland, John van Oldenbarnevelt, in whom were incarnated the finest qualities of Dutch republicanism" (Oog, *Europe in the Seventeenth Century*, 412).

[52] See John Lothrop Motley, *The Life and Death of John of Barneveld, Advocate of Holland; With a View of the Primary Causes and Movements of the Thirty Years' War*, 2 vols. (New York: Harper & Brothers, 1874); Guillaume Groen van Prinsterer, *Maurice et Barnevelt: étude historique* (Utrecht: Kemink et fils, 1875).

53 Although Motley did not spare Maurice for his faults, he defended Maurice's aspirations: "There was nothing criminal on the part of Maurice if he was ambitious of obtaining the sovereignty himself. He was not seeking to compass it by base artifice or by intrigue of any kind. It was very natural that he should be restive under the dictatorship of the advocate. If a simple burgher and lawyer could make himself despot of the Netherlands, how much more reasonable he—with the noblest blood of Europe in his veins, whose direct ancestors three centuries before had been emperor not only of those provinces but of all of Germany and half Christendom besides, whose immortal father had under God been the creator and savior of the new commonwealth, had made sacrifices such as man never made for a people" (Motley, *John of Barneveld*, 2:38–39). See also McNeill, *The History and Character of Calvinism*, 264–65.

54 "The result of the initial struggle between the two was ominous for the future of separatist principles. As usual it was entangled with a religious question. Jacob Harmensz (Arminius) was appointed Professor of Theology at Leyden in 1602. His more relaxed doctrines were favoured by Oldenbarneveldt and by a majority in Holland; Maurice and a large section of the States-General were zealous upholders of orthodox and uncompromising Calvinism" (Oog, *Europe in the Seventeenth Century*, 413).

55 Ibid., 87.

56 Schaff, *Creeds of Christendom*, 511–12; Rattenbury, "The Historical Background and Life of Arminius," 246.

57 "Maurice was not a theologian. He was a steady churchgoer, and his favorite divine, the preacher at his court chapel, was none other than Uytenbogaert....The theological quibble did not interest him much, and he was apt to blunder about it. 'Well, preacher,' said he one day to Albert Huttenus, who had come to him to intercede for a deserter condemned to be hanged, 'are you one of the Arminians who believe that one child is born to salvation and another to damnation?' Huttenus, amazed to the uttermost at the extraordinary question, replied, 'Your Excellency will be graciously pleased to observe that this is not the opinion of those whom one calls by the hateful name of Arminians, but the opinion of their adversaries.' 'Well, preacher,' rejoined Maurice, 'don't you think I know better?' And turning to Count Louis William, stadholder of Friesland, who was present, standing by the hearth with his hand on a copper ring of the chimneypiece, he cried, 'Which is right, cousin, the preacher or I?' 'No, cousin,' answered Count Louis, 'you are in the wrong'" (Motley, *John of Barneveld*, 1:51–52).

58 Oog, *Europe in the Seventeenth Century*, 414–16.

59 The single most important original source for Arminius' life and ministry is Petrus Bertius' oration given at Arminius' funeral (Petrus Bertius, *Oratio De Vita & Obitu Reverendi et Clarissimi Viri D. Iacobi Arminii, Dicta Post tristes ilius exsequias XXII. Octo. Anno CLC.L.C.IX in Auditorio Theologico*, in *Opera Theologica* [Leiden: Goderfridum Basson, 1629]), also available in English as *The Oration of Peter Bertius concerning the life and death of that Reverend and most Famous man, Mr. James Arminius*, in *The Popish Labyrinth*, ed.(London: Ratcliff and Thomson for Francis Smith, 1672); "An Oration on the Life and Death of that Reverend and Very Famous Man, James Arminius, D.D.," in *The Works of James Arminius*, trans. James Nichols, The London ed. (London: Longman, Hurst, Rees, Orme, Brown and Green, 1825; reprint, Grand Rapids: Baker, 1986). However, Carl O. Bangs' research has radically broadened the understanding of Arminius' life, and his social and political milieu. See Carl O. Bangs, "Arminius and Reformed Theology," (Ph.D. diss., University of Chicago, 1958); idem, "Dutch Theology;" idem, "All the Best Bishoprics

and Deaneries;" and especially idem, *Arminius: A Study in the Dutch Reformation*, 2d ed. (Grand Rapids: Francis Asbury Press, 1985). I have closely followed his conclusions. Other important biographies include Nathan Bangs, *The Life of James Arminius* (New York: Harper and Brothers, 1843) and J. H. Maronier, *Jacobus Arminius: Een Biografie (met portret en handteekening)* (Amsterdam: Y. Rogge, 1905). Books which broadly treat the history of the Arminian movement up through the Synod of Dort are Brandt and Brandt, *Historie der reformatie en andere kerkelyke geschiedenissen in en ontrent de Nederlanden* and A. W. Harrison, *The Beginnings of Arminianism to the Synod of Dort* (London: University of London Press, 1926).

60   The idea that Arminius agreed with Beza and then changed his mind after attempting to defend supralapsarianism gains support from Peter Bertius' funeral oration (Bertius, "OVO," 6–7, cf. Bertius, "An Oration," 29–30). Bertius cited Arminius' esteem for Beza (Bertius, "OVO," 4; cf. Bertius, "An Oration," 22). Carl Bangs argued to the contrary, that Arminius was Melanchthonian from the beginning and never had shared Beza's theology of predestination, but gradually made his position clear as circumstances permitted (Bangs, *Arminius: A Study in the Dutch Reformation*, 74–77, 183).

61   Bangs defended 1559 as the year of Arminius' birth (ibid, 25–26).

62   Also present as professors during this time were Kaspar Koolhæs, Johannes Feuguerærus and Joannes Holmannus, all of whom were noted humanists, opposed Beza's ideas on predestination and intolerance. For important Dutch research on the life of Koolhæs, see H. C. Rogge, *Caspar Janszoon Coolhaes, de Voorlooper van Arminius en de Remonstranten* 2 vols. (Amsterdam: Y. Rogge, 1865).The first professor to represent Calvin's theology was Lambert Dannæus, who arrived on the faculty in 1581 (Bangs, "Arminius and the Reformation," 161). For an extended discussion of the theological diversity of the university at its founding, see idem, *Arminius: A Study in the Dutch Reformation*, 46–55.

63   Bangs considered Plancius the first to propagate Calvin's doctrine of predestination in Amsterdam (Bangs, *Arminius: A Study in the Dutch Reformation*, 119). His opinion agrees with that of Keuning, Plancius' biographer, who wrote that prior to Plancius, the preaching at Amsterdam was "based more on the Bible than on dogma, on piety than on theology, without reference to predestination" (J. Keuning, *Petrus Plancius, Theoloog en Geograaf, 1552–1622* [Amsterdam: P.N. van Kampen & Zoon, 1946], 7).

64   Arminius' commentaries on Romans 7 and 9 were eventually published. For his interpretation of Romans 7, see Jacobus Arminius, *Dissertatio De Vero & Genuino Senso Cap. VII Epistolæ ad Romanos*, in *Opera Theologica* (Leiden: Goderfridum Basson, 1629); cf. James Arminius, *Dissertation on the True and Genuine Sense of the Seventh Chapter of the Epistle to the Romans*, in *The Works of James Arminius*, trans. James Nichols, London ed. (London: Longman, Hurst, Rees, Orme, Brown and Green, 1828; reprint, Grand Rapids: Baker, 1986). For Romans 9, see Jacobus Arminius, *Analysis Capitis IX ad Romanos*, in *Opera Theologica* (Leiden: Goderfridum Basson, 1629); cf. James Arminius, *An Analysis of the Ninth Chapter of St. Paul's Epistle to the Romans*, in *The Works of James Arminius*, trans. William Nichols, London ed. (London: Longman, Hurst, Rees, Orme, Brown and Green, 1875; reprint, Grand Rapids: Baker, 1986). Bangs provides summaries of both (Bangs, *Arminius: A Study in the Dutch Reformation*, 192–98).

65   Bangs, *Arminius: A Study in the Dutch Reformation*, 255–56.

66   H. C. Rogge's inventory of the library of the Remonstrant church at Amsterdam (H. C. Rogge, *Beschrijvende Catalogus der Pamfletten-Verzameling van de Boikerij der Remonstrantsche Kerk te Amsterdam*, vol. 1, part 1 [Amsterdam: J. H. Scheltema, 1863])is

of great value for brief biographical sketches on Remonstrant pastors and leaders and information on their written work.

67   Jacobus Arminius, *Collatio Amica cum D. Francisco Iunio de Prædestinatione per Litteras Habita*, in *Opera Theologica* (Leiden: Goderfridum Basson, 1629), cf. James Arminius, *Friendly Conference of James Arminius, The Illustrious Doctor of Sacred Theology, With Mr. Francis Junius, About Predestination*, in *The Works of James Arminius*, trans. William Nichols, London ed. (London: Thomas Baker, 1875; reprint, Grand Rapids: Baker, 1986).

68   The distinction between them is the logical order of God's decrees with respect to predestination. Did God decree to first decree to save some and condemn others, and then decree to create man and provoke the fall to provide a just basis for the prior decree (supralapsarianism), or were the decrees logically contemporaneous (infralapsarianism), or did God first decree to permit the fall and then elect to save some and permit others to remain in their lost condition (sublapsarianism). For further explanation, consult William Klempa, "Supralapsarianism," in *The Encyclopedia of the Reformed Faith*; and John M. Frame, "Infralapsarianism," in *The Encyclopedia of the Reformed Faith*. Although modern scholarship considers Calvin infralapsarian, Arminius classed both Calvin and Beza as supralapsarians.

69   Arminius' title indicates he worked from the second edition (William Perkins, *De Prædestinationis Modo et Ordine: et de amplitudine gratiæ divinæ Christiana & perspicua disceptatio* [Basel: C. Waldkirchii, 1599]). For Arminius' response see Jacobus Arminius, *Examen Modestum Libelli, quem D. Gulielmus Perkinsius apprimé doctus Theologus De Prædestinationis Modo et Ordine, Itemque de Amplitudine Gratiæ Divinæ*, in *Opera Theologica* (Leiden: Goderfridum Basson, 1629); cf. James Arminius, *Dr. James Arminius' Modest Examination of a Pamphlet, Which That Very Learned Divine Dr. William Perkins, Published Some Years Ago, On The Mode and Order of Predestination, and On the Amplitude of Divine Grace*, in *The Works of James Arminius*, trans. William Nichols, London ed. (London: Thomas Baker, 1875; reprint, Grand Rapids: Baker, 1986). It is noteworthy that Arminius did not respond to Perkins' first work on predestination (William Perkins, *Armilla Aurea, id est, Theologiæ Descriptio Mirandam Seriem Causarum & Salutis & Damnationis Iuxta Verbum Desproponens: eius synopsin contriet annexa ad finem tabula*, 2d ed. (Cambridge: Johannis Legatt extant Londini apud Abrahamum Kitson ad insigne solis in Cimiterio D. Pauli, 1591); cf. idem, "The Golden Chain," in *The Work of William Perkins*, ed. Ian Breward, The Courtenay Library of Reformation Classics (Abingdon, England: Sutton Courtenay Press, 1970), which depended more directly upon Beza.

70   Arminius, *Examination of Perkins' Pamphlet*, 3:281, 283–92.

71   Ibid., 3:293–94.

72   Simon Kistemaker, "Leading Figures at the Synod of Dort," in *Crisis in the Reformed Churches: Essays in the Commemoration of the Great Synod of Dort, 1618–1619*, ed. Peter Y. De Jong (Grand Rapids: Reformed Fellowship, 1968), 47.

73   Caspar Brandt, *The Life of James Arminius*, trans. John Guthrie (Nashville: E. Stevenson & F.A. Owen, Agents for the Methodist Episcopal Church South, 1857), 173–181. Gomarus would later try to clear his name by saying that Arminius had deceived him. The most complete biography on Gomarus is G. P. Van Itterzon, *Franciscus Gomarus* (The Hague: M. Nijhoff, 1930); biographical summaries are available in Robert D. Linder, "Gomarus, Franciscus (1563–1641)," in *Encyclopedia of the Reformed Faith* and in Kistemaker, "Leading Figures at the Synod of Dort," 42–46. Gomarus' theological works are available in Franciscus Gomarus, *Opera Theologica Omnia*, 3 vols. (Amsterdam: Joannis Janssonii, 1644). Unfortunately, no copy was available at the writing of this dissertation.

74 Arminius' rejoinder does not appear in the *Opera Theologica* of 1629, but was included in James Arminius, *Examination of the Theses of Dr. Francis Gomarus Respecting Predestination*, in *The Works of James Arminius*, London ed. (London: Thomas Baker, 1875; reprint, Grand Rapids: Baker, 1986).

75 The first was a brief reply to a survey requested by delegates from a local synod (Jacobus Arminius, *Quæstiones Numero Novem, Nobliss. DD. Curatoribus Academiæ Leidensis exhibite à Deputatis Synodi, in hunc finem, ut ad eas à Professoribus S. Theologia responderetur*, in *Opera Theologica* (Leiden: Goderfridum Basson, 1629); cf. idem, *Nine Questions Exhibited for the Purpose of Obtaining An Answer From Each of the Professors of divinity: and the replies which James Arminius gave to them: with other nine opposite articles*, in *The Works of James Arminius*, trans. James Nichols, London ed. (London: Longman, Hurst, Rees, Orme, Brown and Green, 1828; reprint, Grand Rapids: Baker, 1986); see also Jacobus Arminius to Ioannes Uytenbogard, 31 January, 1606, in Christiaan Hartsoeker and Philippus van Limborch, eds., *Præstantium ac Eruditorum Virorum Epistolæ Ecclesiasticæ et Theologicæ* (Amsterdam: Henricum Wetstenium, 1660), 202–05, henceforth *PEVE*). The second was a letter to Hippolytus à Collibus, written in early 1608 (Jacobus Arminius to Hippolytus à Collibus, 5 April, 1608, *PEVE* (1660), 917–36, cf. Jacobus Arminius, *Epistola Ad Hypolytum à Collibus*, in *Opera Theologica* (Leiden: Goderfridum Basson, 1629); James Arminius, *A Letter to His Excellency, the Noble Lord, Hippolytus à Collibus*, in *The Works of James Arminius*, trans. James Nichols, London ed. [London: Longman, Hurst, Rees, Orme, Brown and Green, 1828; reprint, Grand Rapids: Baker, 1986]). The third was a response to thirty-one statements attributed to Arminius and Adrian Borrius. It first appeared in Dutch (Jacobus Arminius, *Vierderley Theses of Articulen* [The Hague: Hillebrant Iacobsz, 1610]), then Latin (idem, *Apologia Adversus Articulos quosdam Theologos in vulgus sparsos, saltem in quorundum, in Belgio et extra Belgium manibus versante, quibus tum ille tum Adranus Borreus Ecclesiastes Leidensis novitatis et heterodoxias in Religione, erroris et hæreseos suspecti reddentur*, in *Opera Theologica* [Leiden: Goderfridum Basson, 1629]) and English (James Arminius, *The Apology or Defence of James Arminius, D. D. Against Thirty-One Articles*, in *The Works of James Arminius*, trans. James Nichols, London ed. [London: Longman, Hurst, Rees, Orme, Brown and Green, 1825–28; reprint, Grand Rapids: Baker, 1986]). Although Calvinists have consistently accused Arminius of dissimulation, not only did he make his beliefs clear in these three works, but also he had already openly defended conditional predestination before the consistory at Amsterdam as early as 1593. For a rehearsal of all the old accusations and recriminations, see Homer C. Hoeksema, *The Voice of Our Fathers* (Grand Rapids: Reformed Free Publishing Association, 1980), 3–10.

76 Arminius' "sentiments" or opinions appeared immediately in Dutch (Jacobus Arminius, *Verclaringhe Iacobi Arminii* [Leiden: Thomas Basson, 1610]), then Latin (Jacobus Arminius, *Declaratio Sententiæ I. Arminii de Prædestinatione, Providentia Dei, Libero arbitrio, Gratia Dei, Divinitate Filii Dei, et de Iustificatione hominis coram Deo*, in *Opera Theologica* [Leiden: Goderfridum Basson, 1629]). Along with the *Nine Questions*, this was the first of Arminius' works to appear in English (Jacobus Arminius, *The just man's defence, or, The declaration of the judgement of James Arminius concerning the principal points of religion before the states of Holland; to which is added nine questions with their solution*, trans. Tobias Conyers [London: Printed for Henry Eversden, 1657]).

77 Bangs' description of Arminius' death is informative and confirms Episcopius' extended presence with him (Bangs, *Arminius: A Study in the Dutch Reformation*, 328–30).

78 *Der Grosse Brockhaus*, 16th ed., s.v. "Arminianer." A significant number of pastors predated Arminius. Concerning this expulsion, see Harrison, *The Beginnings of Arminianism*, 378–80; Frederick Calder, *Memoirs of Simon Episcopius* (London: Simpkin and Marshall, 1835), 390–94; and Brandt, *History of the Reformation*, 3:330–381.

79 Important biographical sources on Episcopius are Stephanus Curcellæus' preface for Episcopius' *Opera Theologica* (Stephanus Curcellæus, *Præfatio Ad Lectorem Christianem*, in *Opera Theologica* [Amsterdam: Ioannis Blæv, 1650]), and Philip van Limborch's longer and more complete *Leven van Mr. Simon Episcopius* (In *Predicatien van M. S. Episcopius*, [Amsterdam: Isaak Pieterz., 1693]), which he republished as *Historia Vitæ Episcopii* (Amsterdam: Georgium Gallet, 1701). The only significant biography in English is Calder's *Memoirs of Simon Episcopius*. Although Calder stated he relied heavily on van Limborch for historical details (Calder, *Memoirs*, 71), much of his analysis is unique. These biographies do not discuss the content of Episcopius' theological works. Henrik Haentjens filled many such *lacunæ* with his 1899 doctoral dissertation, *Simon Episcopius als Apologeet van het Remonstrantisme in zijn leven en werken geschetst* (Anton Hendrik Haentjens, *Simon Episcopius als Apologeet van het Remonstrantisme in zijn leven en werken geschetst* [Leiden: A. H. Adriani, 1899]). In the 1960's, Gerrit J. Hoenderdaal provided important information concerning the relationship between Arminius and Episcopius in Gerrit J. Hoenderdaal, "Arminius en Episcopius," *Nederlands Archief voor Kerkgeschiedenis* 60 (1980): 203–35.

80 Bangs, *Arminius: A Study in the Dutch Reformation*, 147.

81 Van Limborch, *Historia Vitæ Episcopii*, 2; Haentjens, *Episcopius als Apologeet*, 9.

82 Van Limborch, *Historia Vitæ Episcopii*, 4–5. Episcopius' thesis was "Is the study of philosophy necessary for the theological candidate?" See Simon Episcopius, *Oratio Generis Deliberativi, An Philosophæ studium necessarium sit Theologiæ candidato? Habita cum Magister artium createtur*, in *Operum Theologicorum, Pars Altera*, ed. Philip van Limborch (Rotterdam: Arnoldum Leers, 1665).

83 Van Limborch, *Historia Vitæ Episcopii*, 5–7.

84 "Bij de bekende twisten tusschen Arminius en Gomarus trok hij partij voor den eerste. Maar ook tot de persoon van Arminius voelde Episcopius zich aangetrokken. Er ontstond een vriendschap tusschen beiden, waaraan Arminius' dood te spoedig een einde maakte. Bijkans in elken brief aan zijn broeder Rem spreekt over Arminius. Moet Arminius eene conferentie bijwonen, hij spreekt vol hoop over hem, de 'altijds met groot courage Godt loff' is. Zal er onder leiding van Arminius eene belangrijke "disputatio" gehouden worden, hij zijn leermeester en vriend zeer" (Haentjens, *Episcopius als Apologeet*, 11).

85 Simon Episcopius to Dr. Arminius, n.d., *PEVE* (1660), 285.

86 Van Limborch, *Historia Vitæ Episcopii*, 7.

87 Calder, *Memoirs*, 53–54.

88 Van Limborch, *Historia Vitæ Episcopii*, 8–9.

89 Calder, *Memoirs*, 56.

90 Antonides asked for a complete explanation of Arminius' positions. When Episcopius began to answer, he confirmed Antonides' fears that Episcopius was too free-spoken with his opinions, and warned Episcopius not to debate while at Franeker (Ibid., 59–60).

91 Van Limborch, *Historia Vitæ Episcopii*, 9–10. Lubbertus went so far as to try to get Episcopius expelled, first by paying other students to get him drunk and break windows, and when that failed, he accused him of Socinianism. See Calder, *Memoirs*, 77–81.

[92] Adrianus Borrius, to Simon Episcopius, Leiden, July 30, 1609, *PEVE* (1660), 291–295. Adrianus Borrius (1565–1630) was president of the University at Leiden, a firm believer in conditional predestination and a close friend of both Arminius and Episcopius.

[93] Haentjens found a letter in the Remonstrant Library in Amsterdam from Episcopius to Borrius in which he poured out his grief over Arminius' death, closing with 2 Kings 2:12, "Vale, Pater! Currus Israëlis et ejus equi!" (Haentjens, *Episcopius als Apologeet*, 12).

[94] Van Limborch, *Historia Vitæ Episcopii*, 16–18 (van Limborch provided the text of the testimonials); Haentjens, *Episcopius als Apologeet*, 15–16; and Calder, *Memoirs*, 91–93. Concerning this ruse, a twentieth century Dutch Reformed pastor wrote, "Likewise the attestation of the Remonstrant Simon Episcopius, who in 1611 came with a good attestation from Franeker and a couple of months later handed it into the commission for attestations in Amsterdam, and without having to wait for an answer, was refused by the session" (Johannes Jansen, *Korte Verklaring van de Kerkenordening* (Kampen: J. H. Kok, 1923), Article 21).

[95] Calder, *Memoirs*, 94–111; Haentjens, *Episcopius als Apologeet*, 16–19.

[96] The Remonstrance of 1610 can be found in Johannes Wtenbogaert, *Kerkeliicke Historie Vervatende verscehdyen Gedenckwærdige Sæcken in de Christenheyt voorgevallen van het Jær vier hondert af, tot in het Jær sestien hondert ende negentien, Voornamentlijck in dese Geunieerde Provincien*, 2d ed. ([Amsterdam]: Ghedruckt in't Iær ons Heeren, 1647), 524–29; Jacobus Triglandius, *Kerckelycke geschiedenissen: begrypende de swære en bekommerlijcke geschillen in de Vereenigde Nederlanden voor-gevallen : met derselver beslissinge: ende ænmerckingen op de Kerckelycke historie van Johannes VVtenbogært: uyt autentycke stucken getrouwelijck vergadert: ende op begeerte der Zuyd en Noort-Hollantsche synden uytgegeven, tot nodige onderrichtinge* (Leiden: Adriæn Wyngærden, 1650), 522–33, and two places in Schaff, *Creeds of Christendom*, 1:516–19 and 3:545–49 (English, Dutch and Latin). McNeill gives the following summary: "Briefly, this document states (1) that the eternal decree of salvation refers to those who shall believe and persevere in faith; (2) that Christ died for all men, though believers only are benefited; (3) that man can do nothing truly good until he is born again through the Holy Spirit; (4) that grace is not irresistible; and (5) that the faithful are assisted by grace in temptation and are kept from falling if they desire Christ's help and are 'not counteractive'" (McNeill, *The History and Character of Calvinism*, 264).

[97] The seven articles of the Counter Remonstrance appears in *Schriftelicke Conferentie, Gehouden in s'Gravenhaghe inde Iare 1611 tusschen sommige Kercken Dienaren ængænde de Godlicke Prædestinatie metten van dien.*, (The Hague: Hillebrandt Jacobsz., 1612), 13–29; Triglandius, *Kerckelycke geschiedenissen*, 545–52, and Jan Nicolaas Bakhuizen van den Brink, *Documenta reformatoria; teksten uit de geschiedenis van kerk en theologie in de Nederlanden sedert de Hervorming*, 2 vols. (Kampen: J. H. Kok, 1960), 1:293–300. They are summarized as "Appendix D" in Peter Y. De Jong, ed., *Crisis in the Reformed Churches: Essays in the Commemoration of the Great Synod of Dort, 1618–1619* (Grand Rapids: Reformed Fellowship, 1968), 209–213. The *Schriftelicke Conferentie* is the secular record of the first meeting between Remonstrants and Contra–Remonstrants in 1612.

[98] Michel Le Vassor, *The History of the Reign of Lewis XIII, King of France and Navarre Containing the Most Remarkable Occurrences in France and Europe During the Minority of that Prince*, trans. Mr. Fontvive (London: Printed for Thomas Cockerill, 1700), 2:20. Episcopius was skeptical that anything less than a national synod could settle their differences, and wrote to his brother Rem that he tried to exempt himself from the conference (Simon Episcopius to Rembert Bisschop, Amsterdam, 5 March, 1611, at the Remonstrant Library in Amsterdam; quoted by Haentjens, *Episcopius als Apologeet*, 19).

The source for Episcopius having spoken only once at the conference is Haentjens, *Episcopius als Apologeet*, 18.

99 Van Limborch, *Historia Vitæ Episcopii*, 42–44.

100 Simon Episcopius, *De optima regni Christi exstruendi ratione*, in *Operum Theologicorum, Pars Altera*, ed. Philip van Limborch (Rotterdam: Arnoldum Leers, 1665).

101 Simon Episcopius, *Lectiones Sacræ in 1 & 2 Caput Apocalypseos*, in *Operum Theologicorum, Pars Altera*, ed. Philip van Limborch (Rotterdam: Arnoldum Leers, 1665).

102 Simon Episcopius, *Lectiones Sacræ in I. Epistolam Catholicam Apostoli Ioannis*, in *Operum Theologicorum, Pars Altera*, ed. Philip van Limborch (Rotterdam: Arnoldum Leers, 1665).

103 Simon Episcopius, *Notæ Breves in Matthæum*, in *Operum Theologicorum, Pars Altera*, ed. Philip van Limborch (Rotterdam: Arnoldum Leers, 1665).

104 Simon Episcopius, *Paraphrasis & Observationes in Caput VIII, IX, X & XI Epistolæ S. Paulo ad Romanos*, in *Opera Theologica*, ed. Stephanus Curcellæus (Amsterdam: Ioannis Blæv, 1650) Hugo Grotius, a constant supporter of the Arminians and close friend of Episcopius, encouraged him to publish them. Regarding Grotius' friendship with the Arminians, see E. J. Kuiper, "Hugo de Groot en de Remonstranten," *Nederlands Theologisch Tijdschrift* 38 (1984): 111–25.

105 Simon Episcopius, *Præfatio in Novi Testamenti, brevem interpretationem, de lectione Scripturæ*, in *Operum Theologicorum, Pars Altera*, ed. Philip van Limborch (Rotterdam: Arnoldum Leers, 1665).

106 Episcopius' public and private disputations were first published as Simon Episcopius, *Disputationes Theologiæ Tripartæ* (Amsterdam: Ioannem Blæv, 1644), and then included in idem, "Disputationes Theologicæ Tripartitæ," in *Operum Theologicorum, Pars Altera*, ed. Philip van Limborch (Rotterdam: Arnoldum Leers, 1665).

107 Van Limborch, *Historia Vitæ Episcopii*, 43–44.

108 As in Arminius' case, the most serious accusations of Socinianism were made by Festus Hommius, to the point that Episcopius made formal charges against him for slander and won (Ibid., 55–78; Calder, *Memoirs*, 158–186), cf. Simon Episcopius to Conrad Vorstius, January 9, 1617 in the Remonstrant Library in Amsterdam, quoted by Haentjens, *Episcopius als Apologeet*, 31, and Simon Episcopius to Ioannus Scholtlers, April 11, 1617, in *PEVE* (1660), 478–480).

109 Calder, *Memoirs*, 189–91.

110 "De Polyandro nihil certi polliceri audeo. Si ex aliorum uti solet, judiciis pendebit, acrius paulum meui: se ex suopte ipsius ingenio, mitius" (Simon Episcopius to Conrad Vorstius, July 11, 1616, in Christiaan Hartsoeker and Philippus van Limborch, *Præstantium ac Eruditorum Virorum Epistolæ Ecclesiasticæ et Theologicæ*, 3d ed. (Amsterdam: Henricum Wetstenium, 1704), letter #273, quoted in Haentjens, *Episcopius als Apologeet*, 24).

111 "Heri disputabat D. Polyander de peccato Originali, eheu quam misere! Vix dixerim quam multa ἄτοπα et absurda responsa sint!" (Ibid.).

112 "Polyandri simulata clandestina et nullis rationibus subnixa in Remonstrantes invidia atque amarulentia" (Simon Episcopius, *Antidotum Continens Declarationem Sententiæ Quæ in Synodo Nationali Dordrecena Asserta & Stabilita Est*, in *Operum Theologicorum, Pars Altera*, ed. Philip van Limborch (Rotterdam: Arnoldum Leers, 1665), 2:19).

113 Van Limborch, *Historia Vitæ Episcopii*, 44; Calder, *Memoirs*, 136.

114 Calder, *Memoirs*, 132.

[115] Van Limborch, *Historia Vitæ Episcopii*, 90–91; Harrison, *The Beginnings of Arminianism*, 250; Motley, *John of Barneveld*, 2:287–289. Brandt illustrated the part which Calvinist pastors played in these affairs in a quote from Ursinus, one of the ministers at the church at Amsterdam. "Somebody since asked the Minister Ursinus, why his people could not disswade (*sic*) and withhold their children from such riots, as had been committed against the house of Rem Bishop, as well as the Lutherans and Mennonites did theirs? His answer was, '*We have our reasons for not doing it*'" (Brandt, *History of the Reformation*, 2:95, emphasis in the original). For a modern, scholarly examination of the conflict from 1612–18 at the Hague, written by a 20th century Reformed pastor, see L. Wüllschleger, *Scheurmakers en Nieuwlichters: Over Remonstranten en Contra-Remonstranten te 's-Gravenhage (1612–1618)* (Leiden: Uitgeverij J. J. Groen en Zoon, 1989).

[116] This was poignantly pictured in a print entitled "Op de Wæg-schæl" ("On the weigh-scale," 1618). On one side of a large scale lie the works of Calvin and the sword of Maurice, backed by Maurice and his soldiers Behind them stands Gomarus. On the other side lies a book that contains the laws that guaranteed the rights of the provinces, resting upon the mantle of Oldenbarnevelt, backed by Oldenbarnevelt and the officers of the government. Arminius stands behind them all. The print shows Maurice as having just laid his sword in the balance, which shifts toward him, Calvin and Gomarus. Military might has conquered law, justice and the Arminians. The print appears in G. J. Heering, ed., *De Remonstranten Gedenkboek bij het 300-jarig bestaan der Remonstrantsche Broederschap* (Leiden: A. W. Sijthoof's Uitgevers, 1619), 125, and as the frontispiece in Gerrit J. Hoenderdaal and P. M. Luca, eds., *Staat in de vrijheid: de geschiedenis van de remonstranten* (Zutphen: De Walburg Pres, 1982).

[117] Simon Episcopius to Conrad Vorstius, February 27, 1617, *PEVE* (1660), 476–77; Simon Episcopius to Conrad Vorstius, February 12, 1618, *PEVE* (1660), 481–82.

[118] For translations of the Canons of Dort, see Thomas Scott, *The Articles of the Synod of Dort and its Rejection of Errors, with the History of Events Which made Way For That Synod, As Published By the Authority of the States-General; and the Documents Confirming Its Decision* (Utica, NY: William Williams, Genesee Street, 1831); Schaff, *Creeds of Christendom*, 3550–597, Peter Y. De Jong, "Appendix 1: The Canons of Dort," in *Crisis in the Reformed Churches: Essays in the Commemoration of the Great Synod of Dort, 1618–1619*, ed. Peter Y. De Jong (Grand Rapids: Reformed Fellowship, 1968); Hoeksema, *The Voice of Our Fathers*. For modern defenses of these canons, which have universally come to be called the "five points" of Calvinism, see Fred H. Klooster, "The Doctrinal Deliverances of Dort," in *Crisis in the Reformed Churches: Essays in the Commemoration of the Great Synod of Dort, 1618–1619*, ed. Peter Y. De Jong (Grand Rapids: Reformed Fellowship, 1968); Edwin H. Palmer, *The Five Points of Calvinism*, Enlarged ed. (Grand Rapids: Baker, 1980) and David N. Steele and Curtis C. Thomas, *The Five Points of Calvinism: Defined, Defended, Documented*, ed. J. Marcellus Kirk (Phillipsburg, NJ: Presbyterian and Reformed, 1963). The canons of Dort did not exactly correspond to the "five articles" of Remonstrance, and many have questioned whether they accurately reflect the theology of John Calvin with respect to limited atonement. See Brian G. Armstrong, *Calvinism and the Amyraut Heresy* (Madison: University of Wisconsin Press, 1969), 137–38, and John S. Bray, *Theodore Beza's Doctrine of Predestination*, vol. 12 (Nieuwkoop: De Graaf, 1975), 60.

[119] The Contra-Remonstrants not only insured themselves a majority of representatives at the Synod, but also excluded any Remonstrant representation at all. In provinces with a Remonstrant majority, the Contra-Remonstrants held their own meetings and gained the

right to send half the number of delegates allotted to the province. In provinces with a Contra-Remonstrant majority, they excluded the Remonstrants and quashed similar attempts at separate meetings. When some Remonstrant did arrive at the Synod, the Contra-Remonstrants refused to seat them. See Calder, *Memoirs*, 243–44.

120 The phrasing is Tyacke's (Nicholas Tyacke, *Anti-Calvinists: The Rise of English Arminianism, c. 1590–1640* (Oxford: Clarendon Press, 1987), 95). Dewar attempts an unbiased appraisal of Remonstrant treatment (M. W. Dewar, "The British Delegation at the Synod of Dort," *Evangelical Quarterly* 46 [1974]: 107–109).

121 Beza's tract was Bèze, *De hæreticis a ciuili magistratu puniendis libellus, aduersus Martini Bellii farraginem, & nouorum academicorum sectam*; translated into Dutch as Théodore de Bèze, *Een schoon tractæt des godtgheleerden Theodori Bezæ vande straffe, welcke de wereltlijcke overicheydt over de ketters behoort te oeffenen, teghen Martini Bellii tsamenræpsel, ende der secte der nieuwe Academisten*, trans. Johannes Bogerman (Franeker: Gillis van den Rade, 1601). For a sympathetic treatment of Johannes Bogerman, see Kistemaker, "Leading Figures at the Synod of Dort," 39–41.

122 Harrison, *The Beginnings of Arminianism*, 302. Harrison was vice-principal of the Westminster Training School.

123 See, for example, De Jong, "Rise of the Reformed Churches in the Netherlands," 17.

124 "Our Synod goes on like a watch, the main wheels on which the whole business turns are least in sight. For all things of moment are enacted in private sessions. What is done in public is only for show and entertainment" (John Hales, "Letters from Dort," in *Golden Remains, of the Ever Memorable, Mr. John Hales, of Eaton-Colledge, &c* [London: Printed by Tho. Newcomb for Robert Pawlet, 1673], 92).

125 For the most complete account of Episcopius' role at the synod and his conflict with Bogerman from the Remonstrant perspective, see L. Knappert, "Episcopius en de Synode," in *De Remonstranten Gedenkboek bij het 300-jarig bestaan der Remonstrantsche Broederschap*, ed. G. J. Heering (Leiden: A. W. Sijthoof's Uitgevers, 1619).

126 Kistemaker's opinion that the synod cited Episcopius because he refused to attend as a theological advisor has no support in any of the biographical material consulted (Kistemaker, "Leading Figures at the Synod of Dort," 202).

127 *Acta ofte Handelinghen des Nationalen Synodi* (Dordrecht: Isaack Jans. Canin, 1621), 68–79, as well as Simon Episcopius, "Oratio Habita in Synodo Nationali Dordrecena," in *Operum Theologicorum, Pars Altera*, ed. Philip van Limborch (Rotterdam: Arnoldum Leers, 1665), 2:1–4, and in Van Limborch, *Historia Vitæ Episcopii*, 145–167. Both Calder (Calder, *Memoirs*, 284–315) and Brandt (Brandt, *History of the Reformation*, 3:52–61) published English translations. The speech was left out of the *Acta Synodi Nationalis* (Dordrecht: Isaaci Ioannidis Canini Et Sociorum, 1620).

128 Wtenbogært heard about the speech in exile and wrote to congratulate Episcopius (Johannes Wtenbogært to Simon Episcopius, April 25, 1619, in the Remonstrant Library in Rotterdam; quoted by Haentjens, *Episcopius als Apologeet*, 50).

129 Brandt, *History of the Reformation*, 3:151–52; Dewar, "The British Delegation at the Synod of Dort," 113.

130 Some of the strongest evidences of misrepresentation of Remonstrant beliefs by the Synod come from the letters of Walter Balcanqual. He served as a British delegate, was a committed Calvinist and held to particular redemption (Nicholas Tyacke, *English Arminianism*, 44–45, 92, 95–98). These letters were reports on the synod to the British

ambassador Sir Dudley Carleton. He wrote that the British delegation had been criticized for attempting to define Remonstrant beliefs from those books in which "they spake best and soundest," while the tendency was to gather their sentiments "out of all places in their books, where they spake most absurdly, which we thought was very far besides the rule of charity." (George Balcanqual, Dort, to Dudley Carleton, February 9, 1619, in Hales, "Letters from Dort;" quoted by James Nichols, "A Brief Account of the Synod of Dort, Taken Out of the letters of Mr. Hales and Mr. Balcanqual, written from Dort, to the Rt. Hon. Sir D. Carleton, Lord Ambassador then at the Hague," in *The Works of Arminius*, London ed. [London: Longman, Hurst, Rees, Orme, Brown and Green, 1825; reprint, Grand Rapids: Baker, 1986], 1:545). He noted that when Bogerman read from Episcopius, "the President picked out the worst part of it…which contained nothing but a bitter satire against Calvin, Beza, Pareus, Piscator, Whitaker, Perkins, Bogerman, Festus and twenty more. But in truth, through unhappily, yet it was finely penned" (George Balcanqual, Dort, to Dudley Carleton, February 15, 1619, in Hales, "Letters from Dort;" quoted in Nichols, "The Synod of Dort," 1:546). Finally, he criticized the delegates for distorting Remonstrant sentiments when he wrote, "They are so eager to kill the Remonstrants, that they would make their words have that sense which no grammar can find in them…. They condemned the thing itself as a thing most curious, and yet would have it retained only to make the Remonstrant odious, though they find the very contrary of that they would father upon them in their writings" (George Balcanqual, Dort, to Dudley Carleton, February 19, 1619, in Hales, "Letters from Dort;" quoted in Nichols, "The Synod of Dort," 1:546). Blaising provides several examples of these misrepresentations (Craig A. Blaising, "John Wesley's Doctrine of Original Sin," [Ph.D. diss., Dallas Theological Seminary, 1979] 111–124).

[131] Calder, *Memoirs*, 517–18.

[132] See *Acta Synodi Nationalis*, 248; see also Tyacke, *English Arminianism*, 96; Kistemaker, "Leading Figures at the Synod of Dort," 44; Godfrey, "Tensions within International Calvinism," , and Godfrey, "Calvin and Calvinism in the Netherlands," 107–08. Martinus was over 80 years old.

[133] Dewar, "The British Delegation at the Synod of Dort," 106–09; Tyacke, *English Arminianism*, 87–105.

[134] This was done through signing the *Acte van Stilstand*, a promise to either actively support the *Confession* and *Catechism* as interpreted by the Canons of Dort, or keep silent about any criticisms. Those who signed were guaranteed the continuation of their salary and the possibility of remaining in the ministry. Those who did not had their property confiscated and were exiled. More than 200 pastors refused (Gerrit Jan Hoenderdaal, "Arminius, Jacobus / Arminianismus," in *Theologisch Realenzyklopädie*).

[135] An engraving by Clæs J. Visscher pictures the Remonstrants in their wagons, including a table of who was in which wagon (see Gerrit J. Hoenderdaal, "Begin en beginsel," in *Staat in de Vrijheid: de Geschiedenis van de Remonstranten*, ed. Gerrit J. Hoenderdaal and P. M. Luca [Zutphen: De Walburg Pers, 1982], 43). Oldenbarnevelt was not so fortunate; Maurice had him beheaded. Theodore Diodate's boast that the Synod of Dort provided powder and ball to the "cannons" which shot off the grand pensioner's head confirms its part in the "judicial murder" death of this Dutch hero. For the history of Oldenbarnevelt's execution, see Calder, *Memoirs*, 369–86. A copy of an engraving of his execution appears in Kamen, *The Rise of Toleration*, 155.

[136] Concerning this meeting, see Johannes Tideman, *De stichting der Remonstrantsche Broederschap, 1619–1634: Uit en Met de Oorspronkelijke Bescheiden Medegedeeld*, 2 vols.

(Amsterdam: Y. Rogge, 1871), 1:118. Although Wtenbogært was present, the Remonstrants chose Episcopius to chair the meetings.

[137] Simon Episcopius to Assuerus Matthisius, August 4, 1623, at the Remonstrant Library in Rotterdam, cited in Haentjens, *Episcopius als Apologeet*, 69–70.

[138] Simon Episcopius, to Francis van Limborch, June 2, 1623, in the Remonstrant Library in Amsterdam; quoted in ibid., 69. See Calder's description of the persecution of the Remonstrants in Calder, *Memoirs*, 409–447.

[139] Simon Episcopius, *Onbillijcke wreetheyt der Dortsche Synode: Midtgaders der ghener / die het beleyt dær over hebben ghehadt / Teghen de Remonstranten in de Nederlandtsche Gheunieerde Provincien* (n.p.: 1619); cf. idem, *Crudelis Iniquitas Synodi Dordracenæ, et Eorum Qui Illi Præfuerunt, in Belgio Remonstranties, quos vocant, exposta*, in *Operum Theologicorum, Pars Altera*, ed. Philip van Limborch (Rotterdam: Arnoldum Leers, 1665); idem, *Antidotum, ende Nærder Openinghe Van het eyghene ghevoelen des Nationalen Synodi 1618, en 1619* (n.p.: 1619); cf. idem, *Antidotum Continens Declarationem Sententiæ*, and idem, *Corte ende Næckte Ontdeckinghe Vande Bedrijghelijckeheydt des Dortschen Synodi* (n.p.: 1619).

[140] The Remonstrants originally chose three, but the work fell to Episcopius alone.

[141] The Dutch version appeared first (Simon Episcopius, *Belijdenisse, ofte, Verklaringhe Van't ghevoelen der Leeraren : die in de Neder-landen Remonstranten worden ghenæmt* [n.p.: 1621]), then the Latin (idem, *Confessio, sive, Declaratio, Sententiæ Pastorum, qui in Foederato Belgio Remonstrantes Vocantur, Super Præcipuis Articulis Religionis Christianæ* [Harderwijk: Theodorum Danielis, 1622]; Simon Episcopius, "Confessio, sive Declaratio, Sententiæ Pastorum qui in Foederato Belgio Remonstrantes vocantur, Super præcipuis articulis Religionis Christianæ," in *Operum Theologicorum, Pars Altera*, ed. Philip van Limborch [Rotterdam: Arnoldum Leers, 1665]). The English translation was published fifty-five years later (idem, *The Confession or Declaration of the Ministers or Pastors which in the United Provinces are called Remonstrants, Concerning The Chief Points of Christian Religion* [London: Francis Smith, 1676]). The *Confessio* produced good results in both the Netherlands and other countries as well by helping to overcome the stigma of Socinianism and Pelagianism. For more on the writing of the Remonstrant confession, see Calder, *Memoirs*, 387–408. For a statement of the Remonstrant faith from the 1960's, see J. van Goudoever et al., *De Remonstrantse Broederschap* (Lochem: De Tijdstroom, 1964).

[142] Simon Episcopius, *Nieticheyt Van den Calvinischen Ban, ofte, Brief Over Het Onrecht-værdigh Bannen* (n.p.: 1624); idem, "Bodecherus Ineptiens, hoc est, Evidens demonstratio, qua ostenditur N. Bodecherum, ut plus quam servili adsentatione efficacem Contra-Remonstrantium gratiam demereatur, inepte admodum & nugatorie Confessionem Remonstrantium Socinismi arcessere nuper esse aggressum," in *Opera Theologica*, ed. Stephanus Curcellæus (Amsterdam: Ioannis Blæv, 1650).

[143] These were Simon Episcopius, *Epistola Ad Clarissimum Virum Petri Wadingi, Iesuitæ Antuerpiensis, De Regula Fidei*, in *Opera Theologica* (Amsterdam: Ioannis Blæv, 1650); idem, *Responsio ad Epistolam Petri Wadingi, Iesuitæ Antuerpiensis, Theol. Profess., De Regula Fidei*, in *Opera Theologica*, ed. Stephanus Curcellæus (Amsterdam: Ioannis Blæv, 1650) and idem, *Responsio ad Epistolam Petri Wadingi, Iesuitæ Antuerpiensis, Theol. Profess., De Cultu Imaginum*, in *Opera Theologica*, ed. Stephanus Curcellæus (Amsterdam: Ioannis Blæv, 1650), followed by a general refutation of Catholic arguments for papal authority, idem, *Labyrinthus, sive, Circulus Pontificius: Versio ex Belgico*, in *Opera Theologica*, ed. Stephanus Curcellæus (Amsterdam: Ioannis Blæv, 1650). For the history of Episcopius' conversations with Wadding, see Calder, *Memoirs*, 448–55. See P. H. Winkelman for the

friendly relationship between Arminians and Catholics from Arminius to the end of the century (Winkelman, *Remonstranten en Katholieken*), and pages 160–65 concerning this conversation between Episcopius and Wadding.

[144] Episcopius had already written a letter against some of Cameron's ideas in 1613 (Simon Episcopius to Hugo Grotius, n.d., in *PEVE* (1660), 630–32), and Grotius asked him to write again when Cameron attacked the Remonstrants in his theses on grace and freewill (Hugo Grotius to Simon Episcopius, June 7, 1622, in *PEVE* [1660], 632–33; cf. John Cameron, *Theses de Efficacia Gratiæ Dei, et us Liberi Hominis Arbitrii in negotio salutis humanæ*, in *TA ΣΩZOMENA, sive opera partim ab auctore ipso edita*, ed.[Geneva: Iacobi Chouet, 1642]). For Episcopius' response, see Simon Episcopius, *Examen Sententiæ Ioannis Cameronis, Scoto-Britanni, De Gratia Dei & libero hominis arbitrio*, in *Opera Theologica*, ed. Stephanus Curcellæus (Amsterdam: Ioannis Blæv, 1650).

[145] See Simon Episcopius, *Responsio Ad Defensionem Ioannis Cameronis, quam opposuit Epistolæ cuidam, in qua expensa fuerat ejus sententia de gratia & libero arbitrio, sive de determinatione voluntatis per intellectum*, in Opera Theologica, ed. Stephanus Curcellæus (Amsterdam: Ioannis Blæv, 1650); idem, *Tractatus De Libero Arbitrio*, in *Opera Theologica*, ed. Stephanus Curcellæus (Amsterdam: Ioannis Blæv, 1650). He also responded to Jacobus Capellus' disputation in 1623 in which the latter called for the condemnation of Remonstrant theology (idem, *Examen Thesium Theologicarum Iacobi Capelli, quais inscripsi De Controversiis quæ Foederatum Belgium vexuant, &, Satius-ne fuerit doctrinam Arminii tolerari quam damnari*, in *Opera Theologica*, ed. Stephanus Curcellæus [Amsterdam: Ioannis Blæv, 1650]).

[146] Simon Episcopius to Petrus Cupus, March 22, 1625, in the Remonstrant Library at Rotterdam; quoted in Haentjens, *Episcopius als Apologeet*, 74.

[147] Nicholas Grevinchoven to Simon Episcopius, June 12, 1626, the Remonstrant Seminary Library at Amsterdam; quoted in Ibid., 78–79.

[148] Ibid.

[149] The other pastors approved them at the Society's meeting in Rotterdam on October 15, 1631, with a few modifications. See Haentjens, *Episcopius als Apologeet*, 87–88. Two of Episcopius' writings combined pastoral and theological concerns. He wrote to encourage a Calvinist doctor that the doctrine of predestination did not render void his efforts to save lives (*Responsio ad Duas Epistolas Ioannis Breverovicii, Sabini & Medici Dordrechtani, De Vitæ termino, Fatalisne is sit, an vero Mobilis*, in *Opera Theologica*, ed. Stephanus Curcellæus [Amsterdam: Ioannis Blæv, 1650]).

[150] H. W. ter Haar, *Jacobus Trigland* (The Hague: Nijhoff, 1891).

[151] Johannes Polyander et al., *Censura in Confessionem, sive, Declarationem pententiæ corum que in foederato Belgio Remonstrantes vocantur: super præcipius articulis Christianæ religionis* (Leiden: Bonaventuræ & Abrahami Elzevir, 1625).

[152] Antonius Walæus, *Disputatio Theologica de Quatuor Controversis Remonstrantium articulis vulgo notis. In qua status controversiæ nude proponitur et Remonstrantes ad Ecclesiæ Unitatem invitantur integra veritate*, in *Opera Omnia Walæi* (Leiden: n.p., 1643).

[153] Simon Episcopius, *Examen Disputationis Theologicæ Antonii Walæi, quam inscripsit de Quatuor controversis Remonstrantium artriculis vulgo notis, in qua status controversiæ sed proponitu, & Remonstrantes ad Ecclesiæ Belgicæ unitatem invitantur integra veritate*, in *Operum Theologicorum, Pars Altera*, ed. Philip van Limborch (Rotterdam: Arnoldum Leers, 1665).

154 Simon Episcopius, *Apologia Pro Confessione sive Declaratione Sententiæ eorum, Qui in Foederato Belgio vocantur Remonstrantes, super præcipuis articulis Religionis Christianæ, Contra Censuram Quaturo Professorum Leydensium*, in *Opera Theologica*, ed. Stephanus Curcellæus (Amsterdam: Ioannis Blæv, 1650). Episcopius felt it necessary to justify the strong language in the *Apologia* (Simon Episcopius to Caspar Barleus, April 3, 1630, in *PEVE* (1660), 685).

155 Simon Episcopius to Johannes Wtenbogært, August 10, 1626, in *PEVE* (1704), letter 433.

156 Iohannes Polyander, et al., *Specimen Calumniarum atque Heterodoxarum Opinionum ex Remonstrantius Apologia Excerptarum* (Leiden); Johannes Polyander and Johannes Wollebius, *Pointen bij de Professoren tot Leyden geextreheert uit de Apologie van de Confessie der Remonstranten* (Leiden: 1630).

157 Simon Episcopius, *Responsio Remonstrantium ad Libellum Cui Titulus Est, Specimen calumniarum atque heterodoxarum Opinionum, ex Remonstrantium, Apologia excerptarum*, in *Operum Theologicorum, Pars Altera*, ed. Philip van Limborch (Rotterdam: Arnoldum Leers, 1665). Nicholas Vedelius, another professor of theology but at a different university (Deventer) also tried his hand at refuting the Apologia (*De Arcanis Arminianismi Libri Duo, seu Quæstio, Quænam sit Religio et Fides Theologorum Remonstrantium, decisa ex Confissione et Apologia Ipsorum* [N.p., 1630]). His lack of care in his quotations elicited a biting response from Episcopius entitled *Vedelius Rhapsodus, Sive Vindiciæ Doctrinæ Remonstrantium à criminationibus & calumnijs Nicolæ Vedelii* (In *Operum Theologicorum, Pars Altera*, ed. Philip van Limborch [Rotterdam: Arnoldum Leers, 1665)]. A "rhapsodus" referred to either a cobbler or a rag-collector, and indicated Episcopius' opinon about Videlius' academic abilities.

158 Triglandius' anti-Arminian works before this are too numerous to list here. The readers is directed to the bibliography.

159 Triglandius attacked Poppius based on the latter's devotional work, *De enge Poorte: ofte, Predicatien Over eenighe voortreffelijke Texten, ofte Spreucken der heyligher Schrifture* (Goude: Jasper Tournap voor Andries Burier, 1616).

160 Triglandius' books included *Den Krachteloosen Remonstrant Vermorselt Door de Krachte vande Leere der Wærheydt* (Amsterdam: Marten Iansz Brandt, 1632) and *De Ware Religie: Verantwoort teghen de lasteringen der Remonstrantsche Societeyt* (Amsterdam: Marten Jansz Brandtm, 1633).

161 Simon Episcopius, *De Crachteloosheyt der Godsalicheyt, van de Leere Iacobi Triglandii: In Syn Boeck Teghen de Enghe-poorte D. Edvardi Poppii* (n.p.: 1632); idem, *De Kracht der God-Salicheit: Vermorst en Vernorselt Deur Iacobi Triglandii in het Boeckxken Krachteloosheyt der Godzaligheyt* (n.p.: Voor de Societeyt der Remonstranten, 1632); idem, *De War-Religie, ofte, De verwarde: valsche en reden-loose Religi Iacobi Triglandii in syn boeck De ware Religie verantwoort.* (n.p.: Voor de Societeyt der Remonstranten, 1634). Two other Remonstrant theologians also wrote again Triglandius both before and after the Synod of Dort, Jacob Taurinus (*Van de onderlinge Verdraagsammheydt: tegen Jacobi Triglandi Recht-Gematigden Christen* (Utrecht: Ian Evertsen van Doorn, 1615). and Wtenbogaert (*Clare Iustificatie Van seeckere Passagien: Dær over Jacobvs Triglandi* [The Hague: Hillebrant Jacobsz., 1616], *Trouhertighe Aenwijsinghe Der Bedriegelijckheden de Vermaninghe Iacobi Triglandij.* Herderwijck: [n.p., 1623]; *Goedt ende Christelijck Bescheydt Ghegheven op Jacobi Triglandij Tweede Vermaningh ende verdedigingh van de Trouwe Aenwijsingh* [n.p., 1627.]).

162 Simon Episcopius to Johannes Wtenbogært, November 11, 1634, in Johannes Wtenbogært, *Brieven en Onuitgegeven Stukken*, ed. H. C. Rogge, 3 vols. (Utrecht: Kemink en Zoon, 1868), letter 1060.

163 Abraham van der Heyden, *Proeve ende Weerlegginghe des Remonstrantschen Catechismi* (Leiden: Paulus Ærtsz van Revesteyn, 1641).

164 Simon Episcopius, *Antwoort Op de Proeve van Abrahamus Heydanus: Tegen de Onderwysinge in de Christeligcke Religie, na de Belijdenisse der Remonstranten* (Rotterdam: Joannes Næranus, 1644). Undeterred by Episcopius' death, Heyden published his reply to the *Antwoord* a year later (*De causa Dei, dat is: De sake Godts, verdedight tegen den Mensche: ofte, Wederlegginge van de Antwoorde van M. Simon Episcopius, wijlen Professor der H. Theologie, op de Proeve des Remonstrantschen Catechismi* [Leiden: Paulus Ærtsz van Ravesteyn, 1645]).

165 Simon Episcopius, *Verus Theologus Remonstrans, falso ac spurio oppositus*, in *Operum Theologicorum, Pars Altera*, ed. Philip van Limborch (Rotterdam: Arnoldum Leers, 1665).

166 Simon Episcopius to Johannes Wtenbogært, November 1, 1634, in Wtenbogært, *Brieven en Onuitgegeven Stukken van Johannes Wtenbogært*, 1056. Episcopius would later complain to Wtenbogært that the Calvinist clergy were "tireless people" who never ceased their attacks (Simon Episcopius to Johannes Wtenbogært, May 28, 1639, *BJW*, 1102).

167 For an effusive presentation of the history of the Remonstrant seminary and Episcopius' impact upon the lives of his students, see the "festschrift" written in celebration of the 200th anniversary of the seminary, Abraham des Amorie Van der Hoeven, *Het Tweede Eeuwfeest van het Seminarium der Remonstranten te Amsterdam op den 28 October MDCCCXXXIV plegtig gevierd* (Leeuwarden: G. T. N. Suringar, 1840). A more modest and scholarly treatment occurs in the book commemorating the 300th anniversary, again with information about Episcopius and the history of the founding of the seminary scattered throughout (G. J. Heering and G. J. Sirks, *Het Seminarium der Remonstranten Driehonderd Jaar: 1634–1934* [Amsterdam: Lankamp & Brinkman, 1934]).

168 Haentjens, *Episcopius als Apologeet*, 100.

169 Simon Episcopius to Johannes Wtenbogært, May 28, 1639, *BJW*, 1089.

170 Simon Episcopius to Johannes Wtenbogært, December 14 1639, *BJW*, 1115.

171 Mercier to Simon Episcopius, February 13, 1632, in a letter at the Remonstrant Library in Amsterdam; quoted in Haentjens, *Episcopius als Apologeet*, 105.

172 Simon Episcopius, *Institutiones Theologicæ, privatis lectionibus Amstelodami traditæ*, in *Opera Theologica* (Amsterdam: Ioannis Blæv, 1650).

173 Simon Episcopius, *Responsio ad Quæstiones Theologicas sexaginta quatuor, ipsi a discipulis in privatio disputationem collegio Amstelodami propositas*, in *Opera Theologica* (Amsterdam: Ioannis Blæv, 1650).

174 Maria died unexpectedly some time before (Calder, *Memoirs* , 488).

175 Van Limborch, *Historia Vitæ Episcopii*, 320.

Arminius' Doctrine
of Original Sin

T his chapter examines Arminius' theology of original sin and its attendant doctrines in order to establish a basis of comparison with Episcopius' theology and theological method. It also compares and contrasts Arminius' thought with Calvin, Junius and other Christian thinkers.

Arminius' conflicts over original sin began with a series of sermons on Romans 7 which he preached soon after entering his pastoral ministry. While none is extant, we can gather his ideas from a lengthy exegetical treatment of the passage[1] that he was editing for publication when he died.[2] In it he argued that the person in Romans 7 was neither Paul nor a believer under grace, but the unregenerate under the convicting work of the Law. He based this on Paul's description of the person as dead in sin, under the bondage of sin indwelling him (*inhabitans*), and in need of the liberating work of Christ. He thought none of these conditions could be true in the regenerate. Even though Calvin and Beza interpreted the chapter as the experience of the believer in his struggle against sin, Arminius drew support from Beza's analysis of "things which precede regeneration" and "regeneration itself,"[3] and from Calvin's concept of servile fear in the unsaved.[4] He also appealed to ancient and contemporary theologians with whom he found agreement.[5] He knew his handling of the text would not be not acceptable to his contemporaries, and anticipated accusations of Pelagianism and denials of original sin.[6] Calvinists so accused him in Articles 13 and 14 of the *Thirty-One Articles*[7] and Question 3 of the *Nine Questions*,[8] and brought similar indictments after his death.[9] Thus they are important sources for understanding what Arminius thought about original sin.

Aside from his responses to the *Thirty-One Articles* and the *Nine Questions*,[10] we find Arminius' fullest statements in *Certain Articles to be Diligently Weighed and Examined*,[11] and in his private and public disputations.

He also commented on original sin the *Fourth Oration* and in the *Declaration of Sentiments*,[12] and it occupied a large part of his interactions with Junius and Perkins.[13] He referred to original sin with respect to providence, free will and predestination in the *Letter to Hippolytus à Collibus*.[14]

Adam as Created
in the Image of God

While Arminius used the phrase *imago Dei* throughout his writings, Private Disputation 26[15] and Proposition 10 in *Conference with Junius*[16] are most important. Both are models of scholastic presentation, with careful distinctions and definitions, syllogistic argumentation and discussions of causality. Arminius began Disputation 26 affirming God's creation of Adam. Like Calvin, he adopted the dichotomous understanding of Adam as "a body and a rational soul,"[17] stating that the body was "created from pre-existing material, namely earth thoroughly perfused with aqueous and ethereal liquid." God created the soul, however, *ex nihilo*, by the inspiration (*insufflationem*) of the Spirit.[18] He first considered the body and its physical mortality.[19] If immortality and incorruptibility were hypothetically possible, this was "by the grace of God" and not natural conditions. Adam violated the condition of immortality by sinning, and "summoned (*accersivisset*) death upon himself." Arminius concluded his discussion of the body noting "the wise creator" made it the "receptacle of the soul," equipped with "various and excellent organs" for the soul's use.

The soul was remarkable because of its "origin, substance, faculties and habits."[20] Regarding its origin, it was "created by infusion and infused by creation." Just as the body was prepared to receive the soul, the soul is united with the body by a "natural bond" (*nativo vinculo*) so that they form a composite unity.[21] The soul seeks the good of the body, while the body provides a ready vehicle for the desires of the soul.[22] Just as God created the soul in Adam, so he "still daily creates a new soul in each body."[23] This statement is unique for Arminius because, while he usually left the question of the origin of the soul unanswered, he affirmed creationism here.[24] Its substance is "simple, immaterial and immortal," but not infinite.[25] It is simple in that it is not a composite of material substances. It does not depend upon the body for existence, and can exist and maintain functionality outside the body. Like other Reformed theologians,[26] Arminius accepted faculty psychology and attributed two abilities to the soul: intellect and will (*intellectus & voluntatis*).[27] In a previous disputation on the essence of God, he defined intellect and will as the activity of God's inward life. By divine intention, humanity shares in these immaterial components (*intellectus* and *voluntas*) as the basis for the *imago Dei* in humans.[28]

Arminius' discussion of the will anticipated the denial of free will by Augustinians such as Luther and Calvin. [29] He followed Bernard of Clairveaux's paradigm of distinguishing three modes of human liberty: freedom from necessity, freedom from sin and freedom from misery in heaven.[30] Of these three, only freedom from necessity cannot be lost, because it is by nature situated in the will as its proper attribute, so that there cannot be any will if it be not free. By distinguishing these modes of liberty, Arminius could affirm freedom from necessity and still affirm the enslavement of the will to sin. The will inclines toward the universal and highest good, the *summum bonum*, but it is truly free and may also incline itself to "other ends." This provides an essential aspect to Arminius' definition of free will: the power of contrary choice.[31] A state of freedom exists "when all the requisites for willing or not willing are laid down, man is still indifferent to will or not to will, to will this rather than that… which requires not only free capability, but also free use in the very exercise of it." [32] As he urged in the *Dissertation on Romans 7*, the unregenerate will is enslaved to sin because it voluntarily inclines toward an incorrectly perceived good. In this, Arminius agreed with both Augustine and Calvin.

Arminius departed from Calvin by affirming that the will could refuse the offer of salvation even when accompanied by sufficient grace. He also conflicted with Calvinists over their belief that Adam sinned freely with respect to his own will, but necessarily with respect to the divine decree.[33] It was in this manner that they could insist that an act could be both voluntary and so deserving punishment, but still necessary as the unavoidable consequence of the decree.[34] Arminius rejected this as an irreconcilable contradiction.[35] He thought that when Adam "came out of the hands of his Creator, Adam was endowed with such a portion of wisdom, holiness and power, as enabled him to understand, esteem, consider, will and to perform the true good, according to the commandment delivered to him." [36]

"Wisdom, holiness and power" were the *habiti* of the unfallen soul. [37] By *habitus*, Arminius did not intend an acquired behavior, but character qualities or dispositions. By means of wisdom, the intellect "clearly and sufficiently understood the supernatural truth and goodness both of felicity and of righteousness." Through righteousness and holiness, the will was prepared and enabled to follow what wisdom commanded. These three "habits" compose the other "half" of Arminius' definition of the image of God. While intellect and will are "native" aspects of the *imago Dei*, wisdom, righteousness and holiness are the supernatural aspects,[38] supernatural because they are actually the presence and ministry of the Holy Spirit operating within the intellect and will.[39] Being the presence of God in Adam, they formed the foundation of the primitive relationship between them.[40]

Calvin and Arminius agreed on this definition of the supernaturals. Both arrived at it by working back from the restorative effects of redemption mentioned in Colossians 3:10, Ephesians 4:24 and 2 Peter 1:1–4.[41] Arminius speculated that if Adam had continued in his integrity, he would have passed the supernaturals to his posterity. By this, Arminius set up an interesting comparison between original righteousness and original sin. He reasoned that just as Adam's posterity now suffers from the result of his disobedience, they would have benefited by inheriting the full image of God had he obeyed.[42]

Regarding the body, though "nothing physical can properly be said to bear the image of God," there is still "something divine in it." Its dignity arises from its potential immortality, its superiority to the animals and its design for fulfilling God's purposes for Adam.[43] Even if its purpose was, in part, to rule over the earth, it was not dominion that composed the image, but the image which permitted dominion.

Arminius returned to examine more fully the natural and supernatural aspects of the image.[44] The natural comprises the essential being without which humanity would not be human. The soul was permanently granted (*præditam*) the powers of intellect and will, the intellect operating within the constraints of its nature (i.e., human reason does not have infinite abilities), and the will operating on the principle of liberty. Without liberty there is no will, and without will one is not human. The "supernaturals" were character-istics not essential to humanness, but God imparted them in creation. Wisdom, "the knowledge (*notitia*) of God, and of things pertaining to eternal salvation," was foremost. Since this knowledge was supernatural, humanity could gain no understanding of God or salvation by intuition or reason.[45]

From one perspective this is a significant departure from Calvin, who stressed that all people, even the most vile and reprobate, have an intuitive understanding of God's existence.[46] From another, it agrees with Calvin's appraisal that people apart from God's grace are "blind" to the things of God. Calvin and Arminius both thought that if God did not reveal himself, humanity has no avenue by which to approach God or the things of God. This revelation is an act of "grace." The will, affected by this knowledge (*secundum illam notitiam*), then would be capable of righteousness and holi-ness (*rectitudo & sanctitas*). Uprightness and holiness are not native to the human essence, but rather result from the knowledge of God and his truths.

Why then did God create humanity? Arminius' answer, that "man was created, that he might know, love and worship God his creator, and live with him in eternal happiness," reminds us of the Westminster Confession.[47] However, he did not stop here. Supralapsarians had reduced creation to a necessary means for the fulfilling the decrees of election and reprobation,[48] reprobation being the means by which God would show forth his power and justice.[49] Arminius denied reprobation was necessary for this. God needed nothing more to demonstrate his power, wisdom and goodness than to display his power in creation, his wisdom in the ordering of the universe and his goodness in the provision for the happiness of all living creatures. God's soteriological activities had as their objective the "praise of the glory of his grace."[50]

Such a powerful, wise, good creator deserved Adam's worship, and because of his natural and supernatural abilities, Adam was able to do so and merited either reward or punishment for his actions.[51] God's demand was not based on Adam's abilities, however, but on God's worthiness, and he could justly require of Adam (or of anyone) what he either did not provide, or had provided and withdrawn.[52] Another implication of Arminius' connection of intellect and will with religious duties led to what became a hallmark of Arminian theology, that theology is not speculative, but practical.[53] The intellect must receive revelation, but always with the objective of living in righteousness and holiness.

In sum, humans are composed of two parts, the physical and the spiritual, body and the soul. While the body is not part of the *imago*, it provides the soul all that is necessary for it to function in a physical world. The *imago Dei* has both natural and supernatural aspects. The "naturals" are essential to the soul's being. These naturals are twofold: the intellect, or the ability to examine and comprehend objects and ideas outside oneself, and the will, the freedom to accept or reject such objects and ideas. Supernaturals are blessings of grace which God added to the naturals. They did not change the naturals, but permitted them to function beyond their native abilities. To the intellect, he added the right understanding of himself and his truths. To the will, he added righteousness and holiness, so that all decisions could conform to the truths of God. Thus, unfallen humanity received everything necessary to maintain a right relationship with God.

The Fall of Adam

The Adamic Covenant

Arminius separated both human history and theology between "legal" and "evangelical" covenants.[54] God structured his relationship with Adam by means of a covenant (*fœdus*) or contract (*contractum*).[55] Although founded on God's rights as creator and benefactor, the purpose for the covenant was to elicit Adam's "voluntary and free obedience." The word "covenant" was legitimate because it consisted of two equal parts: the work or law commanded and a promised reward. Nevertheless, we see it was not between equal parties because God also affixed (*adjungitur*) the threat of the penalty.

Like other Reformed scholastics, Arminius thought the command not to eat the fruit was symbolic of a deeper law,[56] symbolizing the "two great commandments" of the Mosaic Law. First, God "placed and imprinted on the mind of Man" the "natural duty" of "loving God and his neighbor." On this "chief principle" the rest depended, and the right ordering of the whole law was contained. Love was the "first and proximate cause" by which "man could live with man" (*ut homo secundum hominem vivat*).[57] The relationship between Adam and Eve was not just social, but spiritual. Thus "they were the church of God, neither redeemed by the blood of Christ, nor formed anew by regeneration of the Spirit, nor by a new creation, but they were instituted as a church by the primitive creation of God." Second, the act of eating was indication of whom Adam loved more, himself or God, an outward "profession of willingly yielding obedience" and an acknowledgment that he was "willingly subject" to God.[58]

Arminius speculated about the potential results of obedience to these commands. The first result would have been "life eternal, the complete satisfying of the whole of our will and desire."[59] Adam and Eve would have gained the "power to eat of the tree of life, by the eating of which man was always restored to his pristine strength." Second, God eventually would have transformed their natural, mortal bodies into "spiritual, immortal and incorruptible" ones, and granted them eternal happiness in heaven. He concluded God would have extended almost the same covenant to their posterity.

The Inclusion of Humanity In Adam

The extension of these benefits from "our first parents" to their descendants raises another question central to the Pelagian debate: what was the relation between Adam and his descendants? According to Pelagius, Adam's sin only served as a bad example, but caused no corruption of nature. Arminius rejected this idea and based significant aspects of his theology upon the Augustinian idea that all humanity was seminally present in Adam. He gave this as the reason for the prohibition against murder (Genesis 9:5–7). Nevertheless, he took seminal presence far beyond his opponents in his arguments against reprobation. While the Adamic covenant "was enjoined on Adam and Eve as the roots and principal individuals of the human race, in whom, as in its origin and stock, the whole of humanity was then contained,"[60] all in Adam were also the recipients of the promise of the Savior, and it "appertains to all men considered in Adam."[61] He used this against Beza's interpretation of Romans 9. If God created Adam a vessel of blessing, and all people in him, then he created all to be vessels of blessing as well. They made themselves vessels of sin, and only then did God consider the unrepentant as vessels of wrath.[62]

Arminius extolled human ability in a pre-fallen condition. In describing Adam's powers under his original integrity, three times Arminius declared, "he was able" (*potuit*): able to worship, able to trust in God, and able to serve Him.[63] This ability was the result of the strength imparted by the super-naturals included in the *imago Dei*.[64] The fruit of these excellent gifts was a will that was free in all its modes. "This is my opinion concerning the Free-will of man," Arminius proclaimed to Lords of the States of Holland, "in his primitive condition as he came out of the hands of Creator, man was endowed with such a portion of knowledge, holiness and power, as enabled him to understand, esteem, consider, will and to perform the true good, according to the commandment delivered to him."[65] As Hicks concludes, "The freedom of the will was essential to the covenantal relationship which God had established between himself and Adam."[66] Only free will brought about Adam's fall.

The Fall of Adam

The fall of Adam marks the meeting of two central emphases in Arminius' theology: Adam sinned freely, and neither God's prescience nor decree imposed any form of necessity for Adam to sin. Otherwise, if by the decree God imposed a necessity of sinning, then God is the author of sin. Arminius was unwilling to speculate how long Adam remained in original righteousness before he ate of the tree of knowledge,[67] but it was an act of disobedience which contained within it the denial of subjection and the renunciation of obedience."[68] Two foci emerge from his treatments of Adam's sin: the cause of the transgression and its effect. Public Disputation 7.3 gives a summary statement of both before he considered each individually: "This sin…was perpetuated by the free will of man, from a desire to be like God, and through the persuasion of Satan that assumed the shape of a serpent. On account of this transgression, man fell under the displeasure and wrath of God, rendered himself subject to a double death, and deserving to be deprived of the primeval righteousness and holiness in which a great part of the image of God consisted."

Arminius' examination of the causes of the fall is a careful application of Aristotelian causality. The efficient cause was twofold. The immediate and proximate efficient cause was Adam himself, "who of his own free will and without any necessity either internal or external, transgressed the Law which had been proposed to him, which had been sanctioned by a threatening and a promise and which it was possible for him to have observed."[69] The remote and mediate cause was the devil. Motivated by envy of the divine glory and human blessings, he attacked the woman because he considered her weaker than the man, but useful to persuade the man to sin.[70] Satan's arguments provided the "inwardly moving causes" of the usefulness of the fruit and the desire to be like God, and the "outwardly moving cause," the invalidation of the threat of punishment.[71] The instrumental cause was the serpent. However, none of these imposed a necessity of sinning. Adam could have resisted by "repelling and rejecting the causes which operated outwardly, and by reducing into order and subjecting to the Law and to the Spirit of God those which impelled inwardly."[72]

Next, he denied that God was in any way the cause of sin. Arminius quoted his opponents statements, such as "men were predestined to eternal death by the naked will or choice of God without any demerit on their part,"[73] or that "God has predestined whatsoever men he pleased not only to damnation, but likewise to the causes of damnation,"[74] to show that in the Calvinist model God was the only true cause for sin and damnation. Arminius rebutted similar statements by Perkins and Gomarus.[75] Arminius thought it contradictory to say God not only foreknew Adam's fall but both had planned it and decreed it, and then deny that God was the author of sin.[76] He appears to have structured his comments in response to *Institutes*, 3.23. To Calvin's retort that limited and ignorant people should not question the justice of God, Arminius responded that Calvin and Beza's appeal to Romans 9:19–22 offered no answer at all, but rather was an abuse of the passage based upon an incorrect understanding of Paul's purpose.[77] Calvin had appealed to a distinction between the revealed and hidden wills of God,[78] but Arminius rejoined that this answer had its roots in scholastic theology,[79] with no basis in Scripture.[80] We may see his fuller treatment of this in an extensive quotation from *Analysis of Romans* IX:

> But omnipotence does not always accompany God's will in whatever way consi-dered. For God wills that his law should be performed by all; which is not done. But it does not thence follow that there are two wills in God, contrary to each other; the one willing that his law be performed by all; the other, that it be not performed: for so it would not be wonderful that the law is not performed by many, when this will armed with omnipotence hinders the other from being done. But when some men endeavor to explain how it can be, that those wills are not contrary to each other, they say that God's will may be considered in a twofold light, as it is hidden, and as it is revealed; that the revealed will is respecting those things which God likes or dislikes; the hidden, concerning those things which he simply and absolutely wills to be done or not to be done; and that it is perfectly fitting that he by his revealed will should will one and the same action to be done, and by his hidden will should will it not to be done, since he wills it in a different manner. But it may be disputed whether a hidden will can be maintained in God, by which he may will to be done or not to be done what his revealed will wills not to be done or to be done. Others say that the will of God is of well-pleasing or of the sign; which amounts to the same thing: for is not the well-pleasing will of God signified by his word as a sign? Others assert that one will of God is efficacious, the other inefficacious. But this is the same as saying, that the one can be resisted, the other cannot. And it is wonderful in what labyrinths they involve themselves, blinded either by unskilfulness or by prejudice, or rather by both. [81]

Arminius denied that a "hidden" versus "secret" will could be found in Romans 9,[82] and reasserted, "(O)mnipotent will takes away the cause for just anger, if by it man is moved to sin, and with such force as cannot be resisted; and therefore by that will those who are "hardened" will be excluded from the number of those with whom God can be justly angry, if they have done that, on account of which they are hardened, through being moved by that omnipotent will which no one can resist."[83]

Calvin made some of his strongest statements about providence with respect to God's relation to evil.[84] Arminius lingered long over the subject, in part to challenge Calvinism's assertions regarding the relation between the eternal decree and personal sin.[85] Regarding permission, Calvin denied one could say God merely permitted something to occur. God did not merely per-mit human acts, but by sovereign will actively determined that they should be.[86] Arminius argued to the contrary. Perkins[87] and Gomarus[88] had modified their terminology to include the word "permission" in their theses, but Armi-nius demonstrated they had redefined "permission" to mean predetermina-tion.[89] Calvin stated God foreknew because he had so ordained.[90] Arminius devoted considerable effort to his defense of foreknowledge as simple apprehension of future contingent acts.

One of Arminius' preferred methods of disputing was to appeal to Augustine's later works against the predestinarians of his day regarding the relationship between Adam's fall and God's foreordination. Arminius usually quoted Augustine to show that his opponents had misused him, and that even the later Augustine would not have agreed with them regarding foreknowledge and permission,[91] foreordination,[92] synergism,[93] the supralapsarian interpretation of Romans,[94] perseverance[95] or the effects of baptism.[96] Junius also recognized these discrepancies. In his disputations with Arminius, he cited Augustine to defend the idea that "ordain" does not mean "to cause" but "to order."[97] Concerning personal sin, he wrote, "I answer, therefore, with Augustine, in his book *Against the Articles* falsely imputed to him (Article 10), 'Not the falls of the falling, nor the malignity of the wicked, nor the wrong desires of the sinful, did God's predestination excite or persuade or impel.'"[98] Junius agreed with Arminius on the definition of foreknowledge as mere prescience of evil and quoted Augustine for support: "God the creator does not predestinate all he knows, for bad things he only foreknows, and does not predestinate, but good things he both foreknows and predestinates."[99] Arminius was quick to point out Beza and Calvin would not have agreed with this opinion.[100] He insisted, that if "God ordained that man should fall and become sinful, in order that he might in this manner open the way for his eternal counsels, (then) he who ordains that man shall fall and sin is the author of sin."[101] He noted, "Beza himself confesses it is to be incomprehensible how God can be free from blame, and man exposed to blame, if man has fallen by the ordination of God and necessarily."[102]

This led Arminius to conclude that even if Calvin's doctrine was not precisely Manichean or Stoic, its fundamental premise regarding the source of evil was the same.[103] Calvin's concept, however, was worse. The Manicheans demanded two gods, one good and the other evil, while Calvin's God first made humanity good, then willed them to be damned for sin which they committed as the result of his decree. He concluded such a "God is the supreme evil."[104] This understanding of God violates the Scripture's statements regarding his wisdom, justice and goodness.[105] Nor was he impressed with arguments from sovereignty, that man could not hold God to a standard of justice but rather God therefore acted justly by choice. Rather, God is essentially holy; he cannot act contrary to his own nature, and therefore is necessarily just and good.[106]

The Results of the Fall

By their free will and with divine acquiescence, Adam and Eve ate the forbidden fruit and suffered the consequences threatened in their covenant with God.[107] The first and immediate effect was that they offended God by their disparagement of his authority, denial of his desires and contempt for his commandment. This resulted in a sense of guilt.[108] Arminius suggested their flight from God was the first evidence of a wounded conscience, [109] caused by their awareness of their nakedness, fear and dread.[110]

Arminius accepted the terms *privatio* and *reatus* as a means of distinguishing between the types of punishment imposed for the fall.[111] Of the three general punishments inflicted, the most important for Arminius was *privatio*, the withdrawal of the Holy Spirit from fallen humanity. The Holy Spirit ceased to lead and direct Adam, and assure his heart of favor with God.[112] Arminius did not explain the effects of this deprivation here, but elsewhere he delineated the results in far darker tones. The Holy Spirit was the "grace of God" operating in their lives, and his withdrawal was the "privation of grace, whether habitual or assisting.[113] Arminius disparaged the condition of fallen humanity. The privation of the Spirit resulted in the corruption or depravation of the natural aspects of the *imago Dei* as well.[114] First, the mind (*mens*) "in this state is dark, destitute of the saving knowledge of God and…incapable of those things which belongs to the Spirit of God."[115] The soul (*anima*) has been "encompassed about with clouds of ignorance" so that the mind is "darkened"[116] and "blind." [117] The intellect, by itself, would "never receive the truth of the Gospel externally offered to it," because it judges it to be foolish (*stultitiam*). He agreed with Calvin that while natural revelation is accessible to humanity, the fallen intellect perverts it.[118] Divisions in the church are the fruit of "human perversity which corrupts the clear light of this Divine truth, by aspersing and beclouding it with the blackest errors." Thus, the mind cannot be trusted to apprehend either practical or theoretical truths.[119]

Second, the will "is not only wounded, maimed, infirm, bent and attenuated, but also captive, ruined (*perditum*) and useless." "Having abused his liberty, he lost it."[120] The will was powerless with respect to the things of God without the assistance of grace, and like Calvin, he supported this by quoting Augustine on John 15:5. The unregenerate still have free will, but only as the "capability of resisting the Holy Spirit, of rejecting the proffered grace of God, of despising the counsel of God against themselves, of refusing the Gospel of grace, and of not opening to Him who knocks at the door of their hearts."[121]

Third, the affections and the heart are perverse (*perversitas*).[122] The fallen heart hates and avoids what is good and pleasing to God, and loves and pursues what is evil.[123] The heart is deceitful and perverse, uncircumcised, hard and stony,[124] the imagination is evil,[125] and from the heart can only come evil thought, murders, and adulteries.[126] The sum of these depravations is the utter weakness to perform the good and avoid evil.[127] In sum, humanity is incapable of subjecting itself to the law of God.[128]

The result of depravity is that, instead of being guided by the Spirit, "man…is said to be under the power of sin and Satan, reduced to the condition of a slave and 'taken captive by the Devil.'"[129] God has delivered them "to the power of evil," either by giving sinners over to a reprobate mind, the power (*efficaciam*) and desires (*desideria*) of the flesh and lusts (*cupiditates*),[130] or to the power of Satan himself.[131] Consequently, Adam and his descendants lost the right of priesthood before God,[132] alienated from the life of God, estranged from to the covenant, oppressed under the intolerable burden of sin, fainting under the weight of the wrath of God, born sons of the accursed earth, devoted to hell,[133] and children of wrath.[134] Arminius rivals Calvin in his description of fallen "Adam."

Arminius defined temporal (physical) death as "the separation of the soul from the body," and eternal (spiritual) death as "the separation of the entire man from God his chief Good."[135] Ejection from Paradise was an indication or token of these two final punishments. It was a token of temporal death, because "Paradise was a type and figure of the celestial abode, in which consummate and perfect bliss ever flourishes, with the translucent splendour or the Divine Majesty." It was a token of eternal death, "because in that garden was planted the tree of life, the fruit of which when eaten was suitable for continuing natural life to man without the intervention of death: This tree was both a symbol of the heavenly life of which man was bereft, and of death eternal which was to follow."[136] He observed that "the punishment inflicted on the man had regard to his care to preserve the individuals of the species; and that on the woman, to the perpetuation of the species."[137]

Original Sin and Its Imputation

Arminius affirmed some aspects of a Calvinist understanding of original sin. He reiterated that God's covenant with Adam and Eve included the transmission of their blessings to their descendants: "If by disobedience they rendered themselves unworthy of those blessings, their posterity likewise should not possess them, and should be liable to the contrary evils."[138] He noted it was this punishment that was called "a privation of the image of God" and "original sin."[139] He agreed with the Augustinian dictum that all humanity had sinned in Adam. "The whole of this sin," he wrote, "is not peculiar to our first parents, but is common to the entire race and to all their posterity, who, at the time when this sin was committed, were in their loins, and who have since descended from them by the natural mode of propagation, according to the primitive benediction: For in Adam 'all have sinned.'"[140] Adam served as a representative for his descendants,[141] and God made the Adamic covenant with all Adam's offspring as well.[142] He did not think it strange that people could sin before they had personal existence.[143]

However, he was also open to new ideas. Arminius employed Adamic unity to argue against unconditional reprobation. If, as the supralapsarians asserted, sin was a consequence of the decree of reprobation, "then it follows that Adam, and all men in him, are reprobates, for Adam, and in him all men, sinned."[144] He insisted that one must consider people either in the primeval state of integrity, or in the defective state of sin. If the former, they must be considered as holy and just. But if the latter, "in the state of sin all are considered in one who has sinned, and all are considered to have sinned in him." It was impossible to break this unity, because "all are considered in one, whether standing or fallen, there is no predestination, no preterition or reprobation, no predamnation. For so all would be predestined and none reprobated, or all reprobated and none predestined."[145] Instead of an act of predestination or reprobation, Arminius insisted that God permitted Adam and all within him to fall through "general providence," for even the elect had sinned in Adam.[146]

Beza defended supralapsarianism from Romans 9:10–13, that neither Jacob nor Esau had done anything good or evil which could have explained the differences in their treatment. Arminius countered that when God spoke this, the twins were already in the womb. Thus "they were both already conceived in sin"[147] and Beza's contention was moot. Perkins declared the condemnation of the reprobate just because "they had already received saving grace, righteousness and a life of bliss, together with ability to persevere in the same, in Adam, if they had been willing." Arminius answered by denying they had received the grace of Christ, because grace was for sinners and being unfallen they had no need of a savior.[148] In sum, Arminius affirmed that all of humanity had been present in, and represented by, Adam. His sin was their sin, his loss their loss and their essential unity prevented individual predestination or reprobation.

How did God impute original sin? Although his statements that Adam acted as a representative for all humanity hint at federalism, Arminius' most common explanation is the Augustinian doctrine of "natural propagation."[149] He refused to say more because the question was "useless" and the discussion of transmission "scarcely necessary."[150]

Arminius' Questions

Arminius tempered his strong affirmations of humanity's essential unity and guilt in Adam by departing from Calvin's understanding of a corrupted nature. He asked, "Is original sin only the absence or want of original right-eousness and of primeval holiness, with an inclination to commit sin, which likewise formerly existed in man, though it was not so vehement nor so inordinate as now it is, on account of the lost favor of God, his malediction, and the loss of that good by which that inclination was reduced to order? Or is it a certain infused habit (or acquired ingress) contrary to righteousness and holiness, after that sin had been committed?"[151] He answered this same question elsewhere: "Must some contrary quality, beside the absence of original righteousness, be constituted as another part of original sin? Though we think it much more probable, that this absence of original righteousness only is original sin itself, as being that which alone is sufficient to commit and produce any actual sins whatsoever."[152] Here he contrasted the loss of original righteousness with the acquisition of an "infused habit." By this question, he was contrasting two theories of original sin: the Thomist idea that "supernaturals were lost but the naturals remain uncorrupted," and the Calvinist understanding that the naturals were also corrupted.[153]

Arminius' answers suggest he was moving toward a Thomist under-standing of original sin, nevertheless, he did not stop here. He was also moving away from the Reformed understanding of the penalty (*poenus*) for original sin. Two "heretical" statements had been attributed to Adrianus Borrius (Adrian van Borre): (1) "Original sin will condemn no man," and (2) "In every nation, all infants who die without actual sins, are saved."[154] Arminius admitted that Borrius had discussed these ideas with some of the former's students and gave Borrius' supporting arguments.[155] First, God had initiated a covenant of grace with Adam and his posterity, promising the forgiveness of sins "to as many as stand steadfastly, and deal not treacherously" with it. God renewed this covenant of grace with Noah and perfected it in Christ. Infants have not transgressed this covenant, so they are not liable to condemnation. If infants were condemned, it would not be for any fault or demerit of their own, but because it pleased God to alienate them both from the covenant of grace and from the promise of a savior. Second, God pardoned Adam for his sin, so infants would have benefited from this pardon. If he pardoned Adam, why would he not also pardon infants who had sinned in Adam before they had any personal existence or volition? Finally, if God condemned infants for the sin of Adam, he treats infants worse than demons. He condemned demons for a crime they had personally perpetrated and could have avoided, while he damned infants for the crimes of another and for which they had no recourse to avoid.

If Borrius' statements alarmed Calvinists, Arminius' response would have amplified their concerns. Arminius thought these arguments "were of great importance," and before anyone could condemn them, they were bound to refute them. Nor could Calvinists look to "antiquity" for support, because the ancients believed that all who died without baptism were damned, and God saved all the baptized, even if not predestined.[156] Moreover, the ancients thought that the damnation of unbaptized infants "would be in the mildest damnation of all," not of pain but of loss (of the beatific vision). What kind of damnation was this?, he asked. He knew no Calvinist would accept these ideas.[157] He then cited Junius in support of Borrius, that "all infants who are of the covenant and of election, are saved, but he presumes, in charity, that those infants whom God calls to himself, and timely removes out of this miserable vale of sins, are rather saved."[158] If Junius could hold this, why not Borrius? Arminius then concluded that his Calvinist colleagues' opinions, the affirmation that all unbaptized infants were damned and the refusal to affirm the salvation of baptized children of believers, was scandalous and unsupported by any other Christian church.

Hicks minimized the implications of this answer by suggesting it was merely the sympathetic defense of a friend and that Arminius elsewhere affirmed infant damnation.[159] Arminius' unqualified defense of Borrius suggests otherwise, as do his other writings. He chided Perkins: "(Your) argument deduced from fools and infants is altogether childish. For who can dare deny that many fools and little children are saved?"[160] Arminius had synthesized an understanding of the relation between Adam's sin and original sin that looked Reformed because of his use of *reatus/poenus* terminology and because of his description of human depravity. However, he had redefined *reatus* in such a way that he could deny eternal damnation of children as a universal result of the fall. Arminius asked, "Does original sin render men obnoxious to the wrath of God, when they have been previously constituted sinners on account of the actual sin of Adam, and rendered liable to damnation?"[161] How could Arminius distinguish between being "liable (obnoxious) to the wrath of God" and "liable to damnation?"

Arminius answered this question both in his response to the third of *Nine Questions*,[162] and in his reply to the last of the *Thirty One Articles*.[163] In the former, his Calvinist opponents had asked, "Does original sin, of itself, render man obnoxious (*reum*) to eternal death, even without the addition of any actual sin? Or is the guilt of original sin taken away from all and every one by the benefits of Christ the Mediator?" His questioners desired a straightforward treatment of the *reatus* of original sin and their contrast between original sin and actual sins invoked the question of infants. Arminius asked, "If some men are condemned solely on account of the sin committed by Adam, and others on account of their rejection of the Gospel, are there not two peremptory decrees concerning the damnation of men, and two judgments, one Legal, the other Evangelical?" Were the reprobate condemned twice in the *ordo salutis*, once for violation of the Adamic covenant, and once for rejecting the covenant of grace? If Calvinists affirmed rejection of the gospel as a means of implementing reprobation, did this not force them to abandon condemnation for original sin?

Both Arminius' rephrasing of the question and his answer indicates he thought they must. Arminius treated the question first as a whole, and then divided it into its parts. Treated as a whole, the halves must agree: if God holds all people guilty for Adam's sin, then God can forgive them all in Christ. Then he denied the first member of the equation. By definition, original sin is not a sin, but the punishment of Adam's actual sin. Therefore, it was confused to say "original sin renders a man obnoxious to death," because original sin is in itself the punishment inflicted by God. It was illogical to reckon God's act of punishment as another's personal sin, or that divine punishment for sin could be the source for all other sins. If children are born in original sin, then this both proved they sinned in Adam, and merited no further punishment. In answering the other half of the question, he pressed for hypothetical universal atonement. One must distinguish between soliciting, obtaining and applying the benefits of Christ. The work on the cross was for all, but applied to those who believe. Consequently, Christ's work was sufficient for all who fell in Adam, but efficient in believers.

Arminius built his reply to Article 31 on the same distinction. First, God could not be angry because of original sin because it was not sin, but punishment for sin. If original sin could provoke God's anger, it would create an infinite cycle of imputation and punishment. Second, he denied original sin was a sin based on Romans 7. Original sin provokes actual sins, but only actual sins result in spiritual death (7:8–11). Finally, he affirmed that original sin produced all other sins. Thus, his responses to both Question 9 and Article 31 denied that original sin brought with it guilt and condemnation.

Regarding children of Christians, Arminius approached their salvation in two ways. God included all humanity in the covenant of grace that he made with Adam. God always reckons children as being a part of their parents. Therefore if their parents are a part of the covenant community, then children are saved by their inclusion in their parents, "for the arrangement is a perpetual covenant, that children are comprehended and reckoned in their parents."[164] Hence, contrary to his opponents, Arminius affirmed the covenant of grace incorporated all children of believing parents until they repudiated it. He did not, however, link this inclusion to baptism. He spoke of "baptized infants" here, but elsewhere wrote, "It is unwisely asserted that, through it (baptism) grace is conferred, that is, by some other act of conferring than that which is done through typifying and sealing. For grace cannot be immediately conferred through water."[165] This left open the idea that an unbaptized infant of believing parents could still be a part of the covenant. Perhaps this explains why infant baptism was not as important in the Remonstrant Brotherhood.[166] Arminius based his second approach on the principle that God could not demand what he did not also provide his grace to perform. God cannot demand faith of those who cannot believe. Therefore, God does not demand faith of infants.[167]

Arminius' Doctrine of Grace

Because of God's holiness, the entrance of sin required a change if humanity were to maintain a relationship with God. It could no longer be legal, because "man, being liable to the condemnation of God, needs the grace of restoration."[168] Although Arminius contrasted the legal character of the Mosaic covenant with the "Evangelical,"[169] he thought even the Mosaic was one of grace because it provided for the remission of sins. Forgiveness is an act of grace that rests on the work of Jesus Christ.[170] The basis for the evangelical faith is God's gracious response to human inability, and "God's love of miserable sinners, on which likewise the Christian religion is founded."[171] Arminius taught prolifically on the theme of grace. Four aspects of grace are important for our discussion: its definition, necessity, operation and relation to free will.

Grace Defined

Arminius' definition of grace depended upon its context. He could define grace as an attribute of God, a "certain adjunct of (God's) goodness and love."[172] At times, he defined it according to function, as when he distinguished between the grace of conservation and the grace of restoration.[173] In another place he defined grace as a gratuitous affection, an infusion of the gifts of the Spirit, the perpetual assistance and continued aid of the Holy Spirit.[174] His employed the scholastic categories of common, sufficient and efficient grace,[175] and based his refutation of the Calvinist doctrine of irresistible grace on his distinction between sufficient and efficient grace, and most importantly, on his definition of the essence of grace.[176]

The most significant of Arminius' definitions is that "grace" is an abstraction for the Holy Spirit.[177] Because Arminius sometimes spoke of grace as an "infusion,"[178] some have erred in thinking Arminius regarded grace "as a kind of quasi-metaphysical substance or energy."[179] Nor is grace merely the operation of the Holy Spirit before or after the moment of faith. Grace *is* the Holy Spirit, and the renewing of grace is a renewal of immediate union between God and humanity through the indwelling of the Spirit, "for God unites himself to the understanding and to the will of his creature, by means of himself alone…in which consists the Chief Good of a rational being, which cannot find rest except in the greatest union of itself with God."[180] Grace includes both the perpetual assistance of the Spirit, moving people through "infusing healthy thoughts and inspiring good desires into him,"[181] and the restoration of the gifts of the Spirit.[182] This definition of grace agrees well with his understanding of privation of the Holy Spirit as the penalty (*poenus*) for the fall.

The Necessity and Operation of Grace

The Necessity of Grace

Arminius employed various synonyms for sufficient and efficient grace. He used terms such as "preceding,"[183] "prevenient,"[184] "preparative," "preventing and exciting,"[185] and "operating" for sufficient grace and "following and cooperating"[186] or "subsequent or following"[187] for efficient grace. Nevertheless, his preferred terms were "sufficient" and "efficient" grace. His distinction between them rested on two emphases in his theology: the absolute necessity of grace, and the freedom of the will to reject grace. Arminius spoke about both in the "Declaration of Sentiments":

> In this manner, I ascribe to grace the commencement, the continuance and the consummation of all good, and to such an extent do I carry its influence, that a man, though already regenerate, can neither conceive, will nor do any good at all, nor resist any evil temptation, without this preventing and exciting, this following and cooperating grace. From this statement it will clearly appear, that I am by no means injurious or unjust to grace, by attributing, as it is reported of me, too much to man's free-will. For the whole controversy reduces itself to the solution of this

question, "Is the grace of God a certain irresistible force?" That is, the controversy does not relate to those actions or operations which may be ascribed to grace (for I acknowledge and inculcate as many of these actions or operations as any man ever did), but it relates solely to the mode of operation, whether it be irresistible or not, with respect to which, I believe, according to the scriptures, that many persons resist the Holy Spirit and reject the grace that is offered.[188]

The necessity of grace issued both from humanity's creation (the supernaturals being a central component of the divine image), and from the results of sin entering into the "world." Original sin makes it impossible for people to either do good or please God on the basis of their natural abilities, and necessitates the renewal of the presence and operation of the Spirit. Nevertheless, the will is free to reject the grace of God, dividing the ministry of the Spirit between what he performs up to the point of faith (sufficient grace) and what he performs afterward (efficient grace).

Arminius gave his most complete explanation of grace in *Examination of Perkins' Pamphlet*. It began with his rebuttal of Perkins' treatment of what the English divine had called the "eighth error" of his opponents, that believers could finally fall from grace,[189] and the "ninth error,"[190] that the will can resist grace. Arminius provided a more correct version of what Perkins denied:

> But this is what they hold: that a man receives by his own free choice the grace which comes to him from above, of whatever kind it may be. For, as grace saves, so the free will is saved, and the subject of grace is man's free will. Wherefore it is unavoidable that the free will should concur in preserving the grace bestowed, assisted, however, by subsequent grace; and it always remains within the power of the free will to reject the grace bestowed, and to refuse subsequent grace; because grace is not an omnipotent action of God, which cannot be resisted by man's free will. And since the matter stands thus, the same parties suppose that man can throw away grace, and fall.[191]

In this we have both the anterior and posterior aspects of grace, and the power of the will to reject both. Perkins objected that this made the will "flexible to either side by grace." Arminius responded it was flexible "even without grace," and though addicted to evil it is capable of good. However, the will never achieves this capacity except by grace, which "brings forth the power and capacity of matter into action."[192] Here he introduced the distinction betwen sufficient and efficient grace, citing Augustine from *De Vocatione Gentium*. Arminius' ideas on the relationship between grace and the will are clear. Sufficient grace is capable of effectiveness, but is not considered efficacious until it produces the intended effect.[193] Sufficient and efficacious grace are identical in their essential properties, the difference between them being the acceptance of the will.

Perkins had noted Augustine's distinctions and rejected them because "no grace is sufficient for conversion which is not efficacious," and because "free will is wanting to man in spiritual things." Arminius countered by asking, "But if grace restores the liberty of the will, can it not then in a free will act sufficiently, or does it act efficaciously?" Cannot grace remove impotence, "and cause man to receive the offered grace, to use it when received and to preserve it?" There exist two hindrances to the work of grace: passive resistance because of inborn sin and active resistance because of acquired sinfulness. Grace may remove the first, but the second continues.[194] On the contrary, if grace were to act irresistibly upon the will, then grace does not free the will but destroys it. If it acts resistibly, then grace "corrects the nature itself wheresoever it has become faulty."[195]

Perkins had denied certain arguments drawn from Scripture to support grace as sufficient but not efficacious. Arminius noted the source of Perkins' examples, Robert Bellarmine, the *bête noire* of the Reformed, and defended the cardinal's reasoning.[196] Nevertheless, Arminius maintained Reformed orthodoxy's use of "vocation" for the operation of grace by which God draws men to himself."[197] He defined vocation as "a gracious act of God in Christ by which through his Word and Spirit he calls forth sinful men…into fellowship with Jesus Christ and of his kingdom and benefits."[198] After considering the roles of the Father and Son in vocation, he discussed that of the Word and Spirit. He divided calling between the external call of the preaching of the word of God, and in the internal call of the Spirit by the illumination of the mind and the moving of the heart.[199] Both are forms of persuasion, and both "are almost always joined together."[200] While admitting, "the preaching of the word without the co-operation of the Spirit was useless," he appealed to Isaiah 55:11 that preaching "has that cooperation always joined with it." As with sufficient grace, Arminius affirmed people could resist this call. "Those who are obedient to the vocation or call of God freely yield their assent to grace," he affirmed, and "at the very moment in which they actually assent, they possess the capability of not assenting."[201] Arminius also accepted that God could call people apart from the written word. Arminius believed God ordinarily uses the preaching of the Gospel, but allowed for extraordinary means "without human assistance, when God immediately proposes the word inwardly to the mind and the will."[202]

Arminius declared that faith is a gift of God. He defined faith as "that by which men believe in Jesus Christ, as in the Savior of those universally who believe, and of each of them in particular, even the Savior of him who, through Christ, believes in God who justifies the ungodly."[203] "It is the effect of God illuminating the mind and sealing the heart," God's "mere gift"[204] made necessary by humanity's fallen condition,[205] but not granted to all.[206] However, Arminius' understanding of "faith as a gift" was not Calvinist. By "gift" he did not mean that God infused faith into a person. Rather, faith is a gift in that all people have the ability to believe, but not the will. The grace of God enables them to become willing, and because God has brought about an otherwise impossible condition, Arminius considered this otherwise entirely human act a gift.[207] Arminius' opponents had detected this. In Article 27, they accused him of teaching that "faith is not the pure gift of God, but depends in part upon the grace of God, and in part upon the powers of free will, that, if a man will, he may believe or not believe." Arminius denounced this statement: "I never said this, I never thought of saying it, and relying of God's grace I will never enunciate my sentiments on matters of this description in a manner thus disparate and confused." He declared, "I simply affirm that this enunciation is false: 'faith is not the pure gift of God;' that this is likewise false if taken according to the rigor of the words, 'Faith depends partly on the grace of God, and partly on the powers of the will,' and that this is also false when thus enunciated, 'If a man will, he can believe or not believe.'" Nevertheless, consider the analogy he employed to explain his meaning.

> A rich man bestows on a poor and famishing beggar alms by which he may be able to maintain himself and his family. Does it cease to be a pure gift because the beggar extends his hand to receive it? Can it be said with propriety that the "alms depended partly on the liberality of the Donor, and partly on the liberty of the Receiver," though the latter would not have possessed the alms unless he had received it by stretching out his hand? Can it be correctly said, because the beggar is always prepared to receive, that "he can have the alms, or not have it, just as he pleases?" If these assertions cannot be truly made about a beggar who receives alms, how much less can they be made about the gift of faith, for the receiving of which far more acts of Divine Grace are required![208]

We may presume the Gomarists would have responded to Arminius' question, "Does it cease to be a pure gift, because the beggar extends his hand to receive it," with a resounding "Yes." They would have rejected that the sinner is as "always prepared to receive" grace as a beggar is alms. Arminius believed faith was a gift in that it was grace which enabled the will to respond with faith, but it was not the gift of faith as defined by Calvinism.

The Operation of Grace and Free Will

We may summarize Arminius' understanding of the relation between grace and free will in two sentences. First, grace is absolutely necessary to persuade the will to faith in Christ, and without grace, the will cannot do so. He wrote, "Those who are obedient to the vocation or call of God, freely yield their assent to grace, yet they are previously excited, impelled, drawn and assisted by grace."[209] Grace has the power to bend the will, and the will is powerless to accomplish any spiritual good without grace.

Second, at any moment the will is free to reject the grace of God. The necessity of grace does not violate the domain of human freedom. Arminius based his belief on the rejectability of grace on Scriptural examples of those who had resisted God's Spirit and grace, and termed such rejection an "accidental" consequent of vocation.[210] There is a sense of cooperation between the divine and the human, for "God concurs with man in willing and carrying out into action that good for which he has received sufficient strength, unless man, on his part, placed or has placed a hindrance in the way."[211] It is grace which draws, but "in the very moment in which they actually assent, they possess the capability of not assenting."[212] Arminius argued that all of church history supported this. He cited support from no less than Prosper of Aquitaine: "This aid is afforded to all men by innumerable methods both secret and manifest, and the rejection of this assistance by many persons is to be ascribed to their negligence; but its reception by many persons, is both of Divine Grace and of the human will."[213] One statement in particular demonstrated his opinion regarding the interplay between grace and free will:[214]

> What then, you will ask, does free will do? I reply with brevity, it saves. Take away free will, and nothing will be left to be saved. Take away grace, and nothing will be left as the source of salvation. This world of salvation cannot be effected without two parties: one, from whom it may come, the other, to whom or in whom it may be wrought. God is the author of salvation; only free will is capable of being saved. No one except God is able to bestow salvation, and nothing except free will is capable of receiving it.[215]

Arminius defended both divine justice and human freedom. He believed his paradigm of sufficient and efficient grace allowed for both, and hold them in balance. As he penned to Hippolytus à Collibus, "that teacher obtains my highest approbation who ascribes as much as possible to Divine grace, provided he so pleads the cause of grace as not to inflict injury on the justice of God and not take away from the free will to do that which is evil."[216]

Conclusion

Arminius' doctrine of the *imago Dei* was similar, if not identical, to other scholastic Reformed theologians of his era. God created mankind with two constituent parts, body and soul. While God did not create the body in the *imago Dei*, still it showed forth the handiwork of God and provided a perfect vehicle for the soul. The *imago Dei* rested with the soul, which God breathed into Adam, and creates and places within each person at conception. Arminius held to faculty psychology, common among Dutch Reformed theologians of his day, by further dividing the soul between *intellectus* and *voluntas*. The intellect performs activities of reason, but the will exercises the powers of dilection and choice. Added to these were the "supernaturals," divine *habitus* that illumined the mind and sanctified the will. These divine enablings were in essence the grace of God, an abstraction for the presence of the Holy Spirit in the soul. Adam's disobedience in the garden cut short this divine arrangement, resulting in the loss of the indwelling presence of the Holy Spirit (deprivation) and the consequent corruption of the naturals that remained (depravation). In this, Arminius agreed with Aquinas. He did not believe the fall added some principle of evil to human nature. Rather, the effects of sin were the consequences of the naturals functioning without the guidance of grace and the attendant qualities of right reason and pure affections. Furthermore, he affirmed the "in Adam" theology of Augustine. However, he took this further than the Calvinists when he taught that not only had all humanity fallen in Adam, but also God blessed all people in Adam before the fall and universally promised the Savior to them afterward. Humanity inherited this also from Adam by natural generation.

Arminius acknowledged the absolute necessity of God's grace. Grace provided the propitiatory, expiatory sacrifice for sins through the death of the Lord Jesus Christ, and grace alone provides for human freedom from the bondage and slavery of sin. Arminius believed the privation of the Spirit resulted in an Augustinian division between freedom and liberty. Humanity is in bondage to sin, and freely desires and chooses those things that were in accordance to sin. People are unable to turn toward the things of God without the calling of God through the preaching of the Gospel and the internal calling of the Spirit. Even so, Arminius did not believe that people experienced salvation because they wanted it, or chose to believe, but because they chose not to resist the Spirit. Thus, he was neither Pelagian nor Semi-Pelagian.

Although Arminius died in the middle of a vigorous defense of this theology, the theological movement he represented did not. He left behind a small but committed group of colleagues and disciples, one of whom was Simon Episcopius. We consider him in our next chapter.

Notes

1. Jacobus Arminius, *De vero & genuino sensu cap. VII. Epistolæ ad Romanos dissertatio* (Leiden: Ex Officina Godefridi Basson, 1612); cf. James Arminius, *Dissertation on the True and Genuine Sense of the Seventh Chapter on the Epistle to the Romans*, in *The Works of James Arminius*, trans. James Nichols, London ed. (London: Longman, Hurst, Rees, Orme, Brown and Green, 1828; reprint, Grand Rapids: Baker, 1986).

2. Carl O. Bangs, *Arminius: A Study in the Dutch Reformation*, 2d ed. (Grand Rapids: Francis Asbury Press, 1985), 186.

3. Theodore Beza, *Refutation of the Calumnies of Tilman Heshusius*; cited by Arminius, *Dissertation on Romans 7*, in *WA*, 2:495.

4. John Calvin, *Institutes of the Christian Religion*, ed. John Thomas McNeill, trans. Ford Lewis Battles (Philadelphia: Westminster Press, 1960), 3.2.27; 3.3.2; cited by Arminius, *Dissertation on Romans 7*, in *WA*, 2:496.

5. Ibid., 2:552–61. By his list Arminius demonstrated a wide familiarity with the early fathers. The medieval scholastics are absent.

6. Ibid., 2:489–91.

7. See Bangs, *Arminius: A Study in the Dutch Reformation*, 300. These objections are provided in the headings of Arminius' responses. See Jacobus Arminius, *Apologia Adversus Articulos quosdam Theologos in vulgus sparsos*, in *Opera Theologica* (Leiden: Goderfridum Basson, 1629), 153–55; cf. James Arminius, *The Apology or Defence of James Arminius, D. D. Against Thirty-One Articles*, in *The Works of James Arminius*, trans. James Nichols, London ed. (London: Longman, Hurst, Rees, Orme, Brown and Green, 1825–28; reprint, Grand Rapids: Baker, 1986), 2:10–14.

8. Jacobus Arminius, *Quæstiones Numero Novem, Nobliss. DD. Curatoribus Academiæ Leidensis exhibite à Deputatis Synodi, in hunc finem, ut ad eas à Professoribus S. Theologia responderetur*, in *Opera Theologica* (Leiden: Goderfridum Basson, 1629), 184; cf. James Arminius, *Nine Questions Exhibited for the Purpose of Obtaining An Answer From Each of the Professors of Divinity: and the replies which James Arminius gave to them: with other nine opposite articles*, in *The Works of James Arminius*, trans. James Nichols, London ed. (London: Longman, Hurst, Rees, Orme, Brown and Green, 1828; reprint, Grand Rapids: Baker, 1986), 2:65.

9. See Frederik Broecker, *F. Broeckeri Joh. F. Horn Dispvtatie vant rechte verstant des 7. Cap. des Briefs Pauli tot den Rom: teghens D.V. Coornhert in sijn Nadencken opt 7. Cap. tot den Romeynen: Ende teghens Arminium* (Enchuysen: Jacob Lenærtsz Meyn, 1613). Note Broeker's linking of Coornhert with Arminius.

10. Arminius, *Nine Questions*, 2:65; Arminius, *Thirty-One Articles*, 2:10–14.

[11] James Arminius, *Certain articles to be diligently examined and weighed*, in *The Works of James Arminius*, trans. James Nichols, London ed. (London: Longman, Hurst, Rees, Orme, Brown and Green, 1828; reprint, Grand Rapids: Baker, 1986), 3:714–18 (Articles 5–14); cf. Jacobus Arminius, *Articuli nonnulli diligenti examine perpendendi*, in *Opera Theologica* (Leiden: Goderfridum Basson, 1629), 951–57.

[12] James Arminius, *Oration IV: The Priesthood of Christ*, in *The Works of James Arminius*, trans. James Nichols, London ed. (London: Longman, Hurst, Rees, Orme, Brown and Green, 1825; reprint, Grand Rapids: Baker, 1986)2:409–10; idem, *A Declaration of the Sentiments of Arminius on Predestination, Divine Providence, The Freedom of the Will, the Grace of God, the Divinity of the Son of God, and the Justification of Man Before God*, in *The Works of James Arminius*, trans. James Nichols, London ed. (London: Longman, Hurst, Rees, Orme, Brown and Green, 1825; reprint, Grand Rapids: Baker, 1986), 1:618. He did not present his own opinions, however.

[13] James Arminius, *Friendly Conference of James Arminius, The Illustrious Doctor of Sacred Theology*, in *The Works of James Arminius*, trans. William Nichols, London ed. (London: Thomas Baker, 1875; reprint, Grand Rapids: Baker, 1986)3:93, 145, 151–53, 161–63, 178–79, 219, 224–27; idem, *Dr. James Arminius' Modest Examination of a Pamphlet, Which That Very Learned Divine Dr. William Perkins*, in *The Works of James Arminius*, trans. William Nichols, London ed. (London: Thomas Baker, 1875; reprint, Grand Rapids: Baker, 1986), 3:278, 300, 314, 314, 329, 330, 341, 497.

[14] James Arminius, *A Letter to His Excellency, the Noble Lord, Hippolytus à Collibus*, in *The Works of James Arminius*, trans. James Nichols, London ed. (London: Longman, Hurst, Rees, Orme, Brown and Green, 1828; reprint, Grand Rapids: Baker, 1986), 2:696–701.

[15] "Disputation 26. On the Creation of Man after the Image of God," in James Arminius, *The Private Disputations of James Arminius on the Principal Articles of the Christian Religion*, in *The Works of James Arminius*, trans. James Nichols, London ed. (London: Longman, Hurst, Rees, Orme, Brown and Green, 1828; reprint, Grand Rapids: Baker, 1986), 2:362–64. Arminius did not address the image of God in his public disputations.

[16] Arminius, *Conference with Junius*, 3:94–95, 109–21, 161–62.

[17] "...ex corpore & anima rationali constans" (Jacobus Arminius, *Disputationes Publicæ de Nonnullis Religionis Christianæ capitibus, ab ipso compositæ*, in *Opera Theologica* (Leiden: Goderfridum Basson, 1629), Thesis 26.1. In one of his rare criticisms of Augustine, Calvin judged he had "speculated with excessive refinement" in order to establish a "trinity" in the human constitution. He attributed Augustine's speculation to Aristotle's concept of the three faculties of the soul (intellect, memory, and will), and while admitting the soul possesses such abilities, preferred "a simpler division into two parts" as more in keeping with the Scriptures (John Calvin, *Commentaries on the First Book of Moses Called Genesis*, trans. John King [Edinburgh: Calvin Translation Society, n.d.; reprint, Grand Rapids: Baker, 1981], 1:93–95). This was also the position of the pre-Augustinian fathers. See John Norman Davidson Kelly, *Early Christian Doctrines*, rev. ed. (San Francisco: Harper & Row, 1978), 166, 344.

[18] *Priv. Disp.* 26.1.

[19] *Priv. Disp.* 26.2. This question of whether Adam was created mortal occupied an important place in the discussions of early Christian theologians.

[20] *Priv. Disp.* 26.3–4.

[21] Arminius' expression, "cum eo unum componeret ὑφιολάμενους" is difficult. Nichols left the word untranslated in the text.

22 Priv. Disp. 26.12.

23 Priv. Disp. 26.3, emphasis added.

24 In this, Arminius was in general agreement with other Reformed scholars. See Heinrich Heppe, *Reformed Dogmatics: Set Out and Illustrated from the Original Sources*, ed. Ernst Bizer, trans. G. T. Thomson (London: George Allen & Unwin Ltd., 1950; reprint, Grand Rapids: Baker, 1986), 227–233.

25 Priv. Disp. 26.4.

26 "A strong case can be made, however, for the continuity of faculty psychology of Christian Aristotelianism during the period of the Reformation," and that Protestant scholastics accepted "without question the entire language of faculty psychology as one of the presuppositions of their discussions of human knowing" (Richard A. Muller, *Post-Reformation Reformed Dogmatics: Prolegomena to Theology* [Grand Rapids: Baker, 1987], 227–228). See Calvin, *Institutes*, 1.15.7.

27 Priv. Disp. 26.5. In some places (Arminius, *Certain Articles*, in WA, 2:712; Priv. Disp. 20), he clarified the affections as a function of the will.

28 Priv. Disp. 16.6; cf. Priv. Disp. 17 concerning the understanding of God, and Priv. Disp. 18–20 concerning the divine will.

29 Pub. Disp. 11.

30 Arminius' analysis is identical to that of Bernard of Clairveaux in *De Gratia et Libero Arbitrio* (*Opera Omnia*, Patrologiæ Cursus Completus, sive biblioteca universalis, integra, uniformis, commoda, oeconomica, omnium SS. Patrum, doctorum scriptorumque ecclesiasticorum. Series Latina Prior, ed., J. P. Migne. [Paris: Migne, 1844–64], col. 1005). See also Calvin's discussion of the same (*Institutes* 2.2.5).

31 By distinguishing freedom from necessity from freedom from sin, Arminius could insist that with respect to the first freedom of choice remained after the fall, but on the basis of the second man was enslaved to sin. Blaising concluded this was an "obvious deficiency" was the "total lack...of a necessity toward the good" (Craig A. Blaising, "John Wesley's Doctrine of Original Sin," [Ph.D. diss., Dallas Theological Seminary, 1979] 80–81). Perhaps this is not so great a deficiency, since a "necessity for the good" implies some form of perfectionism.

32 "The liberty of the will consists in this, when all the requisites for willing or not willing are laid down, man is still indifferent to will or not to will, to will this rather than that. This indifference is removed by the previous determination, by which the will is circumscribed and absolutely determined to the one part or to the other of the contradiction or contrariety: And this predetermination, therefore, does not consist with the liberty of the will, which requires not only free capability, but also free use in the very exercise of it...Internal necessity is as repugnant to liberty as external necessity is; nay, external necessity does not necessitate to act except by the intervention of that which is internal" (*Certain Articles*, 6.8–9). Contrast this with Heppe's presentation of the Reformed doctrine of Adam's freedom, which was not the freedom to choose whether to obey, but only the freedom to choose to obey (Heppe, *Reformed Dogmatics*, 243.)

33 See Franciscus Junius, *Theses Theologicæ Quæ in Inclyta Academia Lugdunobativa Ad Exercitia Publicarum Disputationum, Præside D. Francisco Iunio Variis temporibus à Theologiæ Candidatis aduersus oppognantes propugnatæ sunt*, in *Opuscula Theologica Selecta*, ed. Abr. Kuyperus (Amsterdam: Fredericum Muller Cum Soc. et Joannem Hermannum Kruyt, 1882), Theses 18.9.

[34] For contemporary discussions of an act as being both free and necessary, see Franciscus Junius, *Opuscula Theologica Selecta*, ed. Abr. Kuyperus (Amsterdam: Fredericum Muller Cum Soc. et Joannem Hermannum Kruyt, 1882), Thesis 11.10 (140), Thesis 17.7–9 (159–60), and especially Thesis 18 (161–166); William Perkins, *The workes of that famous and worthie minister of Christ in the University of Cambridge* (Cambridge,: Printed by John Legate Printer to the University of Cambridge, 1608), 2:618; William Perkins, "The Golden Chain," in *The Work of William Perkins*, ed. Ian Breward, The Courteny Library of Reformation Classics (Abingdon, England: Sutton Courtenay Press, 1970), 184, 190; Franciscus Gomarus and Jacobus Arminius, *Twee Disputatien van de Goddelicke Predestinatie* (Leyden: Ian Pæts Iacobscoon, 1609), Johannes Corvinus, *Schovvve over D. Francisci Gomari Proeve, van D. M. P. Bertii Ænspræck, By een van sijn disciplulen*, (n.p.: Ian Pædts Iacopszoon, 1610), Theses 8–12, (8); cf. Thesis VIII in James Arminius, "Examination of the Theses of Dr. Francis Gomarus Respecting Predestination," in *The Works of James Arminius*, London ed. (London: Thomas Baker, 1875; reprint, Grand Rapids: Baker, 1986), 3:543. See also Heppe, *Reformed Dogmatics*, 303–11 for a summary of Musculus, Witsius, Wollebius and the *Synopsis Purioris* on the same.

[35] "Internal necessity is as repugnant as is external necessity; nay external necessity does not necessitate to act except by the intervention of that which is internal" (*Certain Articles*, 6.9).

[36] Arminius, *Declaration of Sentiments*, 1:659.

[37] Priv. Disp. 26.6. For an definition of *habitus* and its use among Reformed scholastics, see Muller, *Post Reformed Dogmatics*, 226–230.

[38] See *Certain Articles*, 6.5, and *Conference with Junius*, Proposition 10. Arminius rebuked Perkins, "There is, however, one thing about which I may admonish you. You seem to me wrongfully to exclude God's image, consisting in righteousness and holiness, from supernatural grace. For though that image be conferred upon man in creation, and together with his nature itself, for in that position I place it, yet is it supernatural, and exceeding the nature itself of man" ("Examination of Perkins' Pamphlet," in *WA*, 3:439).

[39] Pub. Disp. 6.15.2.

[40] Priv. Disp. 12.2.

[41] Arminius appears to follow Calvin's arrangement here. See *Conference with Junius*, Proposition 10. He also wrote, "God's image in us, recreated by the regenerating Spirit, is the knowledge of God agreeing with the image of God, in which at the beginning we were created." (*WA*, 1:114). Regarding Calvin's use of this definition, see Calvin, *Commentaries on Genesis*, 1:94–95.

[42] Priv. Disp. 29.9, discussed below.

[43] Priv. Disp. 26.7.

[44] Priv. Disp.26.8; see also "Certain Articles" 6.5.

[45] Arminius had affirmed the inaccessibility of God to man by natural means in *Oration II*, (*WA* 1:350–51): "For since God is the Author of the universe, (and that, not by a natural and internal operation, but by one that is voluntary and external, and that imparts to the work as much as he chooses of his own, and as much as the nothing from which it is produced, will permit,) his excellence and dignity must necessarily far exceed the capacity of the universe, and, for the same reason, that of man See also *Oration III*, *WA* 1:380.

[46] Calvin, *Institutes*, 1.3.

[47] Priv. Disp. 26.10. The Latin reads "Atque ita creatus est homo, ut Deum creatorem suum agnosceret, diligeret, coleret, & cum eo beatus in æternum viveret" (*OT*, 370).

48 Arminius was particularly incensed when some of his adversaries suggested that even having been created in the image of God in no way served to bless the reprobate, but merely advanced a means of greater damnation. (*Declaration of Sentiments*, 9.6) He considered "horrid" Gomarus' thesis that "the way of reprobation is creation in the upright state of original righteousness" (*Certain Articles*, 5.6). See also Perkins, "The Golden Chain," 185–86.

49 See Calvin, *Institutes*, 3.23.

50 Arminius' argument here regarding the creation demonstrating God's goodness, wisdom and power is identical to Tertullian's arguments against Marcion regarding the causes of the fall (Tertullian, *The Five Books Against Marcion*, in *Latin Christianity: Its Founder, Tertullian*, Ante-Nicene Fathers, ed., Alexander Roberts and James Donaldson.[n.p.: Christian Literature, 1885; reprint, Peabody, MA: Hendrickson], 2.5).

51 Priv. Disp. 26.11.

52 "For Adam was able, with the aid of God, to fulfil the Law by those powers which he had received in Creation; Otherwise, transgression could not have been imputed to him for a crime" (Pub. Disp. 13.3).

53 Arminius gave his definitions for speculative and practical theology in his first oration: "For the theology which belongs to this world is practical and through faith; theoretical theology belongs to the other world, and consists of pure and unclouded vision.... For this reason we must clothe the object of our Theology in such a manner as may enable it to incline us to worship God, and fully to persuade and win us over to that practice. " (Arminius, *Oration I*, in *WA*, 1:328). In the same passage he excluded metaphysics from the realm of theology.

54 This distinction between legal and evangelical theology forms a basic paradigm in Arminius' theology. He introduced it midway through *Oration I* (*WA*, 1:332), and continued to employ it as a basic approach throughout most of his other addresses. Arminius did not distinguish between a "covenant of works" and a "legal covenant," but called both legal covenants, one with Adam and the other through Moses. Arminius was very specific in how the Adamic and Mosaic covenants, though both were legal, were still very different from one another. See Pub. Disp. 13:3.

55 *WA*, 2:204–205, cf. *OT*, 270–271 and *OT*, 374–375; See also *Conference with Junius*, Proposition 14 especially.

56 For a survey of Reformed theologians who saw the Decalogue as somehow included in the command, even if in summary form, see Heppe, *Reformed Dogmatics*, 291–94.

57 *OT*, 375.

58 Priv. Disp. 29.5–7.

59 Priv. Disp. 29.8.

60 *Conference with Junius*, Proposition 14.

61 "Examination of Perkins' Pamphlet;" in *WA*, 3:451.

62 *Analysis of Romans IX*, in *WA*, 3:511. William Perkins had used similar argumentation to the contrary in defense of reprobation, that men had rejected Christ and saving grace in Adam. See *Examination of Perkins' Pamphlet*, in *WA*, 3:376.

63 *Oratio* 1, in *WA*, 1:332–333; cf. *OT*, 32–33.

64 Pub. Disp. 13.3.

65 *Declaration of Sentiments*, 3.

66   John Mark Hicks, "The Theology of Grace in the Thought of Jacobus Arminius and Philip van Limborch: A Study in the Development of Seventeenth-Century Dutch Arminianism," (Ph.D. diss., Westminster Theological Seminary, 1985) 28.

67   Priv. Disp. 30. Arminius also discussed "the first sin of man" at length in Pub. Disp. 7. On August 3, 1604 Arminius wrote a lengthy letter to Uitenbogaert regarding this disputation (Jacobus Arminius to Ioannes Uitenbogaert, 3 August, 1604, in PEVE, 167–179). He gave the disputation in the presence of Gomarus and Trelcatius, and Arminius wished Uitenbogaert could have been present to witness their responses (vellem te interfuisse). This disputation was given just before Gomarus completed his lectures on Romans nine and highlighted the differences between the two doctors.

68   Pub. Disp. 7.2.1.

69   Pub. Disp. 7.4.1; cf. Priv. Disp. 30.3 and 30.4.

70   Priv. Disp. 30.3.

71   Priv. Disp. 30.4, Pub. Disp. 7.5. Arminius wondered whether the arguments he used against them were akin to the ones by which "he himself might have been enticed to the commission of sin" (Pub. Disp. 7.4.2).

72   Pub. Disp. 30.7. Junius similarly wrote, "Ac proinde lapsus istius extra eos causa efficiens non est quærenda, nec Satanæ simpliciter, quamuis consuluerit, aut Creatori, quod permiserit, tribuenda, quia non nisi bonarum omnium causa efficiens est Deus" (Theses Theologicæ 18.6).

73   Institutes 3.23, cited by Arminius in Certain Articles, 5.9. Arminius thought Calvin's statement in Institutes 3.23 was scandalous, and quoted Institutes 3.23.4 at length.

74   "Beza, vol. 1., fol. 417," quoted in Arminius, Certain Articles, 5.8.

75   Examination of Perkins' Pamphlet, in WA, 3:281–292; Examination of Gomarus, in WA, 3:588–611.

76   Cf. Institutes 3.23.7: "Nor ought it to seem absurd when I say, that God not only foresaw the fall of the first man, and in him the ruin of his posterity; but also at his own pleasure arranged it." Quoted in Arminius, Certain Articles, 11.8.

77   James Arminius, "An Analysis of the Ninth Chapter of St. Paul's Epistle to the Romans," in The Works of James Arminius, trans. William Nichols, London ed. (London: Longman, Hurst, Rees, Orme, Brown and Green, 1875; reprint, Grand Rapids: Baker, 1986), 3:507–509.

78   Institutes 3.23.8: "Wherefore, let us in the corruption of human nature contemplate the evident cause of condemnation, (a cause which comes more closely home to us,) rather than inquire into a cause hidden and almost incomprehensible in the predestination of God. Nor let us decline to submit our judgment to the boundless wisdom of God, so far as to confess its insufficiency to comprehend many of his secrets. Ignorance of things which we are not able, or which it is not lawful to know, is learning, while the desire to know them is a species of madness."

79   As opposed to a merely scholastic method of presentation.

80   Conference with Junius, in WA, 3:237.

81   Analysis of Romans IX, in WA, 3:504–505.

82   Examination of Perkins' Pamphlet, in WA, 3:504; cf. Certain Articles, 2.7.

83   Analysis of Romans IX, in WA, 3:505–506.

84   Institutes 1.17–18.

85 See the letter to Uitenbogært in WA, 1:175; *Declaration of Sentiments,* in WA, 1:657–658; Pub. Disp. 4.43; Pub. Disp. 9–10. See also "Letter to Hippolytus a Collibus," in WA, 2:696–98, and *Certain Articles,* 8.

86 *Institutes* 1.18.1, 3.

87 Perkins, *The workes of that famous and worthie minister of Christ in the University of Cambridge,* 2:617, quoted in *Examination of Perkins' Pamphlet,* in WA, 3:379.

88 Gomarus' Thesis 23, quoted in Arminius, *Examination of Perkins' Pamphlet,* 588.

89 "But as for your defining 'permission' by 'the denial of grace necessary to avoid sin,' I do not grant it you. For this is not to permit a man to sin freely, but to cause him to sin necessarily, as has been often said already…I pass by the nonsense of calling necessity 'avoidable'" (*Examination of Perkins' Pamphlet,* in WA, 3:385).

90 "The decree, I admit, is, dreadful; and yet it is impossible to deny that God foreknew what the end of man was to be before he made him, and foreknew, because he had so ordained by his decree…. Nor ought it to seem absurd when I say, that God not only foresaw the fall of the first man, and in him the ruin of his posterity; but also at his own pleasure arranged it" (Calvin, *Institutes* 3.23.7).

91 WA, 3:271.

92 WA, 3:268.

93 *Ad Simplicianum* 1.2, quoted by Arminius in WA, 3:313.

94 WA, 3:510–11.

95 WA, 3:586–587. Augustine believed all who were baptized were regenerated, but most lost their salvation for lack of perseverance. Only those who received the gift of perseverance continued in a state of grace and salvation.

96 *De Anima & Ejus Orig.,* 3.9, quoted by Arminius in *Thirty-One Articles,* 14.3.2.

97 "He both makes and ordains the species and natures themselves, but the shortcomings of the species and the defects of the natures He does not make, but only ordains" (*Conference with Junius,* WA, 3:60).

98 Ibid.

99 *Conference with Junius,* WA, 3:58, citing Augustine's "Sixth Book Against the Gnostics." However, Junius' statements on foreknowledge in *Theses Theologicæ* reflected a more traditional orthodox reconciliation between necessity and freedom with respect to Adam's sin. Though he denied any efficient cause for Adam's sin other than his free will, "Necessitatem igitur huic lapsui à causa efficiente ullam foris allatam esse pernegamus, sed contingenter lapsum hominem statuimus: ut pote constitutum in statu liberæ voluntatis," he acknowledged "Etsi non negamus, si respicias ad Dei Providentiam & Præscientiam fuisse necessarium: siquidem omnia sunt ei præsentia, *secundum modum divinum* ipsius" (Junius, *Theses Theologicæ,* Thesis 12.8). He wavered on this short point shortly thereafter: "Scientiam verò, aut præscientiam nemo iure existimaverit necessitatem huic prævaricationi imposuisse: Nam illa in mente divina est, se ad res exteras minimè conferens, sed eas concipiens, ac proinde extrà se non agens in eis quicquam, aut eas cogens, Estque rerum, cùm æternarum, tùm corruptibilium, veri, falsi, entis, non entis, possibilis & impossibilis: omnium denique quæ sunt γνῶσιν in se, ut scientia est," and "quod vesanæ impietatis esset hac necessitate Dei Providentiam, qua gubernat & ordinat res omnes, obligare" (Junius, *Theses Theologicæ,* Thesis 18.10).

100 "If God merely foresaw human events, and did not also arrange and dispose of them at his pleasure, there might be room for agitating the question, how far his foreknowledge

amounts to necessity; but since he foresees the things which are to happen, *simply because he has decreed that they are so to happen*, it is vain to debate about prescience, while it is clear that all events take place by his sovereign appointment" (*Institutes* 3.23.6; quoted in part by Arminius, *Certain Articles*, 11.7.

[101]   *Conference with Junius*, Proposition 6, in *WA*, 3:74.

[102]   *Conference with Junius*, Proposition 6, in *WA*, 3:76. Arminius did not cite his source for this quotation. Through his interaction with Junius, Arminius replied to some of Calvin's logical defenses of God from this accusation. Calvin had appealed to scholastic distinctions between act and criminality, necessity and compulsion, decree and execution, efficaciousness and permissive decrees, and the divine and human natures. Junius himself rejected Calvin's idea that God permitted the fall by withdrawing his grace (Junius denied that man needed grace prior to the fall.) Arminius replied, "But when those antecedents have been laid down, that a law was given to man which he cannot perform without grace, and that grace was not given to that man, the conclusion follows that the cause of sin is not man, but he who had laid down such a law, and has not bestowed the faculty of performing it, or to speak more correctly, the transgression of that law cannot then be called sin, when the law is unjust, as if God were reaping where He had not sowed, which is far from a just and good God" (*Conference with Junius*, Proposition 16).

[103]   *Examination of Perkins' Pamphlet*, in *WA*, 3:381–382; see also *Thirty-One Articles*, Art. 30. For one discussion of philosophical influences on Augustine with respect to predestination, including Manicheanism, see Adolf von Harnack, *History of Dogma*, ed. T. K. Cheyne and A. B. Bruce, trans. Neil Buchanan, (Boston: Little, Brown and Company, 1903), 5:100–05.

[104]   *Examination of Gomarus*, Thesis 23. For a brief introduction to Manichean doctrine and its impact on Christianity, see Kelly, *Early Christian Doctrines*, 13–14.

[105]   *Declaration of Sentiments*, 1.3.5.1–3; cf. *Analysis of Romans IX*, in *WA*, 3:511. Arminius' refutation of Gomarus' defense of supralapsarianism involved the abstract argumentation that God was not sovereign over uncreated man as considered creatable, because this is a non-existent non-entity. God can communicate his likeness to a non-entity, but the result would be a vessel of glory, not of wrath. But there can be "no communication between God and the merely possible," and consequently "Over the possible God has no right of dominion, much less of judgment" (*WA*, 3:537).

[106]   Cf. Priv. Disp. 15, 19–20, respectively, and especially Priv. Disp 22:3–6.

[107]   Arminius specifically discussed the effects of the fall and original sin in Pub. Disp. 11, Priv. Disp. 31, and *Certain Articles*, 17.

[108]   Priv. Disp. 31.2.

[109]   Priv. Disp. 31.3.

[110]   Priv. Disp. 31.4.

[111]   Pub. Disp. 7.15.1–2.

[112]   Priv. Disp. 31.5. Arminius appealed to Romans 8:14–15 and 1 Corinthians 2:12 to support that the Spirit was the "seal of God's favor and good will" (Priv. Disp. 7).

[113]   Pub. Disp. 9:21.

[114]   Except where noted, I have drawn the quotations which follow from Arminius' fullest explanation of the results of the fall upon the natural aspects of the *imago* (Pub. Disp. 11.7–11; cf. *OT*, 263–264). Arminius' scripture citations are in his footnotes.

115 1 Corinthians 2:14. Elsewhere Arminius preached, "The certainty of the mind, while it is engaged in the act of apprehending and knowing things, cannot exceed the truth and necessity of the things themselves; on the contrary, it very often may, like a spent arrow, not reach them, through some defect in its capacity: For the eyes of our mind are in the same condition with respect to the pure truth of things, as are the eyes of owls with respect to the light of the Sun" (*Oration III*, in WA 1:378; see also *Oration V*, in WA, 1:392).

116 Romans 1:21–22; Ephesians 4:17–18; Titus 3:3.

117 *Oration V*, in WA, 1:454–55. Aside from depravity, Arminius listed Satanically induced deceptions which prevail "even in the face of special revelation" (*Oration III*, in WA, 1:392).

118 "For whatever clear and proper conception of the Divine Being the minds of the Heathens had formed, the first stumbling block over which they fell appears to have been this, that they did not attribute that just conception to whom it ought to have been given" (*Oration I*, in WA 1:330–331).

119 *Oration V*, in WA, 1:436.

120 Pub. Disp. 20.5. See also *Declaration of Sentiments*, 3.

121 *Certain Articles*, 17.5.

122 Arminius further examined the effects of the fall on the affections in *Oration V*, in WA, 1:454–458.

123 Romans 8:7.

124 Jeremiah 13:10, 17:9, Ezekiel 36:26.

125 Genesis 6:5, 8:21.

126 Matthew 15:9.

127 Matthew 6:18, 12:34, John 6:44. Unlike his opponents who had said people (fallen or unfallen) could not do more good nor less evil than they do, for all they do conforms to God's decree, Arminius thought "an unregenerate man is capable of omitting more evil external works than he omits, and can perform more outward works which have been commanded by God than he actually performs," though even if he were to do so they would not bring him merit before God (*Certain Articles*, 17:2).

128 Romans 8:7.

129 Romans 6:20; 2 Timothy 2:26.

130 Romans 1:28; 2 Thessalonians 2:9–11; Romans 1:24.

131 2 Corinthians 4:4; Ephesians 2:2; cited in Pub. Disp. 9.21, in WA, 2:175–176.

132 *Oration IV*, in WA, 1:409.

133 *Oration IV*, in WA, 1:429.

134 Arminius commonly referred to the unregenerate as "children of wrath." See WA, 1:333, 156; 2:244, 729; 3:329, 342. Arminius' appeal to Ephesians 2:2 will form a strong contrast with Episcopius.

135 Priv. Disp. 31.6.

136 Priv. Disp. 31.7. Arminius' analysis seems to be inverted. It would seem that exclusion from Paradise as a type and figure of heaven would have represented eternal death, i.e. separation from God, while exclusion from the tree of life would have indicated temporal death, i.e. separation of body and soul.

137 Priv. Disp. 8.

138 "Before the Fall, this church in reality consisted only of our first parents, Adam and Eve; but in capacity it embraced the whole of the human race that were included in their loins, and that were afterwards to proceed from them by natural propagation: This was done by God's constant and perpetual ordinance, according to which he included all their posterity in the covenant into which He had entered with the parents, provided the parents continued in this covenant. (Gen. 7:7; Rom. 5:2, 14) And in this respect, the church before the Fall may take to itself the epithet of 'Catholic'" (Pub. Disp. 18.4).

139 Priv. Disp. 9. In Pub. Disp. 18, Arminius used this covenant as the basis for his assertion that Adam and Eve were the first church. But when "they fell from the covenant (they) ceased to be the church of God," and "were expelled...out of Paradise."

140 Pub. Disp. 7.16; cf. Pub. Disp. 14.7. "But all men have in Adam transgressed the law respecting the forbidden tree" (Conference with Junius, Proposition 14, in WA, 3:153). God had "imputed the guilt of the first sin to all Adam's posterity, no less than to Adam himself and Eve, because they also had sinned in Adam" (Conference with Junius, Proposition 24).

141 "But he did not fall alone. All whose persons he at that time represented and whose cause he pleaded (although they had not then come into existence) were with him cast down from the elevated summit of such a high dignity" (Oration IV, in WA, 1:409). "All men have been given up to themselves and left in the hand of their own counsel, being represented in Adam, and allowed to sin" (Conference with Junius, Proposition 20).

142 Conference with Junius, Proposition 14.

143 In contrast to angels who could only sin personally, "Men sinned, only in Adam their parent, before they had been brought into existence" (Declaration of Sentiments, in WA, 1:637).

144 Conference with Junius, Proposition 18. However, Arminius did hold that God had left "Adam, and in him all men, with that relection" (Conference with Junius, Proposition 12).

145 Conference with Junius, Proposition 26.

146 Examination of Perkins' Pamphlet, in WA, 3:341–42.

147 Conference with Junius, Proposition 9.

148 "Examination of Perkin's Pamphlet," in WA, 3:421.

149 "All men who were to be propagated from them in a natural way became obnoxious to death temporal and death eternal" (Pub. Disp. 14.7).

150 Priv. Disp. 11, emphasis added.

151 Priv. Disp. 31.10.

152 Certain Articles, 12.2.

153 Regarding this, Aquinas wrote, "Finis autem ad quem homo ordinatus est, est ultra facultatem naturæ creatæ.... Unde oportet naturam humanam taliter institui ut non solum haberet illud quod sibi ex principiis naturalibus debebatur, sed etiam aliquid ultra, per quod facile in finem perveniret.... Ideo ut illa pars libere in Deum tenderet, subjectæ sunt sibi vires inferiores, ut nihil in eis accidere posset quod mentem retineret & impediret ab itinere in Deum; pari ratione corpus hoc modo dispositum est ut nulla passio in eo accidere posset per quam mentis contemplatio impeditur. & quia hæc omnia ex ordine ad finem...homini inerant, ideo facta deordinatione a fine per peccatum, hæc omnia in natura humana desiere, & relictus est homo in illis tantum bonis quæ eum ex naturalibus principiis consequuntur" (Aquinas, Commentary on the Sentences, 2.30, 1.1).

For an excellent study concerning Aquinas' definition of the effects of the fall as deprivation, see W. M. Clune, *Human Nature after the fall according to St. Thomas Aquinas* (Rome: Ædes Universitatis Gergorianeæ, 1939). See also Calvin, *Institutes*, 2.1.12.

[154] *Thirty-One Articles*, 13 & 14.

[155] This admission demonstrates that Arminius was aware that there was theological diversity within what would become the Remonstrant movement.

[156] Regarding the first, Arminius quoted Augustine to support that "Antiquity maintains, that all infants who depart out of this life without having been baptized, would be damned; but that such as were baptized and died before they attained to adult age, would be saved." Augustine wrote, "If you wish to be a Catholic, be unwilling to believe, declare, or teach, that infants who are prevented by death from being baptized can attain to the indulgence of original sins." (*De Anima et ejus Orig.*, 3.9). His second quotation, to show the ancients believed "the grace of baptism takes away original sin, even from those who have not been predestinated," was from Prosper of Aquitain (*Ad Cap. Gallorum*, Sent. 2).

[157] For Altaus' affirmation and Beza's denial of these same positions, see Jill Raitt, "Probably They are God's Children: Theodore Beza's Doctrine of Baptism," in *Humanism and Reform: The Church in Europe, England, and Scotland, 1400–1643. Essays in Honour of James K. Cameron*, ed. James Kirk, Studies in Church History. Subsidia, 8 (Oxford: Published for the Ecclesiastical History Society by Basil Blackwell, 1991).

[158] Arminius cited Junius' thesis *De Natura et Gratia*, response 28.

[159] Hicks, "Theology of Grace in Jacobus Arminius," 40. Hicks argued that Arminius held to infant damnation based upon his affirmation of imputation, and cited both Arminius and other scholars to support his conclusions. He noted those with whom he disagreed (Curtiss, Shedd and Meeuwsen), to which list we could add Craig A. Blaising (Blaising, "John Wesley," 85–87). See Hicks, "Theology of Grace in Jacobus Arminius," 37–41.

[160] *Examination of Perkins' Pamphlet*, in *WA*, 3:499. Elsewhere, Arminius emphasized the children of the covenant community were the recipients of grace. However, he denied that baptism served any function in the communication of grace, the normal means by which infants were included in the covenant community.

[161] *Certain Articles*, 7.3.

[162] *WA*, 2:65.

[163] *WA*, 2:57–60. The circumstances of both questions originated from hostile conversations between Arminius and Calvinist pastors. The *Nine Questions*, were answered before the curators of the University of Leiden, the *Thirty-One Articles*, before the Lords of Holland.

[164] *Examination of Perkins' Pamphlet*, in *WA*, 3:344–345.

[165] Priv. Disp. 63.

[166] Philip van Limborch, Episcopius'nephew, was not baptized until after childhood.

[167] *Nine Questions*, Question 5. See also, *Examination of Perkins' Pamphlet*, in *WA*, 3:448.

[168] Priv. Disp. 11:3.

[169] Pub. Disp. 12–13.

[170] Priv. Disp. 11:6.

[171] *Declaration of Sentiments*, in *WA*, 1:637.

[172] Priv. Disp. 20.8.

[173] *Conference with Junius*, Proposition 26.

174 Arminius, *Declaration of Sentiments*, 4.

175 One might unnecessarily multiply Arminius' categories of grace by not observing either his use of synonyms for them, or when he adopts the vocabulary of his opponent. Hicks confused Arminius with Perkins when he wrote "In his dispute with Perkins, Arminius acknowledged that grace has a five-fold nature" (Hicks, "Theology of Grace in Jacobus Arminius," 51–52). Arminius had cited Perkins' five-fold distinction, but then showed how it fit within his own divisions of sufficient and efficient grace (*Examination of Perkins' Pamphlet*, WA, 3:472–473).

176 Though Arminius used the terms "universal" or "general" grace as a synonym for "common" grace (*Examination of Perkins' Pamphlet*, in WA, 3:271, 444–445), he denied that "saving grace" is given to all.

177 See *Declaration of Sentiments*, 4.2–3, *Thirty-One Articles*, 15, Pub. Disp. 11–12, Priv. Disp. 72.9; *Romans VII* (2:587) and *Examination of Perkins' Pamphlet*, in WA, 3:474.

178 *Declaration of Sentiments*, 4.

179 Howard Slaatte, *The Arminian Arm of Theology: The Theologies of John Fletcher, First Methodist Theologian, and his Precursor, James Arminius* (Washington DC: University Press of America, 1977), 54.

180 *Oration II*, in WA, 1:362.

181 "Infundendo ei salutares cogitationes, inspirandoque bona desideria" (*OT*, 122).

182 *Declaration of Sentiments*, 4.

183 Pub. Disp. 11.14, in WA, 2:196.

184 *Certain Articles*, 19.10.

185 *Declaration of Sentiments*, 4.

186 Ibid.

187 Pub. Disp. 11:14.

188 *Declaration of Sentiments*, 4; *Examination of Perkins' Pamphlet*, in WA, 3:445.

189 Arminius began his refutation of Perkins' defense of final perseverance, "I should not readily dare to say that true and saving faith may finally and totally fall away, although several of the Fathers often seem to affirm that," and then defended that a believer could lose his faith and salvation (*Examination of Perkins' Pamphlet*, in WA, 3:454–470).

190 *Examination of Perkins' Pamphlet*, in WA, 3:470.

191 Ibid.

192 Ibid., in WA, 3:471.

193 Ibid., in WA, 3:472.

194 Ibid., in WA, 3:473.

195 Ibid., in WA, 3:474.

196 Some have suggested Reformed theologians during this period were hesitant to cite non-Reformed sources, but this does not appear to have been true of Arminius. Arminius expressed the highest respect for Aquinas' genius (WA, 3:340–341), and he could easily have avoided associating himself with Bellarmine (WA, 3:472–483).

197 Calvin, *Institutes*, 2.2; 3.2. For an extended discussion of the Reformed doctrine of calling, see Heppe, *Reformed Dogmatics*, 510–42.

198 Pub. Disp. 16:2.

199   Pub. Disp. 16.11.

200   *Examination of Perkins' Pamphlet*, in WA, 3:315.

201   *Certain Articles*, 17.16.

202   Pub. Disp. 16.5.

203   *Certain Articles*, 19.6.

204   *Nine Questions*, 6. See also *Certain Articles*, 19.9: "Faith is a gracious and gratuitous gift of God, bestowed according to the administration of the means necessary to conduce to the end."

205   Priv. Disp. 41.3.

206   *Certain Articles*, 19.10.

207   *Thirty-One Articles*, 26.

208   Ibid.

209   *Certain Articles*, 19.9.

210   Priv. Disp. 42.12.

211   *Examination of Perkins' Pamphlet*, in WA, 3:272.

212   *Certain Articles*, 19.9.

213   Prosper of Aquitaine, *The Vocation of the Gentiles*, 2.5; quoted by Arminius in *Thirty-One Articles*, 28.

214   I use the word "interplay" because the terms "synergism," "collaboration" and "cooperation" cannot adequately express the relation Arminius suggested between grace and free will. First, Arminius, following Paul, consistently placed faith in contradistinction to works. Second, he gave a nearly passive quality to the assent of the will to the illumination of the mind by the Spirit. Arminius responded to Perkins' accusation of Pelagianism by writing that man's willingness to follow divine grace was one of "remote ability, and that which is purely passive." (WA, 3:482). A person is saved not so much because they chose to accept, but because they did not chose to reject.

215   Pub. Disp. 11:14.

216   *Letter to Hippolytus a Collibus*, 4.

CHAPTER THREE

Episcopius on Original Sin
Up To 1621

The death of Arminius initiated a series of events which led to Episcopius' induction into the faculty at the University of Leiden. The curators of the university first sought to maintain balance between Arminians and Calvinists by calling Conrad Vorstius, who appeared to share Arminius' beliefs. Vorstius was a competent German theologian at Heidelberg who Beza had invited to Geneva. Instead, he chose to come to the Netherlands, where he created serious problems for the Remonstrants and played a significant part in their loss of credibility. While at Heidelberg, Vorstius had denied the traditional scholastic understanding of the omnipresence of God as an incorrect extrapolation of divine omniscience. Sibrandus Lubbertus seized upon this as an opportunity to slander him as a Socinian (and consequently the Remonstrants along with him), and rallied the Contra-Remonstrants against him.[1] Worse, the Remonstrants felt compelled to defend Vorstius and so alienated themselves from the good graces of James I of England. The only benefit from this debacle for the Remonstrants was that Franciscus Gomarus refused to teach at the same institution with Vorstius and resigned.[2] This opened a position for Episcopius on the faculty. When twenty-nine-year-old Episcopius entered the University of Leiden as one of three professors of sacred theology, many thought him too young for the position.[3] Remonstrant leadership, however, already viewed him as their best chance to carry on Arminius' intellectual leadership. They hoped the combination of Episcopius' theological abilities and the political efforts of Wtenbogaert and Oldenbarnevelt could turn the growing Contra-Remonstrant tide.

Although officially professor of Bible exposition, he was free to give both public and private disputations in theology. We will use these theses in order to synthesize Episcopius' doctrine of originally sin, remembering that they are just the theses. We lack the argumentation and defense which accompanied them in the classroom.[4] We will consider his public and private disputations separately in order not to lose important comparisons and contrasts between Arminius' and Episcopius' thought.

Comparison of Arminius' and Episcopius' Public Disputations

Preliminary Comparisons

Episcopius' public disputations closely followed Arminius'. Both dedicated their first three lectures to the authority, perfection and sufficiency of the Scriptures, followed by several disputations on the nature and attributes of God. Like Arminius, Episcopius focused on God's essential qualities in terms of *intellectus* (or *scientia*) and *voluntatio*, and he appears to have drawn from Arminius' comparisons between Law and Gospel. Both followed their disputations on original sin with a treatment of actual sins. Episcopius often used or paraphrased Arminius' words and phrases, such as Arminius' three-fold analysis of the will of God.[5] However, there are striking differences. While Junius gave three disputations on the *essentia Dei & attribuis illius*,[6] Arminius treated the whole of God's nature in Disputation 4, the relation between Father and Son in Disputation 5 and the Holy Spirit in Disputation 6. Episcopius departed from both Junius and Arminius, devoting four disputations to theology proper,[7] and although he included language which presumed trinitarianism,[8] he did not mention, much less defend it.

Episcopius also deviated from Arminius in his placement of the doctrine of providence. Rather than treating it after the fall, as did Arminius, Episcopius followed Junius by separating it from predestination and putting it between the creation and the fall of Adam. He also handled the work of Christ uniquely. Arminius reserved an entire disputation for the work of Christ considered in itself,[9] while Episcopius used it practically as the primary basis for his comparisons between the old and new covenants.[10] Both addressed the role of magistrates, but Episcopius better reflected the Remonstrant ideology and provided a stronger defense of Erastianism.[11] He exceeded both Junius and Arminius by including disputations on schisms in the church[12] and on good works,[13] but left out public disputations on predestination, freewill, calling, justification, Christian liberty or the church.

Episcopius' *Disputatio IX: de Primo Adami Peccato* strongly paralleled Arminius' *Thesis 7* regarding original sin. Junius began his *Disputatio XVII: De Primo Adami Lapsus* with a discussion of the *imago Dei* and then addressed the effects of the fall on Adam's posterity. Neither Arminius nor

Episcopius lectured on creation or the *imago Dei* in their public disputations. Instead, they launched into the definition of Adam's first sin.[14] Arminius treated the definition of the sin, its causes, its heinousness and its effects. Episcopius limited his treatment to the definition of original sin and its causes. This is an early indication that Episcopius was moving away from the full range of implications of the Reformed doctrine of depravity. What he did include, however, he modeled after Arminius.

The Definition and Occasion of the Fall

Episcopius began his ninth disputation by defining Adam's transgression, first by listing the Pauline vocabulary for it,[15] and then providing a definition based upon the book of Genesis: "Peccatum primum…est voluntaria & libera legis primæ, de non comedendo fructu arboris scientiæ boni & mali, severa mortis comminatione sancitæ, transgressio."[16] He did not see this law as an end in itself; it was *positiva & symbolica* of a deeper matter.[17] But he did not broaden the command as having contained veiled or unrecorded references to the Decalogue or any other command.[18] There was only one command, not to eat of the fruit, for which Adam was able to obey given his creation in the image of God.[19]

Even though Episcopius and Arminius agreed that this command was symbolic of Adam's voluntary submission to the lordship of God, his creator,[20] Episcopius developed this in greater depth. He judged that God imposed this law upon Adam so that "ei obsequendo & obtemperando, palam publiceque veluti testaretur, se, cui dominium rerum omnium creatarum à Deo delatum erat." It served as a public sign of submission under authority, not in spite of such great privilege, but made necessary because of it.[21] The commandment was not imposed as a sign that Adam's existence depended on his creator, but as evidence of his voluntary submission to God.[22] His obedience was a reasonable response to the great love and blessings that God had showered upon him.[23] The rebellion in eating the fruit, coupled with the privileges conferred by his participation in the *gloriæ divinæ*, his lordship, the ease with which Adam could have obeyed God, justified such a severe punishment of such an innocuous act.[24]

The Fall and Questions of Causality

Like Arminius, Episcopius followed the definition of original sin with an examination of the causes of the fall. But while Arminius dealt with sufficient, efficient, near, remote, instrumental, inwardly moving causes, etc., Episcopius treated causation as a general idea, often without offering any specific category, as in his treatment of Satan's role in Adam's sin. While Arminius had classified Satan as the "remote and mediate efficient cause" of Adam's sin,[25] Episcopius was content to state, "Causa, quæ ad peccandum hominem impulit atque instigavit, prima, fuit Diabolus."[26] In doing so he avoided attributing even remote efficient causation to Satan. He also simplified Arminius' complex analysis of the basis for the temptation. Episcopius saw Satan's attack as two-fold. First he sought to remove their fear of punishment, and then "utque id commode fieret, ejus loco spem magni alicujus & summe desiderabilis boni, puta similitudinis cum Deo, primis statim auspiciis injicere & suggerere." Episcopius' abandonment of Aristotelian categories of causation in the examination of original sin was a significant departure from Reformed scholastic analysis.

Episcopius gave little attention to the fruit for at least two reasons. First, it was not the woman's role but the man's which was important, and the man was not deceived into eating the fruit.[27] Consequently, the fruit itself did not attract Adam. Rather, the brunt of the temptation offered by Satan was in the desire to be like God. It was for this, the greatest of all goods, which *"enixissime & fervidissime homo concupivit atque desideravit."*[28] Second, because not eating the fruit was symbolic of Adam's submission to God as Lord and Master, the essence of the sin was not hungering for, picking or eating the fruit. Rather, eating the fruit symbolized his renunciation of obedience to God.[29] In the end, however, there was no sufficient reason for Adam to succumb to the temptation: "Vana & stulta Diaboli tentatio: denique frivola, si perstitisset homo, obedientia."[30]

Episcopius expanded beyond Arminius by devoting an entire thesis to Eve's participation in the fall. Junius mentioned her as having stood with Adam and her role in the temptation,[31] and Arminius eliminated her as a possible cause.[32] Episcopius, however, speculated about how Eve's participation moved Adam to sin. She was a conduit through which the devil gained access to Adam. What made him susceptible to Eve's suggestion was "specialis quidam conjugis propriæ amor, quo adductus in gratiam illius, affectui suo proclivius indulsit, & tentationi Sathanæ facilius cessit auremque præbuit." Thus, Adam's love for Eve was even more significant than the desire to be like God. Episcopius' discussion of Eve is interesting. In terms of causation, Eve was as much the instrumental cause of sin as was the serpent. Episcopius at first stated she was a *transgressionis causam*, then he mollified this by adding *sive potius, ἐν παραβάσει fuisse.* She was not the cause of Adam's decision, but participated through being deceived.[33]

Episcopius then arrived at the central controversy of the disputation: Adam sinned freely without responding in any way to divine necessity. For the first time he employed scholastic categories in defining the "Proxima tamen & immediata causa transgressionis" as "libera hominis voluntas, intrinseco, proprio, spontaneo & libero ab omni necessitate motu, sese determinans ad objectum vetitum."[34] He maintained Arminius' analysis of the fall in terms of intellect and will, that "à mente seducta propositum & ab affectu desideratum tum ac concupitum." Nevertheless, while the mind and affections (the latter a function of the *voluntatio*) played a part in Adam's sin, the weight of the sin was "ab hac voluntate, esus locomotivæ facultati imperatus & ab eadem exercitus est."[35] The *formalem rationem* for eating was *à voluntate imperato*.[36] He was emphatic that "fieri nequit ut ulla causa, vel externa, vel interna hominem ad peccatum hoc perpetrandum necessitaverit." Neither Satan nor God were in any way responsible for Adam's sin.[37]

Episcopius set aside Satan as an efficient cause, because he can only tempt through persuasion. Persuasion does not carry with it necessity (and so eliminates efficiency), but attempts to attract and draw the will.[38] A free person may abandon their integrity in the face of persuasion, or frustrate Satan from achieving his purposes.[39] Given Satanic malevolence, if he could force men to sin, he would not limit himself to mere persuasion.[40]

Nor was God the efficient cause of sin. God did not seek to persuade Adam, nor did he employ secondary means to infallibly effect it, nor did he command it.[41] To the contrary, God prohibited the eating of the fruit. If someone imposed a different, hidden and imperceptible will which demanded that Adam sin, this would be irrational because "circa unum autem eundemque numero actum, contrariis aut contradictoriis volitionibus occupari sapientissimum & optimum Deum, impossibile est."[42] If God effected sin, whether directly or indirectly, then he alone would be the cause of sin and the person would be free from guilt.[43] And although others (including Augustine[44]) had written that God was not the efficient cause of sin but rather the deficient cause, in that he omitted that which could have helped Adam to stand, Episcopius disagreed. He countered that although God omitted nothing which was necessary for Adam to persevere in obedience,[45] to assert that he did would not resolve the problem: "Si enim alterutrum factum dicamus, necessum est, ut in causam efficientem, deficientia hæc tandem resolvatur, Deusque peccati author statuatur. Deficiens enim in necessariis, posita legislatione efficiens transgressionis causa fiat necesse est."[46] Neither did Episcopius accept Calvinist appeals to "permission."[47] He insisted that common definitions, "quæ vel gratiæ ad standum sive non peccandum necessariæ sufficientis, subtractionem, vel ejusmodi desertionem auxiliique negationem," still introduced the necessity of sinning, which "Deo fine injuria tribui non potest."[48]

Episcopius gave a three-fold reply to Calvinist appeals that a person could sin both necessarily and freely. First, the statement involved a logical contradiction, and he had yet to see someone reconcile freedom with coercion or necessity.[49] Second, it was vain to substitute "spontaneity" for freedom, for spontaneity is not a legitimate mode of freedom.[50] His third argument dealt with an appeal to coercion. "Coactio vero etiam (se rem presse urgere velimus) in iis quæ agunt, locum habere non possit. Coacte enim agere nemo potest, sed tantum pati. Quod adeo verum est, ut voluntatem, ne à Deo quidem ipso cogi posse, ut hoc vel illud agere velit, asserere non dubitemus. Soli enim actus imperati cogi possunt, non eliciti."[51] His answer anticipates Thomas Hobbes' ideas on freedom:[52] no one can say they were forced to do anything, because in the end the will still must choose to acquiesce.

Episcopius rejected Calvinist appeals to the decree, permission and determinative foreknowledge. Calvin wrote that, even if Adam fell because God "wished it to be done," nevertheless he fell freely, as proved by his sense of shame and guilt. [53] Episcopius strongly disagreed: "Neque vero respectus decreti & præscientiæ divinæ," he wrote, "quicquam facere nobis posse videntur, ad hoc, ut actus liberi necessarii etiam dici possint."[54] Episcopius argued that if an act arose necessarily from the decree, then God must also have provided for the implementation of the decree. God wills not only the ends, but also the means to accomplish the ends. If so, it follows that God is the cause of that sin and the guilt must be attributed solely to him.[55] Nor did he accept that God's choice not to intervene is merely another mode of willing, an idea which he attributed to Calvin. Rather, "Decretum vero de permittendo, tantum abest ut potentiæ hujus usum includat, ut eam plane excludat. Qui enim, permittit voluntati actum, non agit in voluntatem, sed omnem actionem & agendi potentiamque usurpandi volitionem, suspendit."[56]

Finally, he denied that foreknowledge introduced necessity. He wrote, "Præscientia vero, cum actum ipsum modumque agendi tanquam objectum suum præsupponat, tantum abest, ut necessitatem afferret voluntati, ut necessario seipsam destructura fuisset, si necessitatem attulisset."[57] Episcopius defined foreknowledge as merely "presupposing" an act and its means. By "presupposing," he denied that the object of foreknowledge was the decree and its consequences, but simple prescience of free human decisions and acts. If prescience imposed necessity, then it is no longer prescience but determination.

Having denied God a causal role in the fall, Episcopius attacked the foundational motivation of lapsarian predestination. Calvinists stated God had determined to save some in order to glorify his grace and condemn others to glorify his justice, thus necessitating Adam's fall and all men in him.

Episcopius countered that, if by "justice" one understands true *æquitas*, then one cannot demonstrate justice by necessitating sin. Punitive and vindictive justice are not demonstrated merely by punishing, but in punishing one who is guilty. If God's decree necessitated someone to sin, that person cannot be held liable or guilty of sin.[58] Neither can it establish God's glory. How can one worship a god who created Adam only to necessitate his fall? Rather than reveal God's glory, it obscures it, destroys His claim to justice, and gives people every excuse to reject God.[59]

The Effects of Adam's Sin

When we come to Episcopius' treatment of the effects of original sin, we see momentous deviations from both Arminius and the Augustinian tradition. Unlike Arminius, Episcopius was silent about the effects of Adam's sin, the concepts of *reatus* and *privatio*, seminal presence in Adam and whether Adam's descendents shared in his punishment for that sin.[60] These are important indicators of change, and they only continue in his next disputation, *De Peccatis Actualibus*.[61] Arminius, in his treatment of actual sins, defined them as sins that a person commits *ex naturæ suæ corruptione*.[62] The only source Episcopius mentioned was free will: "Peccata actualia cum dicimus, ea intelligi volumus, quæ nos ipse sponte propria, & prorsus libera nostra voluntate, contra divinam voluntate, sive legem perpetramus: *propria voluntate* dico, non aliena: *prosus libera*, quæ non tantum coactionem (quamquam voluntas cogni non possit per ullam potentiam) sed etiam necessitatem quamlibet sive determinationem ad unum excludit."[63] He made no mention of corruption. This deviation is even more telling when we consider that Episcopius followed Arminius for the rest of the disputation. It is also here that we first encounter a direct statement that a believer could fall from faith and be eternally lost.[64]

The Necessity of Grace

Episcopius concentrated his instruction on the grace of God in *DTT* 1.11, *De Convenientia & Discrimine V. & N. Testamenti*.[65] We may make three observations. First, once again he followed very closely Arminius' corresponding disputation, in this case Disp. Pub. 13, "De Legis & Euangelij Comparatione."[66] Arminius drew comparisons between the Mosaic and New Covenants, and then regressed to the Abrahamic covenant as the basis of the promises provided in the New. With few exceptions Episcopius did the same. Arminius initially referred to the Abrahamic covenant by the words διαθήκη and *fœdus*, and then by *pactum*. Episcopius used only the word *pactum*, reserving the formal *fœdus* for the Mosaic and New Covenants. Second, the two disputations are nearly identical in structure, as the following diagram shows:

Arminius	Episcopius
Definition, two-fold division of Law.	Definition, two-fold division of Law
Agreements between Law and Gospel.	Agreements between Law and Gospel
The Adamic Law	(No Adamic covenant)
Differences between Law and Gospel	Differences between Law and Gospel
The Covenant of Abraham and the Covenant of grace compared and contrasted	The Pact of Abraham and the New Covenant compared and contrasted
Comparison of Law, Promise and Gospel	The Old Covenant is typical of the New

The third and greatest difference is that Episcopius did not include a thesis on Adamic Law. Although this may have been because he had sufficiently treated Adamic law in *DTT, 1.9, De Primo Adami Peccato*, more probably the reason was he denied there was any scriptural evidence for a covenant of grace prior to the Abrahamic covenant. He wrote, "Pactum promissionis cum dicimus, illud tantum foedus intelligimus, quod primum cum Abrahamo tanquam capite & principio populi totius, initum in Scriptura esse dicitur (prioris enim mentio in ea non sit, etsi factum esse inficiari non audeamus) postmodum vero etiam aliis & tandem toti populo revelatum est."[67]

Episcopius' denial of a *pactum* prior to Abraham is significant for three reasons. First, both he and Arminius had avoided any mention of an *eternal* covenant of grace, a noteworthy deviation from other Reformed theologians. Second, Episcopius avoided theological inference and limited himself to the explicit content of the biblical text. In humanist fashion, Episcopius interpreted the text without deducing additional content through the application of Aristotelian logic and syllogisms.[68] This is a notable indicator of Episcopius' theological method, and one we will see in future disputations. Third, Episcopius continued to borrow heavily from Arminius. He reiterated all fourteen of Arminius' comparisons between Law and Gospel and most of his fourteen comparisons between the covenant of Abraham and the

Covenant of Grace. Having followed Arminius so closely, we may deduce that where he differed, he did so with purpose.

Episcopius' dependence upon Arminius appears in the structure of the disputation, and extends to the repetition or rewording of Arminius' words and phrases. This can be seen in the following comparison of their theses:

Arminius:	Episcopius:
1. Generali authoris unius consideratione. Est enim Deus unus idemque author utriusque.... Gen. 2:17, Ex. 20:2, Rom. 1:1.[69]	Conveniunt ergo primò, in generali causæ efficientis consideratione, utriusque enim Deus author est & institutor primarius. Exod. 20:2, Rom. 7:22. Rom. 1:1.[70]
3. Fine generatim considerator: qui est gloria sapientiæ bonitatis, & justitiæ Dei.[71]	Tertio, in fine generaliter spectato…qui est illustratio sapientiæ, bonitatis & justitiæ divinæ.[72]
4. Subjecto per speciales respectus non discriminato, hominibus enim & Lex posita, & Euangelium patefactum est.[73]	Quarto, subjecto indistinctè considerato: homines enim sunt, & quidem peccatores, quibus lex posita & Euangelium patefactum est.[74]
Vetus enim pactum feci ut iratus peccatis, quæ sub priori fœdere manebunt inexpiate. Novum verò instituit ut reconciliatus, vel saltem reconciliationem illo peracturus in Filio dilectinis suæ & sermone gratie.[75]	Pactum enim vetus insituit Deus ut reconciliationem peractus. Novum verò ut reconciliatus, in filio dilectionis suæ & sermone gratia acquiscens (Eph. 2:16–17).[76]
Nam Lex lata cum signis planissimis iræ & horrendi judicij divini adversus peccata & peccatores. Euangelium verò cum indicijs certis benevolentiæ, εὐδοκία, & armois Christo.[77]	Quare & illius promulgationi, signe & indicia planissima iræ & horrendi judicii divini: hujus vero patefactioni manifesta favoris & εὐδοκία documenta adhibita sunt.[78]
Differunt loco promulgationis. Vetus enim promulgatum est de monte Sina. Novum verò ex Sion & Hierusalem exivit.[79]	Differunt & loco promulgationis. Verò enim ut promulgatum est in deserto de Monte Sinai. Novum verò ex Sion & Hierusalem exivit.[80]
Decima differentia statuetur in tempore tum promulgationis utriusque, tum durationis. Vetus Testamentum promulgatum, quum Deus populum Isræliticium educeret ex Aegypto. Novum verò novissimis & postremis temporibus…. Novum vero manet in æternum, utpote sanctitum sanguine Sacerdotis, qui ex vi indissolubilis vitæ per sermonem juramenti constitutus est Sacerdos, & per Spiritum æternum Deo se obtulit. Ex hoc postremo discrimine forte Veteris & Novi appellationis ortum duxerunt.[81]	Duodecimo, differentia statui potest in tempore, tum promulgationis utriusque, tum durationis. Vetus foedus cum patribus pepigit die illo, quo prehensa manu illorum, eos eduxit ex Aegypto. Euangelium vero novissimis & postremis temporibus…quod in æternum manet, ibidem, utpote sancitum sanguine sacerdotis, qui ex vi indissolubilis vitæ, per sermonem juramenti constitutus est Sacerdos, & per Spiritum æternum Deo se obtulit: …Ex qua postrema differentia Veteris & Novi appellationem.[82]

Episcopius substituted synonyms, reworked phrases and word order, and augmented Arminius' comments with insights of his own, but is clearly dependent.

Nevertheless, we note important differences. Some show he was not afraid to correct Arminius, as when he deletes verses which Arminius included in his analysis of the Adamic Law, but which refer to the Mosaic.[83] Two dissimilarities, however, are especially noteworthy. First is his treatment of the Mosaic Law. Arminius dedicated an entire thesis to the Law. He followed Calvin's "three uses" of the Law, an analysis of the three divisions of the Law (moral, ceremonial and judicial), and the degree to which they were abrogated by the New Covenant. Episcopius gave no separate treatment of the Law. We cannot overemphasize his perception of the Law as only a type and shadow of grace.[84] He concluded, "Denique (ut breviter *rem totam comprehendamus*) quicquid veteri isto pacto contentum fuit plane typicum fuisse, umbramque rerum futurarum continuisse arbitramur; corpus vero Christi: Col. 2:17."[85] He insisted that the whole law was abrogated with respect to the believer. The Mosaic covenant was only made with the Jews, not the rest of humanity,[86] and the Old was abrogated by the New. The whole law, including the moral law, contained only a minimal part of true religion,[87] while the Gospel is entirely spiritual, a truly "pure and spotless religion" from which nothing can be added or removed.[88]

A fundamental argument for the superiority of the Gospel was the lack of supernatural quality in the Mosaic Law. While not denying its precepts were given by revelation, still they were deducible from nature. In contrast, the wisdom of the Gospel exceeds human understanding, and could only have come through special revelation.[89] He stated that the new abolished the old,[90] "in every part," though not absolutely, but $\kappa\alpha\tau\alpha\ \tau\iota$, that is, to the degree to which its contents belonged as a part of the Law. The gospel thoroughly "struck down the Law's shadows by its rising light," and to return to the law was to do grave injury to Christ and his grace and risk loss of salvation.[91]

While the Gospel provides forgiveness, life and the empowerment of the Spirit,[92] the Law could only make known its demands, reveal sins, and convict people of their inability to fulfill it, while the Gospel sanctified and justified through faith in Christ.[93] The law was a ministry of death and condemnation, while the Gospel was a life-giving, spiritual ministry.[94] The law could only irritate and stimulate concupiscence, kill those whom it commanded and instill a spirit of fear, while the Gospel brings hope by liberating from sin, purifying from our carnality and restoring His likeness.[95] Through the Gospel, the Holy Spirit and grace are abundantly bestowed upon the believer.[96] Provision of grace is both the glory of the gospel and the basis for human freedom and obedience:

Euangelium verò tantam gratiæ efficacitatem tantam promissionum magnitudinem, & tam firmam solidamque earundem in animis hominum obsignationem continet, ut, salvo interim manente tum rationis, tum voluntatis usu, necesse quodammodo sit, si modo debito sed proponantur, auxilio gratiæ divinæ obedire in eaque obedientia perseverare. Inscribitur enim lex hæc spiritus in cordibus nostris, perque idem Euangelium spiritus filiationis, amoris & roboris ita instillatur, ut ferè opus non sit ut doceamur à proximo nostro, moneamurve ut cognoscamus dominum (Heb. 8:1), sed arcanis quasi funibus ad Christum trahamur: & semel in eo radicati, virtute Dei ad salutem æternam, per fidem custodiamur (Jerem. 31:31, &c. Rom. 8:15, Ioh. 6:44; 1 Petr. 1:5). Unde & potentia Dei ad salutem ab Apostolo, Rom. 1:16.[97]

These are expansive statements on human inability and affirmations of the nature, necessity and efficacy of the Spirit of grace.

A second departure from Arminius is striking. Episcopius did not give separate disputations on predestination, calling, free will or grace. All one needed to understand the Gospel of grace was that, although people are sinners, Christ provided forgiveness of sins, sanctification and eternal life for all who believe.[98] His treatment of grace reads like an inductive Bible study, devoid of speculative questions or inferences. Rather than merely citing references, he built his theses upon the very wording of the Scriptures.

Comparison of Arminius' and Episcopius' Private Disputations

Both Arminius and Episcopius gave private lectures to their students. These lectures were open to all and were a common practice among the professors at Leiden. However, their opponents viewed them with suspicion as being a convenient forum for teaching false doctrine. Both Arminius and Episcopius gave significantly more private disputations than public,[99] and the differences between professor and protégé are more pronounced. Arminius gave one series of private disputations; Episcopius gave two.

One may draw informative comparisons from Arminius' and Episcopius' arrangements of their private lectures. Arminius began with three lectures on theological method.[100] Here Episcopius was silent. Arminius dedicated six disputations to the person and work of Christ, while Episcopius incorporated Christology into his lectures on grace and the new covenant. Once again he gave less emphasis to some subjects, such as predestination, and far more to others, such as the nature and effects of the new covenant. Nevertheless, marked similarities continue. Episcopius reflected Arminius' treatment of Scripture, theology proper, ecclesiology (which Episcopius titled *De Foederatis*), the sacraments, and the Decalogue. Both placed their discussions about providence after their discussion of the creation of Adam in the image of God, but before their consideration of God's covenant with Adam, and his fall.

Episcopius affirmed the absolute authority of the Bible,[101] placing it above any other.[102] He recognized there were difficulties in interpreting the Scriptures[103] and that not all parts were equally clear,[104] but accentuated the perspicuity and clarity of the Scriptures for the person who had both the Spirit of God and the proper disposition to be taught by the Spirit.[105] In his first disputation on theology proper, he upheld Arminius' emphasis on practical theology. He wrote, "Cognitio Dei & Jesus Christi in qua salus ponitur, practica sine dubio est. Notitia enim theoretica impiius and Diabolis cum piis communis est. At verò quia cognitio practica præcedaneam sibi semper habet cognitionem theoreticam, de hac primum videbimus."[106] One does not need perfect knowledge of the divine nature, only enough to worship and serve God[107] as dictated from the Scriptures.[108]

Arminius and Episcopius differed significantly in their treatment of creation. Arminius gave a standard scholastic lecture based upon the efficient, material, formal, and final causes of creation.[109] Episcopius introduced his lecture by repeating his emphasis on biblical, practical theology,[110] limited by the constraints of the text.[111] His analysis of angels is an inductive study of Scripture, in stark contrast between Arminius' traditional, scholastic treatment of angels within the scheme of creation.[112] He wrote, "Creationis angelorum considerationem in Theologia necessarium esse non putamos," and with regard to the rest of creation, "Sufficit si eos sciamus esse, & ut internuncios à Deo in hunc mundum ablegari, quo jussa ipsius bono aut malo hominum exsequantur."[113] He followed with a straightforward exposition of the creation week.[114] He thought there was no need for subtle disputations concerning creation. First, everything depends upon God for its existence, and all things are subsequently subject to his commands. Second, Adam was created with the power to subject all things to himself, and himself to God.[115]

The Creation of Adam

Although Episcopius began his disputation *De Creatione Hominis*[116] in a way similar to Arminius,[117] he had his own agenda. Arminius began with a summary of the creation of body and insufflation of the Spirit, touched on the conditional immortality of the body, moved on to the origin, substance, faculties and habits of the soul, including the image of God, and then distinguished between naturals and supernaturals.[118] He focused on the native mortality and corruptibility of the body. The body depended on internal heat and humidity, and unless food and water replenished these, the body would die unless sustained by special grace.[119] Adam shared corruption and mortality with the rest of creation.[120] Arminius avoided direct reference to the native mortality of the body, perhaps in order to escape any association with Pelagius' thought that Adam was created mortal.[121]

In Episcopius' first series, he wrote that the soul was a "spiritus vivificus, principium vitæ sensus & motus, omniumque operationum vitalium: quin & fruitionis omnis, jucundæ simul ac dolorificæ, fundamentum."[122] He immediately warned, "Natura hujus spiritus etsi sub sensum nullum cadat, proinde cognitu difficilis fit; tamen materialis, crassæ & corporeæ, terrenæque molis expers est." He suggested that it was indivisible, intimately joined with the whole body though specially centered in the heart, and immortal.[123] The soul moves the body, but it is through the body that the soul draws its stimulus from the external world.[124] In the second series he did not address the soul's essence. In both he moved to their respective principal considerations: the discussion of the soul's faculties in the first series, and the God-given freedom and power of the soul in the second. In both he departed from Arminius.

In the first series he rejected the scholastic paradigm of intellect and will as a false dichotomy. Humanity is composed of body and soul.[125] Intellect and will are merely two ways by which the soul approaches ideas or objects: if by reason, this act is *intelligere*; if by love, it is *velle*. It appears he purposefully avoided the nouns *intellectus* and *voluntate*.[126] Freedom is not an act of knowing, for one either agrees or disagrees with what he perceives. Freedom is found "in willing," and then under certain conditions: "libertate non solum quæ à coactione, sed etiam quæ ab omni necessitate sive interna sive externa immunis est; sive illa sit contrarietatis sive contradictionis; dummodo bonum in quod fertur, tale sit cui aliud bonum conferri præferri aut postponi potest."[127] Without this liberty, there can be no legislation.[128] The freedom of the will is the foundation of religion. Without it there can be no true subjection and obedience to God.[129]

Episcopius moved even further from Arminius. Rather than placing the *imago Dei* in terms of both the naturals and supernaturals as Arminius had done, Episcopius placed the *imago Dei* in the soul alone, and denied the *imago* was in any way lost because of the fall:

> Hisce faculatibus præditus homo, fuit viva quædam imago Dei. Imago enim Dei nihil aliud est quam refulgescentia splendor divinæ similitudinis, qui in homine beneficio harum qualitatum divinarum reluxit: per quem ipsi reverentia dignitas quædam principalis, noti aliter quam Deo alicui inter animantia omnia conciliata fuit. Sit hæc imago in homine etiam post lapsum, hæc per peccatum deleta non est. Manserunt enim, in ipso facultates illæ per quas principalem in omnia dignitatem ad Dei ipsius similitudinem ipsius similitudinem exercere poterat.[130]

Arminius had affirmed the idea that "supernaturals were lost, and naturals were corrupted." Episcopius conceded only that *if* the supernaturals existed ("Quod si alias excellentiores qualitates naturalibus hisce postea superinfusas à Deo fuisse, cum Theologis statuamus"), then "eas non pertinuisse ad Dei veritatem constituendam, sed ad eam ornandam tantum & illustrandam."[131] Adam's natural powers were sufficient for him to keep the commands of God.[132] Junius had defended the same opinion against Arminius.[133] Still, neither Junius nor Episcopius teaching Pelagianism, as Pelagianism dealt with human ability and need for grace after the fall, not before. Episcopius did not deny that either "in intellectu hominis scientiam rerum divinarum in voluntate & affectibus rectitudinem quandam sive justitiam originalem locum habuisse." Nevertheless, he observed first that everything God created was good, but certainly all of creation was not infused with original righteousness. Second, the gift of supernatural grace to Adam, including the ability to will freely, cannot be supported from the text.[134]

Episcopius believed God created Adam with all he needed to obey God. This formed the basis for his examination of the fall. He warned that those who insisted that the ability to sin could not coexist with the "supernaturals" were not to be believed, for then God must necessarily have removed them from Adam and killed him as surely as if "he had given him deadly poison to drink."[135] He concluded if God removed the supernaturals from Adam so that he would fall, then God also destroyed the whole purpose of creation and religion. If God removed what was necessary for him to remain upright, then God alone necessitated Adam's fall, creation was not an act of kindness, and this gave people a just excuse to not worship such a God.[136] Rather, he gave Adam a healthy, well-adapted body and a competent soul, the foundations for true religion.[137]

The Fall and Its Effects

Episcopius affirmed in his private disputations what he had implied in public. There was no Adamic covenant, only the Law.[138] Like Arminius, he discussed how providence could be ordered so as not to overthrow free will.[139] Arminius followed with a treatment of the Adamic covenant; Episcopius followed his discussion of providence with *De Legislatione Prima*.[140] Regarding God's right and the rationale for the imposition of the command, Episcopius repeated the content of his public disputation.[141]

At this point, Episcopius wrote regarding the promises associated God's command to Adam. He believed a promise of eternal life could possibly be inferred from God's justice. Unlike Arminius, he was unwilling to say whether "eternal life" would have been a continuation of a "happy and delightful" physical life, based on continued access to the tree of life, or whether people would have been transported to a higher, spiritual existence.[142] He reiterated the mortality of the physical body without the tree of life, and "did not dare to assert" that if Adam had obeyed, he could have secured that promise for his offspring. Like Arminius, he believed this same test would have been extended to them.[143]

In *De Inobedientia Prima*,[144] God's work of redemption was demanded (*fuit præstandi*) by individual, personal sins, precipitated "partim ex inevitabili naturæ, quam ex primo parente, suo peccatore trahunt lege, partim ob propria etiam sua peccata, multa ac varia, involuti atque impliciti jacebant."[145] This is the extent to which he discussed Adam's sin. The rest followed closely his public disputation, and need not be repeated here.

We must carefully consider what Episcopius did and did not say concerning the effects of this first sin. It had two immediate effects: "offensio Numinis ob antegressam prohibitionem, & reatus vel obligatio ad poenam, ob adjunctam prohibitioni poenæ comminationem."[146] Adam and Eve's sense of shame over their nudity and flight from the presence of God were the signs of their fear of God and the impending penalty.[147] But note how Episcopius defined "eternal death:"

> Ex offensione data nata fuit ira; quæ quia est affectus depulsionis, quæ per punitionem fieri debet, causa poenæ fuit, id est mortis æternæ omniumque quæ ad eam ducunt calamitatum & miseriarum. Poena hæc non fuit inflicta actu aliquo positivo, sed tantum puro puto negativo; quatenus Deus hominem, cujus fragilitatem & mortalitatem per gratiam suam in actum exire permissurus non erat, si obedivisset legi ipsius, sibi & naturæ suæ mortali reliquit; quin etiam ad debilitandum & frangendum, eam laboribus & doloribus variis mancipavit.[148]

This "eternal" death is that which, accompanied by "calamity and misery," resulted from expulsion from the garden ("causa poenæ fuit, id est mortis æternæ omniumque quæ ad eam ducunt calamitatum & miseriarum"), and having been deprived of the tree of life, the natural fragility and mortality of their bodies took its natural. The "eternal death" in view is purely and simply physical death.[149] This death passed to their descendants by the law of natural generation, and so "totum genus humanum per primum Adami peccatum morti æternæ mancipatum fuit; punitione divina necessitate naturali in illud, descendente & redundante nullo prorsus discrimine."[150] Since all were cut off from the tree of life, all suffered the consequences of the punishment of Adam and Eve's sin.

But what of eternal damnation? Arminius affirmed that all Adam's descendants sinned in him, and so were guilty and liable for his sin, avoiding infant damnation by insisting that only the punishment they suffered was being deprived of the Holy Spirit. Episcopius did not require such complicated explanations. In *Appendix: De Reprobatione,* he frankly declared, "Deus neminem ob solum peccatum originale rejecti, aut æternis poenis destinavit."[151] This implies some type of *peccatum originale.* People sin personally and suffer for it not only because they are prostrated by their desires, but also because they are inevitably drawn by the sin nature they received from their first parent.[152] Their sin first resulted in the inevitability of physical death, and then in personal sin, both of which are attended by human misery. But we wait, vainly, for any mention of hell.

When we compare this disputation with Arminius' *De Effectis peccati primorum parentum,*[153] the most marked difference concerns the privation of the Holy Spirit. While central to Arminius' theology, it is absent from Episcopius. This creates a quandary. Arminius affirmed that privation of the Holy Spirit was sufficient to account for original sin.[154] If Episcopius did not hold to privation of the Spirit, what is this "sin nature" which draws people? This Episcopius did not answer.

The Necessity of Grace

Adam's offspring needed redemption from death and misery,[155] and unable to help themselves,[156] they found their only hope for redemption in divine grace and mercy.[157] He emphasized God always dealt with fallen people on the basis of grace; however, everything prior to the New Covenant was merely types and shadows of Jesus Christ. Prior to the Abrahamic covenant, God's dealings with humanity included only the most basic instructions concerning grace and acceptable sacrifices, securing the salvation of the pious and the punishment of the rebellious.[158]

At this point, Episcopius provided his unique approach to the covenants. He divided the Abrahamic and Mosaic covenants between their promises and stipulations, and their typical (and hence defective) nature. The Abrahamic covenant provided land, seed and blessing,[159] and was conditioned upon Abraham's obedience.[160] God's covenant with Abraham and his people was a type of the New Covenant between the Messiah and His people. The Old Covenant's blessings and stipulations foreshadowed those of the New.[161] In his treatment of the Mosaic Covenant, Episcopius examined the classic divisions of moral, ceremonial and judicial laws,[162] but only to show them as feeble precursors to the New Covenant. The moral law "veniam non dat, sed absque misericordia condemnat," the ceremonial was "varia & sordida," and the judicial was "accommodata…naturæ & ingenio populi seu reipublicæ."[163] The promises of the Old Covenant "fuerunt carnales & terrenæ,"[164] and its purpose "per cancellos legum istarum rigidarum contineretur in officio, ne contagio populorum circumjacentium afficeretur, utque tanquam infans sub curatela & tutela legis divinæ degeret."[165] Its greatest benefit was that it pointed to the coming Messiah and prepared the people for grace.[166] God's acts prior to the New Covenant were "rudimentary lessons" and "vague sketches" of the grace to come, designed to "inflame men's desire for it."[167]

At the apex of Episcopius' soteriology was the "new covenant." He defined this covenant as "aliud nihil est quam constans & æterna voluntatis ipsius divinæ dispositio, de peccatoribus resipiscentibus in gratiam rursus assumendis seu salvandis per fidem & obedientiam."[168] This definition shows his standard approach to the two components of every covenant: blessings and stipulations.[169] In addition, and more directly related to original sin, the new covenant provided "Ad propositam gratiam amplectendam, & ad fidem atque obedientiam debitam præstandam collationem virium sufficientem, & propositioni convenientem."

Episcopius divided the New Covenant into three divisions: its provision for the penalties of sin, its stipulations of repentance, faith and obedience, and finally the operation of grace throughout. While God's mercy and grace moved him to remedy the fallen human condition,[170] nevertheless "æquitas…sive iustitia postulabat, ut divina comminatio frustra facta non esset."[171] God's justice had to be satisfied. Episcopius built his theology of salvation around the two-fold demands of God's justice: an expiatory sacrifice and obedience on the part of the redeemed.[172] These demands were so fixed by God's justice, that even in his sovereignty he could not have denied them.[173] Jesus Christ's ministry set the pattern for human obedience through his subjection to the Father and provision of an expiatory sacrifice for sin through his death.[174] Episcopius' insistence on an expiatory, blood sacrifice is particularly important in view of the suspicion under which later Arminianism fell because of the Remonstrants' close associations with Hugo Grotius. Grotius had espoused a "governmental" view of the atonement in *De Satisfactione Christi* in 1617.[175] Episcopius, however, declared firmly and repeatedly that the death of Christ was a "sacrificium pro peccato,"[176] an "expiatio pro toto genere humano fieret."[177] It was, therefore, "propriè & verè propitiatoria," and the means by which "non obstante amplius justitiâ, salutatis spem iis facere, ostiumque vitæ aperire, sive novum foedus sancire voluerit."[178]

Justitia and *æquitas* provided the basis for the stipulation of repentance.[179] It was fitting that God, who loved justice and hated sin, demanded it from sinners seeking forgiveness.[180] Otherwise, "ac proinde peccatori ansa semper relicta fuisset, non obstantibus minis, licet severissimis, veniæ tamen, remissionis & impunitatis spem, denuo concipiendi, eaque spe sibi gradum faciendi ad novam peccandi licentiam, maximo profectò cum suo malo atque detrimento; cui ut occurreret gratia divina, æquitas omnino postulavit."[181] However, Episcopius' understanding of repentance shifted while at Leiden. In his first private lectures, in keeping with the scholastic tradition, he defined repentance as *dolor*, the pain of the soul when confronted with sin.[182] This pain creates the desire to be free from both the penalty and inclination of sin,[183] and to lead a life in keeping with the Scriptures.[184] He vigorously denied that repentance was equal to the works that might result from it.[185] Because it prepared the soul to seek for mercy, it preceded faith.[186] This definition contrasts sharply with his treatment of repentance in his second series of private lectures, a modification reflected in changing the title of the disputation from *De Præcepto Poenitentiæ* to *De Resipiscentia*.[187] Based on his study of the Bible and the Greek concept of μετάνοια, he no longer defined repentance as remorse, but as a change of mind.[188]

This modification permitted two important shifts. First, it removed the subjective aspect of repentance and made it a matter of confronting truth. Repentance was no longer an emotion but an act of the will, which agreed with his analysis of faith. He defined faith as assent to the truths presented to the *intellectus* by divine revelation, coupled with *voluntas* by the twofold act of repenting of one's sins and confiding in the message of the Gospel.[189] Therefore, faith was not a frivolous and superficial consideration of revelation, but the act of the willing to turn from sin and believe in the gospel.[190] More importantly, this redefinition permitted Episcopius to reconcile the principle of *sola fide* with loss of salvation.[191] On the one hand, he defended justification by faith. He wrote, "Euangelium vero, ut benignus, reconciliatus & clemens pater, acquiescens in filio suo dilecto, quem placamentum nobis omnibus proposuit, per fidem in sanguine ipsius (Rom 3:25),"[192] and "vero finis est sanctificatio nostri, aut potius nostri per fidem in Christum justificationem."[193] He thought Old Testament typology led to two truths: "1. Iesum esse Christum. 2. Per *solam fidem* in illum salutem contingere omnibus."[194] Nevertheless, if one turned back to sin, then they would cease believing, fall from grace "& totaliter & finaliter excidere & perire posse."[195] While he went so far as to state that faith was the minimum obedience necessary for the initial reception of grace,[196] he thought it difficult for one to renew repentance once it was lost.[197]

Episcopius feared that the preaching of salvation by grace through faith alone would promote unrestrained sin. He did not write on salvation by grace without mingling with it the necessity of obedience. For example, in *De Justificatione*,[198] he insisted justification was dependent upon continued faithfulness to the covenant, i.e. obedience, though he conceded that the demands of the Gospel were not rigorous and the obedience required was not perfect.[199] He concluded this disputation with the question, "An cum

Apostolos Paulos, per fidem solam sine operibus legis justificari nos dicit, legis tantum ceremonialis opera, an etiam moralis intelligat?" His response is astounding: "Legis omnis opera intelligit, etiam Euangelicæ, quatenus opera significant omnibus numeris absolutam & perpetuam obedientiam."[200] In end, it was only by redefining faith to include repentance that Episcopius resolved the Pauline contrast between faith and works.

Episcopius gave grace a central role in the two-fold blessings of the New Covenant: the forgiveness of sin by faith in the expiatory sacrifice of Christ, and "ad propositam gratiam amplectendam, & ad fidem atque obedientiam debitam præstandam collationem virium sufficientem" through the provision of the Holy Spirit.[201] Nevertheless, he did not make broad and repeated statements on the necessity of grace as did Arminius. In *De Præcepto Pœnitentiæ*, Episcopius attributed repentance and the desire for freedom from sin to the preaching of the Law, but did not mention the role of the Spirit.[202] In *De Præcepto Fidei in Christum*, the efficient causes of faith are an accurate understanding of the truths of the Gospel, and the willingness to confide in the truth,[203] but again there is no mention of the role of the Spirit. In his disputation *De Fide* in the second series, he defined faith only as the response to external and internal arguments that are sufficient for belief.[204] The ministry of the Holy Spirit is implied in his use of "internal arguments," but he made no explicit references.

Regarding the provision of grace by the New Covenant, he wrote, "Hujusmodi gratia non potest esse vis quædam irresistibilis aut immediata, voluntatem ad credendum determans: nec potest esse infusio habitus fidei, obedientiæ aut justitæ, quam vocant, per quam homo justificetur. Hæc enim duo totam fœderis, & illius propositionis, naturam perimunt & evertunt."[205] He denied that faith or repentance were gifts of God in the sense of an infused *habitus*,[206] denied that a *habitus* could be infused, and rejected the idea as "a scholastic innovation."[207] Nevertheless, we encounter strong statements of the necessity of grace and human inability at the end of *De Præcepto Obedientiæ*. He wrote, "Tota autem hæc obedientia sicuti neces-saria est ad salutem æternam consequendam, ita etiam difficillima est homini, imprimis circa conversionis initium. Carnali autem, animali & naturali homini ea omnino est impossibilis. Fideli vero & converso, imprimis ei qui jam aliquamdiu in obediendo exercitatus est, per gratiam Spiritu Sancti non tantum est possibilis, se etiam facilis."[208] This clearly teaches the inability of *carnali animali & naturali homini*, even after salvation, and the necessity of the Holy Spirit in the life of the mature believer. However, these assertions of the necessity of grace are less emphatic than those of Arminius.

Episcopius reiterated Arminius' identification of the Holy Spirit with grace when he delineated their necessity and operation in *De Promisso*

Spiritus Sancti and *De Spiritus Sancti, & vitæ hujus promisso.*[209] The promise of the Holy Spirit is the promise of *gratiæ spiritualis*.[210] He affirmed the role of the Spirit in both redemption and sanctification: "…quaque tum de bono isto primo, vitæ scilicet æternæ præmio, certiores redduntur, tum ad actiones sanctas, facilius, hilarius & constatius exercendas acrius incitantur & roborantur."[211] "Restoring," "inciting" and "strengthening" all emphasize the fundamental function of grace. While giving some attention to the role of grace in salvation, he devoted the larger part to the ministry of the Spirit in the life of the believer. By the sealing of the Spirit, God confirms His favor and blessing through the outpouring of His gifts and by granting peace and joy.[212] Episcopius' understanding of the working of the Spirit becomes even clearer when he describes the enabling of the Spirit. He described it as a "motio, ἐνεργείαν, agitatio seu inspiratio quædam arcana & imperceptibilis, per quam spiritus sive animus credentium alacer, idoneus, atque agilis redditur, ad officium foedere contentum lubentius & facilius præstandum."[213] Consistent with his definition of faith, Episcopius limited the enabling and movement of the Spirit almost entirely to the *intellectus*, leaving the *voluntas* free to accept or reject the Spirit's leading. He wrote,

> Actio hæc primum & potissimum circa mentem *occupatur*, & quidem aut immediate, per illustrationem & illuminationem eius in veritatis cognitione: aut mediate per objectorum obscurorum elucidationem, impedimentorum amotionem, specierum novarum oblationem, mediorum ad firmandas species suppeditationem, denique organorum totiusque temperamenti in corpore dispositionem. Tam enim liberaliter Deum largiri Spiritum suum fidelibus, & ex fide eum petentibus, credimus, ut non tantum anima eorum, sed & corpus corporisque organa animæ servientia, ab eo idonea reddantur ad voluntatis ipsius obsequium.[214]

The Spirit affects mind and even body in revealing truths and removing barriers; even so Episcopius tempered his exuberance concerning the relation between Spirit and *voluntas*:

> An vero in ipsum affectum & voluntatem fidelium, etiam porro immediate agat Spiritus Sanctus imprimendo iis motionem aliquam qua in virtutem potenter inclinentur, *non audemos nec necesse habemos vel adserere vel negare*. Certum est mentem hac ratione illustratam, facile affectum jam obsequendi studio, imo obsequio aliquatenus inclinatum ulterius impellere, eique adspirare vim & ἐνεργείαν, qua correptus affectus, voluntatem deinde moveat ad actiones affectui similes exercendas: ita tamen ut pro libertate sua, in contrariam partem nihilominus ferri semper & moveri possit.[215]

While ready to say that the Spirit and knowledge powerfully affect the will, in Episcopius' desire to preserve human freedom he was cautious about specifying how. In the end, free will reigns supreme. As he wrote in *De Præcepto*

Obedientiæ, "voluntatis, ut tum mens tum cor, tum actus omnes ad finem debitum dirigantur & ordinentur."[216] In sum, Episcopius addressed the role of grace in both salvation and sanctification, and clearly enunciated its effects in terms of both illumination and empowerment. He did not confuse grace with nature, but identified grace with the person and ministry of the Holy Spirit.

Episcopius put important clarifications or declarations in the *corollaria* of his disputations. *De Promissio Spiritus Sancti* is no different. We have seen that in the body of the disputation, he attributed an important role to the Holy Spirit and grace in the conversion process. Nevertheless he posed this question in the *corollaria:* "An ulla Spiritus Sancti actio immediata in mentem aut in voluntatem hominis necessária sit, aut in Scripturis promittatur, ad hoc ut quis credere possit verba extrinsecus proposito?"[217] Episcopius' answer was a single letter affixed to the end of the question, the letter "N." This letter communicated that all he had written in this disputation demonstrated that grace was almost indispensable for the illumination of the mind and subjugation of the human will, but not absolutely.

In the end of his second series, Episcopius focused upon the existential benefits of grace for believers in their daily lives, *vitæ præsentis felicitas,* in spite of "trials and tests," "temptations and crosses."[218] He concluded by defending that a believer could indeed fall away finally and fatally from grace,[219] and discussed the appropriate mentality toward God's promises of reward and punishment to the believer.[220]

The *Confessio Remonstrantium*

The Synod of Dort ended bitterly for the Remonstrants, terminating Arminian dreams of influencing Reformed theology. Episcopius wrote the *Confessio Remonstrantium* after entering exile, the first word of the leader of a new movement.[221] Despite the revisions of his fellow Remonstrants, it was truly his work, filled with his peculiar phrases and constructions. The opening sentence is unmistakably Episcopian: "De horum essentia, ordinibus, gradibus, numero, &c. multa subtilier extra Scripturas definire, nec necessarium, nec utile, imo periculosum arbitramur."[222] Also, the outline of the *Confessio* is very similar to the outline of the first series of private disputations. We will pass over large portions of repeated materials, in order to focus either on their differences, or on texts that help confirm or identify developing trends in Episcopius' theology.

The Creation of Humanity

Episcopius' chapter on the creation of Adam is a distillation of his disputations. Here for the first time he mentioned the means of the woman's creation, and joined her with Adam when he used the plural *dominos principesque*.[223] He included a practical application of the doctrine of creation,[224] and a lengthy diatribe against the predestinarian view of the purpose of creation.[225] He emphasized that the Calvinist understanding of creation unavoidably made God the author of sin and excused human guilt.

The Fall and Its Effects

Unlike the public disputations, Episcopius introduced his covenantal paradigm of blessings and stipulations under his consideration of providence.[226] He discussed God's command to Adam and the causes for the fall for chapter 7, *De Peccato & Miseria Hominis*.[227] He treated the threefold results of Adam's sin: eternal death, misery and ejection from the garden.[228] Having suggested earlier that Episcopius redefined eternal death as physical death, this provides a test of that interpretation. Given Episcopius' understanding of the garden as a type of heaven, ejection from the garden appears to imply eternal damnation until we examine the references associated with each result of Adam's sin. Under *reus æternæ mortis*, Episcopius listed "Genes. 2.16, 3.16 & seq.; Rom. 5.12 & seqq.," all of which are usually taken (even if incorrectly) as references to physical death. Instead, Episcopius listed references to eternal punishment ("Apoc. 2.7 & 21:14.") under the penalty of separation from the tree of life. It would seem Episcopius had these reversed, that expulsion from the garden should symbolize exclusion from heaven and exclusion from the tree of life would indicate the penalty of physical death, but his appeal to biblical texts supports our contention that he defined *mortem aeternam* as mere physical death.

Episcopius also delineated the implications of Adam's sin upon his posterity:

> Quia vero Adamus stirps ac radix erat totius generis humani, ideo non seipsum tantum, sed omnes etiam posteros suos (qui quasi in lumbis impius conclusi erant, & ex ipso per naturalem generationem produturi) eidem morti ac miseriæ involvit, & una secum implicuit:[229] adeo ut omnes homines, sine ullo discrimine, excepto solo D. N. Iesu Christo, per hoc unicum Adami peccatum privati sint primæva illa felicitate, & destituti vera justitia, ad æternam salutem consequendam necessaria, adeoque morti illi, quam diximus, & multiplici miseriæ etiam nunc obnoxii nascantur. Atque hoc vulgo peccatum originis dici solet.[230]

Except for the denigrating statement "atque hoc vulgo peccatum originis dici solet," an initial reading might suggest that Episcopius agreed with Reformed orthodoxy. For example, he mentioned the association between Adam and his offspring. However, the phrase "qui quasi in lumbis impius conclusi erant" is not the firm declaration of Arminius that "all have sinned in Adam." Rather, he understood death, sin and misery as the natural results of Adam's sin; they do not result from either mediate or immediate imputation.

We also meet with further indications that only physical death comes upon Adam's posterity. Episcopius specified it was *that death (morti illi)*[231] which was passed to his posterity. Why did he need to specify *that* death? His opponents understood that Adam rendered all men liable to *every* form of death. Once again, we find the references he cited for "that death" are references to physical death. Another evidence of this redefinition comes in his treatment of personal sins, in which he adopted an expanded version of Arminius' idea of degrees of sin. In the *Confessio* 6.6, he asserted that "Quædam vero sunt talia, ut leviores lapsus potius dici mereantur, quam crimini, per quæ juxta gratiosum Dei fœdus & paternam benignitatem, *non excluditur homo a spe vitæ æternæ*," and then "Pro diversa quantitate & qualitate peccatorum, varia quoque pœna à Deo constituta est: puta tum damni, tum sensus, tum temporalis, tum æterna, tum deniqua corporalis, tum spiritualis."[232] Thus, not all sins deserve eternal condemnation in hell, and Adam's personal sin was not worthy of "hellish pains." If Adam's sin did not result in infernal condemnation for himself, then it could not have done so to his descendants.

His assault on the Augustinian doctrine of original sin continued in the next paragraph: "Præter hoc peccatum sunt & alia *propria*, seu *actualia* unius cujusque hominis peccata, a quæ & reatum nostrum coram Deo revera multiplicant, & mentem in rebus spiritualibus obscurant, imo paulitam excæcant, denique voluntatem nostram magis ac magis adsuetudine ipsa peccandi depravant."[233] His declaration that one's own personal sins "obscured the mind, blinded men, and perverted the will" completely broke with the Augustinian tradition, which considered them the results of original sin. However, he was not denying the existence of a sin nature or the necessity of divine grace. Adam deprived his posterity of happiness and true righteousness, and "Duplex autem illa peccati vis & efficacia…damnatio, seu mors æterna, & servitius peccati, seu captivas sub peccati consuetudine."[234] Few before the time of Christ "gratiæ istius divinæ auxilio uti in Deum crediderunt, & per fidem coram ipso integre ac sincere ambulaverunt." Only by grace did they "dominium peccati excusserunt, & per eandem vivam fidem etiam vere justificate fuerunt, sive à reatu peccatorum absoluti, & æternæ vitæ præmio donati."[235] Nevertheless, "magis etiam magisque peccatum auctum, & veluti aculeo indito per legem exstimulatum, reatusque mortis & condemnationis usque adeo *aggravatus est, ut universus mundus sub peccatum conclusis, & condemnationi factus fuerit obnoxius.*"[236] He concluded by declaring it was the hopelessness of the human condition that necessitated divine grace. "Ex quo tandem summa *gratiæ divinæ*," he wrote, "in Christo Servatore nobis ante secula præparatæ, necessitas simul & utilitas evidenter apparuit: quippe sine qua nec miserable peccati jugum excutere, nec quicquam in tota Religione vere bonum operari, nec denique mortem æternam, aut ullam veram peccati poenam, effugere unquam possimus; nedum ut salutam æternam dine illa per nos ipsos, aut per alias creaturas, consequi aliquando possimus."[237]

The Necessity of Grace

In chapter eight, *De Opere Redemptionis, deque Persona & Officii Iesus Christi*, Episcopius expanded on the necessity of grace. He defined the need and purpose for redemption as "opus *Redemptionis* sive novæ *creationis*, quo hominem, per peccatum mortis ac condemnationis æternæ reum factum, & sub servitute peccati misere jacentum, ex sua gratia & misericordia à reatu illo liberaret, & in spem vitæ æternæ atque immortalis restitueret, viresque sufficientes, imo exuberantes, ad peccati dominium excutiendum, & divinæ voluntati tot corde obsequendum suppeditaret."[238] People are unable either to initiate or complete the work of salvation, and only God can restore them. Episcopius put forward his Christology more fully here than in any other disputation,[239] defending Christ's death as a necessary, bloody, expiatory sacrifice for the sins of the whole world.[240] He ended the chapter contrasting this with his opponents' beliefs in election, reprobation, and the dispensability of the death of Christ.[241]

In chapter nine, "*De Cognitione voluntatis divina in Fœdere Novo patefacta*," Episcopius laid out the promises and stipulations of the New Covenant. The promises of salvation and eternal life, including adoption, justification and sealing by the Holy Spirit, depended upon stipulations of faith and obedience. He reinforced, however, the necessity of supernatural grace if people were to believe. He wrote, "Decrevit ejusmodi efficacem gratiam, per eundem filium suum, omnibus vocatis, quantumvis miseris peccatoribus, conferre; per quam reipsa in Christum Servatorem suum credere, Euangelio ejus obedire, atque à dominio & reatu peccati liberari possint: imo etiam per quam reipsa credant, obedient & liberentur, nisi nova contumacia & rebellione gratiam Dei oblatum rejiciant."[242]

Chapter nine also includes an interesting reversion to Arminius' theology when, for the first time, Episcopius presented grace in terms of decrees. His *ordo salutis* was, however, much more simple. First was the decree of predestination to save those who persist in faith and obedience. Second was the decree of vocation or election to grace, by which "statuitur vera necessitas simul atque utilitas gratiæ divinæ, seu mediorum nobis necessariorum ad fidem & obedientiam Jesu Christo, juxta voluntatem Dei, Evangelio ipsius revelatum, ex parte nostra præstandum. Quia verò de *Voluntate* illa Dei, quam ipse à nobis præstari vult, prius constare nobis debet; quam de *gratia* ad voluntatem illam præstandam necessaria."[243] If his use of the phrase *efficacem gratiam* were a nod to Arminius, it was slight. He did not expand the contrast between sufficient and efficacious grace. Nevertheless, this is a simplified restatement of Arminius' theology: grace is necessary for salvation and sanctification, and is a supernatural power provided by God. It is efficient in those who believe, but rejectable.

In chapters ten, *De Præceptis Iesu Christi Intenere, deque fide ac pœnitentia, seu conversione ad Deum*, and eleven, *De fide in Iesum Christum*, Episcopius again reconciled justification by faith alone and maintenance of salvation by works by redefining "faith" to include repentance and obedience.[244] He quoted Paul, that "imo fides ipsa in justitiam credenti imputari dicitur," only to appeal to James 2:24, 1 Timothy 4:8, and Hebrews 12:14. Thus, when one reads "faith" alone is necessary for salvation, "quam quatenus proprietate sua naturali obedientiam fidei includit, & tanquam foecunda bonorum operum mater est."[245] True repentance must be *efficax, sincera,* and *continua.*[246] In chapter eleven, he further developed the definition of faith as understanding plus willful assent, adding three implications. First, faith is entirely voluntary, and cannot be either forced or produced by irresistible strength.[247] Second, faith "secum necessario trahit observationem mandatorum Jesu Christi, sive bona opera."[248] Finally, faith can be lost, and a person who was once a sanctified believer "& sic totaliter, tandemque etiam finaliter, nisi serio in tempore resipiscant, divina gratia excidant."[249]

In his disputations, Episcopius left his readers without a clear understanding of the operation of grace in drawing the sinner to salvation. This was not the case in the *Confessio.* In chapter seventeen, *De Beneficiis & Promissis Divinis; ac primo de Electione ad gratiam, seu Vocatione ad fidem*, Episcopius explained God provides His grace, and the promise of "excellent and beautiful things far beyond his imagination." By this God hopes to render people *idoneus & aptus* to fulfill his commands, and also "quorum desiderium, ac certa spec voluntatem hominis ad obsequium actu præstandum accendere… atque inflammare." God "lavishes" the gift of the Holy Spirit upon us (*largari nobis*) because of his kindness toward the sinner, and seeks to overcome human inability and sinful intransigence in a way agreeable to the human will.[250] Then, after providing sinners sufficient grace for faith and obedience, and he calls them to himself by means of the Gospel. For the first time, Episcopius distinguished two types of election, one "to grace," and one "to glory" or to salvation itself. He believed the Scriptures made this distinction.[251] The preaching of the Gospel effects and performs election to grace, together with the power of the Spirit (*adjunctum virtutem Spiritus*), with serious intention to bring to faith and to save all who hear. If someone were to reject the Gospel, the cause would not be God, but their own obstinate refusal.[252]

For the first time Episcopius identified two types of callings: one effective (*vocatio efficax*),[253] and the other merely sufficient (*vocatio sufficiens*).[254] The *vocatio sufficiens* is not effective because "per singularem & arcanum quandam Dei sapientiam sic administretur, ut fructuose congruat voluntati ejus," or "quod in ea efficaciter, per potentiam irresistibilem, aut vim quanduam omnipotentem…voluntas ejus, qui vocatur, ad credendum determinetur."[255] People are called with the possibility of refusal, yet if they do not resist it is because they have been sufficiently prepared by grace. If that calling were not accepted, the fault would lie with the person alone, because the essence of the call is the same. Arminius' influence is apparent. Episcopius used the term *vocationem* in place of *gratiam*, but it embodies Arminius' distinction between sufficient and efficient grace.

Episcopius' return to Arminius continued in his discussion of the source of faith. In a statement that seems at odds with his emphasis upon free will thus far, Episcopius wrote,

> Homo itaque salvificam fidem non habet ex se ipso, neque ex arbitrij sui liberi viribus regeneratur, aut convertitur: quandoquidem in statu peccati nihil boni, quod quidem salutare bonum sit, (cujusmodi imprimis est conversio & fides salvifica) ex seipso, vel à seipso, vel cogitare potest, nedum velle, aut facere: sed necesse est, ut à Deo, in Christo, per Evangelij, eique adjunctam Spiritus S. virtutem regenetur, atque totus renovetur, puta intellectu, affectibus, voluntate, omnibusque viribus, ut salutaria bona recte possit intelligere, meditare, velle, ac perficere.[256]

This statement of human inability and the power of grace is remarkably parallel to Arminius' declaration concerning the powers of free will *post lapsum* and the necessity of grace:

> …in statu vero lapsus & peccati; ex seipso, quod quidem vere bonum est, neq. cogitare, neque velle aut facere posse; sed necesse esse, ut a Deo in Christo per Spiritum sanctum ipsius regeneretur & renovatur in intellectu, affectionibus sive voluntate, omnibusque viribus, ad id quod vere bonum est recte intelligendum, æstimandum, considerandum, volendum & faciendum. Hujus vero regenerationis participem factum, statuo eum utpote liberatum à peccato, posse bonum cogitare, velle & facere, sed tamen non nisi cum auxilio semper gratiæ Dei.[257]

Faith is a gift of God. People are neither born again nor converted by their free will. They cannot think, much less will, the good. Regeneration preceded the act of faith. These statements sound so Reformed, but Episcopius was once again following Arminius' lead by saying that people maintains true freedom through the power of contrary choice and the ability to resist grace.

This faithful communication of Arminius' theology continued as Episcopius attributed all the good that happens to the effects of grace:

> Gratiam itaque Dei statuimus esse principium, progressum, & complementum omnis boni: adeo ut ne ipse quidem regenitus absque præcendente ista, sive præveniente, excitante, prosequente, & cooperante gratia, bonum illum salutare cognitare, velle aut peragere possit, nedum ullis, ad malum trahentibus, tentationibus resistere. Ita ut fides, conversio, & bona opera omnia, omnesque actiones piæ & salutares, quas quis cogitando potest assequi, gratiæ Dei in Christo, tanquam caussæ suæ principali & primariæ, in solidum sint adscribendæ.[258]

This is an extraordinary assertion of the effects of grace by Episcopius. However, it is very much in keeping with Arminius' declaration before the States of Holland: "Atque hoc modo gratiæ adscribo initium, continuationem atque consummationem omnis boni; etiam eousque, ut homo jam regeneratus sine hac præveniente & excitante sequente & cooperante gratia, bonum prorsus neque cogitare, velle aut facere possit, ac ne quidem ulli tentationi malæ resistere.[259] This is also the capstone of a series of unprecedented repetitions of Arminius' theology. I conclude it provides a clear indication that the other Remonstrants demanded that the *Confessio* be more reflective of Arminius. I believe this also indicates that, at this point in the development of the theology of the Remonstrant movement, Episcopius' colleagues were not supportive of his departure from Arminius in several of the key issues of the Arminian controversy. They demanded a return to Arminius.

This return, however, did not continue. Arminius denied that sufficient grace was given to all men. He also insisted God would not hold men responsible unless he gave them grace sufficient to believe or obey, and that the Spirit did not always accompany the Word. Episcopius was unwilling to accept such a limitation. After a nod to Arminius ("Etsi vero maxima est gratiæ disparita, pro liberrima scilicet voluntatis divinæ dispensatione"), he went beyond:

> …tamen Spiritus S. omnibus & singulis, quibus verbum fidei ordinarie prædicatur, tantum gratiæ confert, aut saltem conferre paratus est, quantum ad fidem ingenerandum, & ad promovendum suis gradibus salutarem ipsorum conversionem sufficit. Itaque gratia sufficiens ad fidem & conversionem non tantum ijs obtingit, qui actu credunt & convertuntur; sed non tantum ijs, qui actu ipso non credunt, nec reipsa convertuntur. Quoscunque enim Deus vocat ad fidem & salutem, eos serio vocat: id est, non externa tantum specie, aut verbo duntaxat vocali (quatenus

scilicet in eo seria opsius præcepta, & promissa vocatis generatim declarantur) sed cum sincera etiam, ac minime simulata salvandi intentione…[260]

God's grace may attend the preaching of the Word with different degrees of intensity, but it was always sufficient for the conversion of the hearers. The fault of unbelief can never be attributed to some secret, hidden will of God, but only to the flagrant, rebellious will of the sinner. Thus he concluded his opinions on original sin and the work of grace, clearly drawing on Arminius but unhesitant to go beyond him.

Parallels Between Episcopius and the Greek Fathers

Outside of Arminius, if we find any parallels with Episcopius' theology they are in the Greek Fathers. Although space does not permit us to make a full comparison, some brief observations will suffice. The Greek Fathers insisted that the cause of the fall was free will, and specifically denied God in any way decreed it.[261] They defined foreknowledge as simple prescience of the future, without compromising the freedom of future contingents.[262] Justin Martyr, responding to philosophical questions regarding foreknowledge, future contingents and freedom, argued:

> But lest some suppose, from what has been said by us, that we say that whatever happens, happens by a fatal necessity, because it is foretold as known beforehand, this too we explain. We have learned from the prophets, and we hold it to be true, that punishments and chastisements, and good rewards are rendered according to the merit of each man's actions. Since if it be not so, but all things happen by fate, neither is anything at all in our power. For if it be fated that this man be good, and this other evil, neither is the former meritorious nor the latter to be blamed. And again, unless the human race have the power of avoiding evil and choosing good by free choice, they are not accountable for their actions, of whatever kind they be. That it is by free choice they both walk uprightly and submit, we thus demonstrate.[263]

Concerning foreknowledge and the decree, Justin wrote, "So what we say about future events being foretold, we do not say it as if they came about by a fatal necessity, but God foreknowing all that shall be done by all men, and it being his decree that the future actions of men shall all be recompensed according to their several value, he foretells by the Spirit of prophecy that he will bestow meet rewards according to the merit of the actions done, always urging the human race to effort and recollection."[264] In Justin's opinion, the object of God's foreknowledge was not some decree, but the "future actions of men."[265] Furthermore, the Greek Fathers limit the universal results of the fall to physical death, misery and corruption; only personal sins result in eternal damnation.[266] They affirmed the sinlessness of infants.[267] They continually spoke of Christ's sacrifice for the whole of humanity,[268] and that men must use their free will in order to turn to God.[269] They placed great emphasis on the power of Satan and the demons which enslave and blind people, so that even though people possess free will they cannot see the truth.[270] They taught one could return to the paths of death and lose ones salvation. Episcopius' theology resonates well with these early theologians of the church. Even if he departed from Augustinian theology as reinterpreted by Reformed orthodoxy, he had good precedents for his faith.

Summary

We have seen measurable and significant change between Arminius and Episcopius. Returning to Hicks' three categories for comparing Arminius' thought (equation, logical entailment and radical distinction),[271] we can quickly eliminate "equation." Episcopius' rejection of the Adamic covenant, the "in Adam" formula and his redefinition of *mors æterna* are sufficient evidence that Episcopius did not merely maintain his mentor's theology. But neither is there the "radical distinction" between Arminius and Episcopius that Hicks found between Arminius and van Limborch. Hicks wrote, "it will become apparent that the theology of Arminius *is that of the Reformers* while that of Limborch belongs to the Semi-Pelagianism of Tridentine Catholicism or even the Pelagian tendencies of Socinianism."[272] Episcopius was neither Pelagian nor Semi-Pelagian. He held to a continuing principle of evil within people that inevitably led to sin, spiritual blindness and moral servitude to sin that could only be removed by the Holy Spirit. He did not define grace in terms of mere nature, or the external preaching of God's word. "Grace" for Episcopius was the illuminating, persuading, and enabling ministry of the Holy Spirit initiated in the unsaved and continuing in the redeemed. Episcopius was neither Calvinist, nor Pelagian, nor Socinian, but he was an Arminian.[273] He tended to maintain Arminius' thought, borrowing Arminius' words and phrases and closely following his lectures. His theology was a logical development of Arminius' theology in both content and method, affirming A. H. Haentjens' opinion.[274]

However, there are marked differences. We may attribute some of these differences to Episcopius being unafraid to state openly what Arminius was only willing either to imply or defend in others but not claim for himself, and nowhere was this more obvious than in their treatment of original sin. But it is also clear that Episcopius a creative theologian in his own right. He had no qualms in modifying Arminius' theology in the areas of the Adamic covenant, the essence of the temptation, the use of the *ordo salutis*, and especially with regard to original sin. He did not believe anyone sinned in Adam, nor in imputation, and most importantly, he did not repeat Arminius' definition of depravity in terms of the deprivation of the Spirit and its consequents. Although he reaffirmed the necessity of grace, he was not as expansive in his descriptions of the need and operation of grace.

We may say the same regarding his theological method. Junius fully utilized classic scholastic method and categories, and drew heavily upon pagan philosophers (Aristotle in particular), Catholic scholastics (especially Aquinas) and to a lesser degree the early Christian writers. Arminius also wrote as a scholastic. He was, however, more moderate than Junius in his implementation of scholastic causality. Even if he expressed appreciation for Aquinas' genius, when he quoted Aquinas it was usually to disagree with him. He preferred to quote from the early Christian writers, especially Augustine. Episcopius used scholastic categories only in an attenuated form. His heavy borrowing from Arminius did not permit him to do away with them entirely. However, the only source he cited was the Scriptures. This represents a significant change in the use of theological sources, and methods, in the movement from Junius to Arminius and then Episcopius.

In this chapter, we have established that Episcopius maintained fundamental aspects of Arminius' theology. We have seen he was willing to carry Arminius' theological methods and conclusions beyond the point at which his teacher had stopped, even to the point of correction and contradiction. In the next chapter, we will consider Episcopius' later writings, and see the degree to which he was willing to go in working out the implications of Arminius' deviations from Reformed Augustinianism and scholasticism.

Notes

1 Simon Kistemaker, "Leading Figures at the Synod of Dort," in *Crisis in the Reformed Churches: Essays in the Commemoration of the Great Synod of Dort, 1618–1619*, ed. Peter Y. De Jong (Grand Rapids: Reformed Fellowship, 1968), 46, 49–50.

2 In retrospect, Gomarus acquiesced too soon. Because of the conflict, the curators at Leiden never permitted Vorstius to teach a single class.

3 Some wanted Episcopius to take Arminius' place in 1609, but others considered him too young at 26 years.

4 Episcopius' Leiden disputations are cited from Simon Episcopius, *Disputationes Theologiæ Tripartæ* (Amsterdam: Ioannem Blaev, 1644), with occasional references to Simon Episcopius, *Disputationes Theologicæ Tripartitæ*, in *Operum Theologicorum, Pars Altera*, ed. Philip van Limborch (Rotterdam: Arnoldum Leers, 1665). The *Disputationes Theologiæ Tripartæ* is, as the name indicates, made up of three series of disputations. The *pars prima* is Episcopius' series of public disputations, Simon Episcopius, *Disputationes Theologicæ, Publicè olim in Academia Leydensi habitæ*, in *Disputationes Theologiæ Tripartæ* (Amsterdam: Ioannem Blaev, 1644), 1–142. The *pars secunda* is his first series of private disputations, Simon Episcopius, *Disputationum Theologicarum, à M. Simone Episcopio in Academia Leydensi privatim olim habitarum, Collegium Primum*, in *Disputationes Theologiæ Tripartæ* (Amsterdam: Ioannem Blaev, 1644), 143–332, delivered from November 13, 1612 until December 4th, 1615, and the *pars tertia* is his second series of private disputations, Simon Episcopius, *Disputationum Theologicarum, à M. Simone Episcopio in Academia Leydensi privatim olim habitarum, Collegium Secundum*, in *Disputationes Theologiæ Tripartæ* (Amsterdam: Ioannem Blaev, 1644), 333–428, delivered from November 4, 1616 to February 26, 1618.

5 See *DTT*, 1.6.1.

6 Franciscus Junius, *Theses Theologicæ Quæ in Inclyta Academia Lugdunobativa Ad Exercitia Publicarum Disputationum, Præside D. Francisco Iunio Variis temporibus à Theologiæ Candidatis aduersus oppognantes propugnatæ sunt*, in *Opuscula Theologica Selecta*, ed. Abr. Kuyperus (Amsterdam: Fredericum Muller Cum Soc. et Joannem Hermannum Kruyt, 1882), Theses 7, 8, and 9.

7 *De Natura Dei* (4), *De Scientia Dei* (5), *De Voluntate Dei* (6) & *De Dominio Dei* (7). Note how these reflect Arminius' analysis of the *essentia Dei*, without traditional consideration of the *ens Dei*.

8 *DTT*, 1.1.12 treats the eternal generation of the Son, and *DTT*, 1.1.20 treats the persons of the Godhead.

9 Pub. Disp. 14, in James Arminius, *Disputations of some of the principle subjects of the Christian religion*, in *The Works of James Arminius*, trans. James Nichols, London ed (London: Longman, Hurst, Rees, Orme, Brown and Green, 1828; reprint, Grand Rapids: Baker, 1986), 2:211.

10 Even though he entitled the disputation *De Convenientia & Discrimine Vetum & Novum Testamenti*, Episcopius made it clear his intention was to compare the old and new covenants: "Vetus & novum Foedus, sive quod idem est, Vetus & Novum Testamentum (quam appellationem cum alia quæ utrique foederi cum testamento proprie dicto communia sunt: tum imprimis Novi Foederis sanctio per mortem testoris peracti introduxisse videntur (Hebr. 9:15 & seqq.) ordinarie in S. literis pro lege & Euangelio usurpari solent." (*DTT*, 1.11.1). Although he established some similarities between the old and new covenants (*DTT*,1.11.3), following Arminius he dedicated the majority of his analysis on their differences. He based almost all differences on the work of Christ.

11 *DTT*, 1.7.

12 *De Schismate* (*DTT*, 1.16). Junius' famous work on resolving divisions among believers is *Eirenicum de Pace Ecclesiæ Catholicæ*, in *Opuscula Theologica Selecta*, ed. Abr. Kuyperus (Amsterdam: Fredericum Muller Cum Soc. et Joannem Hermannum Kruyt, 1882), cf. Franciscus Junius, *Den Vreedsamen Christen, Of, Van de Vrede der Catholijcke Kercke* (Delft: Adriaen Gerritsz., 1612). Arminius preached on Christian unity in *Oratio de Componendo Dissidio Religionis inter Christianos*, in *Opera Theologica* (Leiden: Goderfridum Basson, 1629); cf. James Arminius, *Oration V: On Reconciling Religious Dissentions Among Christians*, in *The Works of James Arminius*, trans. James Nichols, London ed (London: Longman, Hurst, Rees, Orme, Brown and Green, 1825; reprint, Grand Rapids: Baker, 1986). For a recent analysis of Junius' doctrine of toleration, see Christiaan de Jonge, "De irenische ecclesiologie van Franciscus Junius (1545–1602)," (Ph.D. diss., University of Leyden, 1980).

13 *DTT*, 1.8.9.

14 While Arminius did not define the *imago Dei*, he mentioned it throughout; cf. Disp. Pub., Thesis 7.2, in *OT*, 239; *WA*, 2:151, and Disp. Pub., Theses 7.6–7, in *OT*, 240; *WA*, 2:151.

15 Episcopius listed Paul's words in Greek, while Arminius provided their Latin translations. "Peccatum primum, quod ἁμαρτίας, παραπτόματος, παρακοῆς, & παραζάσεως nominibus indigetat Apostolus…;" cf. Arminius, "Peccatum autem hoc commodissime ab Apostolo inobedientia & offensa sive lapsus appellatur" (Disp. Pub., Thesis 7.2, in *OT*, 239; *WA*, 2:153).

16 *DTT*, 1.9.1.

17 See Disp. Priv., Thesis 29, in *OT*, 374.

18 "Et fuit, eaque unica; non continens , decalogi aut legum aliarum instar, præcepta multa; neque præscribens actuum variorum & multiplicium præstationem & omissionem; nec difficile aut molestum obsequium" (*DTT*, 1.9.2). For a survey of Reformed theologians who saw the Decalogue as included in the Covenant of Works, see Heinrich Heppe, *Reformed Dogmatics: Set Out and Illustrated from the Original Sources*, ed. Ernst Bizer, trans. G. T. Thomson (London: George Allen & Unwin Ltd., 1950; reprint, Grand Rapids: Baker, 1986), 291–94.

19 "Sed pronam facilemque ab unico & singulari tantum facto abstinentiam, videlicet ab esu fructus unius, cujus usum sibi, jampridem, tamquam domino ad imaginem Dei condito, indultum aut adsignatum in solidum, homo credebat." *DTT*, 1.9.2.

20 Arminius wrote the law "symbolica fuerit, data ad testificandum hominem esse sublegem Deo, & obedientiam ejus explorandum, ejusque præstatio futura erat manifesta devotæ submissionis & debitæ obedientiæ professus" (*OT*, 239).

21 "Utque idipsum signo, indicio atque experimento aliquo palam fieret."

22   This opinion is very close, if not identical, to Calvin's (John Calvin, *Commentaries on the First Book of Moses Called Genesis*, trans. John King [Edinburgh: Calvin Translation Society, n.d.; reprint, Grand Rapids: Baker, 1981], 1:126).

23   "Cum enim omnia Deo naturaliter subessent, utpote a quo in esse dependerent, nulla vero res creata alteri, sine speciali Dei voluntate atque arbitrio, subesset, æquissimum profecto erat, ut homo qui beneficio dominii speciali super alia omnia à Deo affectus ac præditus erat, eidem tamen Deo, feudatarii instar, cum reliquis rebus omnibus creatis, nihilominus subesse demonstraretur" (*DTT*, 1.9.3).

24   "Quam caussam etiam fuisse credimus, quod lex hæc prima sancita fuerit à Deo comminatione poenæ severissima, quia intererat gloriæ divinæ, ut hoc dominium ipsius supra hominem sanctum atque inviolatum constaret; & legis facillimæ transgressio, non poterat aliud quid videri quam universalis quædam subjectionis atque obsequii renunciatio" (*DTT*, 1.9.4.) Again, the parallels with Arminius are marked: "Sane ejus transgressio non potest *commodiore* quam inobedientiæ nomine insigniri, continentis in se *subjectionis* negationem & obedientiæ *renunciationem*" (Disp. Pub., Thesis 7, in *OT*, 240, italics added.). Arminius also placed Adam's ability to resist in his creation in the *imago Dei*: "quibus omnibus ut per imaginem Dei resistere potuit" (Disp. Priv., Thesis 30.6, in *OT*, 376).

25   *WA*, 2:152.

26   The entire thesis reads, "Causa, quæ ad peccandum hominem impulit atque instigavit, prima, fuit Diabolus, Serpentis, homini nondum satis noti, involucro tectus, qui, humanæ fælicitati divinæque gloriæ invidens, primitus & ante omnia obicem sive repagulum atque obstaculum transgressioni impendiendæ à Deo positum, tollere atque submovere, id est, supplicii sive mali, comminatione denunciati, metum, animo hominis eximere, ac proinde fidem, de poena certo eventura, convellere ac labefactare conatus est, utque id commode fieret, ejus loco spem magni alicujus & summe desiderabilis boni, puta similitudinis cum Deo, primis statim auspiciis injicere & suggerere" (*DTT*, 1.9.5).

27   "Scriptura non dubitet asserere, Adamum non fuisse seductum, sed Evam" (*DTT*, 1.9.8).

28   "Huic proposito Sathanæ subserviit: Tum fructus ipse vetitus, in quem, nulla accedente suasione Diaboli, ob pulchritudinem & gratam oculis speciem, primum naturali quodam appetitu, deinde vero prohibitione Dei superveniente, acrius multo irritato atque exstimulato, pronus homo ferebatur: Tum similitudinis, à Diabolo primum homini suggestæ atque indicatæ, majestas & excellentia, quam procul omni dubio, simulatque ejus mentio facta à Diabolo fuit, enixissime & fervidissime homo concupivit atque desideravit" (*DTT*, 1.9.9).

29   "Non enim in ipsa edendi nuda voluntate vel concupiscentia, quamquam sine ea actualis esus peractus non sit, & ab eâ denominationem habeat quòd malus sit, sive quòd peccatum fuerit. Nec in ipsa fructus decerptione, quæ verisimiliter esum præcessit. Nec denique in alia aliqua sive qualitate, sive qualitatis carentia aut privatione, ab actu ipso edendi diversa vel distincta, rationem mali & peccati positam esse credimus, sed in ipso actu, contra præceptum exercito, qui, licet metaphysicè, quatenus ens, bonus fuerit; moraliter tamen, quatenus à Deo vetitus, malus fuit, ita ut post legem latam malitia ab eo nec separari nec distingui potuerit" (*DTT*, 1.9.10).

30   *DTT*, 1.9.8.

31   "Et quamuis eum Deus formarit mutabilem, non tamè è bono factus est malus, nisi invidia Santanæ, qui Euam aggressus infirmioris sexus decepit, & decepta ad Adamum debellandum usus est (1 Tim. 2;14)" (Junius, *Theses Theologicæ*, Thesis 18.2).

32   "Non Eva. Hæc enim exemplo tantum præire potuit, aut aliqua ratione allicere, non cogere" (Disp. Priv., Thesis 30.6, in *OT*, 376).

33 Ibid.

34 *DTT*, 1.9.9. Junius also affirmed this: "Transgressionis autem istius causam Efficientem, dicimus, Euæ & Adami liberam voluntatem, seu liberæ illus voluntatis abusum.... Liberam dicimus, quod illa cum cogi non potuit ad peccandum & esse voluntas, sic peccare coacta nequiut, alioquin ei peccatum minime imputatur si non consenssit. Deceptus igitur uterque à Diabolo, mandatum Dei ludificante, abusus est libera voluntate, & libere lapsus est" (Junius, *Theses Theologicæ*, Thesis 18.6).

35 Episcopius denied the affections had a final say in decision-making, because the will is able to resist even their most vigorous impulses: "Affectus hominis aliter statui causa non potest; quam, quatenus morali quodam impulso voluntatem quasi ferit ac verberat. Qui impulsus etsi vehemens valde atque potens esset, voluntatis tamen imperio atque arbitrio semper egressus ejus in actum subjiciebatur. Poterat enim, voluntas, divinæ voluntatis consideratione armata, resistere illi, eumque in ordinem ista vi redigere; alioquin enim frustranea fuisset legislatio, qua affectus circumscribebatur & refrænabatur" (*DTT*, 1.9.16).

36 *DTT*, 1.9.10.

37 "...puta, vel Diabolus qui tamen malus ille, sive ὁ πονηρόι est, & ad malum hominem hunc tentavit; vel Deus, qui nec tentari malo potest, nec ad malum quempiam tentat, vel affectus ipse hominis, vel aliud quippiam" (Ibid.).

38 "Diabolus causa talis statui non potest; quia ille suasione sola usus legitur. Suasio autem necessitatem nullam affert, sed moraliter tantum voluntatem ad se allicere atque attrahere conatur" (*DTT*, 1.9.12).

39 "Ubi autem moralis, sive objectiva efficientia, præter eam quæ summi boni est, locum habet, ibi libertas resistendi integra relinquitur, ac proinde frustrari potest fructu suasionis suæ is qui ea utitur" (Ibid.).

40 "Ex hoc plus quam verisimiliter concluditur, Diabolum hominem ad peccandum necessitare ne quidem potuisse: Siquidem enim potuisset, utique, pro malevolentia sua qua tantum non ardebat contra hominem suasione & consilio usus non fuisset" (Ibid.).

41 "Nullo verò modo statui potest causa efficiens Deus, quia, nec suasione ulla circa hominem usas est, quæ etsi non necessariam aliquam tamen, efficientiam, aut saltem efficiendi propositum habet, nec imperio, quia expresse vetiut atque interdixit esum" (*DTT*, 1.9.13)

42 Regarding the idea of two divine wills, one revealed and one hidden, see John Calvin, *Calvin's Commentaries: Harmony Of The Evangelists (Matthew, Mark, And Luke)* [CD–ROM] (Garland, TX: Electronic Edition by Galaxy Software, 1999, [Edinburgh: The Calvin Translation Society, 1845]), cf. Matthew 25:1; John Calvin, *Institutes of the Christian Religion*, ed. John Thomas McNeill, trans. Ford Lewis Battles, vols 20, 21 (Philadelphia: Westminster Press, 1960) 1.17.2. Episcopius' argument is like that of Clement of Alexandria: "For neither did the Lord suffer by the will of the Father, nor are those who are persecuted by the will of God; since either of two things is the case: either persecution in consequence of the will of God is a good thing, or those who decree and afflict are guiltless. But nothing is without the will of the Lord of the universe. It remains to say that such things happen without the prevention of God; for this alone saves both the providence and the goodness of God" (Clement of Alexandria, *The Stromata*, in *The Apostolic Fathers, Justin Martyr, Irenæus*, Ante-Nicene Fathers, ed., Alexander Roberts and James Donaldson [n.p.: Christian Literature Publishing Company, 1885; reprint, Peabody, MA: Hendrickson Publishers, 1994] 4.2.11).

43 "Nec denique potentia aliqua, vel physica, vel hyperphysica: quia hac ratione Deo soli tota peccati efficientia in solidum tribueretur, homo verò extra omnem culpam violatæ legis poneretur" (*DTT*, 1.9.13).

44 "Nemo quærat efficientem causam malæ voluntatis: non enim est efficiens, sed deficiens, quia nec illa est effectio, sed defectio" (Augustine, *The City of God Against The Pagans*, trans. James Houston Baxter (Cambridge: Harvard University Press, 1957), 12.7).

45 "Quia nihil primo homini, vel actu creationis negavit, vel providentia sua postmodum subtraxit, aut omisit Deus, quod ad evitandum transgressionem necessarium erat" (*DTT*, 1.9.14).

46 *DTT*, 1.9.15. Arminius had argued similarly in *Conference with Junius*, Proposition 16 (*WA*, 2:173–174).

47 "But in speaking of permission, I understand that he had appointed whatever he wished to be done. Here, indeed, a difference arises on the part of many, who suppose Adam to have been so left to his own free will, that God would not have him fall…. When I say, however, that Adam did not fall without the ordination and will of God, I do not so take it as if sin had ever been pleasing to Him, or as if he simply wished that the precept which he had given should be violated. So far as the fall of Adam was the subversion of equity, and of well-constituted order, so far as it was contumacy against the Divine Law-giver, and the transgression of righteousness, certainly it was against the will of God; yet none of these things render it impossible that, for a certain cause, although to us unknown, he might will the fall of man. It offends the ears of some, when it is said God willed this fall; but what else, I pray, is the permission of Him, who has the power of preventing, and in whose hand the whole matter is placed, but his will?" (Calvin, *Commentaries on Genesis*, 1:144).

48 *DTT*, 1.9.14.

49 "…necessitatio quælibet, sive illa interna & naturalis sit, sive externa & violenta quæ coactio dicitur, cum libertate consistere nullo modo nobis posse (salvo meliore judicio) videatur" (*DTT*, 1.9.17).

50 "Tantum autem abest, ut id quod sponte aut incoacte agit, libere propterea agere dici possit, ut multa, etiam quæ libera nullo modo sunt, sponte tamen & incoacte agant" (Ibid.).

51 Ibid.

52 See Frederick J. E. Woodbridge, "Hobbes," in *Encyclopedia of Religion and Ethics*.

53 Regarding divine permission, Calvin wrote, "But in speaking of permission, I understand that he had appointed whatever he wished to be done. Here, indeed, a difference arises on the part of many, who suppose Adam to have been so left to his own free will, that God would not have him fall. They take for granted, what I allow them, that nothing is less probable than that God should he regarded as the cause of sin, which he has avenged with so many and such severe penalties. When I say, however, that Adam did not fall without the ordination and will of God…. (F)or a certain cause, although to us unknown, he might will the fall of man. It offends the ears of some, when it is said God willed this fall; but what else, I pray, is the permission of Him, who has the power of preventing, and in whose hand the whole matter is placed, but his will?" (Calvin, *Commentaries on Genesis*, 144–45). Junius, to the contrary, hardly left God a basis for involvement when he wrote that God was neither ignorant, nor approved, nor was unwilling, *sed non nolente*, which he defined as permission ("id est permittere volente;" Junius, *Theses Theologicæ*, Thesis 18.12).

54 *DTT*, 1.9.18.

55 "Decretum enim, cum sit actus, voluntatia divinæ immanens, & intrinsecus, voluntatem hominis ad agendum necessitare non potest, nisi adhibeat potentiam, quâ voluntati, ut in alteram tantum partem determinetur, pondus aut efficax quædam motio imprimatur. Potentiam autem à Deo adhibitam dicere circa Adamum, ut peccaret, est Deo totam peccati efficientiam & culpam transscribere" (*DTT*, 1.9.18),

56 Neither the *intellectus* nor the *voluntatio* of God were causative of man's sin; he had only permitted it. He then wrote concerning permission, "Atque permissio hæc tantum est cessatio ab actu tali qui actum hominis reverea impediturus esset, nihil extra se efficiendo, se efficientiam aliquam suspendo. Itaque cause esse non potest" (Disp. Priv., Thesis 30.5, in *OT*, 376)

57 *DTT*, 1.9.18.

58 "Necessitas denique, ex decreto aliquo illustrandi gloriam justitiæ desumi non potest. Præter ea enim quæ dicta sunt si per justitiam intelligatur æquitas, peccato opus non erat ad eam declarandam. Si justitia punitiva & vindicativa, eam hac ratione illustrare Deus non poterat: Iustitiæ enim non est, punire simpliciter, sed reum & eum qui in culpa est. Reus autem & affinis culpæ esse non potest is, qui necessitate peccat, nisi ipse se liberrime in peccandi necessitatem compegerit, & quasi induerit" (*DTT*, 1.9.20).

59 "Concludimus itaque Adamum, liberrima voluntate lapsum esse, propositionesque illas, quibus adstruitur, Adamum alio aliquo speciali auxilio opus habuisse, ut perseverare posset, aut à Deo necessitate aliqua compulsum fuisse, ut laberetur, cum veritate, consistere non posse. Creationis tanquam actua ex mera & singulari gratia actus profecti, gloriam obscurare; legislationis subsecutæ justitiam evertere, & homini justam semper excusationem & exceptionem contra sententiam Dei relinquere" (*DTT*, 1.9.21).

60 "Totum vero hoc peccatum non est proprium primorum hominum, se commune totius generis & omnium posteriorum, qui tum temporis cum peccabant isti in lumbris illorum erant, & postea naturali propagationis modo secundum primevam benedictionem ab illis descenderunt. *Omnes enim in Adamo peccarunt.* Quare etiam quidquid illatum est poenæ parentibus primis, etiam posteritatem omnem pervasit & urget" (Disp. Pub., 7.16, in *OT*, 242; italics in the original).

61 *DTT*, 1.10.

62 Disp. Pub., Thesis 8.1, in *OT*, 242; emphasis added.

63 *DTT*, 1.10.1; emphasis added.

64 "An itaque is, qui semel vere credidit ea fide quæ justificans à quibusdam dici solet, ita peccare possit, ut à fide illa sua, & consequenter à gratia, & salute æterna, totaliter & finaliter excidat? Affirmatur" (*DTT*, 1.10, *Corollaria* II).

65 Hommius used this disputation to accuse Episcopius of Socinianism.

66 Disp. Pub., Thesis 13.1, in *OT*, 270; *WA*, 2:203–210.

67 *DTT*, 1.11.18.

68 However, we may also see an inclination toward Ramist bifurcations. For example, "Et hic quidem affectus duplex, quo, tum in similitudinem Dei" (*DTT*, 1.9.7); "missa duplicli legis consideratione, quatenus vel primis hominibus in Paradiso, vel per Mosen Israelitis lata est" (*DTT*, 1.11.2.); "Naturæ divinæ cognitio dupliciter considari potest" (*DTT*, 2.3.5); "Natura divina dupliciter…consideri potest" (*DTT*, 2.4.2); "Anima hæc considerari potest dupliciter quà actu est, sive qua corpus informat, & qua aliunde potest moveri" (*DTT*, 2.13.4).

69 Disp. Pub., Thesis 13.2.1, in *OT*, 270; *WA*, 2:203.

70 *DTT*, 11.3.1.

71 Disp. Pub., Thesis 13.2.3, in *OT*, 270; *WA*, 2:203.

72 *DTT*, 11.3.3.

73 Disp. Pub., Thesis 13.2.4, in *OT*, 270; *WA*, 2:203.

74 *DTT*, 11.3.4.

75 Disp. Pub., Thesis 13.6.2, in *OT*, 270; *WA*, 2:204.

76 *DTT*, 1.11.20.

77 Disp. Pub., Thesis 13.6.2, in *OT*, 270; *WA*, 2:204.

78 *DTT*, 1.11.4.

79 Disp. Pub., Thesis 13.7.6, in *OT*, 270; *WA*, 2:204.

80 *DTT*, 1.11.12.

81 Disp. Pub., Thesis 13.10, in *OT*, 270; *WA*, 2:207.

82 *DTT*, 1.11.15.

83 Disp. Pub., Thesis 13.4, in *OT*, 270; *WA*, 2:204.

84 *DTT*, 1.11.6, 16.

85 *DTT*, 1.22.24, emphasis added.

86 "Undecima differentia in adjuncta utriusque amplitudine sive extensione respectu hominum consistit. Lex enim Mosis universalis non fuit, neque omnes omnino homines sed Iudæos tantam aut posteros Iacobi obligavit. Atque hic verum erat illud, Ps. 147 statuta sua patefecit fracti, non sic fecit ulli nationi: itemque" (*DTT*, 1.11.14).

87 "...potius minimaque veræ religionis pars fuerunt" (*DTT*, 1.11.6).

88 Ibid.

89 "Ex hac duplici quarta existit differentia, respiciens modum cognitionis seu formam patefactionis. Legis enim doctrina, qua parte mores respicit, æquitati & rectæ rationi consentaneos, quodammodo per naturam cognita erat, ut ex similibus præceptis & promissis, itemque poenis ab omnes ferè gentes usitatis apparet. At vero doctrina Euangelii cum perfectam sapientiam contineat, non sæculi hujus, aut principum sæculi hujus, sed illam Dei in mysterio absconditam, quam nec oculus vidit, nec auris audivit, neque ullus homo in cor intromisit, non nisi per spiritum Dei innotescit: ea enim quæ sunt Dei nemo novit nisi Spiritus Dei" (*DTT*, 1.11.7).

90 *DTT*, 1.11.15.

91 *DTT*, 1.11.16.

92 "...accedente scilicet plenari luce Euangelii quod in æternum manet, ibidem, utpote sancitum sanguine sacerdotis, qui ex vi indissolubilis vitæ, per sermonem juramenti constitutus est Sacerdos, & per spiritum æternum Deo se obtulit" (*DTT*, 1.11.15).

93 *DTT*, 1.11.10.

94 "Lex est litera cujus nulla efficacia est, & mortis ac condemnationis ministerium in literis positum (2 Cor. 3.6,7). Euangelium vero ministerium spiritus vivificantis, seu ministerium justitiæ ac vitæ spiritualis vocatur (2 Cor. 3)" (*DTT*, 1.11.1).

95 "Quia peccatum ex occasione præcepti legalis non tantum in hominibus omnem concupiscentiam operabatur, & veluti irritatum atque exstimulatum reviviscebat, sicque per præceptum interficiebat, ac morti ob noxios homines reddebat (Rom. 7:8–10). Sed etiam lex peccatum retegebat (Rom 3:20 & 5:20), eoque spiritum timoris instillabat, & tantum ad servitutem, instar Agaris generabat (Rom. 8,15; Gal 4:22–24). At vero Euangelium introductio spei melioris est, per quam Deo; appropinquamus, hoc est, à peccatis liberamur, & à terrenis carnalibusque qualitatibus purgati Deo similes reddimur" (Ibid.).

96 "Euangelium vero tabulis cordis carnes inscribitur: quatenus Spiritus S. gratiam uberrimam sibi conjunctam habet (Exod. 31:18, Jerem. 31:33, 2 Cor. 3:3)" *DTT*, 1.11.12.

97 *DTT*, 1.11.13.

98 Junius, *Theses Theologicæ*, 21–22; Disp. Pub., Thesis 11, in *OT*, 262–65; *WA*, 2:189–96.

[99] Arminius offered 25 public and 78 private disputations; Episcopius offered 17 public and 88 private disputations .

[100] *De Ipsa Theologia* (Disp. Priv., Thesis 1), *De Methodo Qua Theologia Informanda Est* (Disp. Priv., Thesis 2), and *De Beatitudine, Sine Theologia* (Disp. Priv., Thesis 3).

[101] "Utrumque hoc cum de Scripturæ divinæ authoritate agitur considerandum venit, ut nimirum plene persuaderi possimus, tam respectu sensuum contentorum, quam respectu Scriptionis ipsius, authoritatem divinam Scripturæ competere, secundum quam & fidem in dictis propter postestem præscriptionis meretur" (*DTT*, 2.1.3; cf. 3.1.3–8).

[102] *DTT*, 2.1.12; cf. *DTT*, 3.2.8.

[103] *DTT*, 2.2.11; cf. *DTT*, 3.3.4, 6.

[104] *DTT*, 2.2.12.

[105] *DTT*, 2.2.10.

[106] *DTT*, 2.3.2.

[107] *DTT*, 2.3.4.

[108] *DTT*, 2.3.5. Episcopius thought it possible to speak about God's essence, but not on the basis of reason apart from Scripture: "Ut natura Dei recte cognoscatur, non necessario tenenda sunt omnia ea, quæ ad essentiam divinam aliqua saltem ratione pertinent, quæve vel juxta scholatum placita, vel ex discurso rationis probabili atrribui illi solent, sed ea tuntum quæ necessaria sunt ad hoc ut cultus illi optimus, perfectissimusque qualem exigit, præstari possit" (3.4.3). Examinations into the essence of God are considered by some to be a classic mark of scholasticism. Consider Episcopius' comments on this tendency and his rejection of both it and the scholastic method: "Alia itaque omnia quæ de divina naturâ fidenter affimari, subtiliter disceptari, aut probabiliter ventilari solent, absolute necessaria scitu esse non credimus; cujusmodi sunt 1. omnia ea quæ circa essentiam divinam controvertuntur, aut censoria auctoritate tanquam extra omne dubium ponuntur, de distinctione essentiæ ab attributis, & attributorum inter sese, de simplicitatis, immensitatis divinæ modis, de omnipræsentia essentiæ etiam in spatiis imaginariis, de æternitatis ratione ac definitione, aliaque infinita hujusmodi Scholarum placita. 2. omnia ea, quæ circa scientiam divinam, ejusque modum quæri solent, an sit idem quod ipsa essentia, & si hoc verum sit, quomodo alia scientia libera, alia media esse possit; an cognoscat Deus possibilia, an infinita, an scientia ejus sit causa rerum, an sit variabilis, etc…. Certe. si necessarium non fit, merito facessere deberent à Scholis & Ecclesiis intricatæ & spinosæ istæ quæstiones; quæ magno molimine de ejus modo & fundamento agitari solent" (*DTT*, 3.4.10).

[109] Disp. Priv., Thesis 24, in *OT*, 364–66; *WA*, 2:355–58.

[110] *DTT*, 2.12, *De Creatione Mundi*.

[111] He repeated this sentiment in *DTT*, 3.8.1: "Sicut naturæ divinæ excellentia & supereminentia Deum cultu & honore dignum facit; ita opera quæ Scriptura ei tribuit, jus, auctoritatem, & potestatem postulandi à nobis cultum & obsequium eidem conciliant."

[112] Disp. Priv., Thesis 24.11–12, in *OT*, 365; *WA*, 2:357; Arminius continued his examination of angels in Disp. Priv., Thesis 25, in *OT*, 366–68; *WA*, 2:358–62.

[113] *DTT*, 2.12.2.

[114] *DTT*, 2.12.4–10. In the third series, he included his theses on creation under *De Operibus Dei* (*DTT*, 3.4.1–3).

[115] "De hoc opere creationis multa subtiliter disceptari aut quæri necesse non est: sufficere credimus, si duo indubitata teneantar, 1. Quod omnia quæcunque uspiam sunt, a Deo in

esse dependeant; ac proinde supremo ipsius solus dominio ac imperio subdita ita sint, ut pro arbitrio suo eorum usum concedere, negare, restringere, limitare, ac prohibere possit. 2. Quod homo talis creatus a Deo fuerit, qui dominari illis omnibus posset, & interim Deo suo dominium illud coarctare volenti, liberrime subjicere seipsum ac submittere. Reliqua omnia quæ ferè infinitis quæstionibus, circa hanc materiam disceptantur, necessaria scitu non esse, pleraque etiam temerariè adseri non pauca falsò definiri credimus" (*DTT*, 3.8.3).

116 *DTT*, 2.13.

117 Consider Arminius' curious expression concerning the formation of Adam's body, "...quidem secundum corpus ex præexistente materi, nempe terra, liquore aqueo & æthereo perfusa" (Arminius, Disp. Disp., Thesis 26.1, in *OT*, 369), with Episcopius' "Primo efformatum fuit corpus ejus ei; pulvere sive terra rubea, id est ex terra aqueo humore mista & macerata" (*DTT*, 2.13.1).

118 Disp. Priv. Thesis 26.1–8, in *OT*, 369; *WA*, 2:362–63.

119 "...ut eo tanquam glutino partes cohærerent, dissolubiles semper natura sua manentes, & reipsa etiam dissolvenæ propter infusi Spiritus vivifici, calorisque innati continuam & perpetuam in humorem actionem, nisi novo humoris pabulo semper instauraretur. Mansit itaque semper corpus hoc alterationi continuæ obnoxium, ex mutua reactione qualitatum contrariarum; adeo ut nisi extrinseca virtute aut gratia aliqua speciali impediretur corruptio, tandem aliquando corrumpendum esset" (*DTT*, 2.13.1).

120 "Sub hac creatione comprehendi volumus non tantum rerum ipsarum productionem, sed etiam virtutis prolificæ in res quasdam inspirationem, ad speciei cujuslibet creatæ perpetuam quandam conservationem. Eam autem homini communem fuisse cum reliquis sibi similibus, secundum speciem generantibus, defendere conabimur: & quod ex eo consequitur, eidem mortalitatem & corruptibilitatem, non minus quam reliquis generationi dicatis animalibus, ex natura tribuendam fuisse" (*DTT*, 3.8.4).

121 Disp. Priv., Thesis 26.2, in *OT*, 369; *WA*, 2:362.

122 *DTT*, 2.13.

123 "Quantitate & extensione sua, licet ad modum materiæ non divisibili, prædita est: per consequens certo spatio, & loco certo, definita, corporique non per adsistentiam, instar nautæ in navi, sed per intrinsecam & intimam informationem unita, & quidem ita ut uniformiter totum corpus animet. Sedes tamen ipsius principalis in corde est. Intrinsecis corruptionis principiis carere, & sic immortalem eam esse voluit Deus" (*DTT*, 2.13.3).

124 "IV. Anima hæc considerari potest dupliciter quà actu est, sive qua corpus informat, & qua aliunde potest moveri. Quà anima sive forma corporis est, immediatum est vitæ principium, seipsum diffundens vi sua per universum corpus, intiméque corpori toti ita sese uniens, ut ubicunque est ibi necessario animet. Qua aliunde potest moveri, indiget externo aliquo objecto excitante, & per sensus tanquam canales ad se derivato: quod objectum cùm apprehendit Sub ratione veri aut boni, Intellectus dicitur; cum ad illud sese promovet per amorem, voluntas appellatur, sive moveat se extra se actu directo, sive in seipsa actu reflexo" (*DTT*, 2.13.4).

125 His discussion here parallels the Greek Fathers on human composition. See John Norman Davidson Kelly, *Early Christian Doctrines*, rev. ed. (San Francisco: Harper & Row, 1978), 159; 344.

126 "Vnde quæ huic tribuuntur facultates, non tam realiter distinctæ sunt ab ipsa & inter se, quam ratione tantum, sive extrinseca quadam animæ ad objecta relatione. Quatenus enim anima objectum sub ratione veri vel boni aut eligibilis propositum apprehendit, aut cum aliis objectis con ferens dijudicat, intelligere dicitur, & quidem necessario. Adsensus

enim quo verum apprehendit non est liber. Quatenus in objectum subtractione boni propositum tendit per amorem, dicitur velle quidem liberrimè" (*DTT*, 2.13.5).

127 Ibid.

128 "…proinde neque libertas quæ fundamentum legislationis est" (Ibid.).

129 "Cæterum ut præesse aliis omnibus posset, intellectu & scientiâ præditum hominem creari oportuit: ut subesse Deo, & vere obedire posset, liberam insuper ei voluntatem concedi necesse fuit; qua non tantum sponte & incoactè, sed liberrimo atque ab omni internâ & externa necessitate immuni motu, divinæ voluntati sese subjicere vel subducere posset" (*DTT*, 3.8.6).

130 *DTT*, 2.13.6.

131 Ibid.

132 "Et has quidem naturales potentias suffecisse credimus, ut Adamo lex ferri posset. Neque arbitramur, aut infusos, increatos, concreatosvc ullos supernaturales habitus, sive formas, intellectui aut voluntati hominis fuisse, aut ut infunderentur aut concrearentur opus fuisse, cum nihil illi à Deo præscriptum legatur, quod non vi potentiarum istarum creatarum præstari ab illo potuerit ineptam itaque quæstionem illam esse, quâ quæritur, an Adam in primo statu suo non habuerit potentiam credendi in Iesum Christum redemptorem suum cum potentia hæc supernaturalis habitus esse, credatur, & talis cujus usus in statu isto nullus omnino esse, poterat aut debebat" (*DTT*, 3.8.6).

133 *Conference with Junius*, Proposition 21, in *WA*, 3:204.

134 "Vidit enim Deus, quod omnia quæ fecerat, valde bona essent. Sed tales tantum habitus in eo fuisse non legimus, quos à supernaturali aliqua gratia infundi necesse est; quique libertatem voluntatis in unam partem ita determinant, ut unde principium peccandi in homine existere potuerit, haud facile videri queat, tandemque ad subtractionem gratiæ illius, aut aliam nescio quam permissionem divinam, tanquam causam peccati deficientem, recurrendum sit" (*DTT*, 3.5.7).

135 "Et diligenter cavendum esse, ne vel eas tales fuisse credamus cum quibus peccandi potentia consistere non poterat ita ut eas à Deo homini subtrahi necesse esset ut peccare posset: vel tales ut per unum peccati actum, veluti per veneni alicujus mortiferi haustum aboleri protinus potuerint" (*DTT*, 3.5.8).

136 "Hanc totam eversum ire videntur nobis, Primò illi qui statuunt, Deum potentiarum harum usum liberum, vel impedivisse actu aliquo providentiæ occulto, vel ad unum determinasse, vel plane abstulisse, aut subduxisse id, sine quo usus hic liber consistere non potentat, postquam homini legem tulit. Deinde qui statuunt Deum antea tale quid de homine decrevisse, quo posito necesse fuit hominem peccare & labi; imo qui neccessariò lapsum esse hominem affirmare non dubitant…. Quæ omnia non tantum creationis ipsius, tanquam actus ex mera & singulari bonitate profecti, & legislationis subsequutæ justitiam evertunt; sed & universum jus postulandi ab homine cultum, eique legem ferendi, Deo adimunt; homini vero justam semper excusationem, & exceptionem contra Deum relinquunt" (*DTT*, 3.5.10).

137 "Finis hujus creationis est, ut homo creatus aptus & idoneus, esset ad actus religionis & obedientiæ exercendos quos Deus ipsi præscripturus erat. Corpus enim animale datum est homini quod affici poterat pluribus quam opus haberet ad sui conservationem. Spiritus datus ei fuit instructus non tantum potentia intelligendi, ut intelligere posset quibus affici, aut à quibus abstinere deberet si Deo ita videretur, sed & potentia volendi, ut corporis appetitui & locomotivæ imperare posset abstinentiam quando eam Deus præscribere vellet" (*DTT*, 2.13.7).

138   However, he did allow discussion over whether God had in some other way prescribed a moral law to Adam, something that he appears to have denied in his public disputation. Compare *DTT*, 1.9.2 with *DTT*, 2.15.8. However, it is possible he merely meant to say in 1.9.2 that the prohibition of the fruit was not symbolic of an otherwise unmentioned moral law.

139   Priv. Disp. 28, in *WA*, 2:366–369; *DTT*, 2.14.

140   *DTT*, 2.15.

141   "II. Lex autem quæ statim in principio lata est fuit lex positiva, qua præscribebatur homini particularis tantum abstinentia à certo fructus genere, in quem naturali inclinatione propendebat, cujus usus ipsi tanquam domino jam ante concessus verisimiliter fuerat. III. Finis enim propter quem lex hæc homini posita fuit alius nullus esse videtur, quam ut Deus sese Dominum hominis esse & manere semper ostenderet: homo vero sese Deo subjectum subditumque esse intelligeret, idque actu aliquo obedientiæ, veluti certo recognitionis symbolo vassali solent, profiteretur. Uni enim omnia Deo naturaliter subessent & subesse deberent, voluit hominem sibi insuper excellentissimo modo, qui excellentissimam creaturam & reliquarum dominam deceret, videlicet per liberam, spontaneam & voluntariam obedientiam subjicii & subesse" (*DTT*, 3.15.2–3).

142   "An verò ex opposito lex hæc promissione vitæ sancita fuerit, etiamsi non liqueat, tamen verisimiliter vel adseritur, vel saltem gratioso & libero Dei favore subsecutaram vitæ communicationem, fuisse, etiam sine promissione, ex æquitatis divinæ indole statuitur: sive illa esset vitæ ipsius felicis & jucundæ continuatio, mediante arboris vitæ qualitate & vi vivifica ipsi indita, sive tandem aliquando æternæ etiam spiritualis &, incorruptibilis vitæ collatio" (*DTT*, 2.15.5).

143   "Bonum tamen hoc, siquidem promissum fuerit Adamo obedienti, ut stirpi & capiti promissum esse non audemus statuere, sed ut personæ singulari & individuæ; ita tamen ut Deum eadem aut simili ratione acturum fuisse cum posteris verisimile & æquitati consentaneum existimemus" (*DTT*, 2.15.7).

144   *DTT*, 2.16.

145   *DTT*, 3.6.3.

146   *DTT*, 2.16.7.

147   "Hanc poenæ inflictionem antegressa est in Adamo & Eva offensæ conscientia; irati Numinis timor & poenæ metus: quorum signa fuerunt Pub. Disp. or ex agnitioue nuditatis, & fuga sive absconsio à facie judicis" (*DTT*, 2.16.8)

148   Ibid.

149   Episcopius did not explain how this could be called "*mors æterna,*" but one may deduce this from passages such as Deuteronomy 15:17, 1 Samuel 27:12, Isaiah 32:13, 34:10 and 17.

150   *DTT*, 2.16.9.

151   *DTT*, 3.9.2.

152   *DTT*, 3.6.3.

153   Disp. Priv., Thesis 31, in *OT*, 377; *WA*, 2:374–75.

154   "An vero præter carentiam justitia originalis aliqua contrari qualitates constituenda sit, tanquam peccati originalis pars altera, disquiri permittimus: quanquam arbitramur versimilius illam solam carentiam ipsum peccatum originis esse, utpote quæ sola sufficit ad quævis peccata actualia committendum & producendum" (Disp. Priv., Thesis 31.10, in *OT*, 378; *WA*, 2:375).

155   "Misero huic & mortis æternæ necessariæque reatui obnoxio homini, totique ex illo descendenti humano generi, nihil magis necessarium erat, nihilque desideratius fieri aut

contingere poterat, quam ut à malis istis miseriæ & mortis vindicaretur & liberaretur" (*DTT*, 2.17.1).

156   *DTT*, 3.6.3.

157   "At vero cum propter legis divinæ transgressionem, hæc mala illi incumberent, à sola gratia & misericordia divina remedium & auxilium expectandum erat: cujus beneficio, loco miseriæ felicitas, & loco mortis vitæ spes ipsi restitueretur, ejusque consequendæ modus benignior & indulgentior ostenderetur" (*DTT*, 2.17.1)

158   "Quodcunque autem præcedere Deus voluit ea non fuerunt nisi rudimenta quadam gratiæ secuturæ, lineamenta illius qua clarius qua obscurius referentia: cujusmodi fuerunt sacrificiorum approbationes aut improbationes, piorum in coelum traductio, liberatio ex perditionis periculo, benedictio, atque implorum contrariæ punitiones" (*DTT*, 2.17.5).

159   "Et quia foedus omne ex natura contractus duabus constat partibus, sponsione & stipulatione, sive mutua & reciproca obligatione utriusque partis, hinc etiam Deus in foedere suo promissione se hominibus obstringere, & hominem vicissim stipulatione officii voluntaria & spontanea sibi obligari voluit. Ut enim appareret foedus esse inter impares & inæquales, sive inter superiorem & inferiorem, promissione seipsum obstrinxit Deus homini; hominem vero lege sua obstrictum sibi esse voluit. Nec enim homo vicissim Deo se obstrinxit sponte sua, sed à Deo ipsi Deo obstrictus est" (*DTT*, 2.18.2; cf. *DTT*, 2.18.6).

160   *DTT*, 2.18.7.

161   "Sicut autem homines isti typus fuerunt, ita etiam populus qui ex illis ortus est typus fuit Messiæ & populi ipsius. Totum etiam foedus cum populo isto initum, adeoque signum foederis fuit typicum & figurativum. Denique omnia fere quæ in eo fuerunt, tanquam typi quidam fuerunt eorum quæ erant futura. Promissiones etiam quibus foedus illud sancitum fuit à Deo, fuerunt typicæ, habentes tantum umbram futurorum bonorum, non autem ipsam expressam imaginem. Quinimo & præcepta non pauca talia fuerunt, quæ pure pute typica & umbratilia fuerunt: quæ proinde adveniente plenitudine & corpore, evanescere & cessare erat necesse" (*DTT*, 2.18.4–5; cf. 2.18.8).

162   *DTT*, 2.19.10.

163   *DTT*, 2.19.11.

164   *DTT*, 2.18.12.

165   *DTT*, 2.18.16.

166   *DTT*, 2.19.16–18.

167   "…noluit Deus id protenus in clara luce sua videndum proponere mortalibus; sed primum promittere, & eminus quasi, positum ostendere inde vero sub obscuris typis, & involucris prædictionum, prophetiarum, cæremoniarum personarum, rerum, variorumque operum veluti occultatum, per transennam & per umbram exhibere, ut tanto magis desiderium ejus in animis hominum acueretur, mundusque universus tam diu luce clarâ destitutus, & in tenebris veluti positus, ad exortum ejus fervidius exstimularetur, ad agnoscendam & prædicandam gratiæ & misericordiæ divinæ magnitudinem atque excellentiam" (*DTT*, 3.6.14).

168   *DTT*, 2.22.1.

169   See also *DTT*, 3.14: "Constat Fœdus hoc novum, instar foederum aliorum omnium, præcepto sive stipulatione conditionis, & promisso sive sponsione remunerationis."

170   *DTT*, 3.6.5.

171   *DTT*, 3.6.7.

172   "Tum præstandæ fundamentum est hinc sequebatur æquum esse ut gratia homini non fieret sine interveniente *peccatorum expiatione*, & sine *novæ obedientiæ*, saltem fidei, stipulatione (*DTT*, 2.17.3); "Ut autem hujus tum *expiationis*, tum *obedientiæ novæ*

necessitas solidius perciperetur, præire multa voluit Deus per quæ ejus rei fides fieret. Quæ causa etiam fuit Deo, quod *expiationem* hanc & *obedientiæ*, hujus postulationem plenam & apertam, non nisi ultimis temporibus, & in fine sæculorum per Filium suum fieri voluerit" (*DTT*, 2.17.4); "Duo itaque ut hic justitiæ amor in Deo esse patefieret necessaria fuerunt: 1. *Peccatorum expiatio per sanguinem*, sive per sacrificii cruenti oblationem. 2. *Nova obedientiæ* ad mortem usque præstandæ stipulatio" (*DTT*, 2.20.3).

173 "Gratiam tamen cum dicimus, eam intelligi nolumus, quâ Deus simpliciter & absolute pro jure & potestate sua, quam tanquam supremus & nulli obligatus dominus ex se, ipso habet, peccatum homini citra ullam intervenientem satisfactionem, sive propitiationem remisit aut condonavit"(*DTT*, 3.6.6).

174 "Utrique huic voluntati divinæ ut satisfieret, personam idoneam deligi oportuit, *per cujus mortem expiatio pro toto genere humano fieret, & quæ obedientiam istam exemplo suo monstraret*, & doctrina sua aliis traderet. Persona hæc fuit Iesus Nazarenus Dominus Noster" (*DTT*, 2.20.4); cf. *DTT*, 2.20.8 and *DTT*, 2.20.11.

175 Hugo Grotius, *De Satisfactione Christi* (The Hague: n.p., 1617).

176 *DTT*, 2.20.2.

177 *DTT*, 2.20.4.

178 *DTT*, 3.6.8. Thesis 9 continued with even more graphic language: "Quia verò actio hæc propitiatoria esse, non poterat, nisi interveniret Sanguinis effusio, sive violenta & cruenta, mors ejus, qui propitiator futurus erat; (sine sanguinis enim effusione nulla fit remissio peccatorum) hinc est quod eam etiam sanguine filii Dei peragi necesse fuerit, & quod peracta revera etiam sit."

179 Episcopius treated repentance in *DTT* 2.23 and 3.16.

180 "...quod Deus cum hominibus pacisci volebat, & in quo spem, vitæ facere non decreverat, nisi sub hac lege & conditione, si justitiam amarent, & odio haberent peccatum, non satis evidenter constare potuisset, remissione ejusmodi semel factâ, aut impunitate simpliciter concessa, quod serio Deus justitiam amaret & odio haberet peccatum" (*DTT*, 3.6.7).

181 Ibid.

182 "Pœnitentia enim aliud nihil est quam serious animi dolor, conceptus ex agnitione peccatorum perpetratorum, ex sensu dominantium, & reatus ex utroque existentis metu, cum desiderio & conamine contrariæ justitiæ præstandæ & vitæ obtinendæ" (*DTT*, 2.23.2.).

183 "Verum autem hunc dolorem subsequitur desiderium duplicis liberationis; a peccati comissi reatu, & ab incumbentis & prementis peccati dominio & tyrannide: cui qualem conatum sive tentamen redeundi ad meliorem mentem, non virtualiter tantum & implicite, sed formaliter etiam atque expresse conjunctum esse oportet" (*DTT*, 2.23.6).

184 "Conatus hic versatur circa actus quosdam, aut omittendos si mali sint, aut committendos si boni sint, aut si ad bonos actus melius & facilius exercendos conducere aliquomodo possint, sive illi sint indicati in Scripturis, sive libere & voluntarie suscipiantur: ita tamen ut hi posteriores poenitentiam non constituant, sed tantam poenitentis animum disponant aut aptiorem eum reddant ad poenitentiam debite eliciendam & continuandam" (*DTT*, 2.23.7).

185 "Unde neque actus, hi dici ullo modo possunt partes poenitentiæ, sive essentiales sive integrales. Tantum enim disponunt subjectum ipsius ad poenitentiam recte agendam aut saltem subjectum rite dispositum esse declarant. Proinde nullo modo cum opinione necessitatis aut meriti fieri, nedum voluntarie suscipi debent" (*DTT*, 2.23.8).

[186] *DTT*, 2.23.2; cf. 2.24.1, where he described faith as "Secundum & primo succedaneum præceptum, est præceptum Fidei."

[187] While *pænitentia* refers to displeasure or grief, *resipiscentia* refers to a state of recovering one's senses or to become reasonable, as was with the Greek word μετάνοια [Lewis and Short, s.v. "pænitentia," "pæniteo," "resipiscentia" and "resipisco").

[188] "Resipiscentia est mentis actionumque ex ea promanantium, juxta præscriptum Iesu Christi mutatio" (*DTT*, 3.16.1).

[189] "Actus fidei hujus est duplex; unus qui dicitur assensus sive persuasio de veritate revelationis propositæ, cuius fundamentum est duplex notitia, una qua agnoscitur Deum esse; altera qua cognoscitur esse aliquam divinam revelationem, seu verbum aliquod divinitus patefactum. Utraque tamen notio hæc non est absolute necessaria ad assensum hunc habendum. Alter actus fidei hujus & qui illum consequitur, est confidentia, se filialis fiducia, qua homo veritati illi Euangelicæ, quatenus non tantum ut vera, sed ut optima & necessaria ad salutem ipsi revelatur, inhæret, quidem cum affectu & quiete mentis voluntatisque (*DTT*, 2.24.4).

[190] "Ut recte intelligatur quod de assensu diximus, observandum est assensum duplicem esse unum qui levis est & perfunctorius, quique subito ex superficiaria quadam revelationis quæ consideratione, aut ex intuitu signorum quæ revelationem illam confirmant, aut ex aliis causis ortum ducit. Alterum qui accuratus, & solidus est quique paulatim, partim per solidam internæ veritatis introspectionem partim per signorum quæ ad veritatem confirmandam adhibentur accuratam considerationem, ex voluntate hominis elicitur" (*DTT*, 2.24.4).

[191] *DTT*, 3.16.2–8.

[192] *DTT*, 1.11.4.

[193] *DTT*, 1.11.10. See also *DTT*, 1.11.19: "fides utrobique præscripta, & fidei justitia utriusque pacti cultoribus per gratiam Dei imputata est (Gen. 15:5, 6; Rom. 4:1, &c, Heb. 11 per tot)."

[194] *DTT*, 3.16.11. For later confirmation of the consciousness of this shift and its implications, see note 279 below.

[195] *DTT*, 3.16.10.

[196] "...sequebatur æquum esse ut gratia homini non fieret sine interveniente peccatorum expiatione, & sine novæ obedientiæ, saltem fidei, stipulatione" (*DTT*, 2.17.3; cf. 2.18.9).

[197] "...resipiscentiæque eundem etiam gradum restitui, licet difficulter" (Ibid).

[198] *DTT*, 2.45.

[199] "Norma præstationis est non voluntas nostra propria, aut alterius alicujus moralis præscriptum, sed sola divina, clare atque evidenter enunciata voluntas, quæ mandatis Euangelii continetur. Qua vero voluntas hæc rigore caret, & ἐπιείκεια temperata est, hinc est quod non intelligatur per præstationem, prefectissima & absolutissima illa mandatorum observatio, quæ omnem omnino defectus & vitium excludit, sed talis quæ ad obedientiæ habitu constituendum sufficit: qui habitus in eo situs est, ut opera justæ Euangelio præscriptæ libenter & perplurium faciamus, & ab omnibus manifestis operibus carnis mundos nos conservemus" (*DTT*, 2.25.4).

[200] *DTT*, 2.25, *Corollarium*.

[201] *DTT*, 2.22.2.

[202] "Agnitio peccati est ipsius conscientiæ de peccato testificantis perceptio, quæ lege divina informata, de eo quid peccatum & quæ peccati vis sit persuasa est: memoriæ autem

subsidio adjuta quæ facta sint intelligit, & quæ vires reliquæ sint experiundo compertum habet" (*DTT*, 2.23.4).

203 "Hujus igitur assensus causa efficiens duplex est: una, accurata observatio, revelationis Euangelicæ & intrinsecæ quæ illi, inest veritatis. Altera, argumentorum & signorum externorum, quæ ad illam veritatem confirmandam adhibentur præcipuorum, attenta introspectio" (*DTT*, 2.24.5).

204 "Argumenta, quæ hominem movere debent ut credat, vel sunt externa, puta miracula & opera extraordinaria vi facta: vel interna, quæ ex ipsius Euangelii substantia promuntur, & talia quibus verisimiliter nihil opponi postest, cur credibilia non sint; quæque quod credibilia sint, sufficienter per se fidem facere possint" (*DTT*, 3.15.10).

205 *DTT*, 2.22.2.

206 Cf. *DTT*, 3.14.3, 3.15.2.

207 "Hic enim Scholasticorum novitium commentum est" (*DTT*, 3.15.2).

208 *DTT*, 2.25.8.

209 *DTT*, 2.46 and 3.25.

210 *DTT*, 2.46.1; 3.25.2.

211 *DTT*, 2.46.1.

212 *DTT*, 2.46.1–6. Episcopius acknowledged the distinction between temporary and spiritual permanent gifts. The purpose for the *donorum variorum mirabilium* was for the assurance of the Apostles and the proof of the veracity of the Gospel, but lasted only for such a time as was necessary to confirm *gratiam doctrinæ Euangelicæ veritas* to both Jews and Greeks. He thought "illi inepti merito sunt habendi, qui eam perpetuam esse, & continua successione durare volunt, etiam postquam totus orbis jampridem factus est Christianus; neque infirmitati isti locus amplius est, aut esse saltem nullo jure debet" (*DTT*, 2.46.5).

213 *DTT*, 2.46.8.

214 *DTT*, 2.46.9.

215 *DTT*, 2.46.10, emphasis added.

216 *DTT*, 2.46.5.

217 *DTT*, 2.25, *Corollaria*.

218 *DTT*, 3.25.5–9.

219 "Nunquam tamen eo usque intendi credimus in hac vita, ut ex fide & spe ista, propria culpa sua, fideles ejusmodi simpliciter excidere nequeant: nedum ut ejus beneficio atque auxilio in peccatis suis securi, aut de subsequutura semper pœnitentia certi esse possint" (*DTT*, 3.25.4).

220 "Promissionibus his opponi possunt & debent comminationes, tum æternæ damnationis, tum miseriæ, atque infelicitatis in hac vita temporaria, qua à Deo circa fideles etiam usurpari in Scriptura legimus.... Hisce positis dicimus: 1. Non esse servile & mercenarium, æterni præmii aut mercedis coelestis intuitu, divinis mandatis ac jussibus obsequi. 2. Imo ne quidem servile esse comminationibus æternæ mortis, ac damnationis respectu moveri ad observationem divinæ legis. 3. Quod magis est, ne quidem promisso hujus vitæ incitari ad Deo obediendum, servile esse: si tantummodo moveamur eam ipsam ob causam, quia gratiose à Deo promissio facta est obedientibus. Quo enim argumento utitur Deus ad movendum & persuadendum, eodem moveri nos non est servile" (*DTT*, 3.25.10–11).

221 Simon Episcopius, *Confessio, sive, Declaratio, Sententiæ Pastorum, qui in Foederato Belgio Remonstrantes Vocantur, Super Præcipuis Articulis Religionis Christianæ* (Harderwijk:

Theodorum Danielis, 1622), cf. idem, *Confessio, sive Declaratio, Sententiæ Pastorum qui in Foederato Belgio Remonstrantes vocantur, Super præcipuis articulis Religionis Christianæ*, in *Operum Theologicorum, Pars Altera*, ed. Philip van Limborch (Rotterdam: Arnoldum Leers, 1665).

[222] *Confessio Remonstrantium* 5.3, henceforth referred to as *Conf. Rem.*

[223] *Conf. Rem.*, 5.4.

[224] *Conf. Rem.*, 5.6.

[225] *Conf. Rem.*, 5.7.

[226] *Conf. Rem.*, 6, *De Providentia Dei, Seu Rerum Conservatione & Gubernatione.*

[227] *Conf. Rem.*, 7.1–2.

[228] *Conf. Rem.*, 7.3.

[229] Romans 5:12ff, John 14:1ff.

[230] *Conf. Rem.*, 7.4.

[231] Apparently the English translator noticed this also, and added the word "eternal."

[232] *Conf. Rem.*, 7.7.

[233] *Conf. Rem.*, 7.5

[234] Ibid.

[235] *Conf. Rem.*, 7.8.

[236] *Conf. Rem.*, 7.9, emphasis added.

[237] *Conf. Rem.*, 7.10.

[238] *Conf. Rem.*, 8.1.

[239] *Conf. Rem.*, 8.2–10.

[240] *Conf. Rem.*, 8.7; 8.9.

[241] *Conf. Rem.*, 8.10.

[242] *Conf. Rem.*, 9.2.2.

[243] *Conf. Rem.*, 9.4.

[244] *Conf. Rem.*, 10.1.

[245] *Conf. Rem.*, 10.2.

[246] "Ad hanc constituendam tria sunt necessaria: 1. Mandatorum præscriptorum præstatio. 2. Præstationis sinceritas. & 3. Utriusque tum præstationis tum sinceritatis continuitas" (*DTT*, 2.25.2).

[247] *Conf. Rem.*, 11.3.

[248] *Conf. Rem.*, 11.5.

[249] *Conf. Rem.*, 11.7.

[250] *Conf. Rem.*, 17.1.

[251] Matthew 11:20ff, John 5:34, 40; 6:44–45 and 1st Peter 1:1–4.

[252] *Conf. Rem.*, 17.2.

[253] Romans 8:28–29, 1 Corinthians 1:24, 26.

[254] Proverbs 1:24–25, Ezekiel 12:1, Isaiah 5:1ff, Matthew 23:37, Luke 7:30, John 5:40, Acts 7:5ff, 13:46, 2 Thessalonians 3:1–2. He added "Contra Synodi Dordrac. Canon, cap 3&4."

[255] Ibid.

256 *Conf. Rem.*, 17.5.

257 *Declaratio Sententiæ*, 3, in *OT*, 121–122; *WA*, 1:659–70.

258 *Conf. Rem.*, 17.6.

259 Jacobus Arminius, *Declaratio Sententiæ I. Arminii de Prædestinatione, Providentia Dei, Libero arbitrio, Gratia Dei, Divinitate Filii Dei, et de Iustificatione hominis coram Deo*, in *Opera Theologica* (Leiden: Goderfridum Basson, 1629), 122; *WA*, 1:664).

260 *Conf. Rem.*, 17.8.

261 Supporting material from the Greek Fathers and various pre-Augustinian Latins is so voluminous that I have used Kelly's research in order to present this material more succinctly. Regarding freedom of the will to chose good or evil after the fall, see Kelly, *Early Christian Doctrines*, 166–68 (regarding the Apologists); 171 (Irenaeus); 175 (Tertullian), 182 (Origen), Methodius (183), later Greek Fathers (349–52), etc. Origin's *De Principiis* merits special reference. Section 3.1–4 presents his defense of free will, in which he specifically treated passages used to argue against it. His comments in 3.1.20 anticipate Beza's handling of Romans 9: "For it will be said: If the potter of the same lump make some vessels to honor and others to dishonor, and God thus form some men for salvation and others for ruin, then salvation or ruin does not depend upon ourselves, nor are we possessed of free-will…. For the Creator makes vessels of honor and vessels of dishonor, not from the beginning according to His foreknowledge, since He does not condemn or justify beforehand according to it; but (He makes) those into vessels of honor who purged themselves, and those into vessels of dishonor who allowed themselves to remain unpurged" (Origen, *De Principiis*, in *Tertullian, Part Fourth; Minucius Felix; Commodian; Origen, Parts First and Second*, Ante-Nicene Fathers, ed., Alexander Roberts and James Donaldson [n.p.: Christian Literature Publishing Company, 1885; reprint, Peabody, MA: Hendrickson Publishers], 4:324–35).

262 "For the Lord knows the heart, and knowing all things beforehand he know the weakness of man and the subtlety of the devil, that he will do some evil to the servants of God" (Shepherd of Hermas, *Mandates*, in *The Apostolic Fathers*, The Loeb Classical Library, ed., G. P. Goold [Cambridge, MA: Harvard University Press; London: William Heinemann, 1974], 4.3.4). Their use of the word foreknowledge does not support Zanchi's later reinterpretation of foreknowledge as "foreloved" or "predestined." They attributed foreknowledge even to Moses, the prophets and the apostles (Clement of Rome, *The First Epistle of Clement to the Corinthians*, in *The Apostolic Fathers*, Loeb Classical Library, ed., G. P. Goold [Cambridge, MA: Harvard University Press; London: William Heinemann, 1985], 43.6, 44.2).

263 Justin Martyr, *The First Apology*, in *The Apostolic Fathers, Justin Martyr, Irenæus*, Ante-Nicene Fathers, ed., Alexander Roberts and James Donaldson (n.p.: Christian Literature Publishing Company, 1885; reprint, Peabody, MA: Hendrickson Publishers), 43.

264 *Ibid.*, 44. See also Justin Martyr, *Dialogue of Justin, Philosopher and Martyr, with Trypho, a Jew*, in *The Apostolic Fathers, Justin Martyr, Irenaeus*, Ante-Nicene Fathers, ed., Alexander Roberts and James Donaldson (n.p.: Christian Literature Publishing Company, 1885; reprint, Peabody, MA: Hendrickson Publishers) 141. See also Tatian, *Address to the Greeks*, in *Fathers of the Second Century: Hermas, Tatian, Athenagoras, Theophilus and Clement of Alexandria*, Ante-Nicene Fathers, ed., Alexander Roberts and James Donaldson (n.p.: Christian Literature Publishing Company, 1885; reprint, Peabody, MA: Hendrickson Publishers), 7.2: "And the power of the Logos, having in itself a faculty to foresee future events, not as fated, but as taking place by the choice of free agents, foretold from time to time the issues of things to come."

[265] The Greek Fathers made clear that they understand foreknowledge as simple prescience of future actions. See Clement, *1 Clement*, 43; Justin Martyr, *First Apology*, 45, 49; idem., *Dialogue with Trypho*, 35, 42 ("of those who it was foreknown were to believe in Him"); 70 ("that the people foreknown to believe in him were foreknown to pursue diligently the fear of the Lord"); 140 ("I have proved in what has preceded, that those who were foreknown to be unrighteous, whether men or angels, are not made wicked by God's fault, but each man by his own fault is what he will appear to be"); 141 ("But if the word of God foretells that some angels and men shall be certainly punished, it did so because it foreknew that they would be unchangeably wicked, but not because God had created them so"); Theophilus of Antioch, *Theophilus to Autolycus*, in *Fathers of the Second Century: Hermas, Tatian, Athenagoras, Theophilus and Clement of Alexandria*, Ante-Nicene Fathers, ed., Alexander Roberts and James Donaldson (n.p.: Christian Literature Publishing Company, 1885; reprint, Peabody, MA: Hendrickson Publishers), 28 ("but God foreknew that man would call upon a number of gods. And having this prescience, and knowing that through the serpent error would introduce a number of gods which had no existence..."); Clement of Alexandria, *Stomata*, 13 (" And the Lord, knowing the heart, and foreknowing the future, foresaw both the fickleness of man and the craft and subtlety of the devil from the first, from the beginning")]; Clement of Alexandria, *Who is the rich man that shall be saved?*, in *Fathers of the Second Century*, Ante-Nicene Fathers, ed., Alexander Roberts and James Donaldson (n.p.: Christian Literature Publishing Company, 1885; reprint, Peabody, MA: Hendrickson Publishers, 1994), 6, ("For He foresaw as God, both what He would be asked, and what each one would answer Him").

[266] Kelly, *Early Christian Doctrines* 347

[267] Justin, 1 Apology, 62; Ibid. 176, 179, 349.

[268] Ibid., 164–66.

[269] Ibid. *passim*.

[270] Ibid. 168–69, 182–83.

[271] John Mark Hicks, "The Theology of Grace in the Thought of Jacobus Arminius and Philip van Limborch: A Study in the Development of Seventeenth-Century Dutch Arminianism," (Ph.D. diss., Westminster Theological Seminary, 1985) 13–19.

[272] Ibid., 24.

[273] *DTT*, 2.11 ("Tribui autem in Sacris Scripturis videmus hanc divinitatem Patri, Filio & Spiritui S. & ita quidem ut eadem tribus illis, licèt non eodem ordine, communis sit, sed Patri à se, tanquam principio & fonti divinitatis totius; cui proinde κατά ὑπεροχὴν nomen Dei, proprietates, actiones & cultus in Sacris literis tribuuntur: Filio, non à se sed à Patre; non per creationem, aut essentiæ solam communionem, sed per veram & realem generationem, sive essentiæ propriam, sed divinam tamen, communicationem: Spiritui S. à Patre & Filio, sive per Filium, per ineffabilem...emanationem); cf. *Conf. Rem.* 2.3, 3 *in toto*, 8.3,

[274] Anton Hendrik Haentjens, *Simon Episcopius als Apologeet van het Remonstrantisme in zijn leven en werken geschestst* (Leiden: A. H. Adriani, 1899), iv. Emphasis added.

CHAPTER FOUR

Original Sin in
the *Institutes Theologicæ*

E piscopius lived for 24 years after the Synod of Dort, a period he filled with leading the Remonstrant Brotherhood, pastoring churches in Rotterdam and then Amsterdam, teaching at the Remonstrant Seminary and writing. His theological works fill three large folio volumes and provide a good picture of his theological battles and personal concerns.[1] The most complete theological source is the *Institutes Theologicæ: Privatis Lectionibus Amstelodami Traditæ*, a conscious effort to record his theology, and the subject of this chapter.

The lectures in *Institutes Theologicæ* have a different attitude, scope and authority than the Leiden disputations. The first words of the *Institutes Theologicæ*, "Dilectii Iuvenes,"[2] convey the image of an older, graver and wiser Episcopius sitting before the small group of young men who represented the future leadership of the Remonstrant Brotherhood. He began the prolegomena with a consideration of the personal qualities necessary for the study of theology. He reaffirmed an Arminian hallmark of the practical nature of theology,[3] and denied the possibility of doing theology based on nature and unaided reason. He specifically applied these to proofs for the existence of God. He employed syllogisms and refutations of major and minor premises only when rebutting similar arguments against divine existence. However, when arguing for the existence of God's, unlike Arminius, he did not use Aquinas' "five ways" or similar methods.[4] Instead, he drew his arguments from divine intervention in history, the trustworthiness of the biblical record and the life of Christ. He concluded that natural theology based upon reason was insufficient either to know or to worship God. If true worship were to be established, it would be necessary for God to reveal Himself and initiate a covenant relationship.

The necessity of covenant led to an inductive study of the three covenants between God and his people. Episcopius examined what each revealed about God, their blessings and their stipulations. He considered this the first step in studying theology, reiterating again the inadequacy of reason and nature.

Episcopius' First Explication of Original Sin

One reason Episcopius gave for the inadequacy of reason as a basis for religion was its inability to overcome the power of *cupiditatis*. "Fleshly desires" lead people to ignore what they know is "in keeping with right reason," and do the irrational which leads to pain and sadness.[5] This "was most clearly apparent in the first man himself," who had every reason to obey a simple command. Neither the divine law, nor threats, nor greatness of God's permission and kindness, nor *even right reason itself* were able to control the desires which were birthed in the man as a result of wanting the fruit.[6] Thus, the ultimate proof of the inadequacy of unaided reason is that it could not even guarantee the obedience *in ipso primo homine,* **in spite of** full provision of his needs, a right relationship with a God of kindness, a clear expression of God's will, and threats of punishment for disobedience.

The "birth" and power of these sinful impulses raised the subject of original sin and Episcopius took advantage of this to address his divergences with Reformed theology on this subject. He again rejected the idea that God had made a covenant with Adam, in that the law imposed did not include any promise of blessing for obedience.[7] In fact, the only entity who held out the promise of "better and more excellent blessings" (*promissionem boni novi ac melioris excellentiorisque*) was the devil. This promise powerfully moved Adam to renounce *quod rectæ rationi conveniens ac justum erat.* Episcopius denied what others had insisted: the threat of death implied the promise of eternal life. If anyone were to say that some promise were contained within the threat, the proof would fall entirely upon him, because it was difficult if not impossible to demonstrate such from the Scriptures, and even if such a promise were someone implied, the contents of the promise were not.[8] We meet here with one of Episcopius' preferred methods of argumentation: holding his opponents to a strict reading of the text and denying appeals to logical implication which Contra-Remonstrants used to had built up "chains" of doctrine based on reason.

Disallowing that the promise of eternal life in heaven was implicit in the text would have raised strong objections from the orthodox Reformed. Episcopius followed with an even more radical denial: Genesis 2 not only offered no promise of eternal life, nor did it impose the threat of eternal punishment in hell. He saw no where in the text where "an eternal penalty in the sense being suggested was contained either in the agreement between God and Adam, nor is it in any way permitted by the sentiments which God spoke afterwards to the transgressors."[9] If it had been originally understood in the agreement between God and Adam, there should have been some indication when God imposed punishments for their disobedience.

Episcopius then suggested the possibility that physical death could have had a place in unfallen creation, that God could have allowed a person to die physically in order move on to a better life.[10] Did physical death necessarily preclude translation to a heavenly existence? Could not God have used physical death, even in unfallen Adam, as a means of translating him from earth to heaven? Would it not be possible to distinguish between this type of death, a natural facet in the passing of life, and a miserable death of suffering?[11] Although it does not overthrow his basic assertion, there is a weakness in his argument. The Christian doctrine of resurrection affirms God's purpose for human existence as an eternal union of body and soul.[12] Some painless form of death within the earthly Paradise as a means of advance would have been possible, but not necessary given the possibility of translation. Perhaps this is all Episcopius was seeking to establish: the hypothetical experience of the separation of body and soul in paradise in contrast to the death with which humanity is presently afflicted. In Episcopius' opinion, God threatened Adam and Eve with a miserable, painful existence culminating in the act of dying, but to go beyond this to include punishment in hell was to read into the text what is not there.

Episcopius returned to his denial of an implied promise. He thought it no light argument that life was not promised as a reward for obedience because God had already granted Adam free access to the tree of life. There was no additional promise in God's "pact" with Adam, and even if there were, neither it nor the threat were rationally sufficient for Adam and Eve to maintain the life God had provided.[13]

If reason were insufficient to hinder the fall, neither could it hinder the progressive moral degeneration of those who lived before the flood and invoked it.[14] He framed his description of antediluvian depravity in scriptural. Its iniquity was proven from the Apostle Peter (2 Peter 2:5) and history (Gen. 6, 8), that "God himself saw that the evil of men multiplied upon the earth, and that every imagination of their heart was evil every day. The earth was corrupt before God, and filled with iniquity, and God saw the earth, that it was corrupt, for all flesh had corrupted its way upon the earth."[15] These strong statements concerning the sinfulness of the human condition set the stage for Episcopius to dispute the orthodox Reformed doctrine of total depravity. His challenge came at the conclusion of the citation from Genesis 8:21 ("Quia cogitatio cordis humani prava à pueritia") when he added "non habet sensum istum, *qui vulgo ei tribui solet; quasi sit: Quia omnes homines peccato originali sunt infecti.*" This verse was especially important because the orthodox Reformed used the reference to childhood to prove total depravity even in children. His estimation that original sin the opinion of the *vulgo* may have been an intentional affront to his Dortian opponents.

Instead of proof for original sin, Episcopius saw here the progressive degeneration of humanity as it rejected both wisdom and Noah's prophecies. If this degeneration had resulted from original sin, then the level of depravity would have been constant and there would have been nothing peculiar to that generation which called for God's judgment.[16] Rather, it was that society of Genesis 6:8 which was so corrupt that people were sinning almost from childhood.[17] It was also too much to suppose some *peccati virus* or *peccati contagio* which equally infected all men even from the cradle.[18] Instead, Episcopius attributed these conditions to differences which discipline, upbringing and environment played in the development of personal morality. He compared young children to clay, easily molded and formed when wet, but when once it hardened easier to break than correct. In such a state, it might even appear as if its form was *à natura*.[19]

Episcopius' use of words like "infection" and "contagion" could appear to deny an inherited sin nature in general, but I do not believe that was his purpose. Rather, he was denying that the depraved conditions of humanity before the flood could be applied to all peoples and societies everywhere; they were the specific conditions of that time. We find a clear affirmation of the presence of a sin principle within the world in the next paragraph. Episcopius noted that the evil "was not restrained by the waters of the flood," nor was it "destroyed and suffocated with all the authors or culprits of evil." Like leaven "it diffused itself throughout the new world," and "rebounded in the very ones" who by their righteousness has been delivered from the flood and soon spread "far and wide." Episcopius cited the example of "Noah's youngest son, who had scarcely left the ark," and the evil men of Sodom, who "polluted themselves with enormous shameful acts which were previously unheard of, the names from which which even the most contaminated mind recoils."[20] These were powerful desciptions of the strength and pervasiveness of sin, and his ascription of this progressive depravity to *malitia* within men affirms the presence of a sinful nature. He does not, however, define what this *malitia* is, nor how it spreads.

Episcopius did explain his understanding of other central questions associated with original sin. He did not view eternal punishment in hell as part of the punishment inflicted by God upon Adam and Eve. People experience death and misery only as an effect of expulsion from paradise. Episcopius based this on a strict interpretation of Genesis 2:15–17 and 3:1–24. He again affirmed the presence of a malicious principle in the world, but denied that all people were equally sinful, or that their acts were equally wicked. He supported this be appealing to the effective results of child-training on the moral formation of young children.

The Creation of Adam

After treating the creation of angels and the world,[21] Episcopius lectured on the creation of Adam, but often differently than at Leiden.[22] He examined the definition of body and soul, including the faculties and *habitus*,[23] then rebutted attempts to reconcile necessity and freedom in the fall. Only then did he consider the *imago Dei*, including it within the union of body and soul,[24] a clear departure from Arminius.

Discussions Concerning Body and Soul

Although Episcopius repeated many ideas from the *Disputationes*,[25] in the *Institutes* he made stronger statements concerning the degree to which the appetite and senses could fight against the Law of God. These powerful bodily forces fought against the Law of God, and for this reason the Bible often referred to sin as *mentio fit corporis & carnis, adeo ut peccata ipsa carnis opera, & actiones corporis, cupiditæs carnis vere vocentur, peccati instrumenta dicantur membra corporis, & peccatores dicantur vivere, ambulare secundum carnem, in carne esse, secundum carne esse, carnales & caro ipsa.*[26] While the carnal may be led by "right reason," only the spiritual are guided by the Spirit of God.

In chapter five, Episcopius discussed the soul's origin, immortality and faculties.[27] The source of the soul was the *spiraculum vitarum, potius vitæ, id est, animam viventem* of God into Adam. Rejecting scholastic tradition, he refused to speculate about this inspiration,[28] affirming only what he could substantiate from the Scriptures. Based on Scripture, he taught that the soul could be separated from the body and still function (2 Cor. 12:2) and was unable to die (Matt. 10:28). It returns to God upon separating from the body (Eccl. 12:7), and so "the spirit or soul of man was a substance inspired by God, thus independent from the body, and able to exit without it and beyond it. Thus they do not pass away together in death, for it can neither be extinguished nor perish."[29]

Episcopius repeated his rejection of faculty psychology and with it any reconciliation of necessity with freedom.[30] The Contra-Remonstrants attempted this by placing the act of faith not in the *voluntas*(the will), but in the *intellectus*. The *intellectus* cannot deny the truth put before it, regardless of what one wills. By moving the act of faith to the *intellectus*, they reconciled the necessity of recognizing the truth with the supposed freedom of the *intellectus* in seeing it. Episcopius refuted their argument by rejecting their distinctions; thinking and choosing are intrinsic to the soul. Faculty psychology may be heuristic description of these functions, but has no reality in itself. He wrote that "If two such powers, distinct from one another, are really established to exist in the soul, then it is necessary that the intellectual power be attributed to one part of the soul, whose proper mode is to understand, to consult, and to judge. To the other part is the power of willing or desiring, whose proper mode is not to judge, nor to understand, but to will and to choose. If this be so established, then it necessarily follows that the will is a power blind to all things, and free from all reason and judgment, in as much as it is really distinct from the intellectual power, it does not judge why it chooses, or chose this because it is better than that."[31]

This discussion set the stage for his defense of free will. In chapter six, Episcopius argued that those who "introduce fated act, the necessary occurence of all things, it is necessary that they deny that liberty or free will be attributed to this human soul."[32] While Calvin would have disagreed with idea of "fatal necessity," he would have affirmed that people had been deprived of free choice.[33] Episcopius argued against this on the basis of implied consequences, that it rendered empty and ridiculous all persuasion, exhortation, promises or threats which serve to turn the will one way or another. These arguments would be as effective as light to the blind, fables to the deaf, or a syllogism to the stupid.[34] Even if he admitted that this hypothesis of a real distinction between these two rational faculties of the soul were accepted by the greater community, nevertheless he was constrained to believe this opinion was false and vain. [35] If the will were truly indifferent in matters of judgment, then there could be no sin against the conscience, nor blasphemy against the Holy Spirit. The same is true if all acts are predestined and happen necessarily. He argued that if an act happens because it is predestined, it most certainly cannot be sin, for nothing ought to be more a question of liberty than to sin, and through sin to make oneself liable to the penalty of sin.[36] Thus the denial of free will based on faculty psychology which divided the soul into intellect and will in order to defend the idea that an act could be both necessary and free was was fundamentally flawed because it presented a false dichotomy in human nature, rendered all moral persuasion irrelevant, and in the end removed the possibility of sin.

Episcopius defined free will as "the power to act or not to act,"[37] the possibility of contrary action. He rejected a definition based on spontaneous action. God gave this liberty to the soul at creation, which continued after the fall. Because freedom is inherent in the nature of man and so an inseparable property of the will, the foundation of choice, it not only had a place in the first state of integrity, but in any state, for a residue remains remains in the will in the state of sin. Consequently sin, which is an act of free power, could no more take away the power of freedom than could virtue.[38] God created Adam and Eve knowing everything they needed to know, yet with the capacity of acquiring new knowledge. The *voluntas* was naturally upright and whole, allowing them not to sin against the Law of

God. Their uprightness (*rectitudo*) was consistent with the simplicity and innocence which existed in that first infantile age of Adam.[39]

Why does Episcopius appear to adopt the use of faculty psychology in this is extensive analysis, when he had just dismissed it as "flawed and morally useless?" It was in order to position his response to an anticipated question from his opponents. They asked if there were not, apart from the naturals, supernatural qualities or abilities such as wisdom and prudence superinfused into Adam's natural soul?[40] First, Episcopius rejected the idea of superinfused virtues as distinctions foreign to the Scriptures, and the three passages to which his opponents customarily appealed (2 Cor. 3:18, Eph. 6:22–24 and Col. 3:9–10) were so inadequate to prove their point that he felt neither the desire nor the obligation to refute them. He thought his only reponsibility was to caution against exaggerating either this *habitus* of righteousness or the power of sinning and the sin which followed.[41]

He also argued that the reason his opponents' insisted on the idea of a superinfused righteousness was because it served to preserve the supralapsarian model of God necessitating Adam's fall without being the author of Adam's sin. When God withdrew the supernaturals from Adam and opened the opportunity for Satan to tempt him, Adam faced temptation with perfect but unaided human nature and unavoidably sinned. Nevertheless, God was blameless because he neither withdrew what was rightfully Adam's (the naturals), nor did he himself tempt the man. While this explanation might have been satisfying to the supralapsarians, to Episcopius this transformed the just God into an unjust and most cruel tyrant, even if they insisted the evil one was the author of sin.[42]

Discussion of The *Imago Dei*

Episcopius placed the *imago Dei* in the whole person (*totus homo*), and was unwilling to decide whether the image of God was some special and notable majesty which Adam bore, or if it were the right of having authority, absolute power and dominion over all things.[43] He did not deny that it had a special foundation "with respect to the substances, abilities and conditions"[44] of the soul, but he countered that "Scripture nowhere places the image of God in these things, but in that which merely appears and shines forth in the whole man, just as is seen from the story of creation (Genesis 1:26)"[45] He argued, based on Adam's relationship to his wife, that "it was on account of this in itself that the man is said to be the image and glory of God, and has command and dominion over his wife (1 Cor. 11:7), nor by reason of his soul, abilities or conditions, because in these and other good qualities, *the woman is often more gifted than her husband.*"[46] This suggests Episcopius was more inclined here than in the *Disputationes* to define the *imago* in terms of dominion.

Adam exercised dominion over all other life by the design of his body and the "scepter" of his reason. Episcopius' description of this dominion is expansive. Man had dominion over all things, not just that which is on the earth, but anything beyond the earth which touches on that which pertains below, plants, herbs, fruit trees and others, over metal, water, fire and other things, not to mention all other earthly animal life, by far his inferiors. He can subjugate, dominate, rule, tame and compel them to work and serve him by bit, spur, rod, whip, trumpet, drum, voice and even by his whisper. Man has ruled flying creatures, just by the aid of diligence and reason. Neither swiftness of wing, nor height of nest, nor steepness of mountain, nor sharpness of claw, nor strength of beak, can keep them safe from the snares, traps, nets, lassos, cunning and tricks of the lord man. Aquatic animals of the sea, which seem to hide in its depths, whose bodies have tremendous size, who seem by their speed and agility to be able to flee from man, man is able to take them from the depths of the sea by hooks, drag-nets and barbs, and use them for his own purposes. Neither mussels, nor oysters nor shellfish which lie in the deep are able to escape from his power, if he were to turn his attention to them. What pertains to beyond the earth, the sun, the moon and the stars of the skies, he was able to adapt to his use as he wishes, to admit or exclude, increase or diminish, cut short or prolong, to hurt or to harm. In addition, man has the power of the free will, by which Adam subjugated the animals to himself, and himself to God.[47]

The *imago Dei* also provided the basis for God's just dominion over man, even the right of annihilation, if God desired. Because he who has given all has the right to take it away. He needs neither guilt nor sin in order to intervene. It included the right of enjoying and making his creation, allowing for the rationality of the creature and supported by his justice. It included the right of legislation, or limiting the power of human freedom, save the use of his free will. It extended to the right to punish his creatures, according to the quantity and quality of his failures and disobedience.[48] However, this did not imply that God could abuse man. His justice and equity prohibited this. God's love necessitated that justice not be unlimited, nor could it be extended beyond what the cause permitted, upon which the of justice depended. God "could not justly cause such great pain upon an innocent man, so that it would be better for him not to exist than to live with such pain, not to mention the greatest pain and evil, that of causing infinite and eternal misery."[49] Therefore the idea of the reprobation of man was absolutely injust. God could not punish Adam for a law which was either imperceptible or impossible to maintain, nor could he justly introduce sin into the world solely to provide an opportunity to punish or forgive Adam. He could not righteously act with evil intent toward an innocent man simply because of his omnipotence.[50]

This led Episcopius into a discussion of God's providence, in which he disputed his opponents' views that attributed the initial impetus of sin to God but denied his authorship by interposing secondary causes and means.[51] Episcopius answered these propositions in his formal consideration of the doctrine of original sin and redemption.

Sin and Redemption

The Results of Personal Sin

Episcopius began this section with a discussion of actual, personal sin and worked toward original sin. He declared that the entire New Testament attributed the work of redemption to "that greatest misery in which the whole human race *fell* by the free and deliberate transgression of the divine commands."[52] Two evils caused this misery, "the evil of death or damnation, and the evil of of the domination or slavery of sin."[53]

Episcopius based his understanding of the first "evil" of eternal damnation on the *loci classici* of Ephesians 2:1, 1 Peter 4:6, Matthew 8:22, Colossians 2:13, Romans 3:19, Luke 29:10, Romans 3:23, Romans 1:18, John 3:36, Romans 5:10 and Ephesians 2:13. However, he contrasted eternal damnation for personal sins with physical death as the result of Adam's sin.

> "By 'this death' is not properly understood that death which was caused by the penalty of death of our first parent which we derive from the inevitability of nature or the law of natural generation, as is mentioned in 1 Corinthians 15:21, "Through one man death, through a man the resurrection of the dead," and verse 22, "In Adam all die." Because that death is not the penalty for our sins, but the natural necessity of dying, which indeed arose from the sin of Adam who was punished with the penalty of death, but that penalty is not incumbent upon us nor meets us. But death is understood of which and by which penalty is which is drawn by own own personal behavior, by that which lies within us, not just with our damnation, but also with due proportion of the suffering and the sense of the evil of our sin. "For all have sinned," says the Apostle," and are destitue of the glory of God."[54]

Thus Episcopius explicitly denied that any one would be condemned for the sin of Adam; the death which he passed to his descendents was merely physical. Later in this section, Episcopius would emphatically state that no one experiences torment "in fire and sulpher" on the basis of Adam's sin alone.

The *malum secundum* is that for which all are called "sinners, lying in and under sin, slaves of sin, in whom sin reigns and dominates"[55] This "consists in the habit and custom of sinning, whether by the commission of one or of many sins, continual or repeated, or at least regularly, whenever the occasion offers itself."[56] However, "Hæc vero consuetudo, quia multo maximam generis humani partem tenet." This "habit of sin" afflicts the greater part of humanity, but not the whole,[57] since "all" and "the world" do not necessarily connote every individual but "*totum genus humanum involvat.*" He did not include in this number either "infants, or the insane or demented, or those destitue of the use of reason or freewill." Because these types of persons cannot sin, "it would be unjust to punish them or to make them liable. Therefore, neither were they liable to be enslaved to sin. For the necessity of dying is from nature, so that it has its place in this matter, excluding no one, and because this suffering is of this manner, redemption even extends to them, that they also may be freed from physical death by special divine grace."[58] He returned to emphasize this especially with respect to infants. Sin depended on free will; therefore, it is impossible for infants to be punished for sin. Their physical deaths were not proof of sin, but are the natural consequence of exclusion from the tree of life. We find here a marked difference with Arminius. While Arminius believed infants could die without grace if they were born to unbelieving parents, Episcopius excluded from condemnation all who lacked the mental capacity either to sin or to understand the Gospel because they have no free will.

Episcopius' Refutation of the Reformed Doctrine of Original Sin

Episcopius' Refutation of the Logic of Original Sin

Episcopius gave his most scholarly refutation of the orthodox Reformed doctrine of original sin in *Institutiones* 4.5.2. He identified the *fontem sive caussam* of the universal misery "to be the guilt of each and every man, or better, the most free will of man." He though it "was impossible that a man should become guilty of sin except by his own free will, or of the wretched penalty properly called, unless by his own guilt, and the sin be both overcomable and avoidable."[59] By saying that *reatus* and *pœna* were the results of personal sins alone, he broke with the Augustinian definition of original sin. He went even further when he argued that nowhere do the Scriptures suggest that men were guilty of Adam's sin. He argued from the use of plurals when Ephesians 2:1–5 and Romans address the sins of the human race, this indicates personal sins, committed willfully and against the dictates of their conscience, as in Romans 1:21. The book of Romans develops God's case against humanity based on personal, rational, willful sin against God, not on the imputation of Adam's sin.

Episcopius then rebuffed the Augustinian doctrine of inability. He asked what benefit was there to knowing God's will when inability to perform was either present or could not be removed?[60] If someone could not fulfill God's requirements because of inability (*impotentia*), then "inability is the most just reason for *one's* defense or of an excuse, from whence it is rightly said, that no one is obligated to do the impossible."[61] He anticipated the rejoinder that mankind had brought this impotence upon itself by asking if there were such a thing as "voluntary ignorance?" How could one bring impotence upon oneself? Certainly it was possible to develop a *habitum* through "many repeated evil acts (*actus…multi, continui, mali*), but a *habitus contractus* could not destroy ability. Men could bring upon themselves a *habitum* of inability to do good, but only through repeated evil acts (*per crebras actiones malas*), and even this was not absolutely true, because if inability is said to have been originated from this freely contracted habit, much more is it necessary that their misery be so considered. Furthermore, because Episcopius believed that a power against acting existed in us not only before but also after the habit was contracted, then the two could only be linked with great difficulty.[62]

Episcopius then specifically explained his doctrine of original sin. First, he used a diatribe to raise the objections of his opponents: "You will ask therefore whether that which is called 'original sin' is not the cause of this misery of theirs which we have been treating up to now, and indeed if it is not the most primary, if not the one and only cause of all misery?"[63] For his rejection of this idea he drew upon two sources of authority. First, he rejected their objection on the basis of an appeal to Scripture, because "in no place does Scripture make mention of some original sin, still less did it allege that this sin is the first and most principle, if not only, cause of this misery.[64] No doubt this denial raised immediate exegetical and logical objections in the minds of his opponents.

But even more interesting is his second declaration, that "*neither would reason permit* that Scripture asserts that this must be believed."[65] Episcopius thought it absurd to define original sin as the imputation of Adam's sin or the resulting corruption of nature to his descendants.[66] *Impossibile est* that Adam's actual, personal sin could be ours; one cannot be held liable for the sin or will of another. *Impossibile est* that those who do not exist can sin. *Impossibile est* for one person to sin on another's behalf, unless they personally agree to it. Finally, it is absurd to attribute any sin to children, much less to people conceived thousands of years after the fact.[67] These are extremely strong *a priori* declarations regarding what reason would allow the Scriptures to declare.

Episcopius further argued that, if imputation of sin is impossible, then it is likewise impossible to impose penalties for that sin; for if Adam's sin is not our sin, neither can his punishment be ours. He wrote that humanity indeed suffers the consequences of Adam and Eve's expulsion from Paradise, but one cannot consider these consequences as punishments. Returning to the

Scriptures, he believed they did not teach that people were born in original or heredity corruption, nor that this corruption was *peccatum nostrum originale*. Episcopius used Arminius' argument from the *Declaratio*: if such corruption were both a punishment and a sin, and all sin calls for punishment, then this sin would call punishment upon itself, *ad infinitum*. And if this punishment caused both a necessity to sin and universal corruption, then God was the author of all human sin. Nor was there reason to believe that this first sin had a special power even greater than later sins.[68] Episcopius denied that "because the whole of human nature came forth from Adam, it followed that the whole of human nature was infected by this first sin." Sin can deprave and twist the will, but it cannot infect a "nature." He asked, if a single act cannot generate a *habitum*, how could it infect an entire *naturam*? If a sinful nature is passed on, why are righteousness and virtues not passed on in the same way? Children born to wicked parents and so share in their natures do not necessarily share in their sins. How could a just God have decreed such corruption? Finally, he returned to his appeal to Scripture. One could not gather the least sign or indication in Scripture that all of human nature has been corrupted. Rather, 1 Corinthians 14:20 and Matthew 19:14 assert the innocence of little children.[69]

Episcopius' Refutation of the Exegesis of Original Sin

Romans 5:12–19. Episcopius then attempted to prove false his opponents' appeals to Scripture, beginning with the locus classicus, Romans 5:12–19: He opened the diatribe with "You will say that, nevertheless, the Scripture openly testifies that all sinned in Adam (Romans 5:12), and that through the disobedience of the one the many were constituted sinners (verse 19).[70]

He attacked the grammatical foundations of the interpretation, beginning with the translation of *in quo* for ἐφ᾽ ᾧ: "Nego in textibus istis dici, 1. Quod omnes homines in Adamo peccarint. Atqui, inquies, diserta verba sunt, ἐφ᾽ ᾧ πάντες ἥμαρτον. Fateor: sed ἐφ᾽ ᾧ significare isthic *in quo*, & quidem sic ut aliter exponi non possit, nulla ratio cogit. Quid enim vetat, ut exponatur per, *eo quod*, vel *quatenus*? Neque enim dubium est, quin isto sensu phrasis ista Græca usurpari soleat apud probatos autores, & usurpata etiam sit ab ipso Apostolo, ad Rom. 8:3, & 2 Corinth. 5:4, Heb. 2:12.[71] His understanding of the grammar of the passage agreed with that of early Greek theologians, as did his conception of the theology of the passage.[72] He argued that connecting "whom" with "Adam" was grammatically impossible because there were nearer, legitimate antecedents,[73] an argument Greek theologians had used against their Latin counterparts. The sin in view in the phrase ἐφ᾽ ᾧ πάντες ἥμαρτον was not the "personal and original sin of Adam," but the personal and proper sins of each and every man who is able to sin, excepting those who cannot.[74]

Some of Episcopius' opponents suggested that the original reading was ἐν ᾧ. He countered, based upon the manuscripts available to him, that the traditional Greek reading was the best reading.[75]

Episcopius' own exegesis of Romans 5:12–19 was creative and perhaps unprecedented. He argued that verse thirteen strictly limits the scope of every other referent in the passage only to sinners who lived between the fall of Adam and the giving of the Law. The purpose for Romans 5 was to set up a comparison between Adam and his descendents with Christ and his descendents. Just as Adam's descendents prior to the giving of the Law experienced death even though they had not sinned in the same fashion as he had (against a clearly stipulated law which invoked the penalty of death), so also by their faithfulness, righteousness and holiness, those who had been regenerated by Christ Jesus received righteousness and life, even if their faithfulness, righteousness and holiness were not equal to or even similar to that of Jesus Christ.[76] By limiting the referant of "all" only to Adam's descendents who lived prior to the giving of the Law, Episcopius not only avoided the idea of original sin in Romans 5, but also negated the Reformed doctrine of justification by grace through faith alone without any consideration of their works.

The Gomarists would certainly have been familiar with the argument that "all" is not necessarily inclusive of "all men" in general, but not in this context. They would also have argued strenuously against the sin in Romans 5:12 as being personal sins. Episcopius anticipated his opponents' response in the form of a syllogism. The sin in Romans 5:12 was that which came into the world through the first man. But it was not personal sin which came into the world. Therefore the sin in Romans 5:12 must be original sin. Episcopius answered that they had inverted the order of origins.[77] Original sin did not come into the world and provoke Adam's sin. Rather, Adam's personal sin was the source of both original sin and death.[78] The phrase *intrandi in mundum* was merely an expression of first appearances, as in 1ˢᵗ John 1:9, 3:19, etc.[79] Furthermore, the word "spread" does not indicate a universal corruption of nature, an unsubstantiated use for this verb.[80]

Regarding Romans 5:19, *per unius hominis inobedientiam, dicit peccatores constitutos esse multos*, Episcopius appealed to his understanding of the argument of the passage. The phrase did not mean that "some sinful quality has been naturally diffused to the many, through which they came to be and were constituted sinners." Rather, God treated the pre-Law descendents of Adam as if they were just as sinful as Adam, in spite of having not broken any expressed moral code, as did Adam. Therefore, God treated them together with Adam in the same way he treated obedient believers as if they were as righteous as Christ.[81] Just as justification is not the infusion of a quality of justice, but a divine judgment contrary to the actual condition of the sinner,[82] so also these sinners were not infused with a quality of sinfulness (original sin), but were treated just as if they had sinned as heinously as Adam.

Hebrews 7:9. Episcopius' insistence that sin must be personal and volitional to be culpable led him to consider a second important passage which his opponents customarily appealed to in order to establish that one could be held responsible for acts of his forefathers, even if he were not personally and consciously present, Hebrews 7:9. "You will retort," he wrote, "that the argument that "he who does not exist in the nature of things is unable to act in other matters" does not proceed, because in Hebrews 7:9 it clearly says that Levi, long before he existed in the nature of things, gave tithes through Abraham, that is, he gave tithes to Melchizedek when his father Abraham gave tithes to the king (Genesis 14:20)."[83] Episcopius' reponse was that the phrase ὡς ἔπος εἰπεῖν clearly indicated that this was a figure of speech rather than a personal reference to Levi. To speak this way as a means of showing superiority is reasonable; to apply this to sin is absurd. He drew comparisons between this offering and an inheritance. If a father gives what would have gone to his son, the son is involved in the gift. However, to say that one may sin in his father or grandfather is absurd. Personal sin must be linked to personal responsibility.[84]

Psalm 51:7. Episcopius began his rebuttal of appeals to Psalm 51:7 with an anticipated question. "If David by these words did not mean that he had sinned in his mother, what therefore did he mean?" He suggested David's words were hyperbolic, an exaggeration of his temperamental and even bloody disposition so that God might be induced to show him mercy and grace. He thought this method of speaking was not uncommon either to David or the rest of the Scriptures.[85] Episcopius found parallels to this construction in Psalm 22:10 and 81:5–6.[86] He thought that, rather than finding support for original sin from Psalm 51:7, the doctrine of original sin had more in common with the opinions of the Pharisees in John 9:34, and rejoined, "Quid enim, si in peccatis nasci, est nasci in & cum originali peccato, annon Pharisæis jure à cæco regeri potuisset, & vos in peccatis nati estis toti, & vos me docere vultis?"[87] Therefore, David's self-revelatory and even hyperbolic statements are not necessarily true of everyone. Finally, he appealed to Isaiah's statement to "law-breakers and profane Israelites," that they were apostates from their mothers' wombs (48:8). Isaiah's intent was obviously not to condemn himself of prenatal apostasy, but to speak of the utterly apostate condition of his hearers. If Isaiah's words do not lead one to a doctrine of general apostasy of the unborn, then neither should David's words justify the doctrine that all people are one being born in sin.

The Augustinian understanding of Psalm 51:7 carried implications regarding personal responsibility. If David diverted the responsibility of his personal sin to original sin, and the corruption within him came purely by divine punishment for a sin committed by Adam, then this would render God ultimately responsible. Episcopius parodied with his version of "the (original) sinner's prayer:" "I admit that I have sinned, but truly, you, God were the cause. Certainly it is by your own punishment to me, that before I existed, you willed me to be a sinner in Adam, and you caused such corruption to exist in my entire nature, that unless you restrain me through some irresistible power in me, I could not only not abstain from any sin but indeed am most willingly inclined to all sin. In this sin my mother conceived me, and it is this which has worked all the iniquity which I have committed."[88] Episcopius asked, who would not find such a statement to be nauseating? Could one give any greater insult either to God or David?

Ephesians 2:3. Episcopius argued that *eramusque natura filii iræ, ut & reliqui* does not refer to the pre-birth condition of the Ephesians, but to their condition after they gained the use of reason and free will. He argued the tense of the verb ἤμεθα indicated a condition which had been true in the past but which was not longer so. If being "by nature a child of wrath" results from *original* sin and not *actual* sin, and if original sin is not lost until death, how could the Ephesians cease to be children of wrath even after conversion? If the fallen nature remains, are they not still children of wrath? If the nature remains, but the wrath does not, then wrath was not provoked by nature but by the sins resulting from it.

He then drew attention to parallelisms between the use of the word φύσις in Ephesians 2:3 and Galatians 2:15. In Galatians 2:15, Paul wrote, "we are Jews by nature, and not sinners from among the Gentiles." Did Paul not believe Jews were "sinners by nature and from birth and so children of wrath?" Rather, in Galatians 2:17 Paul explained that a "sinner" was one who lived in violation of the Law. In Galatians 2:15, "a Jew by nature" was not a metaphysical reality which the Gentiles did not share, but a culture of observing the Law.[89] In the same manner, Paul's use φύσις in Ephesians 2 did not refer to original sin, but was a confession that even the Jews were sinners by practice, in need of a savior.[90]

Episcopius briefly supported his argument from Genesis 6:5 ("Omne figmentum cogitationum cordis eorum tantummodo malum erat omni die") and Genesis 8:21 ("Cogitatio cordis hominis, mala est à pueritia sua"). He concluded: "But I ask, who attributes thoughts, imagination and such to newly born infants? No one, unless he is more foolish and childish than a child"[91]

Job 14:4. Finally, Episcopius considered Job 14:4. His opponents asked, "Iobus diserte quærit cap. XIV.4: Quis dabit mundum ex immundo? Id est, non peccatorem ex peccatore?" He responded, "Quæ consequentia?" His adversary replied, "Immundus omnis est peccator." Episcopius answered that they were begging the question. One needed to specify the type of *immunditia*; they could not presuppose that it referred to moral filthiness. Episcopius believed this soliloquy decried not inborn sin, but the miseries of human existence. *Immundities physica* was a metaphor for all the infirmities, imperfection and corruptions from whence came all the suffering, death, misery, pain, and fetid ulcers which deform mankind, since they usually render mankind wretched and unpleasant to see and contemplate. Because it is true that all men who are born from women live their entire lives subject to these infirmities and imperfections, it is for this reason that Job asserts that all men are wretched, having been born in wretchedness, in order that by this argument he might move God to compassion by his discourse. Episcopius suggested that "Job's meaning is, 'You, Lord, have so excessively afflicted me. Why? Am I not also a man born of woman, susceptible to the same conditions to which all are susceptible? Certainly my condition is not better than those of all other mortal men. Fate oppresses us with all types of wretchedness. We appear to be born like beautiful flowers, and behold, we are hardly born when infirmity comes us, so that gradually we languish, fade, and just like dry and wilted flowers. We are given over to wretchedness and ugliness, and afterwards we disappear like shadows and die broken and crushed by evils. Oh God, why, in addition to this condition into which I was born, do you oppress me with these great and manifold evils? Allow me, I pray, to live with the wretchedness which springs from my nature, free from these dire calamities, until I die. For what remains of a man after death? Nothing, except a wretched corpse and a ghastly grave, wherein which lies the greatest saddness."[92]

Episcopius anticipated appeals to Job 15:14, "Quid est homo ut mundus sit, & at justificetur natus ex muliere, id est, ut justus fit?" by pointing out that these were the words of Eliphaz, condemned by God for misrepresenting both God and Job. Furthermore, Episcopius believed this understanding of *immundia* as a reference to the wretchedness of the human condition fit well within the argument of the book, for Job's friends did not condemn him on the basis of original sin, but for the hidden, personal sins which they believed had provoked the wrath of God.

Episcopius' Theology of Grace

Episcopius treated redemption and grace in chapters 3–15. He began uncharacteristically with a scholastic consideration of the causes of God's grace.[93] That which impelled God to the work of redemption was the misery of the human race. The remote cause was the free will of God's grace. The near cause was his mercy and grace. Mercy impelled him to save and grace impelled him not to save based on merit. As in his *Disputationes*, he balanced mercy and grace with justice and equity. God had the absolute right to inflict the penalties for sin and justice did not demand that God save. If he chose to save, he would have to satisfy justice's demands.[94] As in the *Disputationes*, Episcopius stated that God demanded that man love justice and hate evil, setting up the demands of a propitiatory sacrifice and repentance.[95] Only grace could bring man to repentance and free man from the dominion of sin. He concluded with a defense of substitutionary, propitiatory atonement.

Chapter four detailed the revelation of divine grace from the fall to the time of Christ. Astonishingly, Episcopius used the word "faith" only once, buried in a paragraph concerning the necessity of repentance. He concluded, "For the eternal remission of all sin, and the clear promise of eternal life given to those who repent, pertain to that time, because the time of grace is called κατὰ ἔξοχον, because the perfection of divine grace is placed therein, in so far as God desires to make this remission available to the greatest number of repentant sinners, without any discrimination between gentile and Jew."[96] This omission is an unexplainable deviation from both his and Arminius' previous writings. There is no declaration of the *stipulatio duplex* of faith and repentance, and no discussion of the components of faith, *cognitio* and *assensus*. Further on, in his examination of supralapsarian and infralapsarian divines, he would defend election not on the basis of foreseen faith, but foreseen repentance. Finally he wrote briefly concerning *fides electorum*,[97] concluding that "Therefore the faith of the elect is very agreeably set forth in the doctrine of faith, which they gladly receive and accept, not profane, evil or perverse men, but those who, among other other profane mortals, retain an honest and teachable mind, and thus they are the elect, that is, it is those who fear God who are excellent and chosen."[98] Episcopius still maintained the necessity for grace, in that only God could provide the needed sacrifice for sin and only grace could bring a man to repentance. However, the role of faith had radically changed. At this point, Episcopius focused on the need of repentance for salvation, and what was said regarding faith had atrophied almost to non-existence. In his insistence on repentance and works, Episcopius appears to have abandoned justification by grace through faith alone.

We may observe another notable difference in Episcopius' later theology. In his *Disputationes*, the enabling power of the Holy Spirit had comprised half of God's benefits to man in the New Covenant. The *Institutiones Theologicæ* merely suggests that the grace of God was necessary to bring man to repentance. Episcopius died in 1643, before completing the *Institutiones*. The *Institutiones Theologicæ* ended with the ministry of Christ, and logically the sanctifying ministry of the Holy Spirit would have followed. Perhaps he would have written more about the ministry of the Spirit if he had lived longer, but its absence in the section on redemption and grace was a radical variation from both Arminius and his previous writings.

Conclusion

We have traced Episcopius' development from the young Arminian professor at Leiden to the mature theologian of the Remonstrant Brotherhood. There is much continuity between his earlier and later theologies. He affirmed the *imago Dei* while rejecting faculty psychology. He denied the existence of an Adamic covenant, and insisted that the penalty for Adamic sin was mere physical death. He maintained a three-covenant structure in his approach to grace. He continued to view the older covenants as typological of the New Covenant. He insisted grace and mercy were balanced by justice and equity. Perhaps most importantly, he maintained the spirit of Arminius' theology in his defense of the freedom of the will. Episcopius' opposition to absolute predestination and supralapsarianism never waned. In some respects, his method of doing theology solely based on Scripture and common sense reasoning did not change. His appealed to Hebrew and Greek vocabulary, grammar and syntax show he attempted to ground his theology on the Bible.

However, reason was beginning to limit what he was willing to consider in his interpretation of Scripture. He wrote, "Nec ut adseuisse id credatur Scriptura, ratio sinit."[99] There were marked differences, whether by inclusion, deletion or outright modification in his theology. His analysis of the Adamic Law, the causes for the fall and the means by which Satan tempted man had faded or vanished. However, he changed most dramatically regarding the doctrine of original sin. Instead of beginning with original sin and moving to personal sins as both he and Arminius had done before, he focused on the effects of personal rebellion against God. Sin and bondage did not come from fallen nature but from sinful acts. He denied God could condemn those who are without the use of reason, because reason was the foundation for free will. Sin could not corrupt nature, but arose from the will and could not be passed on to future generations. Rather than blaming aberrant behavior on original sin, he emphasized environment and the necessity of child-training. Still, he acknowledged both *cupiditatis* in the human nature which drives men to sin against reason and an principle of evil (*malitia*) both in the world and the person. He made stronger statements concerning how ones physical desires fought against the Law of God. He strongly affirmed the need for the substitutionary death of Christ as a propitiatory sacrifice for sin; however, the role of faith had changed, if not disappeared. The message of the Gospel had become one of repentance, and he no longer gave a dynamic role to the power of the Holy Spirit to overcome the dominion of sin.

We have seen radical change in both Episcopius' theology and method. We must now answer the question of whether it is possible that the mature Episcopius can be considered the legitimate heir of Arminius' theology.

Notes

1. Simon Episcopius, *Opera Theologica*, ed. Stephanus Curcellæus (Amsterdam: Ioannis Blæv, 1650); idem, *Operum Theologicorum, Pars Altera*, ed. Philip van Limborch, (Rotterdam: Arnoldum Leers, 1665); and idem, *Predicatien van M. S. Episcopius*, ed. Philip van Limborch (Amsterdam: Isaak Pieterz., 1693).

2. *IT* 1.1; *OT 1:1*. These are large, folio pages. In order to avoid excessive citations, successive quotations from the same page will not be cited.

3. "Theologiam non est scientiam speculativam, sed practicam: Nec esse, ut quidam volunt, partim speculativam, partim practicam, nedum, ut alii, maximum partem speculativam. Purè practica est" (*IT*. 1.2; *OTE* 1:4)

4. "Rational" meaning arguments drawn from unaided reason, as opposed to arguments drawn from revelation.

5. "Hinc facile evenit, ut nisi homo vel cognoscat, vel cogitet, si actiones rectæ rationi convenientes, appetitu isto intelligibili ductus faciat, futurum ut inde commodum & emolumentum aliquod consequatur, putà vel honorem, vel divitias, vel voluptatem, vel commoda aliqua sensibilia & grata carni suæ, vel quæ his multò sunt majora, contrariaque mala effugiat, actiones istas missas faciat, etiamsi eas alioqui rationis rectæ instinctu impulsus facere vellet; & contra actiones illas quæ rationi rectæ non sunt consentaneæ, faciat, etiamsi istas facere alioquin nollet, & in faciendis istis sentiat atque experiatur luctam, dolorem, & displicentiam aliquam ex rationis rectæ dictamine" (*IT*. 1.10; *OTE* 1:22).

6. "…simulatque ei interdiceretur vesci ex arbore aut fructu arboris unius, quem carni aut sensibus suis gratum esse sentiebat, concessa interim licentia vescendi ex omnibus arborum omnium fructibus quos cuperet ac desideraret. Nec ipsa divina lex ore tenus ei lata, nec sanctio comminationis legi addita, nec magna ista licentia, aut potius divina indulgentia, nec recta ipsa ratio frænarunt appetitum ejus sensibilem; quin imò sola utilitatis ex esu fructus illius consecuturæ spes aut cogitatio aliunde ei injecta, stimulum ei subdidit ut appetitus alterius fræno excutiendo consilium coeperit, adeoque frænum ejus excusserit: usque adeo potens est innatum desiderium in bonum utile & delectabile" (ibid.).

7. "Et notatu dignum est, legem primo homini latam, nulla boni novi aut melioris promissione sancitam fuisse, sed sola malorum aut mortis comminatione" (ibid.).

8. "Si quis dicat promissionem divinam, comminatione oppositam, sub comminatione comprehensam fuisse, illi probatio ejus rei incumbit. In Scriptura promissionis nullam mentionem fieri certissimum est: & posito quod aliqua omnino promissio comprehensa comminatione concederetur, quæ tamen aut quanta ea fuerit, difficile, imo fortè impossibile est designare. Pone enim comminationem esse de morte æternam ac necessaria, quæ pæna damni sit, (pænam enim æternam sensus, quæ dicitur, hac comminatione contineri nullo pacto mihi sit verisimile, nec sententia ipsa Dei postmodum in transgressores lata, id ullo modo sinit) non sequitur, Deus comminatur

primo homini æternam pænam damni si transgrediatur, ergo promittit ei tacite æternam vitam si non transgrediatur" (ibid.).

9 "Pone enim comminationem esse de morte æternam ac necessaria, quæ pæna damni sit, (pænam enim æternam sensus, quæ dicitur, hac comminatione contineri nullo pacto mihi sit verisimile, nec sententia ipsa Dei postmodum in transgressores lata, id ullo modo sinit) non sequitur, Deus comminatur primo homini æternam pænam damni si transgrediatur, ergo promittit ei tacite æternam vitam si non transgrediatur" (ibid.).

10 "Cur enim non potuisset Deus sincere hominem mori, & deinde eum ex morte transferre in meliorem vitam?" (ibid.).

11 "Cur enim non potuisset Deus sincere hominem mori, & deinde eum ex morte transferre in meliorem vitam? Mors enim illa non comprehensa fuisset comminatione ista, nec exclusa promissione. Tum si rem pressius consideremus; nec sequitur quidem, Deus comminatur homini mortem, si edat ex fructu vetito, ergo promittit vitam, si non edat. Aliud enim est mortem comminati ut pænam, aliud permittere ut mors homini naturaliter eveniat sine ratione pænæ. & quid si mors quam comminatur Deus, significare dicatur mortem tristem, immaturam, & ad quam non nisi per molestias ac miserias multas perveniendum erat? Ita certè sententia à Deo deinde lata, mortis vocem accipiendam esse arguit, & sic pænam mortis; lege sua Deus comminatus dicitur prævaricatoribus, quæ distincta erat à morte, quæ omnibus ex naturæ conditione evenit" (ibid).

12 1 Corinthians 15; 2 Corintians 5:1–6.

13 "Non leve mihi argumentum videtur, Deum promissionem non fecisse Adamo, quia arborem vitæ collocaverat in horto, ut ex ea ederet Adamus ipse si vellet: at si promisisset vitam, non permisisset arborem illam libero ejus arbitrio, sed vitâ tanquam præmio obedientiæ ipsum donasset. Ut ut sit, promissionem à talem primis hominibus intellectam non fuisse id satis arguit, quòd promissionem Diaboli pluris fecerint, eaque permoveri se siverint, ut divino jussui morem non gererent" (ibid.).

14 "Et sane si sequentia secula id est fere bis mille annos consecutos videamus, ea promissionum expertia fuisse comperiemus: atque inde fortasse factum esse, quod mortales qui istis seculis vixerunt plerique, si non omnes, usque adeò à rectæ rationis norma & regula deflexerint, & sensibus suis obsecuti fuerint, ac paulatim etiam magis magisque, partim exemplis, partim consuetudine in pejus degeneraverint, vincente rationis rectæ instinctum carnalium ille cebrarum desiderio, ac studio voluptatum: uti in Caino, in Lemecho, cæterisque adeò omnibus mortalibus (exceptis tribus istis, quos diximus solos recenseri, ac fortasse duobus tantum) observare est, usque ad diluvii tempora: quibus adeò invaluerat carnis studium, ut unus tantum Noachus inter eos justus fuisse reliquus legatur, isque nec exemplo, nec præconio suo, nec divinæ misericordiæ & indulgentiæ annunciatione, improbitatem jam grassantem sistere posset ac reprimere" (ibid.).

15 "Unde & mundum illum, mundum impiorum fuisse ait Apostolus Petrus, 2. Epist. 2:5. & historia ipsa testatur, Genes. 6 & 8 cap. ipsum Deum vidisse quod multa esset malitia hominum super terram, & quod omne figmentum cordis eorum tantummodo esset malum omni die. Cap. 6 vers 5. quod aliis verbis effertur vers 11 & 12: Corrupta erat terra coram Deo, & repleta erat ipsa iniquitate; viditque Deus terram, & ecce corrupta erat; nam corruperat omnis caro viam suam super terram. Locus verò cap. 8. 21. Quia cogitatio cordis humani prava à pueritia" (ibid).

16 "Nihil minus, sic enim eadem ratio quæ Deum moverat ad diluvium mundo immittendum, Deum movisset ad diluvium mundo imposterum non immittendum" (ibid.)

17 "Sed sensus est; etiamsi cogitatio cordis humani adeò corrupta foret, ut à teneris quasi unguiculus homines peccarent; (particula כ significat aliquando *quamvis*, ut Hebræi adnotant) tamen non amplius sic cum iis agam uti egi" (ibid.).

[18] "Supponit tantum ista divina locutio factum fuisse ut peccati virus etiam ad primos adolescentes propagaretur, & fieri iterum posse, ut peccati contagio adeo inficiat omnes homines, summos imosque, ut nulla ætas, ne prima quidem, immunis sit quominus statim, atque ab ipsis pene cunabulis, ad nequitiam, dictis, factis, gestibus; moribus, exemplisque peccantium quasi formetur aut contaminetur, atque ita ad malum omne jam prona sit, antequam quid malum sit intelligat" (ibid.)

[19] "Rudis enim ætas cerea est & in vitium ductilis ac sequax, argillæ instar, quæ uda dum est formam facile suscipit quam imprimit fingentis manus; siccata vero eam adeò pertinaciter retinet, ut eam citius frangas quàm corrigas, non aliter quam si à natura sit facta, & in eam formam efficta esset" (ibid).

[20] "Sed nec stetit malitia, aquis diluvii repressa, & extinctis suffocatisque omnibus penè malitiæ auctoribus aut reis, sed veluti fermenti instar sese diffundit in novum orbem, aut potius repullulavit in iis quos sua probitas destinatæ exemisse videbatur sententiæ, adeò ut statim eruperit in iis ipsis, & paulatim iterum longè lateque propagata fuerit. In filio ipso Noachi minimo natu prodidit se vixdum ex arca egresso; & non multò post in populis ac regionibus integris exeruit se tanta cum fertilitate, ut aliquando ne decem quidem in iis reperire fuerit qui integri vitæ & sceleris puri essent, imo ut enormibus flagitiis sese polluerent, quæ inaudita antea fuerant, & à quorum nominibus abhorret etiam contaminatissima mens" (ibid).

[21] *IT.* 4.3.1–2; *OTE* 1:346–49.

[22] *IT.* 4.3.4–7; *OTE* 1:352–60.

[23] *IT* 4.3.5–6; *OTE* 1:353–58.

[24] "Ad imaginem hanc constituendam concurrunt Corpus & Anima" (*IT* 4.3.7; *OTE* 1:359).

[25] Episcopius raised interesting, thought-provoking questions here, only not to answer them: "Quæ porro ad corporis istius structuram & conformationem, partiumque in eo omnium, tum situm, tum fucntiones functionumque proprietates, & nominatim privilegia sive prærogativas eis adsignatas attinent, ea Philosophis & Medicis relinquimus, imprimis Anatomicis" (ibid.). It was sufficient for the theologian to know the reason for which God had formed the body, namely *ad Religionis negotium* (ibid.).

[26] Ibid.

[27] "De anima hominis, ejusque immortalitate & intelligendi facultate."

[28] "Quæ, qualis aut quomodo facta fit hæc inspiratio, nec necesse est anxiè inquirere, nec possibile certò definire, nec tutum hariolari aut conjicere, ne Deo inspiratori aut indignum quid attribuamus, aut dignum detrahamus. Certum est, actione hac particulari, & qua sola atque unica veluti nobili actione Deus uti voluit, excellentiam animæ humanæ supra cætera omnia creata designati" (*IT* 4.3.5; *OTE* 1:354).

[29] "Spiritum sive animam hominis à Deo homini inspiratum, substantiam esse, à corpore ita independentem, ut sine eo & extra illius subsistere possit, ac proinde cum eo per mortem extincto aut pereunt, non extinguatur nec pereat" (ibid).

[30] "Intellectus hic & voluntas potentiæ sive facultates vocatari solent, quæ distinctæ sint realiter, tum ab anima ipsa, tum inter se. *De quo merito dubitari potest.* Quid enim vetat credere animam rationalem esse immediatum principium intellegendi & volendi, & immediatum tum intellectionis tum volitionis subjectum? Certe nihil (*IT* 4.3.5; *OTE* 1:355).

[31] "Si tales potentiæ duæ realiter inter se distinctæ statuantur in anima locum habere, tum necesse est ut animæ tribuatur ex una parte potentia intellectiva, cui proprium quarto modo sit intelligere, consultare, judicare; ex altera parte potentia volendi sive appetendi, cui proprium quarto modo sit non judicare, non intelligere, sed velle atque eligere. Id si statuatur, tum necessario sequetur voluntatem tanquam potentiam omnino cæcam, & rationis ac judicii omnis expertem, puro quodam impetu & motu, id est stulto vel desultorio, ferri in objectum ab intellectu monstratum, vel à judicio rationis practico

necessario trahi ac determinari, ad volendum & appetendum omne id quod intellectus practicus eligendum esse imperat, qui ipsa bruta & cæca potentia existens, utpote ab intellectiva potentia realiter distincta, non judicat quare eligat, aut hoc potius quam illus eligat" (ibid.; *OTE* 1:355).

32 "...fatalem rerum omnium, actionem, eventuum necessitatem inducunt, ii necesse est ut libertatem sive liberum arbitrium in anima humana dari negent" (*IT* 4.3.6; *OTE* 1:356).

33 John Calvin, *Institutes of the Christian Religion*, ed. John Thomas McNeill, trans. Ford Lewis Battles (Philadelphia: Westminster Press, 1960), 2.2. Calvin ridiculed the idea that one could say man has a free will because he sins willingly: "In this way, then, man is said to have free will, not because he has a free choice of good and evil, but because he acts voluntarily, and not by compulsion. This is perfectly true: but why should so small a matter have been dignified with so proud a title? An admirable freedom! that man is not forced to be the servant of sin, while he is, however, ἐθελοδοῦλος (a voluntary slave); his will being bound by the fetters of sin" (Institutes 2.2.7). For Calvin's arguments against free will, see *Institutes*, 2.5.

34 "...vanæ & ridiculæ sint omnes suasiones, horationes, promissiones, comminationes etc. quæ adhiberi solent ad flectendum voluntatem in hanc vel in illam parte. Tantundem quippe sunt voluntati argumenta ista, atque cæco lux, surdo fabula, & bruto Syllogismus" (ibid.; *OTE* 1:357).

35 "...etsi sententiam hanc fateor colorem non tenuem accipere à communi & recepta hypothesi, id est, à distinctione reali, quæ inter duas animæ rationalis facultates esse dicitur, tamen, quia hypothesin illam falsam esse aut vanam supra sum arbitratus, sententiam etiam quæ ei superstruitur falsam esse ut credam necesse est" (ibid).

36 "Si libertas voluntatis in indifferentia ista judicii ponatur, & in lubente judicii practici sequela quam voluntas facit, tum nullum peccatum contra conscientiam, nedum blasphemia in Spiritum sanctum dari potest. Consequentia per se liquet: nisi quis Atheum se profiteatur, & contendat non modo non dari peccatum ullum contar conscientiam, nedum in Spiritum sanctum, sed no peccatum quidem ullum, isto ipso fundamentum nixus, quod omnia necessario ac fataliter fiant. Quod enim necessario fit, id peccatum esse non posse certissimum est. Nihil enim magis liberum esse debet, quam peccare, & per peccatum reum se facere pænæ" (ibid).

37 "...posse agere & non agere," (*IT* 4.3.6; *OTE* 1:358).

38 "...quæque non tantum in primo statu integritatis locum habuit, se in omni statu, etiam in statu peccati in voluntate reliqua manet, quia naturalis, ac proinde inseparabilis à voluntate proprietas est, quatenus voluntas principiam electionis est. Peccatum enim, quis liberæ potentiæ actio est; potentiam ipsam liberam tollere non potest: non magis quam virtum, quæ etiam liberæ potentiæ actio est, libertatem potest tollere" (ibid).

39 "...itaque hæc in simplicitate & innocentia constitat, quæ ætati isti primæ Adami, tanquam infantili, conveniens fuit" (ibid).

40 "Quares: An præter hic naturalia, non etiam superinfusæ animæ Adami, qualitates sive habitus supernaturales; nempe in intellectum scientia rerum non modo naturalium omnium, sed & supernaturalium conjuncta cum sapientia & prudentia in rebus & actionibus, omnibus ad debitum finem ordinandis ac dirigendis. In voluntatem justitia originalis, qua fiebat ut non vellet nisi quod justum esset, & dictamini rationis rectæ sive sapientiæ ac prudentiæ conveniens. In affectus sanctas, qua motus omnes tum appetitus concupiscibilis, tum irascibilis contra rationem insurgentes comprimebantur; ita ut nulla esset in homine rationis & sensuum rebellio, sed mera quies & concordia, tum inter corpus & animam, tum inter inferiorem animæ partem & superiorem, tum inter superiorem & Deum ipsum" (ibid).

41 (N)on video id fundamentum ullum in Scriptura certum habere: loca enim illa tria, 2 Corinthios 3:18, Ephesios 6:22–24, Colossenses 3:9–10 quæ fundandæ isti sententia adduci solent, non videntur mihi; idonea, nedum sufficientia ad eam comprobandam

esse; tamen cur receptæ & passivæ opinioni isti refragari aut velim aut debeam non reperi: dummodo unum hoc diligenter caveatur, ne habitus istos sic extollamus, ut potentia peccandi, & peccatum quod secutum est, cum illis non videantur consistere aut componi posse (ibid.; *OTE* 1:358–59).

[42] "Quo fine? ut nempe Deum faciant $\dot{\alpha}\nu\tau\epsilon\xi o\acute{\nu}\sigma\iota o\nu$, qui jus habet agendi cum homine pro suo arbitrio, id est, dandi habitus per quos à peccato immunis conservertur, & rursus adimendi istos ipsos: ut in peccatum incidere tam necesse ei fit, quam lapidi, super medio se leviore posito, ex alto in imum cadere: id est, ut uno verbo dicam ut Deum liberum faciant, injustum eum, Tyranno quovis crudeliorem & Diabolum, id est peccati autorem faciunt" (ibid.; *OTE* 1:359).

[43] "…vel majestatem aliquam egregiam & insignem, divinæque similem, inter creata omnia gerens, vel jus, authoritatem, imperium & dominium habens in omnia, Dei instar."

[44] "…respectu substantiæ, facultatum & habituum."

[45] "Scriptura nuspiam in iis imaginem Dei collocet, sed in eo dumtaxat quod in toto homine apparet ac relucet; uti manifestum est ex creationis historia, Gen. 1:26" (ibid).

[46] "…ex eo quod ob id ipsum quod vir imperium ac dominium habeat in uxorem suam, *imago* & gloria Dei vocetur, 1 ad Corinth. XI.7, non ratione animæ aut facultatum, aut habituum; *quia iisdem & sæpe melioribus, prædita est uxor quam maritus* (ibid., emphasis added).

[47] "Dominari potest homo in omnia, non sublunaria tantum sed & supralunaria quod ad sublunaria attinet, ut de plantis, herbis, fruticibus, arboribus, metallis, aqua, igne ac re, &c. nihil dicam, animantia omnia terrestria, quamquam viribus longe iis impar, subigere, domare, regere, flectere, atque ad operas & ministeria sua cogere potest, fræno, stimulo, baculo, flagro, tuba, tympano, sistula, voce, ac vel sibilo. Volucria omnia hominem rectorem habent, solius industriæ ac Rationis auxilio. Nec alarum pernicitas, nec nidorum sublimitas, nec montium præcipitia, nec unguium acumina, nec rostrorum robora, ea tuta atque immunia præstare possunt ab insidiis, à cassibus, à retibus, à laqueis, à dolo & fraude hominis dominatoris. Aquatilia, quæ ipsa maris. profunditate abscondita videntur, quæ corporum suorum mole tremenda sunt, quæ celeritate sua ac pernicitate effugere hominem posse videntur, ea homo hamis, retibus sagenis, uncis ex profundo maris educere, & in usum suum convertere potest; adeo ut ne conchylium, ne ostreum, ne mitulus quidem in imo fundo latitare possit, quod ille non sui juris facere possit, si rationem industriam acuat. Quod ad supralunaria attinet; Solis Lunæque & astrorum lumen usibus suis prout vult aptare potest: admittere, excludere augere, minuere intendere, extendere, ad juvandum, ad nocendum adhibere potest. Neque quidquam in rerum universitate dari potest, quo homo aut uti aut frui non possit ope rationis & industriæ suæ ac solertiæ" (ibid).

[48] "1. in jure Annihilationis, si Deus velit. Qui enim totum dedit, is totus tollendi jus habet. Nec culpæ nec peccati meritum ut interveniat necesse est. 2. in jure utendi, & de creatura faciendi, quicquid ration creationis, & æquitas ei innixa, permittit. 3. In jure legislationis, sive voluntatis humanæ potestatem circumscribendi, salvo usu voluntatis liberæ. 4. In jure puniendi creaturam, pro quantitate & qualitate delicti sive inobedientiæ" (*IT* 4.3.6; *OTE* 1:360).

[49] "…non posse tamen jure eum innoxium dolore tanto adficere, ut homini melius esset non esse, quam cum dolore isto esse ac vivere, nedum summo dolore ac malo, id est, infinita & æterna miseria adficere.." (ibid.).

[50] Ibid.

[51] *IT* 4.4; Ibid.

[52] "…summa miseria, in quam humanum genus totum, liberrima & ultronea legum divinarum transgressione" (*IT* 4.5.1; *OT* 1:401; one notes that in this section Episcopius also lectured on questions about the authorship and canonicity of the New Testament, and theological differences between the books of the New Testament).

53 "…malo scilicet mortis seu damnationis, & malo dominii seu servitutis peccati" (ibid.)

54 "Per mortem hanc &c. non intelligitur proprie mors ista, quam ex primo parente mortis pæna adfecto, inevitabili naturæ aut generationis lege trahimus, juxta id quod dicitur I ad Corinth. xv.21. Per hominum mors, per hominem resurrection mortuorum. & vers. 22. In Adam omnes moriuntur. quia mors illa non est pæna peccatorum nostrorum, sed naturalis tantum moriendi necessitas, orta quidem ex peccato Adami, mortis poena puniti, sed nobis tamen non incumbens aut obveniens ut pæna. Sed intelligitur mors, quæ & qua pæna est propria nostra culta attracta, & qua talis nobis incubitura, non cum damno tantum nostro, sed & cum dolore & sensu mali, peccatorum nostrorum, meritis proportionato. Omnes enim peccaverunt, inquit Apostolus, & deficiuntur gloria Dei" (ibid).

55 "…peccatores, in peccato aut sub peccato jacentes, servi peccatorum, in quibus peccatum regnat aut dominatur, &c." (ibid.).

56 "…constitit in habitu & conseutudine peccandi, id est, vel unius, vel plurium peccatorum continua vel crebra, vel saltem ordinaria, si occasio se offerat, patratione" (ibid.).

57 "Hæc vero consuetudo, quia multo maximam generis humani partem tenet" (ibid.).

58 "Infantes…quà tales, uti & fatuos, insanos, amentes aut rationis & voluntatis liberæ usu destitutos, sub iis comprehensos nolumos. Hi enim, quia peccare non possunt, jure etiam puniri, ac proinde miseriæ tanquam pænæ obnoxii fieri non possunt. Servituti ergo peccati ut obnoxii reddantur, impossibile est. Naturalis tamen ista moriendi necessitas, quin in iis locum habeat, nihil vetat, & quia illa ipsa aliquomodo miseria est, redemptio etiam ad eos pertinere potest, qua fiat, ut à morte ipsa illa liberentur, ex divina speciali gratia" (ibid.).

59 "…esse suam propriam cujusque hominis culpam, sive potius liberrimam hominis voluntatem; quia impossibile est ut homo aut peccati reus fiat absque propria voluntate sua libera; aut pænæ sive miseriæ proprie dictæ absque culpa sua, eaque vincibili aut evitabili" (IT 4.5.2; OTE 1:402).

60 "Quid enim scientia ejus, quod faciendum est, juvare potest, ubi impotentia faciendi, quod scitur, adest aut non tollitur?" (ibid.).

61 "…justiorem multo apologias sive excusationis caussam esse impotentiam, quam ignorantiam: unde recte dici solet, ad impossibile nemo obligator" (ibid.).

62 "Quod si ex isto liberè contracto habitu, impotentia nata dicatur fuisse, tanto majori miseria eorum fuisse, ut statuatur, necesse est. Sed vero nos tum ante, tum post contractum habitum, potentiam contra agendi, licet cum magna difficultate conjunctam, remanere credimus" (ibid.).

63 "Quares: An ergo peccatum quod vocant originale, non est caussa miseriæ estius utriusque, de qua hactenus egimus, & prima quidem ac potissima, si non sola atque unica, omnium caussa?" (ibid.).

64 "Scriptura nusquam peccati alicujus Originalis meminit, nedum ut peccatum istud miseriæ hujus caussam, quid dico caussam primam ac potissimam, imo unicam, esse afferat…" (ibid.).

65 "… nec ut adseruisse id credatur Scriptura, ratio sinit" (ibid.).

66 "Aut enim volumus Peccatum Originale significare ipsum primum origine peccatum actuale Adami; aut peccati istius effectum sive consequens, quod vocari solet universalis & à prima nativitate inhærens, totius naturæ humanæ corruptio, qua fit, ut omnes ac singuli homines, non tantum nascantur destituti divinæ voluntatis cognitione, ac proinde impotentes & in idonei ad faciendum ea, quæ Deo per se grata sunt, nisi accedat nova divinæ revelationis gratia; (hoc enim quin certum fit, nemo dubitat) sed & usque adeo distorti & pravi, tum voluntate tum adfectibus, ut non nisi ad malum, & ad omne

malum) adeoque ad odium Dei & proximi sint propensi, ab ipso statim non nativitatis tantum, sed conceptionis etiam momento" (ibid.; *OTE* 1:403).

67 "1. impossibile est, ut actuale & personale peccatum Adami, originaliter nostrum fit peccatum. Peccatum enim, impossibile est ut peccantem aut voluntatem ejus egrediatur. 2. impossibile est, ut qui nondum sunt in rerum natura peccent. 3. impossibile est, ut quis in alio peccet, nisi accedat vel imperium, vel consilium, vel consensus sive tacitus sive expressus, vel saltem (uti quidam volunt) sceleris sive peccati, quod ex lege adjudicem deferri debet, conscientia. At nihil horum potuit locum habere in peccato isto; quia ut infans ullum istorum credatur fecisse aut habuisse, per se absurdum est. quanto minus ergo verosimile videri debet, homines omnes, non modo nondum infantes, sed ne conceptos quidem adhuc, imo non nisi post peccatum peractum, & forte post aliquot annorum millia demum concipiendos & nascituros. ullum istorum in Adamo fecisse?" (ibid.).

68 "Nam 1. Hæc corruptio foret pæna. Atqui ut peccatum pæna peccati & peccati effectus sit, per se absurdum est. Per pænam enim nemo pænæ reus sit. At per peccatum reus quis fit pænæ. Deinde pæna passio est, peccatum actio sive culpa. Denique per pænam fit delicti compensatio, per peccatum meretur quis pænæ compensationem. Ergo si pæna peccatum esse posset compensatio culpæ, compensationem novam culpæ mereretur. 2. multo adhuc absurdius est, peccati unius ac solius pænam & effectum simulesse universalem peccandi necessitatem, & naturæ totius humanæ corruptionem. Nam universalis ista corruptio, effectus esset peccati istius, aut ex vi peccati qua talis, aut ex speciali aliqua ordinatione divina" (ibid.).

69 "Nec idcirco, quia ex Adamo natura tota humana proseminanda erat, naturam totam ex primo peccato sic infectam fuisse, consequitur. 1. quia peccatum naturam non inficit, sed voluntatem tantum ejus, qui peccat, depravat aut detorquer. 2. Actus unus ne habitum quidem gignere potest, quanto minus naturam totam inficere? 3. quia, uti justitia & virtus proseminari non potest, ita nec peccatum, ne quidem si animam per traducem propagari velimus. Nam alioquin filii omnes, qui a parentibus peccatoribus proseminantur, & naturam suam humanam ex iis derivant, naturam etiam eandem peccatricem necessario haberent; quod contra esse experientia satis testatur. ut corruptio ista universalis ex speciali aliqua ordinatione divina fluere dicatur, æquitatis aut justitiæ divinæ ratio non permittit: aut si omnino eam id permittere velis, unde ista ordinatio divina liquet? Certe absurdissimum est, istam corruptionem ex ordinatione divina derivare; cum nec in comminatione, nec in sententiæ executione vel hilum de ista corruptione, ut pæna a Deo ordinata dictum legatur. Denique, corruptionis istius universalis nulla sunt indicia nec signa; imo non pauca sunt signa, ex, quibus colligitur, naturam totam humanam sic corruptam non esse, vide sis, ut alia omittam, hoc unum, quod Scriptura ipsa nos velit fieri pueros malita, id est, expertes malitæ, quales pueri sunt: 1 Corinth. 14:20, quod nos negat regum cælorum ingressuros, nisi fiamus sicut parvuli, aut infantibus similes sunt, regnum cælorum sit: Matt. 19:14" (ibid.).

70 "Dices: Scriptura tamen aperte testatur, Omnes homines in Adamo peccasse: ad Romanos 5:12, & per inobedientiam unius hominibus peccatores multos constitutos esse, vers. 19" (ibid.).

71 Ibid.

72 See Weaver's examination of Romans 5:12 among Eastern Orthodox theologians (Dennis Weaver, "From Paul to Augustine: Romans 5:12 in Early Christian Exegesis," *St. Vladimir's Theological Quarterly* 27 (1983): 187–206; idem, "The Exegesis of Romans 5:12 Among the Greek Fathers and its Implications for the Doctrine of Original Sin: the 5th–12th Centuries," *St. Vladimir's Theological Quarterly* 29 (1985): 133–59; and idem, "Romans 5:12, part 3," *St. Vladimir's Theological Quarterly* 29 (1985): 230–57.

73 "Sed vero manifesta etiam est ratio, cur sic exponi verba ista non debeant; quia ante relativum ᾧ, vox hominis non præcessit immediatè. Natura autem rei & linguæ usus non sinunt, ut referatur ad vocem multo ante positam, cum qua in periodo tota non

connectitur. Hyperbaton hîc fingere, sine caussa, sine connexione commoda, est textum torquere ad sensum suum, non sensum suum textui aptare; præterquam quod hyperbaton foret insolens admodum, cum verba quæ sequotur post verba ista: Per unum hominem peccatum transiit, etc. non contineantur io isto versu tanquam parenthet ῶ̓ι inserta. Sed ut per se, connexa cum præcedentibus. Repetitio autem ut hîc facienda dicatur, nulla ratione probari potest; &, si omnino facienda esset, tum ὑπερβάτῳ locus non esset" (ibid.).

74 "Hoc ergo sensu phraseos hujus sublato, relinquitur, hîc per το peccarunt, intelligi non personale, non originale Adami peccatum; sed omnium ac singulorum hominum (qui quidem peccare possunt, in quorum numero non possunt esse infantes, fatui, etc.) propria ac personalia peccata intelligenda esse" (ibid.).

75 "Dices, In istis locis legitur ἐφ᾿ ῷ̣, non ἐφ᾿ ῷ̣. Fateor; quamquam in secundo, qui est 2 ad Corinth. v. 4, Complutensis editio habet ἐφ᾿ ῷ̣. Sed eo ipso firmatur magis id quod dico, quia etiamsi hic legeretur, ἐφ᾿ ῷ̣, tamen argumentum inde nullum effici posset, cum ista ipsa phrasis ἐφ᾿ ῷ̣, etiam significare posset eo quod, vel quatenus; quanto magis ergo phrasis ἐφ᾿ ῷ̣ quæ si non semper, usitatissimè tamen significare solet, eo quod, vel quatenus, rarissime vero ac fortasse nunquam, in quo; cum videlicet aliquid in aliqua re vel persona esse, aut per eam factum fuisse indicatur" (IT 4.5.2; OTE 1:403).

76 "Quia tamen peccatis eorum mors lege aliqua expresse lata adsignata non erat, uti Adami peccato adsignata fuerat, hinc est, quod Deus Adamum, & quotquot ex eo ante Legem nati fuerunt homines, protypo Iesu Christi, & fidelium qui ex eo nascituri essent, servire voluerit hactenus, quod sicut in istos homines ante legem natos, etsi non similiter peccatores uti Adam fuerat, peccatores tamen ex perfecto peccatore natos, mors pervaserat; ita in hos fideles Iesu Christi discipulos, etsi non pariter nec similiter, uti Iesus, justos & sanctos, ex perfecte tamen Sancto justoque parente Christo regenitos, Iustitia & vita pervasura esset" (ibid.; OTE 1:403).

77 Ibid.

78 Ibid.

79 Ibid.

80 Ibid.

81 Ibid.

82 "Quia, peccatores multos constitui, Apostolo, non significat, in multos peccaminosam qualitatem naturali contagione diffundi, per quam peccatores fiunt et constituuntur, sed significat ita tractari, tanquam si gravissimi peccatores essent; phrasi Hebræis usitata, qua condemnare, tractare aliquem ut peccatorem, solent exprimere per verbum הרשיע, id est, impiificare. Proverb. xvii.15, Esa. v.23, et per simplex nomen התאימ peccatores scilicet esse. 1 Reg. 1.21 etiam quando quis peccator non est, sed innocens et extra culpam. Vide similiter verbum הטה usurpatum Genes. xliii.9 et xliv.32. Primum istud Apostolo, non significare phrasin hanc, ex ipso textu liquet; quia eam opponit phrasi isti qua per unius obedientiam multos juftos constitui ait. At per phrasin multos justos constitui, non intelligit, justitiam veluti contrariam. peccato qualitatem diffundi in multos, sed multos justificari, id est veluti justos tractari et absolutos à peccatis, uti ex scopo loci patet" (ibid.).

83 "Regeres: Argumentum non procedere, Qui in rerum natura non est, is non potest in alio quidquam agere; quia ad Heb. VII.9 disertè dicitur, Levi multo antequam in rerum natura esset, decimatum fuisse in Abrahamo, id est, decimas dedisse Melchizedeco quando Abraham Pater ejus Melchizedeco Regi decimas dabat Genes. XIV.20" (ibid.; OTE 1:405).

84 "Quia peccatum merè personalis actio est, quæ peccantem non egreditur; aut si peccatum etiam velimus fieri in alio, tum necesse est. ut pæna etiam respondens peccato aut culpæ contractæ, in alio ferenda dicatur, & sic peccati simul ac pænæ formalis ratio in eo, qui in alio peccare dicitur, locum non habeat. Sed & impossibile est, ut quis dicatur in alio peccare, qui nondum in rerum natura est, quia ut ei Lex, quid dico Lex pæna

sancita? Feratur, moraliter impossibile est. Ne infanti quidem recens nato Lex ferri potest, quanto minus nondum nato. Nec, si Lex ferretur, peccare posset, quia ne adultus quidem, si rationis usu careat, peccare potest, & ratione etiam optima præditus, in alio tamen peccare non potest, nisi in peccatum sive tacite sive expresse propria sua voluntate consentiat" (ibid.).

85 "Certè, nihil vetat credere hyperbolen, quæ semper ultra verum aliquid addit, quæ verbis his inesse, per quam David significare voluit naturalem temperamenti sui, sanguinei fortasse, ad libidinem à prima statim proclivis ac proni conditionem, non aliter quam si cum ipsa libidine natus & educatus esset, ut ista scilicet ratione Deum ad misericordiam & gratiam sibi faciendum flecteret. Ita ut in peccato genitum esse, idem sit, quod genitum, esse cum eo, quod libidinis & peccati quasi origo fuit. Nam nec inusitata est ejusmodi hyperbolica loquendi ratio, non dico tantum in familiari sermone, sed & ipsi Davidi aliisque Scriptoribus Sacris" (IT 4.5.2; OTE 1:405–06).

86 Isaiah 48:8, Job 31:18.

87 Ibid.

88 IT 4.5.2; OTE 1:405–06.

89 The same argument could be used to elucidate 1 Corinthians 11:14 (φύσι αὐτη).

90 Ibid.

91 "At obsecro, quis recens natis infantibus cognitationes tribuat, quis figmenta cogitationum cordis, & similia? Nemo nisi fatuus & infante infantior" (IT 4.5.2; OTE 1:406).

92 "Immundities Physica per Metaphoram est omnis infirmitas, imperfectio, & corruptibilitas; unde nascuntur omnes ægritudines, morbi, miseriæ, dolores, ulcera fætida, quæ hominem deformem, & veluti immunda solent, ingratum, in visum & contemtum reddunt. Quia vero homines omnes ex mulieribus nati istis infirmitatibus & imperfectionibus, obnoxii semper vivunt, hinc est quod Iob omnes homines veluti immundos, ex immundis nasci asserat, ut isto argumento Deum ad commiserationem sui moveat. Sensus enim Jobi est: "Tu me Domine tam vehementer affligis. Cur vero? An non & ego homo sum ex muliere natus, eidem conditioni obnoxius, cui omnes sunt obnoxii? Non sane melior est conditio mea quam cæterorum mortalium omnium. Eadem nos omnes immundities, eadem fors premit. Nasci videmur ut, flores pulchri, & ecce vix natos nos comitatur infirmitas, qua fit ut paulatim languescamus, defluamus, &, veluti aridi ac flaccidi flores, immundi ac turpes reddamur, tandemque ut umbræ evanescamus, saturi ira, id est, fracti & obruti malis moriamur. Hac conditione, ô Deus! cum natus ego etiam sim, quid est cur me insuper premas magnis & multis hisce malis? Sine me, obsecro, vivere cum naturali saltem ista mea immunditie immunem ab hifce tam diris calamitatibus, usque dum moriar. Quid enim post mortem homini restat? Nihil nisi immundum cadaver, & sepulchrum luridum, in quo erit tristissima" (Ibid.; OTE 1:406–407).

93 IT 4.5.3; OTE 1:407.

94 One may note here that Episcopius' doctrine of atonement is significantly different than that of Hugo Grotius. Grotius' governmental theory of atonement is often (wrongly) used as if it represented the Remonstrants.

95 "Sacrificio propitiatorio peccati perpetrati impunitas tolleretur. Respicientiæ postulato nova peccandi & cum spe impunitatis peccandi licentia" (ibid.).

96 "Æterna enim peccatorum omnium remissio, & immortalis vitæ resipiscentibus dandæ aperta promissio, ad tempus illud pertinet, quod gratiæ tempus vocatur κατὰ ἔξοχου, quia perfectio divinæ gratiæ in eo posita est, quod Deus resipiscentibus peccatoribus, multo maximis, remissionem istam facere velit, absque ullo gentilium & Iudæorum discrimine" (IT 4.5.4; OTE 1:408).

97 Cf. Titus 1:1.

98   "...fides ergo electorum optime exponitur de doctrina Fidei, quam admiserant ac receperant libenter, non profani, non maligni, non perversi homines, sed ii qui inter profanos cæteros mortales, sive Iudæos, sive gentiles, animum adhuc probum & docilem retinuerant, & sic selecti, id est, egregii, eximii & Dei timentes erant" (*IT* 4.5.6; *OTE* 1:414).

99   *IT* 4.5.2; *OTE* 1:414

Summary and Conclusions

The purpose for this study was to measure the theological and methodological changes between Jacobus Arminius and Simon Episcopius, using the doctrine of original sin as the basis for comparison. In part, this comparison sought to provide a basis of assessment for future studies which could consider whether differences between Arminius and later Arminianism arose from Episcopius. As our research progressed, we also examined evidences of methodological reactions against scholasticism by both Arminius and Episcopius.

We have seen that the Arminian controversy should not be separated from other events in the Netherlands. Three factors contributed to the rise of the controversy, including religious renewal movements, Dutch humanism and toleration. But two others created and radicalized divergences among the Reformed. First were the disparate theological sources for the Reformed church in the Netherlands which gave rise to Calvinist and Arminian factions among its members. Second was the alignment of these Reformed factions with the political parties that resulted from vagaries in the Union of Utrecht. This competition between a would-be king and his Calvinists allies against Republicans and Arminians terminated in 1618 with the execution of Oldenbarnevelt and the exile of Arminian leaders.

Coupled with these native issues was the rise of Reformed scholasticism. The definition of and causes for Reformed scholasticism have provoked a debate in the critical literature on this topic.[1] We presented Armstrong's conclusions concerning the tendencies of Reformed scholasticism,[2] Muller's response to Armstrong based upon his own analysis of Reformed scholastics,[3] and concluded on the more "nuanced" conclusions Bray presented in his examination of Beza's doctrine of predestination.[4] We tentatively suggested, without denying the marked differences between scholasticism and humanism, that a synthesis developed through the study of Aristotelian texts by northern Italian humanists. This synthesis later migrated into Reformed theology through Italian humanists in Geneva. We suggested that the search for a meaningful synthesis continued in the theological methods of Arminius and Episcopius.

We proposed that the elements of Dutch toleration, a synthesis between Reformed scholasticism and Dutch humanism, Melanchthonian predestination and Dutch Republicanism provided the distinctive marks of the theologies and ministries of Arminius and Episcopius. Arminius became the leader of what Godfrey termed "the national Reformed" in the Netherlands.[5] His early death left a void in the theological leadership among them, which his student Simon Episcopius later filled. We presented Episcopius as Arminius' legitimate successor, assuming the chair of theology at Leiden, leading the Remonstrant party at the Synod of Dort and becaming the most active of the "directors" of the Remonstrant Brotherhood.

Summary of Arminius' Doctrine of Original Sin

The comparison between Arminius and Episcopius on original sin and its attendant doctrines began with a survey and analysis of Arminius' theological works. We saw how criticisms of his handling of original sin accompanied him from the beginning of his ministry until his death. Consequently, he treated the doctrine not only in his private debates with other Reformed scholars (Junius and Perkins) and in his lectures while professor at Leiden, but also in his answers to various hostile considerations of his theology.

Arminius was a dichotomist, a creationist and used faculty psychology's distinctions of *intellectus* and *voluntas* in his analysis of the soul. These natural qualities formed the *imago Dei* in humans and could not be lost without loss of humanness as well. Joined to these were the supernatural qualities of wisdom, holiness and righteousness, which in reality were the effects of the presence of the Holy Spirit. Arminius denied people had innate or rational access to divine truth without the Spirit's work of illumination.

Although the body did not share in the *imago Dei*, it was adequate both for use by the soul and to fulfill divine commands. Aside from the commands to fill the earth and subdue it, Arminius accepted the idea of an Adamic covenant. This covenant consisted of the command not to eat the fruit of the knowledge of good and evil and the threat of death. He also assumed the command was an abbreviated form of the two summary commands of the Old Testament and included a promise of eternal life if the command were obeyed. Arminius spoke highly of the pre-fall condition of Adam, emphasizing there was nothing lacking which would have hindered him from keeping the command of God.

Arminius used Aristotelian categories of causality in his presentation of the fall. Although he considered other causes as contributing factors, he arrived at two conclusions: Adam sinned only because of the abuse of his freedom of will and nothing in either God's foreknowledge or decree necessitated the fall. The immediate results of the fall were loss of fellowship with God, including the withdrawal of the presence of the Holy Spirit, and Adam and Eve's sense of fear and guilt.

Concerning original sin, Arminius agreed with Aquinas that privation of the Spirit was sufficient to explain human depravity. He strongly affirmed that all humanity was seminally present in Adam and shared the penalty of the fall. Even if at first he defined the punishment for the fall as both physical and eternal death (in the sense of hell), in later conversations he defended that privation of the Spirit was the only inherited penalty for Adam's sin. Thus, original sin was not personal sin, nor even sin, but the dehabilitating loss of the presence of the Spirit. Thus he could defend the salvation of children, for their only penalty for Adam's sin was to be born without being inhabited by the Spirit.

Regarding free will in fallen humanity, Arminius accepted Bernard's three-fold definition of freedom from necessity, sin and misery. He used this paradigm to defend the freedom of the will from necessity, deny the irresistibility of grace, affirm that humanity was enslaved to sin and sustain the necessity of grace.

Arminius described the effects of sin in graphic terms. Slavery and blindness rendered grace absolutely necessary for the "commencement, continuance and consummation" of salvation. He divided grace, an abstraction for the ministry of the Holy Spirit, between sufficient and efficient grace, the difference between them being that the first changed into the second when accepted by faith. Faith is a gift of God, not in the sense of an infused ability, but because the ministry of the Spirit frees a person to utilize their natural ability to believe. Strong affirmations of the necessity of the Spirit in all aspects of salvation disallow accusations of either Pelagian or Semi-Pelagian theology.

The Development of Episcopius' Doctrine of Original Sin

We considered Episcopius' doctrine of original sin in chapters three and four. We examined his early theology on the basis of his public and private disputations at Leiden and found broad repetitions of Arminius' theological distinctives. However, we also observed disputations in which Episcopius included his own material, as when he described the *imago Dei* in both physical and spiritual terms and rejected faculty psychology as an artificial understanding of the soul. He denied that the command to eat the fruit implied the Decalogue or contained hidden promises of eternal life. He considered the causes of the fall in an attenuated form, and then to emphasize that the only reason for Adam's sin was his free will, motivated by his desire to be like God and by love for his wife. In his defense of free will, Episcopius denied that it was affected either by permission, removal of grace, or necessitated by divine foreknowledge or decree. In the end, he insisted supralapsarian and infralapsarian schemas of predestination made God the true author of sin.

He thought the only penalties of the fall were physical death and misery, natural results of expulsion from the Garden. Although he did not repeat Arminius' definition of original sin as privation of the Spirit, he posited an evil force in humanity that inevitably led people to sin against God. People were desperately in need of redemption from sin, misery and death, and completely unable to remedy themselves.

Episcopius thought grace and redemption only occurred in covenant relationship with God. He denied an Adamic covenant because it could not be found in Scripture, and considered the Abrahamic and Mosaic covenants as types and shadows of the New Covenant. Every covenant was comprised of promises of blessings and stipulations. He demonstrated the Law could only inflame sin, and that the New Covenant abrogated it in all its aspects. The New Covenant was the focus of his theology of grace, because by it one receives the blessings of redemption through the expiatory sacrifice of Christ and the enabling power of the Holy Spirit. These are available to the sinner on the conditions of faith and repentance. He defined faith as willful assent to understood truths, and redefined repentance as a change of mind. His mingling of repentance with faith permitted him to import works into the act of believing. Unlike Arminius, he openly stated that the New Covenant could be repudiated and salvation lost.

Even though Episcopius' presentation of original sin in the *Confessio Remonstrantes* closely followed his early disputations, we encountered evidence that in other topics the Remonstrants pressed him to maintain conformity with Arminius. We can see this in expansive affirmations of the necessity of grace and its power to overcome human inability and sinful intransigence, the return to a two-fold scheme of election and a two-fold calling that mirrored Arminius' sufficient and efficient grace. Nevertheless, he went beyond Arminius by teaching that sufficient grace was given to all men. If people rejected the Gospel it was not because of some hidden divine decree, but because they had freely chose not to accept it. Chapter three concluded by showing that although Episcopius decidedly rejected Augustinianism, his theology harmonized with that of Greek Fathers, who later rejected Augustine and condemned Pelagius. Although he appeared Pelagian from a Calvinist perspective, his strong affirmations of the necessity of the Spirit in justification and sanctification indicate otherwise.

In chapter four we examined Episcopius' later theology as found in the *Institutes Theologicæ*. He began with strong affirmations of the inability of reason to apprehend divine truth, even for the establishment of God's existence. He used scholastic argumentation in order to refute atheistic arguments, but when arguing for the existence of God he turned to evidences from history, Scripture and Jesus Christ.

His first discussion of original sin came in conjunction with his discussion of the insufficiency of reason to control the power of *cupiditatis*, the sinful desires that promote sin, pain and sadness. He affirmed the necessity of a divine covenant to control these sinful impulses. He made an interesting inversion of the traditional treatments of original and personal sins by considering personal sins before that of original sin. The fruit of personal sin was damnation in hell and the dominating habit of sinning. Neither applied to either infants or the mentally impaired, because sin can only result from free acts of the will. He denied that sin had any other source than the will. Original sin was only the first sin committed by Adam; he thought to define it in terms of imputed guilt or the corruption of nature was absurd, illogical and impossible. He found equally absurd the idea that one could be punished for another's sin. Sin cannot corrupt nature, only the will, and that only through custom and habit.

He then turned to exegetical examinations of Augustinian proof-texts. Appeals to Romans 5:12–19 were illegitimate because they were based on faulty translations, texts and grammar. They also illegitimately expanded Paul's argument regarding the generation that lived between the time of Adam and Moses (5:13) to the entire human race. In his opinion, appeals to Hebrews 7 ignored clear contextual clues that this was merely an illustration (οἱ ἔποι εἰπεῖν), not a declaration of theological truth. Psalm 51:7 is David's hyperbolic confession of guilt, similar to Psalm 22:10, 81:5–6 and Isaiah 48:8. In Ephesians 2:4, Paul used φύσις not with respect to a sin nature, but as in Galatians 2:17, as a culture of habitual violation of the Law. Finally, he treated Job 14:4 and 15:14. The first was could not have been a declaration of original sin, for this would have violated the argument of Job's friends, that Job was suffering for personal sins. Rather, the verse is a declaration of the universal condition of misery and death, which concurred with Episcopius' theology. The second citation was from Eliphaz, who was criticized by God himself for misrepresenting both God and humanity.

Finally, Episcopius considered the necessity of grace in view of human depravity. In a rare occasion, he made extensive use of Aristotelian categories of causation for the purpose of establishing equilibrium between the mercy and grace with the demands of justice and equity. This permitted him to posit not faith but repentance as the requirement for salvation. In contrast both to Arminius' and Episcopius' earlier writings, he made almost no mention at all of faith. While he strongly affirmed the need for a substitutionary, expiatory sacrifice in order to satisfy the divine demands of justice, the Arminian emphasis on the ministry of the Holy Spirit in the life of the believer has disappeared.

Episcopius As Heir
of Arminius' Theology

We return once again to Hicks' paradigm as a basis for comparing Episcopius' theology with that of Arminius. By the end of chapter two, we had already established significant areas of discontinuity between Arminius and Episcopius. Our examination of the *Institutes Theologicæ* revealed that these differences had widened remarkably. Aside from questions about creation and covenants, his examination of sin (it is almost inaccurate to write of him examining "original sin") focused on the role free will played in the fall, or refutations of his Calvinist opponents' arguments of necessity. He made strong affirmations of *cupiditatis* as a sin-inducing, irrational force in humanity which reason cannot control, but he had abandoned all Arminian emphases on the unity of the race in Adam, the absolute necessity of the Spirit or the primacy of faith.

The question then is whether these were legitimate extrapolations of Arminius' theology, or radical disjunctures signaling that Episcopius abandoned his predecessor's theology. I believe, as distant as they appear from one the other, that in most of these differences Haentjens is still correct: Episcopius' theology reflects the development of ideas which were suggested by Arminius but left undeveloped. Episcopius' declarations regarding infant salvation and the salvation of the mentally impaired mirror Arminius' intimations in article 30 of the "Thirty-One Articles."[6] Consider Episcopius' statement that sin cannot twist nature, and that only actual sin can deprave the will through habit. It is not difficult to see this as a development of Arminius' doctrine of deprivation. Arminius asked if the privation of the Spirit were not sufficient to explain the frankly negative picture he developed of human sinfulness, implying that it was. But if this is the case, then even though Arminius' verbiage at times looks Reformed and Episcopius' never does, they were still affirming the same theological tendencies. More difficult to reconcile are the contrasts between Arminius' declaration of salvation by grace through faith and Episcopius' later gospel of salvation by grace through repentance. But once again, the moment we make explicit Arminius' intimations of the possibility of the loss of salvation, the emphasis moves from faith to something else, to what one does to maintain salvation. Arminius did not think merely renewing one's faith was sufficient to recover salvation. In his "Declaration of Sentiments," he did not question David's salvation on the basis of David's loss of faith, but on the basis of David's sin. In order to renew his salvation, David had to repent, and here we arrive at Episcopius' conclusions. I suggest that even in his most questionable departures from Arminius' soteriology, Episcopius was merely working out what was implicit in his precursor's theology.

A Comparison of Theological Methods

But there are other comparisons that invite analysis in a different direction. We have seen throughout the dissertation that Arminius made extensive use of scholastic categories, syllogisms and recognition of logical errors, first in his disputations with Junius and Perkins and then in his public and private disputations. Arminius was willing to speculate on whether the command not to eat of the fruit included the Decalogue, or whether God would have extended the covenant to Adam's children. He adopted scholastic categories when he analyzed creation or the classes of angels. While there were times when we find this type of analysis in Episcopius, it appears to be due to his wholesale borrowing from Arminius. Unlike Arminius, Episcopius refused to comment on that which he could not substantiate from a close reading of the Scriptures and attacked his opponents' positions when they did not demonstrate their ideas from the same. Like Arminius, Episcopius was skilled in using Aristotelian techniques in debating with his opponents. Nevertheless, we find a different theological method when Episcopius arranged and presented his personal theology.

Hicks suggested Episcopius' method was the rationalism of the Enlightenment. First, we must consider what is "rationalism." Rationalism is not merely the use of reason, as when one uses the ability to reason when testing hypotheses and conducting empirical experiments. Rather, modern philosophers define Rationalism as "any philosophy magnifying the role played in *unaided* reason in the acquisition and justification of knowledge,"[7] "the position that reason has precedence over the other ways of acquiring knowledge, or more strongly, that it is the unique path to knowledge.[8] It stands in contrast to knowledge either obtained through revelation[9] or through empirical and scientific methods.[10]

This is not what we find in either Arminius or Episcopius. Unlike the originators of Rationalism, Descartes or Spinoza, both Arminius and Episcopius strongly denied that reason was adequate to discover anything about God or divine truth. We saw this dramatically confirmed in the opening chapters of Episcopius' *Institutes Theologicæ*, where Episcopus specifically denied the ability of unaided reason to prove the existence of God. Instead, he argued for God's existence on the basis of history. This is a quasi-empirical attempt at proofs for the existence of God, the very opposite of rationalism. If Episcopius were the precursor to the Enlightenment, it was not because he was a rationalist.

To what (or whom) then may we attribute Episcopius' theological method? I would suggest that his rejection of scholastic method, his refusal to speculate and his emphasis of building theology on a close reading of the biblical text indicates a return to the exegetical and theological methods of Desiderius Erasmus and John Calvin. In the introduction, we saw that one of the primary marks of the humanists, and especially Erasmus, was the development of the historical, grammatical, contextual method of interpretation. This was also Calvin's method. Humanist hermeneutics was a decided rejection of the *grammatica speculativa*, and "shifted to a common sense and semantic approach which rejected the artificialities of scholastic analysis,... a shift from the formal and structural approach of the scholastic 'modalists' to a more semantic, historical and relativist conception."[11] Humanist exegetical method demanded the use of reason in sifting between semantic ranges and grammatical categories, but this is not the rationalist hermeneutic of Jean Le Clerc or Richard Simon (1638–1712), the forerunner of modern biblical criticism.

We saw that, from the beginning of his time at Leiden, Arminius criticized excessive use of reason in theology and advocated a return to Calvin and his method of interpreting Scripture.[12] Arminius maintained the scholastic method of teaching, but in reduced form when compared to Junius. Episcopius continued in the same direction. In his earlier works, he curtailed the use of scholastic categories even more than Arminius and refused to go beyond Scripture in his theological content. In his later works, he maintained scholastic analysis only to treat the logical arguments of his opponents. He broke with scholastic tradition when he arranged his *Institutes Theologicæ* inductively from Scripture. He continued to ignore subjects that were not explicit in the text, and denied his opponents' implications and extrapolations. We see this method clearly in Episcopius' handling of original sin. He limited the results of Adam's sin to those explicitly mentioned in Genesis 2 and 3, appealed to textual criticism when dealing with the Augustinian use of Romans 5:12, and interpreted Romans 5:12–20 and other Reformed proof-texts contextually. We see the humanist confidence in "common sense," the native ability of an intelligent person to recognize the irrational, in his responses to Reformed orthodox argumentation. Rather than appeal to Aristotelian categories of logical errors, as Arminius had with Perkins, he simply judged that they were "absurd."[13]

Two other humanist qualities mark Episcopius' theology: his defense of human dignity and freedom.[14] The defense of free will dominated his analysis of creation, the fall and redemption. His defense of human dignity governed what God could and could not have done in predestination. He also shared with Erasmus an affinity for patristic theology. Both his earlier and later works have too many parallels with Justin and Origen to have simply happened. Is it coincidence that these were Erasmus' favorite fathers as well?

In conclusion, we may note significant differences between Arminius and Episcopius in both content and method. These differences, however, are not because Episcopius abandoned Arminius, but because of following through and working out the methodological and theological impulses he received from his master.

Notes

1. Philip C. Holtrop, "Beza, Theodore (1519–1605)," in *Encyclopedia of the Reformed Faith*.

2. Brian G. Armstrong, *Calvinism and the Amyraut Heresy* (Madison: University of Wisconsin Press, 1969), 32.

3. Richard A. Muller, *Christ and the Decree: Christology and Predestination in Reformed Theology from Calvin to Perkins* (Durham, N.C.: Labyrinth Press, 1986), 196–197.

4. John S. Bray, *Theodore Beza's Doctrine of Predestination* (Nieuwkoop: De Graaf, 1975).

5. W. Robert Godfrey, "Calvin and Calvinism in the Netherlands," in *John Calvin, His Influence in the Western world*, ed. W. Stanford Reid and Paul Woolley (Grand Rapids: Zondervan, 1982), 99.

6. James Arminius, *The Apology or Defence of James Arminius, D. D. Against Thirty-One Articles*, in *The Works of James Arminius*, trans. James Nichols, London ed. (London: Longman, Hurst, Rees, Orme, Brown and Green, 1825–28; reprint, Grand Rapids: Baker, 1986).

7. *The Oxford Dictionary of Philosophy*, s.v. "Rationalism," emphasis added.

8. David Garber, "Rationalism," in *The Cambridge Dictionary of Philosophy*.

9. "It may oppose the view that revelation is central to religious knowledge" (Ibid). See also *A Dictionary of Philosophy*, s.v. "Rationalism," 2d ed., and articles on philosophical and theological rationalism in Jan P. Beckmann and Falk Wagner, "Rationalismus," in *Theologische Realenzyklopädie*.

10. "(Rationalism is) opposed to empiricism, the doctrine that experience is a necessary basis to all our knowledge." (J. O. Urmson, "Rationalism," in *The Concise Encyclopedia of Western Philosophy and Philosophers*.

11. Donald R. Kelly, *Renaissance Humanism*, ed. Michael Roth (Boston: Twayne, 1991), 77.

12. See the Introduction, footnote 75.

13. Perhaps it would be legitimate to ask whether he was able to recognize the "absurd" because of his extensive training in Aristotelian and Ramist logic.

14. Paul Oskar Kristeller, *Renaissance Thought: The Classic, Scholastic and Humanist Strains* (New York: Harper and Row, 1961), 170.

Bibliography

Original Sources

Acta Synodi Nationalis. Dort: Isaaci Ioannidis Canini Et Sociorum, 1620.

Acta ofte Handelinghen des Nationalen Synodi. Dort: Isaack Jans. Canin, 1621.

Anglus, Gratianus Civilis [pseud.]. *Remonstrantium in Belgio Semi-Pelagianismus in Pietate Ordinum Hollandiæ ac West Frisiæ defensus per Hugonem Grotious, eorundum Ordinum fisci advocatum*. Basel: n.p., 1616.

Arminius, Jacobus. *Een Cleyn Tractætgen*. Amsterdam: Dirck Pieterssz, 1609.

—————. *Een Cort/ende bundich Tractætgen / vervatende seeckere Theses of Articulen: Dat de Gereformeerde Kercken vande Roomsche Kercke niet afgheweecken zijn*. The Hague: Hillebrant Jacobsz, 1609.

—————. *Corte ende grondighe verclaringhe uyt de Heilige Schrift over het swaerwichtighe pointt van de Cracht ende Rechtvaerdicheyt der Voorsienicheyt Godts*. Leiden: Ian Paets Iajobsz, 1609.

—————. *Vierderley Theses of Articulen*. The Hague: Hillebrant Iacobsz, 1610.

—————. *Verclaringhe Iacobi Arminii*. Leiden: Thomas Basson, 1610.

—————. *Orationes, itemque tractatus insigniores aliquot: in quibus quidnam sentiat de quamplurimis in S. theologia hoc tempore controversis quæstionibus*. Leiden: Ex officina Thomæ Sasson, 1611.

—————. *De Vero & Genuino Sensu Cap. VII. Epistolæ ad Romanos Dissertatio*. Leiden: Ex Officina Godefridi Basson, 1612.

—————. *Vertælde Theses Inhoudende een corte ondervvijsinghe Van de oprechte Regeeringhe der Kercke Christi*. Delft: Ian Andriesz., 1612.

—————. *Opera Theologica*. Leiden: Goderfridum Basson, 1629.

—————. *Analysis Capitis IX ad Romanos*. In *Opera Theologica*, 778–823 . Leiden: Goderfridum Basson, 1629.

—————. *Apologia Adversus Articulos quosdam Theologos in vulgus sparsos, saltem in quorundum, in Belgio et extra Belgium manibus versante, quibus tum ille tum Adranus Borreus Ecclesiastes Leidensis novitatis et heterodoxias in Religione, erroris et hæreseos suspecti reddentur*. In *Opera Theologica*, 134–83. Leiden: Goderfridum Basson, 1629.

—————. *Articuli nonnulli diligenti examine perpendendi, eo quod inter ipsos Reformatæ Religionis Professsores de iis aliqua incidit controversia: illi autem partim asseverantur vel negati, vel affirmati sunt, partim dubitanter vel affirmati vel negati, quod & certis indiciis significatum singulis articulis additis*. In *Opera Theologica*, 948–66. Leiden: Goderfridum Basson, 1629.

————. *Collatio Amica cum D. Francisco Iunio de Prædestinatione per Litteras Habita.* In *Opera Theologica*, 458–610. Leiden: Goderfridum Basson, 1629.

————. *Declaratio Sententiæ I. Arminii de Prædestinatione, Providentia Dei, Libero arbitrio, Gratia Dei, Divinitate Filii Dei, et de Iustificatione hominis coram Deo.* In *Opera Theologica*, 91–133. Leiden: Goderfridum Basson, 1629.

————. *Disputationes Privatæ de Plerisque Christianæ Religionis Capitibus, Incoatæ potissimum ab Auctore ad corporis Theologici informationem.* In *Opera Theologica*, 339–457. Leiden: Goderfridum Basson, 1629.

————. *Disputationes Publicæ de Nonnullis Religionis Christianæ capitibus, ab ipso compositæ.* In *Opera Theologica*, 197–338. Leiden: Goderfridum Basson, 1629.

————. *Dissertatio De Vero & Genuino Senso Cap. VII Epistolæ ad Romanos.* In *Opera Theologica*, 824–947. Leiden: Goderfridum Basson, 1629.

————. *Epistola Ad Hypolytum à Collibus.* In *Opera Theologica*, 937–47. Leiden: Goderfridum Basson, 1629.

————. *Examen Modestum Libelli, quem D. Gulielmus Perkinsius apprimé doctus Theologus De Prædestinationis Modo et Ordine, Itemque de Amplitudine Gratiæ Divinæ.* In *Opera Theologica*, 634–777. Leiden: Goderfridum Basson, 1629.

————. *Oratio de Componendo Dissidio Religionis inter Christianos.* In *Opera Theologica*, 71–91. Leiden: Goderfridum Basson, 1629.

————. *Oratio de Sacerdotio Iesu Christi, habit cum Auctor Doctor S. Theologiæ createtur.* In *Opera Theologica*, 9–25. Leiden: Goderfridum Basson, 1629.

————. *Oratio Prima, de Objecto Theologiæ.* In *Opera Theologica*, 26–41. Leiden: Goderfridum Basson, 1629.

————. *Oratio Secunda, de Authore et fine Theologiæ.* In *Opera Theologica*, 41–55. Leiden: Goderfridum Basson, 1629.

————. *Oratio Tertia, de Certitudine S. Sanctæ Theologiæ.* In *Opera Theologica*, 56–71. Leiden: Goderfridum Basson, 1629.

————. *Questiones Numero Novem, Nobliss. DD. Curatoribus Academiæ Leidensis exhibite à Deputatis Synodi, in hunc finem, ut ad eas à Professoribus S. Theologia responderetur.* In *Opera Theologica*, 184–96. Leiden: Goderfridum Basson, 1629.

————. *Verklaring van Jacobus Arminius Afgelegd in de Vergadering van de Staten van Holland op 30 Oktober 1608.* Edited by Gerrit J. Hoenderdaal. Lochem: De Tijdstroom, 1960.

Arminius, James. *The Just Man's Defence, or, The declaration of the Judgement of James Arminius Concerning the Principal Points of Religion Before the States of Holland; to which is added nine questions with their solution.* Translated by Tobias Conyers. London: Printed for Henry Eversden, 1657.

————. *A Declaration of the Sentiments of Arminius on Predestination, Divine Providence, The Freedom of the Will, the Grace of God, the Divinity of the Son of God, and the Justification of Man Before God.* In *The Works of James Arminius*, trans. James Nichols, 1:580–732. London ed. London: Longman, Hurst, Rees, Orme, Brown and Green, 1825. Reprint, Grand Rapids: Baker Book House, 1986.

————. *Oration I: The Object of Theology.* In *The Works of James Arminius*, trans. James Nichols, 1:321–47. London ed. London: Longman, Hurst, Rees, Orme, Brown and Green, 1825. Reprint, Grand Rapids: Baker Book House, 1986.

————. *Oration II: The Author and the End of Theology.* In *The Works of James Arminius*, trans. James Nichols, 1:348–373. London ed. London: Longman, Hurst, Rees, Orme, Brown and Green, 1825. Reprint, Grand Rapids: Baker Book House, 1986.

————. *Oration III: The Certainty of Sacred Theology.* In *The Works of James Arminius*, trans. James Nichols, 1:374–401. London ed. London: Longman, Hurst, Rees, Orme, Brown and Green, 1825. Reprint, Grand Rapids: Baker Book House, 1986.

————. *Oration IV: The Priesthood of Christ.* In *The Works of James Arminius*, trans. James Nichols, 1:402–433. London ed. London: Longman, Hurst, Rees, Orme, Brown and Green, 1825. Reprint, Grand Rapids: Baker Book House, 1986.

————. *Oration V: On Reconciling Religious Dissentions Among Christians.* In *The Works of James Arminius*, trans. James Nichols, 1:402–433. London ed. London: Longman, Hurst, Rees, Orme, Brown and Green, 1825. Reprint, Grand Rapids: Baker Book House, 1986.

————. *The Works of James Arminius.* Translated by James Nichols and William Nichols. London ed. London: vols. 1–2, Longman, Hurst, Rees, Orme, Brown and Green; vol. 3, Thomas Baker, 1825–75. Reprint, Grand Rapids: Baker Book House, 1986.

————. *The Apology or Defence of James Arminius, D. D. Against Thirty-One Articles.* In *The Works of James Arminius*, trans. James Nichols, 1:733–770; 2:1–79. London ed. London: Longman, Hurst, Rees, Orme, Brown and Green, 1825–28. Reprint, Grand Rapids: Baker Book House, 1986.

————. *Certain articles to be diligently examined and weighed.* In *The Works of James Arminius*, trans. James Nichols, 2:706–31. London ed. London: Longman, Hurst, Rees, Orme, Brown and Green, 1828. Reprint, Grand Rapids: Baker Book House, 1986.

————. *Disputations of Some of the Principle Subjects of the Christian Religion.* In *The Works of James Arminius*, trans. James Nichols, 2:80–317. London ed. London: Longman, Hurst, Rees, Orme, Brown and Green, 1828. Reprint, Grand Rapids: Baker Book House, 1986.

————. *Dissertation on the True and Genuine Sense of the Seventh Chapter on the Epistle to the Romans.* In *The Works of James Arminius*, trans. James Nichols, 2:471–683. London ed. London: Longman, Hurst, Rees, Orme, Brown and Green, 1828. Reprint, Grand Rapids: Baker Book House, 1986.

————. *A Letter to His Excellency, the Noble Lord, Hippolytus à Collibus.* In *The Works of James Arminius*, trans. James Nichols, 2:689–705. London ed. London: Longman, Hurst, Rees, Orme, Brown and Green, 1828. Reprint, Grand Rapids: Baker Book House, 1986.

————. *Nine Questions Exhibited for the Purpose of Obtaining An Answer From Each of the Professors of divinity: and the replies which James Arminius gave to them: with other nine opposite articles.* In *The Works of James Arminius*, trans. James Nichols, 2:64–71. London ed. London: Longman, Hurst, Rees, Orme, Brown and Green, 1828. Reprint, Grand Rapids: Baker Book House, 1986.

————. *The Private Disputations of James Arminius on the Principle Articles of the Christian Religion.* In *The Works of James Arminius*, trans. James Nichols, 2:318–469. London ed. London: Longman, Hurst, Rees, Orme, Brown and Green, 1828. Reprint, Grand Rapids: Baker Book House, 1986.

————. *The Writings of James Arminius, D. D., Formerly Professor of Divinity in the University of Leyden.* Translated by James Nichols and William R. Bagnall, 3 volumes. Auburn and Buffalo: Derby Miller and Orton, 1853.

————. *An Analysis of the Ninth Chapter of St. Paul's Epistle to the Romans.* In *The Works of James Arminius*, trans. William Nichols, 3:485–525. London ed. London: Longman, Hurst, Rees, Orme, Brown and Green, 1875. Reprint, Grand Rapids: Baker Book House, 1986.

————. *Dr. James Arminius' Modest Examination of a Pamphlet, Which That Very Learned Divine Dr. William Perkins, Published Some Years Ago, On The Mode and Order of Predestination, and On the Amplitude of Divine Grace.* In *The Works of James Arminius,* trans. William Nichols, 3:267–484. London ed. London: Thomas Baker, 1875. Reprint, Grand Rapids: Baker Book House, 1986.

————. *Examination of the Theses of Dr. Francis Gomarus Respecting Predestination.* In *The Works of James Arminius,* 3:521–658. London ed. London: Thomas Baker, 1875. Reprint, Grand Rapids: Baker Book House, 1986.

————. *Friendly Conference of James Arminius, The Illustrious Doctor of Sacred Theology, With Mr. Francis Junius, About Predestination.* In *The Works of James Arminius,* trans. William Nichols, 3:16–248. London ed. London: Thomas Baker, 1875. Reprint, Grand Rapids: Baker Book House, 1986.

Bertius, Petrus. *Oratio De Vita & Obitu Reverendi et Clarissimi Viri D. Iacobi Arminii, Dicta Post tristes ilius exsequias XXII. Octob. Anno CLC.LC.IX in Auditorio Theologico.* In *Opera Theologica,* unpaginated. Leiden: Goderfridum Basson, 1629.

————. *The Oration of Peter Bertius Concerning the Life and Death of that Reverend and Most Famous Man, Mr. James Arminius.* In *The Popish Labyrinth,* 1–34. London: Ratcliff and Thomson for Francis Smith, 1672.

————. *An Oration on the Life and Death of that Reverend and Very Famous Man, James Arminius, D.D.* In *The Works of James Arminius,* trans. James Nichols, 1:13–47. The London ed. London: Longman, Hurst, Rees, Orme, Brown and Green, 1825. Reprint, Grand Rapids: Baker Book House, 1986.

Bertius, Petrus, and Jacobus Arminius. *Twee Disputatien.* The Hague: Hillebrant Jacobsz., 1609.

Bèze, Théodore de. *De hæreticis a ciuili magistratu puniendis libellus, aduersus Martini Bellii farraginem, & nouorum academicorum sectam.* Minerva [Geneva]: Unveränderter Nachdruck, Oliua Roberti Stephani, 1554.

————. *Responsio ad defensiones & reprehensiones Sebastiani Castellionis, quibus suam Noui Testamenti interpretationem defendere aduersus Bezam, & eius versione vicissim reprehandere conatus est in hoc libello multi Noui Testamenti loci accuratissimè excutiuntur, quorum indicem adiecimus.* [Geneva]: Excudebat Henricus Stephanus, 1563.

————. *Een schoon tractaet des godtgheleerden Theodori Bezae vande straffe, welcke de wereltlijcke overicheydt over de ketters behoort te oeffenen, teghen Martini Bellii tsamenraepsel, ende der secte der nieuwe Academisten.* Translated by Johannes Bogerman. Franeker: Gillis van den Rade, 1601.

Braght, Thieleman J. van. *Het Bloedig Tooneel, of Martelaers Spiegel der Doops-gesinde of Weerloose Christenen: Versamelt uyt verscheyde geloofweerdige chronijken, memorien, en getuygenissen.* 2nd ed., 2 vols. Amsterdam: H. Sweerts, J. ten Hoorn, J. Bouman, and D. van den Dalen, 1685.

————. *The Bloody Theater, or, Martyrs' mirror.* 17th ed. Scottdale, PA: Herald Press, 1951.

Brandt, Geeraert. *The History of the Reformation and other Ecclesiastical Transactions in and about the Low-countries: From the Beginning of the Eighth Century, Down to the Famous Synod of Dort, Inclusive: faithfully translated from the original Low-Dutch.* 4 vols. London: Printed by T. Wood for T. Childe, 1720.

————, and Johannes Brandt. *Historie der Reformatie en Andere Kerkelyke Geschiedenissen in en Ontrent de Nederlanden.* 2d ed., 4 vols. Amsterdam: Jan Rieuwertsz. Hendrik and Dirk Boom, 1677–1704.

Broecker, Frederik F., and Joh. F. Broecker. *Horn Disputatie vant rechte verstant des 7. Cap. des*

Briefs Pauli tot den Rom: teghens D.V. Coornhert in sijn Nadencken opt 7. Cap. tot den Romeynen: Ende teghens Arminium. Enchuysen: Jacob Lenaertsz Meyn, 1613.

Bullinger, Heinrich. *Der Alt Gloub das der Christen Gloub von Anfang der Wält Gewart Habe der Recht Waar alt und Ungezwyflet Gloub sye Klare Bewysung.* Zürich: Christoffel Froschouer, 1539.

──────. *Sermonum Decades Quinque, de Potissimis Christianæ Religionis Capitibus in Tres Tomos Digestæ.* Zurich: In officina Christoph. Froshoveri, 1552.

──────. *Hvysboec \ Viif Decades.* Emden: n.p., 1563.

──────. *Fiftie Godlie and Learned Sermons Divided into Five Decades: Containing the Chiefe and Principall Points of Christian Religion, Whereunto are Added Certain Epistles Concerning the Apparell of Ministers and Other Indifferent Things.* London: Imprinted by Ralph Newberie, 1587.

──────. *The Decades of Henry Bullinger.* Edited by Thomas Harding. Translated by "H. I." Cambridge: The University Press, 1849.

Cameron, John. *Theses de Efficacia Gratiæ Dei, et us Liberi Hominis Arbitrii in Negotio Salutis Humanæ.* In *TA ΣΩZOMENA, sive opera partim ab auctore ipso edita.* Geneva: Iacobi Chouet, 1642.

Coornhert, Dieryck Volkertszoon. *Vande Erfzonde of Die inde H. Schrifture zoo wert Bevonden als inden Catechismus en by Eenige Predicanten Geleert Wert. Ende: Keplücke vande Predicanten,* 1580.

──────. *Vande Toelatinge ende Decrete Godts: Bedenckinghe of de H. Schrift oock inhoudt sulex als Calvijn ende T. Beza dær van leeren Vermaninghe aen R. Donteclock, Om te verdedighen de Erf-zonde.* Goude: Jasper Tournap, 1610.

──────. *Van de Erfzonde: Disputatie Tusschen de Predicanten tot Haarlem ende D.V. Coornhert. Van de Erfzonde.* Goude: Jasper Tournap, 1610.

──────. *Theriakel Teghen het Vernijnighe Wroegh-schrift by Arent Cornelisz ende Reynier Donteclock, Delfsche Predicanten: aan den H.H. Staten van Hollandt: Vertoonende de Onschuldt van D.V. Coornhert.* Goude: Jasper Tourney, 1610.

──────. *Dolingen des Catechisini Ander-werven Blijckende in des Selfs Beproefde Proeve: Wederlegginge ende de Censuren of Berispingen van Arent Cornelisz, Reynier Donteclock ende Joannes Gerobulus.* Goude: Jasper Tournay, 1610.

──────. *Bootgen VVt het Schip van de Tweede Antwoorde van D.V. Coornhert: Opte Replijcke der Predicanten Disputatie van Erfzonde.* Goude: Jasper Tournap, 1610.

──────. *Vande Verworpelingen: Of Godes Predestinatie oorsake is van jemants eeuwighe Verdoemenisse: Derde Ghesprake tusschen Ghereformeerde Calvinist, ende D.Demostenes.* N.p, 1611.

──────. *Vande Vreemde Sonde, Schulde, Straffe nasporinghe: ende oorsake vande schadelijcke dolingen gheslopen inde Leeringhen vande Vrije-wille, Predestinatie ende Justificatie.* Goude: Jasper Tournap voor Andries Burier, 1616.

──────. *À L'aurore des Libertés Modernes: Synode Sur la Liberté de Conscience (1582).* Paris: Éditions du Cerf, 1979.

Corvinus, Johannes. *Schovve over D. Francisci Gomari Proeve, van D. M. P. Bertii Aenspraeck, By een van sijn discipulen, tot nodige protestatie voor de eere sijns meesters, ende voorbode van de Wederlegginghe van D. Gomari Waerschouinghe utytgegheven.* N.p.: Ian Paedts Iacopszoon, 1610.

Curcellæus, Stephanus. *Præfatio Ad Lectorem Christianem.* In *Opera Theologica,* unpaginated. Amsterdam: Ioannis Blæv, 1650.

Der Remonstranten Vocale Letters, Sijnde Het vervogh van de Verresenen Barneveldt, in't welcke Barnevelts, als oock Grottii (der Remonstranten Vocale Letters) en alle der Remonstrantsche Consonanten schadelijcke maximen ontrent het Kerkelijcke toon gestelt wert. Schiedam: Voor de Liefhebbers der waerheyt, 1664.

Donteclock, Reynier. *Antwoorde Op een seker Schrift / eens Onbekenden / 'tonrechte geintituleert / Christelicke ene erstighe Vermaninghe tot vrede, aen R, Dontelock, over sijne 'tSamentsprekinghe.* Gulden: Ian Andriesz., 1609.

Dwinglo, Bernardus. *Grovvvel Der Ver VVoestinghe Staende in de Heylighe plaetse: Dat is / Claer ende warachtigh Verhael vander voornaemste Mis-handelinghen / Onbillijcke Procedueren ende Nulliteyten des Nationalen Synodi, Ghehouden binnen Dordrechte / inde Jaren 1618 ende 1619.* N.p.: t'Enghuysen, 1622.

Een Kort en Waerachtich Verhael / wat voor een grouwelijck ghevoelen dat de Arminianen / Vortianen / ofte nieuwe Arrianen / Pelagianen / Socinianen / Samosatinianen ghesocht hebben in de Gehereformeerde kercke in te voeren / en in kort heir teghen gestelt het ghevoelen der Ghereformeerde kerche. N.p.: "Ghedruckt buyten Romen," n.d.

Episcopius, Simon. *Antidotum, ende Naerder Openinghe Van het eyghene ghevoelen des Nationalen Synodi 1618, en 1619.* N.p., 1619.

⸻. *Onbillijcke wreetheyt der Dortsche Synode: Midtgaders der ghener / die het beleyt daer over hebben ghehadt / Teghen de Remonstranten in de Nederlandtsche Gheunieerde Provincien.* N.p., 1619.

⸻. *Oratie Van Den Hoogh-gheleerden end Voortreffelijcken Mr. Symon Episcopius, Professoor der Theologie inde Universiteyt binnen.* Leyden. n.p., 1619.

⸻. *Corte ende Naeckte Ontdeckinghe Vande Bedrijghelijckeheydt des Dortschen Synodi.* N.p., 1619.

⸻. *Antidotum Continens Pressiorum Declarationem in Synodo Nationali Dordracena.* Harderwijk: Ex Officina Typographi Synodalis, 1620.

⸻. *Noodige Verantwoordinge der Remonstranten nopende soo wel het stellen van een eyghene en bysondere Confessie, verclaringhe haers Gevoelens, vereeninge met de Luterische: aslo mede / over haere Leere / van den Doop, Avontmael, ende Rechvaerdich-makinge uyt den gheloove / etc. Mistgaeders, van de burchten der Contrapremonstranten ghelove.* N.p., 1620.

⸻. *Simonis Episcopii Brief: in de welcke de gront van de Remonstranten, aangaende hare Belijdenis ontdeckt wort, Met een Voor-reden aende Staten General.* The Hague: Hillebrant Iacobsz., 1620.

⸻. *Brief Van Simon Episcopius Met eenighe Aentyckeninghen ofte Commentaren breeder verclaert. Daer in verscheyden raetslagen ende mysterien der Arminianen ondeckt worden.* Amsterdam: Marten Iansz. Brandt, 1620.

⸻. *Belijdenisse, ofte, Verklaringhe Van't ghevoelen der Leeraren: die in de Neder-landen Remonstranten worden ghenaemt.* N.p., 1621.

⸻. *Confessio, sive, Declaratio, Sententiæ Pastorum, qui in Foederato Belgio Remonstrantes Vocantur, Super Præcipuis Articulis Religionis Christianæ.* Harderwijk: Theodorum Danielis, 1622.

⸻. *Nieticheyt Van den Calvinischen Ban, ofte, Brief Over Het Onrecht-vaerdigh Bannen.* N.p., 1624.

⸻. *Eere Godts, Verdedight teghen den Laste Iacobi Triglandij, Begaen in Seeckere Predicatie.* N.p., 1627.

⸻. *Vrye Godes-dienst, of t'Samenspreeckinghe Tusschen Remonstrant en Contra-*

Remonstrant. N.p., 1627.

————. *Apologia Pro Confessione, sive, Declaratione Sententiæ Eorum, qui in Foederato Belgio vocantur Remonstrantes, Super Præcipuis Articulis Religionis Christianæ: Contra Censuram Quatuor Professorum Leidensium*. N.p., 1629.

————. *Responsio Remonstrantium ad Libellum Cui Titulus Est, Specimen Calumniarum atque Heterodoxarum Opinionum, ex Remonstrantium, Apologia Excerptarum: Instar Prodromi in Lucem Emissum per Quatuor Professores Leydenses*. Harderwijk: Ex officina typographorum Remonstrantium, 1631.

————. *De Crachteloosheyt der Godsalicheyt, van de Leere Iacobi Triglandii: In Syn Boeck Teghen de Enghe-poorte D. Edvardi Poppii*. N.p., 1632.

————. *De Kracht der God-Salicheit: vermorst en vernorselt Deur Iacobi Triglandii in het Boeckxken Krachteloosheyt der Godzaligheyt*. N.p.: Voor de Societeyt der Remonstranten, 1632.

————. *De War-Religie, ofte, De verwarde: valsche en reden-loose Religi Iacobi Triglandii in syn boeck De ware Religie verantwoort*. N.p.: Voor de Societeyt der Remonstranten, 1634.

————. *Vrymoedige Weder-Spraeck: Op de Harde Aen-Spraeck van Abrahamus Heydanus*. [Rotterdam]: J. Naeramus, 1643.

————. *Antwoort Op de Proeve van Abrahamus Heydanus: Tegen de Onderwysinge in de Christeligcke Religie, na de Belijdenisse der Remonstranten*. Rotterdam: Joannes Naeranus, 1644.

————. *Disputationes Theologiæ Tripartæ*. Amsterdam: Ioannem Blæv, 1644.

————. *Disputationum Theologicarum, à M. Simone Episcopio in Academia Leydensi privatim olim habitarum, Collegium Secundum*. In *Disputationes Theologiæ Tripartæ*, 333–428. Amsterdam: Ioannem Blæv, 1644.

————. *Disputationum Theologicarum, à M. Simone Episcopio in Academia Leydensi privatim olim habitarum, Collegium Primum*. In *Disputationes Theologiæ Tripartæ*, 143–332. Amsterdam: Ioannem Blæv, 1644.

————. *Disputationes Theologicæ, Publicè olim in Academia Leydensi habitæ*. In *Disputationes Theologiæ Tripartæ*, 1–142. Amsterdam: Ioannem Blæv, 1644.

————. *Opera Theologica*. Edited by Stephanus Curcellæus. Amsterdam: Ioannis Blæv, 1650.

————. *Apologia Pro Confessione sive Declaratione Sententiæ eorum, Qui in Foederato Belgio vocantur Remonstrantres, super præcipuis articulis Religionis Christiane, Contra Centuraam Quaturo Professorum Leydensium*. In *Opera Theologica*, ed. Stephanus Curcellæus, 2:95–293. Amsterdam: Ioannis Blæv, 1650.

————. *Bodecherus Ineptiens, hoc est, Evidens demonstratio, qua ostenditur N. Bodecherum, ut plus quam servili adsentatione efficacem Contra-Remonstrantium gratiam demereatur, inepte admodum & nugatorie Confessionem Remonstratium Socinismi arcessere nuper esse aggressum*. In *Opera Theologica*, ed. Stephanus Curcellæus, 2:48–58. Amsterdam: Ioannis Blæv, 1650.

————. *Conciones Duæ, de Causis Incredulitatis Iudæorum*. In *Opera Theologica*, ed. Stephanus Curcellæus, 1:431–40. Amsterdam: Ioannis Blæv, 1650.

————. *Epistola Ad Clarissimum Virum Petri Wadingi, Iesuitæ Antuerpiensis, De Regula Fidei*. In *Opera Theologica*, ed. Stephanus Curcellæus, 2:97–100. Amsterdam: Ioannis Blæv, 1650.

————. *Examen Sententiæ Ioannis Cameronis, Scoto-Britanni, De Gratia Dei & libero hominis arbitrio*. In *Opera Theologica*, ed. Stephanus Curcellæus, 2:209–218. Amsterdam: Ioannis Blæv, 1650.

————. *Examen Thesium Theologicarum Iacobi Capelli, quais inscripsi De Controversiis quæ*

Foederatum Belgium vexuant, &, Satius-ne fuerit doctrinam Arminii tolerari quam damnari. In Opera Theologica, ed. Stephanus Curcellæus, 2:165–97. Amsterdam: Ioannis Blæv, 1650.

——————. Examen Thesium Theologicarum Iacobi Capelli, quas inscripsit De Controversiis quæ Foederatum Belgium vexant, et Satisne fuerit tolerari sententiam Arminii, quam damnari et Sedani, anno MDC.XXIII. publice disputandas proposuit. In Opera Theologica, ed. Stephanus Curcellæus, 2:165–197. Amsterdam: Ioannis Blæv, 1650.

——————. Institutiones Theologicæ, privatis lectionibus Amstelodami traditæ. In Opera Theologica, ed. Stephanus Curcellæus, 1:1–430. Amsterdam: Ioannis Blæv, 1650.

——————. Iudicium De Controversia, Quodnam sit ordinarium conversionis medium, Amstelodami exort in illorum cætu qui vulgo Mennonitæ Waterlandi vocantur, inter Nittardum Obbesium ab una, et Ioannem Rysium, Reynerium Wibrandi, Petrum Andreæ et Cornelium Nicolai ab altera parte. In Opera Theologica, ed. Stephanus Curcellæus, 2:372–77. Amsterdam: Ioannis Blæv, 1650.

——————. Labyrinthus, sive, Circulus Pontificius: Versio ex Belgico. In Opera Theologica, ed. Stephanus Curcellæus, 2:148–64. Amsterdam: Ioannis Blæv, 1650.

——————. Paraphrasis & Observationes in Caput VIII, IX, X & XI Epistolæ S. Paulo ad Romanos. In Opera Theologica, ed. Stephanus Curcellæus, 2:388–425. Amsterdam: Ioannis Blæv, 1650.

——————. Responsio Ad Defensionsem Ioannis Cameronis, quam opposuit Epistolæ cuidam, in qua expensa fuerat ejus sententia de gratia & libero arbitrio, sive de determinatione voluntatis per intellectum. In Opera Theologica, ed. Stephanus Curcellæus, 2:219–369. Amsterdam: Ioannis Blæv, 1650.

——————. Responsio ad Duas Epistolas Ioannis Breverovicii, Sabini & Medici Dordrechtani, De Vitæ termino, Fatalisne is sit, an vero Mobilis. In Opera Theologica, ed. Stephanus Curcellæus, 2:378–387. Amsterdam: Ioannis Blæv, 1650.

——————. Responsio ad Epistolam Petri Wadingi, Iesuitæ Antuerpiensis, Theol. Profess., De Regula Fidei. In Opera Theologica, ed. Stephanus Curcellæus, 2:101–30. Amsterdam: Ioannis Blæv, 1650.

——————. Responsio ad Epistolam Petri Wadingi, Iesuitæ Antuerpiensis, Theol. Profess., De Cultu Imaginum. In Opera Theologica, ed. Stephanus Curcellæus, 2:131–47. Amsterdam: Ioannis Blæv, 1650.

——————. Responsio ad Quæstiones Theologicas sexaginta quatuor, ipsi a discipulis in privatio disputationem collegio Amstelodami propositas. In Opera Theologica, ed. Stephanus Curcellæus, 2:1–70. Amsterdam: Ioannis Blæv, 1650.

——————. Tractatus Brevis In Quo Expenditur Quæstio, An homini Christiano liceat gerere Magistratum. In Opera Theologica, ed. Stephanus Curcellæus, 2:71–95. Amsterdam: Ioannis Blæv, 1650.

——————. Tractatus De Libero Arbitrio. In Opera Theologica, ed. Stephanus Curcellæus, 2:198–208. Amsterdam: Ioannis Blæv, 1650.

——————. Extract Uyt het 'Tractaet, 't Welck Mr. Symon Episcopius: Handelnde Van de Vrye Wil, tegen Joannes Camero Geschreven Heeft. Edited by Jacob Johannes Batelier. Rotterdam: Francois van Highstranten, 1664.

——————. Operum Theologicorum, Pars Altera. Edited by Philip van Limborch, 2 vols. Rotterdam: Arnoldum Leers, 1665.

——————. Antidotum Continens Declarationem Sententiæ Quæ in Synodo Nationali Dordrecena Asserta & Stabilita Est. In Operum Theologicorum, Pars Altera, ed. Philip van Limborch, 2:17–47. Rotterdam: Arnoldum Leers, 1665.

——————. Apologia Pro Confessione sive Declaratione Sententiæ eorum, Qui in Foederato Belgio *vocantur Remonstrantes, super præcipuis Articulis Religionis Christianæ, Contra Censuram, Quatuor Professorum Leydensium.* In *Operum Theologicorum, Pars Altera,* ed. Philip van Limborch, 2:95–283. Rotterdam: Arnoldum Leers, 1665.

————. *Confessio, sive Declaratio, Sententiæ Pastorum qui in Foederato Belgio Remonstrantes vocantur, Super præcipuis articulis Religionis Christianæ.* In *Operum Theologicorum, Pars Altera,* ed. Philip van Limborch, 1:69–94. Rotterdam: Arnoldum Leers, 1665.

————. *Crudelis Iniquitas Synodi Dordracenæ, et Eorum Qui Illi Præfuerunt, in Beglii Remonstranties, quos vocant, exposta.* In *Operum Theologicorum, Pars Altera,* ed. Philip van Limborch, 2:5–9. Rotterdam: Arnoldum Leers, 1665.

————. *De optima regni Christi exstruendi ratione."* In *Operum Theologicorum, Pars Altera,* ed. Philip van Limborch, 1:586–589. Rotterdam: Arnoldum Leers, 1665.

————. *Disputationes Theologicæ Tripartitæ.* In *Operum Theologicorum, Pars Altera,* ed. Philip van Limborch, 2:386–460. Rotterdam: Arnoldum Leers, 1665.

————. *Examen Disputationis Theologicæ Antonii Walæi, quam inscripsit de Quatuor controversis Remonstrantium artriculis vulgo notis, in qua status controversiæ ned proponitu, & Remonstranes ad Ecclesiæ Begicæ unitatem invitantur integra veritate.* In *Operum Theologicorum, Pars Altera,* ed. Philip van Limborch, 2:59–68. Rotterdam: Arnoldum Leers, 1665.

————. *Lectiones Sacræ in 1 & 2 Caput Apocalypseos.* In *Operum Theologicorum, Pars Altera,* ed. Philip van Limborch, 1:429–581. Rotterdam: Arnoldum Leers, 1665.

————. *Lectiones Sacræ in I. Epistolam Catholicam Apostoli Ioannis.* In *Operum Theologicorum, Pars Altera,* ed. Philip van Limborch, 1:173–428. Rotterdam: Arnoldum Leers, 1665.

————. *Notæ Breves in Matthæum.* In *Operum Theologicorum, Pars Altera,* ed. Philip van Limborch, 1:1–169. Rotterdam: Arnoldum Leers, 1665.

————. *Oratio Generis Deliberativi, An Philosophæ studium necessarium sit Theologiæ candidato? Habita cum Magister artium createtur.* In *Operum Theologicorum, Pars Altera,* ed. Philip van Limborch, 1:582–90. Rotterdam: Arnoldum Leers, 1665.

————. *Oratio Habita in Synodo Nationali Dordrecena.* In *Operum Theologicorum, Pars Altera,* ed. Philip van Limborch, 2:1–4. Rotterdam: Arnoldum Leers, 1665.

————. *Præfatio in Novi Testamenti, brevem interpretationem, de lectione Scripturæ.* In *Operum Theologicorum, Pars Altera,* ed. Philip van Limborch, 1:593–596. Rotterdam: Arnoldum Leers, 1665.

————. "Responsio Remonstrantium ad Libellum Cui Titulus Est, Specimen Calumniarum atque heterodoxarum Opinionum, ex Remonstrantium, Apologia excerptarum." In *Operum Theologicorum, Pars Altera,* ed. Philip van Limborch, 2:284–321. Rotterdam: Arnoldum Leers, 1665.

————. *Vedelius Rhapsodus, Sive Vindiciæ Doctrinæ Remonstrantium à Criminationibus & calumnijs Nicolæ Vedelii.* In *Operum Theologicorum, Pars Altera,* ed. Philip van Limborch, 2:322–385. Rotterdam: Arnoldum Leers, 1665.

————. *Verus Theologus Remonstrans, falso ac spurio oppositus.* In *Operum Theologicorum, Pars Altera,* ed. Philip van Limborch, 2:508–533. Rotterdam: Arnoldum Leers, 1665.

————. *The Popish Labyrinth: Wherein is made manifest, that the papists are entangled in the Fundamental Article of their Faith, that the Church cannot Erre.* Translated by "J. K." London: Ratcliff and Thomson for Francis Smith, 1673.

————. *The Confession or Declaration of the Ministers or Pastors which in the United Provinces* are called Remonstrants, Concerning The Chief Points of Christian Religion. London: Francis Smith, 1676.

————. Opera Theologica. 2d ed., 2 vols. London: Mosis Pit, 1678.

————. Predicatien van M. S. Episcopius. Edited by Philip van Limborch. Amsterdam: Isaak Pieterz., 1693.

Gomarus, Franciscus. Opera Theologica Omnia. 3 vols. Amsterdam: Joannis Janssonii, 1644.

Gomarus, Franciscus, and Jacobus Arminius. Twee Disputatien van de Goddelicke Predestinatie. Leyden: Ian Pæts Iacobscoon, 1609.

Hartsoeker, Christiaan, and Philippus van Limborch, ed. Præstantium ac Eruditorum Virorum Epistolæ Ecclesiasticæ et Theologicæ. Amsterdam: Henricum Wetstenium, 1660.

————. Præstantium ac Eruditorum Virorum Epistolæ Ecclesiasticæ et Theologicæ. 3d ed. Amsterdam: Henricum Wetstenium, 1704.

Heyden, Abraham van der. Proeve ende Weerlegginghe des Remonstrantschen Catechismi. Leiden: Paulus Ærtsz van Revesteyn, 1641.

————. De causa Dei, dat is: De sake Godts, verdedight tegen den Mensche: ofte, Wederlegginge van de Antwoorde van M. Simon Episcopius, wijlen Professor der H. Theologie, op de Proeve des Remonstrantschen Catechismi. Leiden: Paulus Ærtsz van Revesteyn, 1645.

Hemmingius, Nicolas. Tractatus. Copenhagen: Munksgaard, 1591.

Junius, Franciscus. De Theologia Vera: Ortu, Natura, Formis, Partibus, et Modo Illius. Leiden: Ex Officina Plantiniana Apud Franciscum Raphelengium, 1594.

————. Den Vreedsamen Christen, Of, Van de Vrede der Catholijcke Kercke. Delft: Adriaen Gerritsz., 1612.

————. Opuscula Theologica Selecta. Edited by Abr. Kuyperus. Amsterdam: Fredericum Muller Cum Soc. et Joannem Hermannum Kruyt, 1882.

————. Theses Theologicæ Quæ in Inclyta Academia Lugdunobativa Ad Exercitia Publicarum Dipustationum, Præside D. Francisco Iunio Variis temporibus à Theologiæ Candidatis aduersus oppognantes propugnatæ sunt. In Opuscula Theologica Selecta, ed. Abr. Kuyperus, 104–289. Amsterdam: Fredericum Muller Cum Soc. et Joannem Hermannum Kruyt, 1882.

————. Tractatus de Vera Theologia. In Opuscula Theologica Selecta, ed. Abr. Kuyperus, 37–101. Amsterdam: Fredericum Muller Cum Soc. et Joannem Hermannum Kruyt, 1882.

————. Eirenicum de Pace Ecclesiæ Catholicæ. In Opuscula Theologica Selecta, ed. Abr. Kuyperus, 395–494. Amsterdam: Fredericum Muller Cum Soc. et Joannem Hermannum Kruyt, 1882.

————. "Franciscii Junii Vita." In Opuscula Theologica Selecta, ed. Abr. Kuyperus, 2–36. Amsterdam: Fredericum Muller Cum Soc. et Joannem Hermannum Kruyt, 1882.

Locke, John. A Letter Concerning Toleration. Edited by William Popple. London: Awnsham Churchill, 1690.

————. Lettres Inédites de John Locke à Ses Amis Nicolas Thoynard, Philippe van Limborch et Edward Clarke. Edited by Henri Ollion and T. J. de Boer. La Haye: M. Nijhoff, 1912.

————. Epistola de Tolerantia. A Letter on Toleration. Edited by Raymond Klibansky. Translated by J. W. Gough, with an introduction and notes. Oxford: Clarendon Press, 1968.

Perkins, William. Armilla Aurea, id est, Theologiæ Descriptio Mirandam Seriem Causarum & Salutis & Damnationis Iuxta Verbum Desproponens: eius synopsin continet annexa ad finem tabula. 2d ed. Cambridge: Johannis Legatt extant Londini apud Abrahamum Kitson ad insigne solis in Cimiterio D. Pauli, 1591.

———. *De Prædestinationis Modo et Ordine: et de Amplitudine Gratiæ Divinæ Christiana & Perspicua Disceptatio*. Basel: C. Waldkirchii, 1599.

———. *The workes of that famous and worthie minister of Christ in the University of Cambridge*. Cambridge: Printed by John Legate Printer to the University of Cambridge, 1608.

———. *The Golden Chain*. In *The Work of William Perkins*, ed. Ian Breward, 169–260. Abingdon, England: Sutton Courtenay Press, 1970.

Polyander, Iohannes, André Rivet, Antonius Walæus, and Antonius Thysius. *Specimen Calumniarum atque Heterodoxarum Opinionum ex Remonstrantius Apologia Excerptarum*. Leiden, n. p., 1625.

———. *Synopsis Purioris Theologiæ, Disputationibus Quinquaginta Duabus Comprehensa*. Leiden: Ex Officinâ Elzeviriana, 1625.

———. *Censura in Confessionem, sive, Declarationem pententiæ corum que in foederato Belgio Remonstrantes vocantur: super præcipius articulis Christianæ religionis*. Leiden: Bonaventuræ & Abrahami Elzevir, 1626.

Polyander, Johannes, and Johannes Wollebius. *Pointen bij de Professoren tot Leyden geextreheert uit de Apologie van de Confessie der Remonstranten*. Leiden, 1630.

Poppius, Eduard. De enge Poorte: ofte, Predicatien Over eenighe voortreffelijke Texten, ofte Spreucken der heyligher Schrifture. Goude: Jasper Tournap voor Andries Burier, 1616.

Schriftelicke Conferentie, Gehouden in s'Gravenhaghe inde Iare 1611 tusschen sommige Kercken Dienaren ængaende de Godlicke Praedestinatie metten van dien. The Hague: Hillebrandt Jacobsz., 1612.

Triglandius, Jacobus. *Den Recht-gematichden Christen*. Amsterdam: Paulus van Ravesteyn, 1615.

———. *Antwoorde Op dry Vraghen: dienende tot advijs in de huydendaechse swaricheden*. N.p., 1615.

———. *Clare Aenwijsinge Hoe Iohannes Wtenbogaert Hem gheensins en suyvert / noch verontschuldight in sijn genaemde klare Justificatie / van de ontrouwigheydt ende onbehoorlijcke maniere van doen / die Iacobus Triglandius, so inde Dedicatie aen sijn Princelijcke Excellentie, als inde Voor-reden / gelijck mede in sijn boeck / Verdediginghe genaemt / hem naecktelijck had verthoont, Rakende voornamelijck de Poincten Van't noodtsaken tot de Sonde: Ende d'Onderlinge Verdraeghsaemheyt*. Amsterdam: Martin Iansz, 1616.

———. *Verdediging vande Leere end Eere: der Gereformeerde Kercken ende Leeraren / tegen verscheyden lasteringen / insonderheyt Iohannis Wtenbogardi in zijn boeck t'onrecht geintituleert Verdedigingh vande Resolutie der Mog. Heeren Staten van Hollant ende West-Vrieslant*. Amsterdam: Marten Jansz. Brandt, 1616.

———. *Christelijcke ende nootvvendighe Verclaringhe Vant ghene in seker Formulier gheintituleert Resolutie der Staten*. Amsterdam: Marten Jansz. Brandt, 1616.

———. *Klaer ende grondich Tegen-vertoogh: van eenige Kercken-Dienaren van Hollant ende West-Vrieslandt: ghestelt tegen Remonstranten*. Amsterdam: Marten Jansz. Brandt, 1617.

———. *Geessel Om uyt te dryven den Arminiaenschen Quel-Gheest*. Amsterdam: Marten Jansz. Brandt, 1618.

———. *Verdediging van de Leere end Eere Der Gereformeerde Kercken: tegen Iohannem Wtenbogaerdi in zijn Boeck: Verdedigingh van de Resolutie der Staten van Hollant*. Amsterdam: Marten Jansz. Brandt, 1619.

———. *Brief Van Simon Episcopius Met eenighe Aenteyckeninghen ofte Commentarien breder* verclaert: waer bij noch gevoecht is een kerckelyck ende Politijck Discours. Amsterdam: Marten Iansz. Brandt, 1620.

————. Christelijcke ende Vriendelijcke Vermaninge ten alle af-gedwaelde Remonstrants-Gesinde. Amsterdam: Marten Iansz Brandt, 1623.

————. Den Krachteloosen Remonstrant Vermorselt Door de Krachte vande Leere der Waerheydt. Amsterdam: Marten Iansz Brandt, 1632.

————. De Ware Religie: Verantwoort teghen de lasteringen der Remonstrantsche Societeyt. Amsterdam: Marten Jansz Brandtm, 1633.

————. Kerckelycke geschiedenissen: begrypende de swaere en bekommerlijcke geschillen in de Vereenigde Nederlanden voor-gevallen: met derselver beslissinge: ende aenmerckingen op de Kerckelycke historie van Johannes VVtenbogaert: uyt autentycke stucken getrouwelijck vergadert: ende op begeerte der Zuyd en Noort-Hollantsche synden uytgegeven, tot nodige onderrichtinge. Leiden: Adriaen Wyngaerden, 1650.

————. Antapologia: sive, Examen atque Refutatio Totius Apologiæ Remonstrantium: Ubique Ipso Apologiae Textu Inserto, Ita ut Cum & Sine Ipsa Legi Possit. Amsterdam: Joannem Janssonium Joannem à Waesberge & Elizeum Weyerstraeten, 1664.

Van Limborch, Philippus. A Compleat System, or Body of Divinity, both Speculative and Practical: Founded on Scripture and Reason. Edited by Jean Le Clerc, 2 vols. London: n.p., 1702.

————. Leven van Mr. Simon Episcopius. In Predicatien van M. S. Episcopius, 3–150. Amsterdam: Isaak Pieterz., 1693.

————. Historia Vitæ Episcopii. Amsterdam: Georgium Gallet, 1701.

————. Theologia Christiana ad Praxin Pietatis ac Promotionem Pacis Christianæ Unice Directa. Edited by Jean Le Clerc. 4th ed. Amsterdam: Rodolph. & Gerhard. Wetstenios, 1715.

Vedelius, Nicholas. De Arcanis Arminianismi Libri Duo, seu Quæstio, Quænam sit Religio et Fides Theologorum Remonstrantium, decisa ex Confissione et Apologia Ipsorum. N.p., 1630.

Walæus, Antonius. Disputatio Theologica de Quatuor Controversis Remonstrantium articulis vulgo notis. In qua status controversiæ nude proponitur et Remonstrantes ad Ecclesiæ Unitatem invitantur integra veritate. In Opera Omnia Walæi. Leiden: n.p., 1643.

Wtenbogaert, Johannes. Brieven en Onuitgegeven Stukken. Edited by H. C. Rogge, 3 vols. Utrecht: Kemink en Zoon, 1868.

————. Clare Iustificatie Van seeckere Passagien: Dær over Jacobvs Triglandi. The Hague: Hillebrant Jacobsz., 1616.

————. Trouhertighe Aenwijsinghe Der Bedriegelijckheden de Vermaninghe Iacobi Triglandij. Herderwijck: n.p., 1623.

————. Goedt ende Christelijck Bescheydt Ghegheven op Jacobi Triglandij Tweede Vermaningh ende verdedigingh van de Trouwe Aenwijsingh. N.p., 1627.

————. Kerkeliicke Historie Vervatende verscehdyen Gedenckwaerdige Saecken in de Christenheyt voorgevallen van het Jaer vier hondert af, tot in het Jaer sestien hondert ende negentien, Voornamentlijck in dese Geunieerde Provincien. 2d ed. [Amsterdam]: Ghedruckt in't Iaer ons Heeren, 1647.

————. "The Remonstrance of 1610." In The Creeds of Christendom, with a History and Critical Notes, ed. Philip Schaff, 3:545–549. 6th ed. New York: Harper & brothers, 1919.

Other Books

Aquinas, Thomas. *Questions on the Soul*. Edited by James H. Robb. Translated by James H. Robb. Milwaukee: Marquette University Press, 1984.

Aristotle. *The "Art" of Rhetoric* . Cambridge, MA: Harvard University Press, 1994.

Armstrong, Brian G. *Calvinism and the Amyraut Heresy: Protestant Scholasticism and Humanism in Seventeenth-Century France*. Madison: University of Wisconsin Press, 1969.

Augustine. *The City of God Against The Pagans*. Translated by James Houston Baxter. Loeb classical library, ed. T. E. Page, E. Capps, W. H. D. Rouse, L. A. Post and E. H. Warmington. Cambridge: Harvard University Press, 1957.

Baker, J. Wayne. *Heinrich Bullinger and the Covenant: The Other Reformed Tradition*. Athens, OH: Ohio University Press, 1980.

Venema, Cornelis P. *Heinrich Bullinger and the Doctrine of Predestination: Author of "the Other Reformed Tradition"?* Grand Rapids: Baker Academic, 2002.

Bakhuizen van den Brink, Jan Nicolaas. *Documenta Reformatoria; Teksten Uit de Geschiedenis van Kerk en Theologie in de Nederlanden Sedert de Hervorming*, 2 vols. Kampen: J. H. Kok, 1960.

Bangs, Carl O. *Arminius: A Study in the Dutch Reformation*. 2d ed. Grand Rapids: Francis Asbury Press, 1985.

Bangs, Nathan. *The Life of James Arminius*. New York: Harper and Brothers, 1843.

Barth, Karl. *The Doctrine of God*. Translated by Geoffry W. Bromiley. Vol. 2/2, *Church Dogmatics*. Edinburgh: T. & T. Clark, 1957.

Beardslee, John W, ed. *Reformed dogmatics: J. Wollebius, G. Voetius and F. Turretin*. New York: Oxford University Press, 1965.

Becker, Bruno. *Sébastien Castellion et Thierry Coornhert*. Amsterdam: Hertzberger, 1968.

Bernard of Clairvaux. *De Gratia et Libero Arbitrio*. In *Opera Omnia*. Vol. 182. *Patrologiæ Cursus Completus, sive biblioteca universalis, integra, uniformis, commoda, oeconomica, omnium SS. Patrum, doctorum scriptorumque ecclesiasticorum*. Series Latina Prior, ed. J. P. Migne, vol. 182, cols. 1001–30. Paris: Migne, 1844–64.

Bizer, Ernst. *Frühorthodoxie und Rationalismus*. Theologische Studien, vol. 71. Zürich: EVZ-Verlag, 1963.

Blanke, Fritz, and Immanuel Leuschner. *Heinrich Bullinger: Vater der reformierten Kirche*. Zürich: Theologischer Verlag, 1990.

Blok, Petrus Johannes. *Geschiedenis Van Het Nederlandsche Volk*. 6 vols. Groningen: J. B. Wolters, 1892.

———. *A History of the People of the Netherlands*. New York: G. P. Putnam's Sons, 1899–1900.

Bonger, H. *De Motiviering van de Godsdienstvrijheid bij Dirck Volckertszoon Coornhert*. N.p.: Van Loghum Slaterus, 1954.

———. *Dirck Volckertszoon Coornhert: Dwars Maar Recht*. Zutphen: De Walburg Pers, 1989.

Bouwsma, William James. *The Interpretation of Renaissance Humanism*. Washington: Service Center for Teachers of History, 1959.

———. *John Calvin: A Sixteenth-Century Portrait*. New York: Oxford University Press, 1988.

Brandt, Caspar. *The Life of James Arminius*. Translated by John Guthrie. Nashville: E.

Stevenson & F.A. Owen, Agents for the Methodist Episcopal Church South, 1857.

Bratt, John H., ed. *The Heritage of John Calvin: Heritage Hall lectures, 1960–70.* Heritage Hall publications, no. 2. Grand Rapids: Eerdmans, 1973.

Bray, John S. *Theodore Beza's Doctrine of Predestination.* Bibliotheca Humanistica & Reformatorica, no. 12. Nieuwkoop: De Graaf, 1975.

Büsser, Fritz. *Wurzeln der Reformation in Zürich: zum 500 Geburtstag des Reformators Huldrych Zwingli.* Leiden: E.J. Brill, 1985.

Calder, Frederick. *Memoirs of Simon Episcopius.* London: Simpkin and Marshall, 1835.

Calvin, John. *Institutes of the Christian Religion.* Edited by John Thomas McNeill. Translated by Ford Lewis Battles. The Library of Christian Classics, vols. 20, 21. Philadelphia: Westminster Press, 1960.

————. *Calvin's Commentaries: Harmony Of The Evangelists (Matthew, Mark, And Luke).* Garland, TX: Electronic Edition by Galaxy Software, 1999. [CD-ROM]. (Edinburgh: The Calvin Translation Society, 1845).

————. *Commentaries on the First Book of Moses Called Genesis.* Translated by John King. Edinburgh: Calvin Translation Society, n.d. Reprint, Grand Rapids: Baker Book House, 1981.

Cerny, Gerald. *Theology, Politics, and Letters at the Crossroads of European Civilization: Jacques Basnage and the Baylean Huguenot Refugees in the Dutch Republic.* Dordrecht: M. Nijhoff, 1987.

Clement of Alexandria. *The Stromata.* In *The Apostolic Fathers, Justin Martyr, Irenæus.* Vol. 2, *The Ante-Nicene Fathers. Translations of the writings of the fathers down to A.D. 325,* ed. Alexander Roberts and James Donaldson, 299–568. Buffalo, NY: Christian Literature Publishing Company, 1885. Reprint, Peabody, MA: Hendrickson Publishers, 1994.

————. *Who Is the Rich Man that Shall be Saved?* In *Fathers of the Second Century.* Vol. 2, *The Ante-Nicene Fathers. Translations of the writings of the fathers down to A.D. 325,* ed. Alexander Roberts and James Donaldson, 591–604. Buffalo, NY: Christian Literature Publishing Company, 1885. Reprint, Peabody, MA: Hendrickson Publishers, 1994.

Clement of Rome. *The First Epistle of Clement to the Corinthians.* In *The Apostolic Fathers.* Loeb Classical Library, ed. G. P. Goold, 1:1–122. Cambridge, MA: Harvard University Press; London: William Heinemann, 1985.

Clune, W. M. *Human Nature After the Fall According to St. Thomas Aquinas.* Rome: Aedes Universitatis Gergorianeæ, 1939.

Cochrane, Arthur C. *Reformed Confessions of the 16th century.* Philadelphia: Westminster Press, 1966.

Colie, Rosalie L. *Light and Enlightenment.* New York: Cambridge University Press, 1957.

Coornhert, D. V. *Op Zoek Naar Het Hoogste Goed.* Edited by H. Bonger. Geschiedenis van de wijsbegeerte in Nederland, no. 7. Baarn: Ambo, 1987.

Cunningham, William. *Historical Theology: A Review of the Principal Doctrinal Discussions in the Christian Church since the Apostolic Age.* 2 vols. London: Banner of Truth Trust, 1960.

Cunningham, William. *The Reformers and the Theology of the Reformation.* Edited by James Buchanan and James Bannerman. Edinburgh: T. and T. Clark, 1862. Reprint, Edinburgh: Banner of Truth Trust, 1967.

Cuno, François W. *Franciscus Junius der Ältere, Professor der Theologie und Pastor (1545–1602): sein Leben und Wirken, seine Schriften und Briefe.* Amsterdam: Scheffer, 1891.

Curtis, S. J. *A Short History of Western Philosophy in the Middle Ages.* London: MacDonald and

Co., 1950.

Dabney, Robert Louis. *Syllabus and Notes of the Course of Systematic and Polemic Theology.* 4th ed. Richmond, VA: Presbyterian Committee of Publication, 1890.

Davaine, Alfred. *François du Jon (Junius) Pasteur et Professeur en Théologie, 1545–1602; étude historique.* Paris: Imprimé par C. Noblet, 1882.

De Yong, Peter Y., ed. *Crisis in the Reformed Churches: Essays in the Commemoration of the Great Synod of Dort, 1618–1619.* Grand Rapids: Reformed Fellowship, 1968.

Downey, Edward A. *The Knowledge of God in Calvin's theology.* New York: Columbia University Press, 1952.

Dresden, S. *Humanism in the Renaissance.* London: Weidenfeld & Nicolson, 1968.

Duke, Alastair C. *Reformation and Revolt in the Low Countries.* London: Hambledon Press, 1990.

————, Gillian Lewis, and Andrew Pettegree. *Calvinism in Europe, 1540–1610: A Collection of Documents.* Manchester: Manchester University Press, 1992.

Evans, G. R. *Old Arts and New Theology: The Beginnings of Theology as an Academic Discipline.* Oxford: Clarendon Press, 1980.

Gäbler, Ulrich. *Huldrych Zwingli: His Life and Work.* Translated by Ruth C. L. Gritsch. Philadelphia: Fortress Press, 1986.

Geisendorf, Paul Frédéric. *Théodore de Bèze.* Geneva: Labor et Fides, 1949.

Geyl, Pieter. *Geschiedenis van de Nederlandse Stam.* 6 vols. Amsterdam: Wereldbibliotheek, 1961–62.

Groen van Prinsterer, Guillaume. *Maurice et Barnevelt: étude historique.* Utrecht: Kemink et fils, 1875.

Haar, H. W. ter. *Jacobus Trigland.* The Hague: Nijhoff, 1891.

Haentjens, Anton Hendrik. *Simon Episcopius als Apologeet van het Remonstrantisme in Zijn Leven en Werken Geschestst.* Leiden: A. H. Adriani, 1899.

Haren, Michael. *Medieval thought: The Western Intellectual Tradition from Antiquity to the Thirteenth Century.* New York: St. Martin's Press, 1985.

Harnack, Adolf von. *History of dogma.* Edited by T. K. Cheyne and A. B. Bruce. Translated by Neil Buchanan, 10 vols. Boston: Little, Brown and Company, 1903.

————. *Outlines of the History of Dogma.* Edited by Edwin Knox Mitchell. Translated by Edwin Knox Mitchell. Boston: Beacon Hill Press, 1959.

Harrison, A. W. *The Beginnings of Arminianism to the Synod of Dort.* London: University of London Press, 1926.

Heering, G. J., ed. *De Remonstranten Gedenkboek bij het 300-jarig bestaan der Remonstrantsche Broederschap.* Leiden: A. W. Sijthoof's Uitgevers, 1919.

Heering, G. J., and G. J. Sirks. *Het Seminarium der Remonstranten Driehonderd Jaar: 1634–1934.* Amsterdam: Lankamp & Brinkman, 1934.

Helm, Paul. *Calvin and the Calvinists.* Carlisle, PA: Banner of Truth Trust, 1982.

Heppe, Heinrich. *Reformed Dogmatics: Set Out and Illustrated from the Original Sources.* Edited by Ernst Bizer. Translated by G. T. Thomson. London: George Allen & Unwin Ltd., 1950. Reprint, Grand Rapids: Baker Book House, 1986.

Hodge, Charles. *Systematic Theology.* 3 vols. New York: Charles Scribner's Sons, 1872.

Hoeksema, Homer C. *The Voice of Our Fathers.* Grand Rapids: Reformed Free Publishing Association, 1980.

Hoenderdaal, Gerrit J., and P. M. Luca, ed. *Staat in de Vrijheid: De Geschiedenis van de Remonstranten*. Zutphen: De Walburg Pres, 1982.

Hollweg, Walter. *Heinrich Bullingers Hausbuch: eine Untersuchung über die Anfänge der reformierten Predigtliteratur*. Geschichte und Lehre der Reformierten Kirche, vol. 8. Neukirchen: Krs. Moers, 1956.

Hyma, Albert. *The Christian Renaissance: A History of the "Devotio Moderna."* 2d ed. Hamden, CT: Archon Books, 1965.

————. *The Life of Desiderius Erasmus*. Assen: Van Gorcum, 1972.

Jansen, Johannes. *Korte Verklaring van de Kerkenordening*. Kampen: J. H. Kok, 1923.

Jelsma, Auke. *Frontiers of the Reformation: Dissidence and Orthodoxy in Sixteenth-Century Europe*. Aldershot, England: Ashgate, 1998.

Justin Martyr. *Dialogue of Justin, Philosopher and Martyr, with Trypho, a Jew*. In *The Apostolic Fathers, Justin Martyr, Irenaeus*. Vol. 1, *The Ante-Nicene Fathers. Translations of the writings of the fathers down to A.D. 325*, ed. Alexander Roberts and James Donaldson, 194–270. Buffalo, NY: Christian Literature Publishing Company, 1885. Reprint, Peabody, MA: Hendrickson Publishers.

————. *The First Apology*. In *The Apostolic Fathers, Justin Martyr, Irenaeus*. Vol. 1, *The Ante-Nicene Fathers. Translations of the writings of the fathers down to A.D. 325*, ed. Alexander Roberts and James Donaldson, 159–187. Buffalo, NY: Christian Literature Publishing Company, 1885. Reprint, Peabody, MA: Hendrickson Publishers.

————. *The Second Apology*. In *The Apostolic Fathers, Justin Martyr, Irenaeus*. Vol. 1, *The Ante-Nicene Fathers. Translations of the writings of the fathers down to A.D. 325*, ed. Alexander Roberts and James Donaldson, 188–93. Buffalo, NY: Christian Literature Publishing Company, 1885. Reprint, Peabody, MA: Hendrickson Publishers.

Kamen, Henry. *The Rise of Toleration*. New York: McGraw-Hill Book Company, 1967.

Kelly, Donald R. *Renaissance Humanism*. Edited by Michael Roth. Boston: Twayne Publishers, 1991.

Kelly, John Norman Davidson. *Early Christian Doctrines*. Rev. ed. San Francisco: Harper & Row, 1978.

Kendall, R. T. *Calvin and English Calvinism to 1649*. Oxford: Oxford University Press, 1979.

Keuning, J. *Petrus Plancius, Theoloog en Geograaf, 1552–1622*. Amsterdam: P.N. van Kampen & Zoon, 1946.

Kickel, Walter. *Vernunft und Offenbarung bei Theodor Beza. Zum Problem der Verhältnisses von Theologie, Philosophie und Staat*. Neukirchen-Vluyn: Neukirchener Verlag, 1967.

Klauber, Martin I. *Between Reformed Scholasticism and Pan-Protestantism: Jean Alphonse Turretin and the Enlightened Orthodoxy at the Academy of Geneva*. Selingsgrove: Susquehanna University Press, 1994.

Knappert, L. *Het Ontstaan en de Vestiging van het Protestantisme in de Nederlanden*. Utrecht: A. Oosthoek, 1924.

Kristeller, Paul Oskar. Renaissance *Thought: The Classic, Scholastic and Humanist Strains*. New York: Harper and Row, 1961.

————. *Eight philosophers of the Italian Renaissance*. Stanford: Stanford University Press, 1964.

————. *Medieval Aspects of Renaissance Learning; Three Essays*. Duke Monographs in

Medieval and Renaissance Studies. Durham, NC: Duke University Press, 1974.

————. *Renaissance philosophy and the mediaeval tradition.* Wimmer Lecture, no. 15. Latrobe, PA: Archabbey Press, 1966.

————, and Michael Mooney. *Renaissance Thought and Its Sources.* New York: Columbia University Press, 1979.

Kromminga, Diedrich Hinrich. *The Christian Reformed Tradition: From the Reformation till the Present.* Grand Rapids: Wm. B. Eerdmans, 1943.

Laplanche, François. *Orthodoxie et Prédication: L'oeuvre d'Amyraut et La Querelle de La Grâce Universelle.* Paris: Presses Universitaires de France, 1965.

Le Cornu, Frank. *Origine des Eglises Réformées Wallonnes des Pays-Bas: Étude Historique.* Utrecht: J. van Boekhoven, n.d.

Le Vassor, Michel. *The History of the Reign of Lewis XIII, King of France and Navarre containing the most remarkable occurrences in France and Europe during the minority of that prince.* Translated by Mr. Fontvive. London: Printed for Thomas Cockerill, 1700.

Lindberg, Carter. *The European Reformations.* Oxford: Blackwell Publishers, 1996.

Luther, Martin. "Disputation against Scholastic Theology." In *Early Theological Works,* ed. James Atkinson, 266–73. Philadelphia: Westminster Press, 1962.

Marenbon, John. *Later Medieval Philosophy.* London and New York: Loutledge and Kegan Paul, 1987.

————. *Early Medieval Philosophy.* London and New York: Routledge, 1988.

————., ed. *Medieval Philosophy. Routledge History of Philosophy.* Vol. 3. London and New York: Routledge, 1998.

Maronier, J. H. *Jacobus Arminius: Een Biografie (Met Portret en Handteekening).* Amsterdam: Y. Rogge, 1905.

McCulloch, Gerald O., ed. *Man's Faith and Freedom: The Theological Influence of Jacobus Arminius.* New York: Abingdon Press, 1962.

McGrath, Alister E. *The Intellectual Origins of the European Reformation.* Oxford: Basil Blackwell, 1987.

McKim, Donald K. *Ramism in William Perkins' Theology.* American University Studies, ser. 7, Theology and Religion, vol. 15. New York, Bern, Frankfurt am Main, Paris: Peter Lang, 1987.

McNeill, John Thomas. *The History and Character of Calvinism.* New York: Oxford University Press, 1954.

Motley, John Lothrop. *The Rise of the Dutch Republic: A History.* 3 vols. New York: Harper & Bros., 1856.

————. *History of the United Netherlands: From the Death of William the Silent to the Twelve Years' Truce.* 4 vols. New York: Harper, 1861.

————. *The Life and Death of John of Barneveld, Advocate of Holland; With a View of the Primary Causes and Movements of the Thirty Years' War.* 2 vols. New York: Harper & Brothers, 1874.

Muller, Richard A. *Christ and the Decree: Christology and Predestination in Reformed Theology from Calvin to Perkins.* Durham, N.C.: Labyrinth Press, 1986.

————. *Post-Reformation Reformed Dogmatics: Prolegomena to Theology.* Grand Rapids: Baker Book House, 1987.

————. *God, Creation, and Providence in the Thought of Jacob Arminius: Sources and Directions of Scholastic Protestantism in the Era of Early Orthodoxy*. Grand Rapids: Baker Book House, 1991.

Nichols, James. "A Brief Account of the Synod of Dort, Taken Out of the letters of Mr. Hales and Mr. Balcanqual, written from Dort, to the Rt. Hon. Sir D. Carelton, Lord Ambassador then at the Hague." In *The Works of Arminius*, 1:541–579. London ed. London: Longman, Hurst, Rees, Orme, Brown and Green, 1825. Reprint, Grand Rapids: Baker Book House, 1986.

Nijenhuis, Willem. *Ecclesia Reformata: Studies on the Reformation*. Vol. 2. Leiden: Brill, 1972.

O'Daly, Gerard J. P. *Augustine's Philosophy of Mind*. Berkeley and Los Angeles: University of California Press, 1987.

Ong, Walter J. *Ramus: Method, and the Decay of Dialogue: From the Art of Discourse to the Art of Reason*. Cambridge, MA: Harvard University Press, 1958.

Oog, David. *Europe in the Seventeenth Century*. London: Adam and Charles Black, 1948.

Oorthuys, G. *Anastasius' "Wechwyser," Bullingers "Huysboeck" en Calvyns "Institutie" vergeleken in hun leer van God en mensch*. Leiden: Brill, 1919.

Origen. *De Principiis*. Vol. 4, *The Ante-Nicene Fathers. Translations of the writings of the fathers down to A.D. 325*, ed. Alexander Roberts and James Donaldson, 239–385. Buffalo, NY: Christian Literature Publishing Company, 1885. Reprint, Peabody, MA: Hendrickson Publishers.

Palmer, Edwin H. *The Five Points of Calvinism*. Enlarged ed. Grand Rapids: Baker Book House, 1980.

Parker, Geoffrey. *The Dutch Revolt*. Ithaca, NY: Cornell University Press, 1977.

———. *Spain and the Netherlands, 1559–1659: Ten Studies*. Short Hills, NJ: Enslow Publishers, 1979.

———. *Philip II*. 3d ed. Chicago: Open Court, 1995.

Peter of Ailly. *Peter of Ailly and the Harvest of Fourteenth-Century Philosophy*. Edited by Leonard A. Kennedy. Queenston/Lewiston: Edwin Mellen Press, 1986.

Pettegree, Andrew, ed. *The Early Reformation in Europe*. Cambridge: Cambridge University Press, 1992.

———. *Emden and the Dutch Revolt: Exile and Development of Reformed Protestantism*. Oxford: Oxford University Press, 1992.

———, ed. *The Reformation of the Parishes: The Ministry and The Reformation in Town and Country*. Manchester: Manchester University Press, 1993.

Pierson, Peter. *Phillip II of Spain*. New York: Transatlantic Arts, Inc., 1975.

Pijper, F. "Geestelijke Stroomingen in Nederland Vóór de Opkomst van het Remonstrantisme." In *De Remonstranten Gedenkboek bij het 300-jarig betstaan der Remonstrantsche Broederschap*, ed. G. J. Heering, 37–60. Leiden: A. W. Sijthoff's Uitgevers, 1919.

Platt, John. *Reformed Thought and Scholasticism: The Arguments for the Existence of God in Dutch Theology, 1575–1650*. Leiden: E.J. Brill, 1982.

Poujol, D. F. *Histoire et Influence des Églises Wallonnes Dans les Pays-Bas*. Paris: Fischbacher, 1902.

Prestwich, Menna, ed. *International Calvinism, 1541–1715*. Oxford: Clarendon Press, 1985.

Raitt, Jill. *The Eucharistic Theology of Theodore Beza: Development of the Reformed Doctrine*. Chambersburg, PA: American Academy of Religion, 1972.

———. *The colloquy of Montbéliard: Religion and Politics in the Sixteenth Century*. New York: Oxford University Press, 1993.

Reid, W. Stanford, and Paul Woolley, ed. *John Calvin, His influence in the Western world. Contemporary Evangelical Perspectives.* Grand Rapids: Zondervan Publishing House, 1982.

Reitsma, Johannes. *Geschiedenis Van de Hervorming en De Hervormde Kerk der Nederlanden.* 4th ed. Utrecht: Kemink & Zoon, 1933.

Rogge, H. C. *Beschrijvende Catalogus der Pamfletten-Verzameling van de Boikerij der Remonstrantsche Kerk te Amsterdam.* Vol. 1, part 1. Amsterdam: J. H. Scheltema, 1863.

————. *Caspar Janszoon Coolhaes, de Voorlooper van Arminius en de Remonstranten.* 2 vols. Amsterdam: Y. Rogge, 1865.

————. *Johannes Wtenbogaert En Zijn Tijd.* Amsterdam: Y. Rogge, 1874–76.

Rutgers, F. L. *Calvijns Invloed Op de Reformatie in de Nederlanden, Voor Zooveel Die Door Hemzelven is Uitgeoefend.* 2d ed. Leiden: D. Donner, 1899.

Schaff, Philip. *History of the Christian Church.* 8 vols. New York: Harper and Brothers, 1910.

————. *The Creeds of Christendom, with a History and Critical Notes.* 6th ed. 3 vols. New York: Harper & Brothers, 1919.

Schwarzenau, Paul. *Der Wandel im theologischen Ansatz bei Melanchthon von 1525–1535.* Gütersloh, C. Bertelsmann, 1956.

Schwiebert, Ernest G. *The Reformation.* Minneapolis, MN: Fortress Press, 1996.

Scott, Thomas. *The Articles of the Synod of Dort and its Rejection of Errors, with the History of Events Which made Way For That Synod, As Published By the Authority of the States-General; and the Documents Confirming Its Decision.* Utica, NY: William Williams, 1831.

Scharlemann, Robert. *Aquinas and Gerhard: Theological Controversy and Construction in Medieval and Protestant Scholaticism.* New Haven: Yale University Press, 1964.

Shepherd of Hermas. *Mandates.* In *The Apostolic Fathers.* The Loeb Classical Library, ed. G. P. Goold, 2:1–306. Cambridge, MA: Harvard University Press; London: William Heinemann, 1974.

Slaatte, Howard. *The Arminian Arm of Theology: The Theologies of John Fletcher, first Methodist theologian, and His Precursor, James Arminius.* Washington DC: University Press of America, 1977.

Steinmetz, David Curtis. *Reformers in the Wings.* Grand Rapids: Baker Book House, 1981.

Tatian. *Address to the Greeks.* In *Fathers of the Second Century: Hermas, Tatian, Athenagoras, Theophilus and Clement of Alexandria.* Vol. 2, *The Ante-Nicene Fathers. Translations of the writings of the fathers down to A.D. 325,* ed. Alexander Roberts and James Donaldson, 59–84. Buffalo, NY: Christian Literature Publishing Company, 1885. Reprint, Peabody, MA: Hendrickson Publishers.

Taurinus, Jacob. *Van de onderlinge Verdraagsammheydt: tegen Jacobi Triglandi Recht-Gematigden Christen.* 2d ed. Utrecht: Ian Evertsen van Doorn, 1615.

Tertullian. *The Five Books Against Marcion.* In *Latin Christianity: Fathers Its Founder, Tertullian.* Vol. 2, *The Ante-Nicene Fathers. Translations of the writings of the fathers down to A.D. 325,* ed. Alexander Roberts and James Donaldson, 269–476. Buffalo, NY: Christian Literature Publishing Company, 1885. Reprint, Peabody, MA: Hendrickson Publishers.

Theophilus of Antioch. *Theophilus to Autolycus.* In *Fathers of the Second Century: Hermas, Tatian, Athenagoras, Theophilus and Clement of Alexandria.* Vol. 2, *The Ante-Nicene Fathers. Translations of the writings of the fathers down to A.D. 325,* ed. Alexander Roberts and James Donaldson, 85–122. Buffalo, NY: Christian Literature Publishing Company,

1885. Reprint, Peabody, MA: Hendrickson Publishers.

Thomas, Aquinas. *Aquinas on Creation: Writings on the "Sentences" of Peter Lombard, book 2.* Edited by Steven Earl Baldner and William E. Carroll. Mediaeval sources in translation; 35. Toronto: Pontifical Institute of Mediaeval Studies, 1997.

Tideman, Johannes. *De Remonstrantsche Broederschap: biographische naamlijst van hare professoren, predikanten en proponenten, met historische aanteekeningen omtrent hare kweekschool en gemeenten.* Haarlem: Erven F. Bohn, 1847.

—————. *De Remonstrantie en Het Remonstrantisme: Historisch Onderzoek.* Haarlem: E.F. Bohn, 1851.

—————. *De stichting der Remonstrantsche Broederschap, 1619–1634: Uit en Met de Oorspronkelijke Bescheiden Medegedeeld.* 2 vols. Amsterdam: Y. Rogge, 1871.

—————. *Het Seminarium der Remonstranten te Amsterdam: Afscheid bij den overgang naar Leiden, op den 16den December 1872, in de gehoorzaal van het Amsterdamsche Athenaeum.* Amsterdam: Y. Rogge, 1873.

Tyacke, Nicholas. *Anti-Calvinists: The Rise of English Arminianism, c. 1590–1640.* Oxford: Clarendon Press, 1987.

Van der Hoeven, Abraham des Amorie. *Het Tweede Eeuwfeest van het seminarium der Remonstranten te Amsterdam op den 28 October MDCCCXXXIV plegtig gevierd.* Leeuwarden: G. T. N. Suringar, 1840.

Van der Poel, Marc. *Cornelius Agrippa, The Humanist Theologian and His Declamations.* Leiden: E.J. Brill, 1997.

Van der Walt, B. J. *Natuurlike Teologie, met besondere aandag aan di visie daarop by Thomas van Aquino, Johannes Calvyn en die "Synopsis Purioris Theologiæ."* 2 vols. Franeker: Wever, 1974.

Van Gelder, H. A. Enno. *The Two Reformations in the 16th century: A Study of the Religious Aspects and Consequences of the Renaissance and Humanism.* The Hague: M. Nijhoff, 1961.

Van Goudoever, J., H. J. Heering, Gerrit Jan Hoenderdaal, J. L. Klink, A. M. van Peski, S. Vuyk, and W. R. M. Noordhoff. *De Remonstrantse Broederschap.* Lochem: De Tijdstroom, 1964.

Van Itterzon, G. P. *Franciscus Gomarus.* The Hague: M. Nijhoff, 1930.

—————. *Het Gereformeerd Leerboek der 17de Eeuw: "Synopsis Purioris Theologiæ."* The Hague: M. Nijhoff, 1931.

Van Stam, F. P. *The Controversy over the Theology of Saumur, 1635–1650: Disrupting Debates Among the Huguenots in Complicated Circumstances.* Amsterdam: APA-Holland University Press, 1988.

Venema, Cornelis P. *Heinrich Bullinger and the Doctrine of Predestination: Author of "the Other Reformed Tradition"?* Grand Rapids: Baker Academic, 2002.

Voetius, Gisbert. *Selectæ Disputationes Theologicæ.* In *Reformed Dogmatics,* ed. John W. Beardslee III, 265–334. Grand Rapids: Eerdmans, 1977.

Voogt, Gerrit. *Constraint on trial: Dirck Volckertsz Coornhert and religious freedom.* Sixteenth-Century Essays & Studies, vol. 52. Kirksville, MO: Truman State University Press, 2000.

Wakefield, Gordon S. "Arminianism in the Seventeenth and Eighteenth Centuries." *London Quarterly and Holborn Review* 185, 6th ser., no. 29 (1960): 253–258.

Winkelman, P. H. *Remonstranten en Katholieken in de eeuw van Hugo de Groot.* Nijmegen: Uitgeverij de Koepel, 1945.

Wüllschleger, L. *Scheurmakers en Nieuwlichters: Over Remonstranten en Contra-Remonstranten te 's-Gravenhage (1612–1618).* Leiden: Uitgeverij J. J. Groen en Zoon, 1989.

Encyclopedias and Dictionaries

Audi, Robert. *The Cambridge Dictionary of Philosophy.* 2d ed. Cambridge: Cambridge University Press, 1999.

Blackburn, Simon, ed. *The Oxford Dictionary of Philosophy.* Oxford, New York: Oxford University Press, 1994.

Buchberger, Michael, Josef Höfer, and Karl Rahner, ed. *Lexikon für Theologie und Kirche.* Freiburg: Herder, 1957.

Brockhaus, F. A. *Der Grosse Brockhaus.* 16th ed, 15 vols. Wiesbaden: Brockhaus, 1952.

Craig, Edward, ed. *Routledge Encyclopedia of Philosophy.* London: Routledge, 1998.

Cross, F. L., and Elizabeth A. Livingstone, ed. *The Oxford Dictionary of the Christian Church.* New York: Oxford University Press, 1997.

Eliade, Mircea, and Charles J. Adams. *The Encyclopedia of Religion.* 16 vols. New York: Macmillan, 1987.

Elwell, Walter A., ed. *Evangelical Dictionary of Theology.* Grand Rapids: Baker Book House, 1984.

Galling, Kurt, and Hans Campenhausen. *Die Religion in Geschichte und Gegenwart: Handwörterbuch für Theologie und Religionswissenschaft,* 3d ed. Tübingen, Mohr, 1957.

Fahlbusch, Erwin. *Evangelisches Kirchenlexikon Internationale Theologische Enzyklopädie.* 5 vols. Göttingen: Vandenhoeck & Ruprecht, 1985.

Fahlbusch, Erwin, and Geoffrey William Bromiley. *The Encyclopedia of Christianity.* Grand Rapids: Eerdmans, 1999.

McKim, Donald K, ed. *Encyclopedia of the Reformed faith.* Louisville, KY: Westminster/John Knox Press, 1992.

Meagher, P. K., Thomas C. O'Brien, and Consuelo Maria Aherne, ed. *Encyclopedic Dictionary of Religion.* Philadelphia, PA: Sisters of St. Joseph of Philadelphia, Corpus Publications, 1979.

Rahner, Karl. *A Concise Theological Dictionary.* Edited by Cornelius Ernst. Translated by Richard Strachan. Freiburg: Herder; London: Burns & Oates, 1965.

Articles, Periodicals and Unpublished Dissertations and Manuscripts

Atkinson, Lowell M. "The Achievement of Arminius." *Religion in Life* 19 (Summer 1950): 431–9.

Bangs, Carl O. "Arminius and Reformed Theology." Ph.D. diss., University of Chicago, 1958.

———. "Arminius and the Reformation." *Church History* 30 (June 1961): 155–170.

———. "Recent Studies in Arminianism." *Religion in Life* 32 (summer 1963): 421–8.

————. "Dutch Theology, Trade and War: 1590–1610." *Church History* 39 (Dec. 1970): 470–482.

————. "Arminius As A Reformed Theologian." In *The heritage of John Calvin: Heritage Hall lectures, 1960–70*, ed. John H. Bratt, 209–22. Grand Rapids: Eerdmans, 1973.

————. "All the Best Bishoprics and Deaneries: The Enigma of Arminian Politics." *Church History* 42 (March 1973): 5–16.

Bergsma, Wiebe. "The Low Countries." In *The Reformation in National Context*, ed. Robert W. Scribner, Roy Porter and Mikuláš Teich, 67–79. Cambridge: Cambridge University Press, 1994.

Blaising, Craig. "John Wesley's Doctrine of Original Sin." Ph.D. diss., Dallas Theological Seminary, 1979.

Boughton, Lynne Courter. "Supralapsarianism and the Role of Metaphysics in Sixteenth-Century Reformed Theology." *Westminster Theological Journal* 48 (spring 1986): 63–96.

Brown, Stephen F. "Peter of Candia's Hundred-Year 'History' of the Theologian's Role." In *Medieval philosophy & theology*, ed. Norman Kretzmenn, Mark D. Jordan, Stephen F. Brown, David B. Burrell, Kent Jr. Emery and Eleonore Stump, 156–74. Notre Dame: University of Notre Dame Press, 1991.

Chadwick, Owen. "Arminianism in England." *Religion in Life* 29 (autumn 1960): 548–56.

Clark, F. Stuart. "Arminius' Understanding of Calvin." *Evangelical Quarterly* 54 (Jan–Mar 1982): 25–35.

————. "The Theology of Arminius." *London Quarterly and Holborn Review* 185, 6th ser., no. 29 (1960): 248–53.

Collinson, Patrick. "England and International Calvinism, 1558–1640." In *International Calvinism, 1541–1715*, ed. Menna Prestwich, 197–223. Oxford: Clarendon Press, 1985.

D'Alton, Craig W. "The Trojan War of 1518: Melodrama, Politics and the Rise of Humanism." *Sixteenth Century Journal* 28 (spring 1997): 727–38.

Dantine, Johannes. "Die prädestinationslehre bei Calvin und Beza." Ph.D. diss., Göttingen University, 1965.

————. "Das christologische Problem in rahmen der Prädestinationslehre von Theodor Beza." *Zietschrift fur Kirchengeschichte* 78 (1966): 81–96.

————. "Les Tabelles sur la doctrine de la prédestination par Théodore de Bèze." *Revue de Théologie et de Philosophie* 15 (1966): 365–77.

De Yong, Peter Y. "Rise of the Reformed Churches in the Netherlands." In *Crisis in the Reformed Churches: Essays in the Commemoration of the Great Synod of Dort, 1618–1619*, ed. Peter Y. De Yong, 1–21. Grand Rapids: Reformed Fellowship, 1968.

————. "Appendix 1: The Canons of Dort." In *Crisis in the Reformed Churches: Essays in the Commemoration of the Great Synod of Dort, 1618–1619*, ed. Peter Y. De Yong, 229–62. Grand Rapids: Reformed Fellowship, 1968.

Dewar, M. W. "The British Delegation at the Synod of Dort." *Evangelical Quarterly* 46 (April–June 1974): 103–16.

Dipple, Geoffrey. "Humanists, Reformers and Anabaptists on Scholasticism and the Deterioration of the Church." *The Mennonite Quarterly Review* 68 (Oct 1994): 461–82.

Downey, E. A. "Comments on One of Heinrich Bullinger's Most Distinctive Treatises." In *Calvin: Erbe und Auftrag: Festschrift für Wilhelm Heinrich Neuser zum 65. Geburtstag*, ed. W. van 't Spijker and Wilhelm H. Neuser, 270–78. Kampen: J. H. Kok, 1991.

Duke, Alistair C. "A Footnote to 'Marrano Calvinism' and the Troubles of 1566–1567 In The Netherlands." *Bibliotheque d'humanisme et Ranaissance* 30 (1968): 147–48.

————. "The Ambivalent Face of Calvinism in the Netherlands, 1561–1618." In *International Calvinism, 1541–1715*, ed. Menna Prestwich, 109–34. Oxford: Clarendon Press, 1985.

————. "The Netherlands." In *The Early Reformation in Europe, 142–65*. Cambridge: Cambridge University Press, 1992.

————. "Salvation by Coercion: the Controversy Surrounding the 'Inquisition' in the Low Countries on the Eve of the Revolt." In *Reformation principle and practice: essays in honour of Arthur Geoffrey Dickens*, ed. Peter Newman Brooks, 137–56. London: Scholar's Press, 1980.

Dulles, Avery. "Scholasticism and the Church." *Theology Today* 38 (Oct 1981): 338–43.

Fitzsimmons, Richard. "Building a Reformed ministry in Holland, 1572–1583." In *The Reformation of the Parishes: The Ministry and the Reformation in Town and Country*, ed. Andrew Pettegree, 175–94. Manchester: Manchester University Press, 1993.

Fowler, S. "Faith and Reason in the Period of the Reformation." In *Our Reformational Tradition: A Rich Heritage and Lasting Vocation*, 62–85. Potchefstroom: Potchefstroom University for Christian Higher Education, 1984.

Gamble, Richard C. "Exposition and Method in Calvin." *Westminster Theological Journal* 49 (spring 1987): 153–65.

Godfrey, W. Robert. "Tensions within International Calvinism: The Debate on the Atonement at the Synod of Dort, 1618–1619." Ph.D. diss., Stanford University, 1974.

————. "Calvin and Calvinism in the Netherlands." In *John Calvin, His Influence in the Western world*, ed. W. Stanford Reid and Paul Woolley, 93–120. Grand Rapids, MI: Zondervan Publishing House, 1982.

Groenewegen, H. Y. "Arminius en de Remonstrantie." In *De Remonstranten Gedenkboek bij het 300-jarig betstaan der Remonstrantsche Broederschap*, ed. G. J. Heering, 61–77. Leiden: A. W. Sijthoff's Uitgevers, 1919.

Hales, John. "Letters from Dort." In *Golden Remains, of the Ever Memorable, Mr. John Hales, of Eaton-Colledge, &c.* London: Printed by Tho. Newcomb for Robert Pawlet, 1673.

Hall, Basil. "Calvin Against the Calvinists." In *John Calvin: A Collection of Distinguished Essays*, ed. Gervase Duffield, 19–37. Grand Rapids: Eerdmans, 1966.

————. "The Calvin Legend." In *John Calvin, ed. Gervase E. Duffield and F. L. Battles*, 1–18. Appleford: Sutton Courtenay Publishing, 1966.

Heering, G. J. "Het Godsdienstig Beginsel." In *De Remonstranten Gedenkboek bij het 300-jarig bestaan der Remonstrantsche Broederschap*, ed. G. J. Heering, 5–35. Leiden: A. W. Sijthoof's Uitgevers, 1919.

————. "Episcopius en de Synod." In *De Remonstranten Gedenkboek bij het 300-jarig bestaan der Remonstrantsche Broederschap*, ed. G. J. Heering, 79–108. Leiden: A. W. Sijthoof's Uitgevers, 1919.

Hicks, John Mark. "The Theology of Grace in the Thought of Jacobus Arminius and Philip van Limborch: A Study in the Development of Seventeenth-Century Dutch Arminianism." Ph.D. diss., Westminster Theological Seminary, 1985.

Hoenderdaal, Gerrit Jan. "The Life and Thought of Jacobus Arminius." *Religion in Life* 29 (autumn 1960): 540–7.

————. "Uytenbogaert in Untrecht." *Nederlands Theologisch Tijdschrift* 22 (Jan. 1967): 3–12.

————. "A Dutch Theology of Toleration." *Religion in Life* 42 (winter 1973): 449–55.

————. "Arminius en Episcopius." *Nederlands Archief voor Kerkgeschiedenis* 60 (1980): 203–35.

————. "Begin en beginsel." In *Staat in de vijheid: de geschiedenis van de remonstranten*, ed. Gerrit J. Hoenderdaal and P. M. Luca, 9–55. Zutphen: De Walburg Pers, 1982.

Hommius, Festus. "Appendix A: Acts of the Synod of Dordrecht." In *The Voice of Our Fathers*, ed. and trans. Homer C. Hoeksema, 45–102. Grand Rapids: Reformed Free Publishing Association, 1980.

Ijsewijn, Jozef. "Humanism in the Low Countries." In *Renaissance Humanism: Foundations, Forms, and Legacy*, ed. Albert Rabil, 2:156–215. Philadelphia: University of Pennsylvania Press, 1988.

Jinkins, Michael. "Theodore Beza: Continuity and Regression in the Reformed Tradition." *Evangelical Quarterly* 64 (April 1992): 131–154.

Jonge, Christiaan de. "De irenische ecclesiologie van Franciscus Junius (1545–1602)." Ph.D. diss., University of Leyden, 1980.

Kelly, Douglas F. "A Rehabilitation of Scholasticism? A Review Article of Richard Muller's Post-Reformation Reformed Dogmatics, vol. 1, Prolegomena to Theology." *Scottish Bulletin of Evangelical Theology* 6 (spring 1988): 112–22.

Kingdon, Robert McCune. "Geneva and the Coming of the Wars of Religion in France." Ph.D. diss., Columbia University, 1955.

————. "Popular Reactions to the Debate between Bolsec and Calvin." In *Calvin: Erbe und Auftrag: Festschrift für Wilhelm Heinrich Neuser zum 65. Geburtstag*, ed. W. van 't Spijker and Wilhelm H. Neuser, 138–45. Kampen: J. H. Kok, 1991.

Kistemaker, Simon. "Leading Figures at the Synod of Dort." In *Crisis in the Reformed Churches: Essays in the Commemoration of the Great Synod of Dort, 1618–1619*, ed. Peter Y. De Yong, 39–51. Grand Rapids: Reformed Fellowship, 1968.

Klooster, Fred H. "The Doctrinal Deliverances of Dort." In *Crisis in the Reformed Churches: Essays in the Commemoration of the Great Synod of Dort, 1618–1619*, ed. Peter Y. De Yong, 52–94. Grand Rapids: Reformed Fellowship, 1968.

Knappert, L. "Episcopius en de Synode." In *De Remonstranten Gedenkboek bij het 300-jarig bestaan der Remonstrantsche Broederschap*, ed. G. J. Heering, 79–108. Leiden: A. W. Sijthoof's Uitgevers, 1919.

Knetsch F. R. J. "Church Ordinances and Regulations of the Dutch Synods 'Under the Cross' (1563–1566) Compared With The French (1559–1663)." In *Humanism and Reform: The Church in Europe, England, and Scotland, 1400–1643: Essays in Honour of James K. Cameron*, ed. James Kirk, Studies in church history. Subsidia; 8 (Oxford: Published for the Ecclesiastical History Society by Basil Blackwell, 1991)

Kuiper, E. J. "Hugo de Groot en de Remonstranten." *Nederlands Theologisch Tijdschrift* 38 (April 1984): 111–25.

Letham, Robert. "Theodore Beza: A Reassessment." *Scottish Journal of Theology* 40 (1987): 25–40.

Lorentzen, Carl. "Dieryck Volkertszoon Coornhert: der Vorläufer der Remonstranten: ein Vorkämpfter der Gewissensfreiheit: Versuch einer Biographie." Ph.D. diss., University of Jena, 1886.

MacCulloch, Diarmaid. "Arminius and the Arminians." *History Today* 39 (October 1989): 27–34.

Meeuwsen, James. "Original Arminianism and Methodistic Arminianism Compared." *Reformed Review* 14 (spring 1960): 21–36.

Muller, Richard A. "Perkin's A Golden Chaine: Predestinarian System or Schematized Ordo Saludis?" *Sixteenth Century Journal* 9 (1978): 69–82.

———. "Vera Philosophia cum sacra Theologia nusquam pugnat: Kickermann on Philosophy, Theology, and the Problem of Double Truth." *Sixteenth Century Journal* 15 (fall 1984): 341–364.

———. "Scholastic Protestant and Catholic: Francis Turretin on the Object and Principles of Theology." *Church History* 55 (June 1986): 193–205.

———. "Arminius and the Scholastic Tradition." *Calvin Theological Journal* 24 (Nov 1989): 263–77.

———. "The Priority of the Intellect in the Soteriology of Jacob Arminius." *Westminster Theological Journal* 55 (spring 1993): 55–72.

———. "Calvin and the 'Calvinists': Assessing Continuities and Discontinuities Between Reformation and Orthodoxy." *Calvin Theological Journal* 30 (Nov 1995): 345–75.

Nauert, Charles G, Jr. "The Clash of Humanists and Scholastics: An Approach to Pre-Reformation Controversies." *Sixteenth Century Journal* 4 (April 1973): 1–18.

———. "Humanism as Method: Roots of Conflict with the Scholastics." *Sixteenth Century Journal* 29 (summer 1998): 427–38.

Nijenhuis, Willem. "Variants within Dutch Calvinism in the Sixteenth Century." *The Low Countries History Yearbook* 12 (1979): 48–64.

Nuttall, Geoffry F. "The Influence of Arminianism on American Theology." In *Man's Faith and Freedom: The Theological Influence of Jacobus Arminius*, ed. Gerald O. McCulloh, 46–63. New York: Abingdon Press, 1962.

Perreiah, Alan. "Humanist Critiques of Scholastic Dialectic." *Sixteenth Century Journal* 13 (fall 1982): 3–22.

Praamsma, Louis. "The Background of the Arminian Controversy (1586–1618)." In *Crisis in the Reformed Churches: Essays in Commemoration of the great Synod of Dort, 1618–1619*, ed. Peter Y. De Yong, 22–38. Grand Rapids: Reformed Fellowship, Inc., 1968.

Raitt, Jill. "Probably they are God's children: Theodore Beza's Doctrine of Baptism." In *Humanism and Reform: The Church in Europe, England, and Scotland, 1400–1643. Essays in Honour of James K. Cameron*, ed. James Kirk, 151–70. Oxford: Published for the Ecclesiastical History Society by Basil Blackwell, 1991.

Rattenbury, H. Morley. "The Historical Background and Life of Arminius." *London Quarterly and Holborn Review* 185, 6th ser., no. 29 (1960): 243–8.

Reid, W. Stanford. "The Transmission of Sixteenth Century Calvinism." In *John Calvin, His influence in the Western world*, ed. W. Stanford Reid and Paul Woolley, 34–50. Grand Rapids: Zondervan Publishing House, 1982.

Reitsma, Johannes. "Franciscus Junius: een levensbeeld uit den eersten tijd der kerkhervorming." Ph.D. thesis, Hoogeschool te Groningen, 1864.

Rummel, Erika. "Et cum theologo bella poeta gerit: The Conflict between Humanists and Scholastics Revisited." *Sixteenth Century Journal* 23 (winter 1992): 713–26.

Sinnema, Donald. "Antoine de Chandieu's Call For A Scholastic Reformed Theology (1580)." Unpublished manuscript.

Spaans, Joke. "Unity and Diversity in Dutch Religion." In Unity and Diversity in the Church: papers read at the 1994 Summer Meeting, and the 1995 Winter Meeting of the Ecclesiastical History Society, ed. R. N. Swanson, 221–34. Cambridge, Mass.: Basil Blackwell Publishers for The Ecclesiastical History Society, 1996.

————. "Unity and Diversity as a Theme in Early Modern Dutch Religious History: An Interpretation." In Unity and Diversity in the Church, ed. R. N. Swanson. Oxford: The Ecclesiast, 1996.

Spencer, Stephen R. "Reformed Scholasticism in Medieval Perspective: Thomas Aquinas and Francois Turrettini on the Incarnation." Ph.D. diss., Michigan State University, 1988.

Tideman, Johannes. "Remonstrantisme en Ramisme." Studiën en Bijdragen op't Gebied der Historische Theologie 3 (1876): 389–429.

Van der Walt, Barend Johannes. "The Synopsis Purioris Theologiæ—Is It Really So Pure? Philosophical Impurities in the Post-Dortian Theology." In Our Reformational tradition: a rich heritage and lasting vocation, 378–423. Potchefstroom: Potchefstroom University for Christian Higher Education, 1984.

Van Holk, Lambertus Jacobus. "From Arminius to Arminianism in Dutch Theology." In Man's Faith and Freedom: The Theological Influence of Jacobus Arminius, ed. Gerald O. McCulloh, 27–45. New York: Abingdon Press, 1962.

Van't Hooft, Antonius Johannes. "De Theologie van Heinrich Bullinger in Betrekking tot de Nederlandsche Reformatie." Ph.D. thesis, Rijksuniversiteit te Leiden, 1888.

Vos, Arvin. "As the Philosopher Says: Thomas Aquinas and the Classical Heritage." In Christianity and the Classics: The Acceptance of a Heritage, ed. Wendy E. Helleman, 69–82. Lanham, MD: University Press of America, 1990.

————. "Calvin: The Theology of a Christian Humanist." In Christianity and the Classics: The Acceptance of a Heritage, ed. Wendy E. Helleman, 109–18. Lanham: University Press of America, 1990.

Waterbolk, F. H. "Humanisme en de Tolerantie-Gedachte." In Opstand en pacificatie in de Lage Landen. Bijdrage tot de studie van de pacificatie van Gent, 308–21. Ghent: Snoeck-Ducaju/Nijgh & Van Ditmar, 1976.

Weaver, Dennis. "From Paul to Augustine: Romans 5:12 in Early Christian Exegesis." St. Vladimir's Theological Quarterly 27 (1983): 187–206.

————. "The Exegesis of Romans 5:12 Among the Greek Fathers and its Implications for the Doctrine of Original Sin: the 5th–12th Centuries." St. Vladimir's Theological Quarterly 29 (1985): 133–59.

————. "The Exegesis of Romans 5:12 Among the Greek Fathers and its Implications for the Doctrine of Original Sin: the 5th–12th Centuries." St. Vladimir's Theological Quarterly 29 (1985): 230–57.

Wooden, Warren W. "Anti-Scholastic Satire in Sir Thomas More's Utopia." Sixteenth Century Journal 7 (1977): 29–45.

Index

•A•

Amyraut, Moise, 37
Anabaptists (Mennonites), 26
Arianism, 39
Arminius, Jacobus, 1-6,
    and scholasticism, 11
    biography, 30-31
    on original sin, 63, 68-79
    on grace, 79-84
    on the *imago dei*, 64-67
    on faith, 80-81
Arminianism, 4, 41, 117, 177
    and Reformed Scholasticism, 7
    definition, 1–2
    as a pre-Calvinist Reformed
      movement, 27, 29–30
Armstrong, Brian, 10-11, 177-178
Augustine of Hippo, 5, 7, 31, 65, 72-73,
    81, 85, 105, 130, 180

•B•

Bangs, Carl, 1-2
Beza, Theodore, 4, 5, 10-12, 30-31, 35,
    63, 69, 70, 72, 75, 102, 177
Belgic Confession, 27, 29, 30
Bernard of Clairveaux, 65
Bogerman, Johannus, 35-36
Bray, John, 11, 117
Bullinger, Heinrich, 3, 26-27
Borrius, Adrianus, 33, 76-77.

•C-D•

Calvin, John, 1, 2, 4-5, 7, 9-13, 27-28, 30-
    31, 63-66, 71-76, 106, 154, 184
Calvinism, 2-3, 26-27, 37-38, 83
Cameron, John, 37
Capellus, Jacob, 37
Charles V, 27
Confessio Remonstrantes, 13, 37-38, 40-41,
    121-127
Curcellæus, Stephanus, 39
Descartes, René, 3, 183
Dort, Synod of, 3, 32–36, 121, 149, 178

•E•

Enlightenment, the 3-4, 183-84
Episcopius, Simon, 3, 5, 12
    biography, 32–39
    comparison with the Greek Fathers,
      124-125
    on grace, 103-07, 112-17, 120-24,
      164-65
    on original sin, 99-103, 110-12, 118-
      20, 150-52, 157-64
    on the *imago Dei*, 108-10, 118, 153-
      57
Erasmus, Desiderius, 11–12, 26, 30, 184
Erastus, Thomas, and Erastianism, 28, 30,
    41, 102

•F-G•

Foreknowledge, 7, 72, 106, 128, 179-80
Free will, 5, 7, 38, 64-65, 69-70, 73, 80-
    84, 107, 111, 114, 120, 126-129, 154,
    156, 158, 163-64, 166, 179-80, 182,
    185
Grynaeus, Johannes, 12, 31
Gomarus, Franciscus, 31-32, 34, 36, 70,
    101
Gomarists, 33, 35, 40, 83, 161
Grevinchoven, Nicholas, 3, 37- 38

•H-I•

Haentjens, A. H.
    Relationship between Arminius and
        his followers, 2–3
    Research into the life of Episcopius,
        6, 33, 129, 182
Hales, John, 35
Hemmingius, Nicholas, 25–26, 27.
Heidelberg Catechism, 29
Heyden, Abraham van der, 39
Hicks, John Mark, 2–3, 125
Hommius, Festus, 6, 35
Humanism, 7-9, 40, 177

•J-K-L•

Junius, Franciscus, 5, 12, 31, 63-64, 72,
    77, 102, 104, 114, 130, 178, 183-84
Limborch, Philip van, 1, 2-3, 39, 52, 129,
Luther, 7, 26, 65
Luthernism in the Netherlands, 26-28

•M-N•

Maccovius, Johannes, 36
Martinus, Matthias, 36
Melanchthon, Philip, 3, 9, 11, 26-27
Maurice of Nassau, 29, 34, 37
Muller, Richard, 10-12, 178

Netherlands, the
    events leading up to the
        Reformation, 25–30
    Arminian controversy, 30-32

•O•

Original sin, 1-2, 5, 63-64, 66, 74-78, 102-
    4, 116-17, 123, 128-130, 150-52, 157-
    64, 166, 177-82, 184
Oldenbarnevelt, Johannes, 29, 32, 34,
    102, 177

•P-Q•

Pelagius, 5, 69, 113, 180
Perkins, William, 3, 31, 64, 70, 71, 75, 77,
    81-82, 178, 183-84
Pelagianism, 2, 5, 35, 37-38, 63, 114,
Plancius, Petrus, 29, 32-33
Platt, John, 6, 11
Polyander, Johannes 31
Poppius, Eduardus, 38
Predestination, 2, 5, 11, 26-32, 38, 64, 72,
    75, 102, 106, 111, 125, 166, 177-78,
    180, 185

•R-S•

Remonstrant Brotherhood, 36-38, 41, 79,
    149, 166, 178
Sybrandus, Lubbertus 23–24
Scholasticism, 5-12, 26, 64, 68, 70, 80, 85,
    101, 104, 112-113, 118-19, 130, 153,
    164, 177-78, 181, 183-84
Semi-Pelagianism, 2, 35, 85, 129, 179
Socinianism, 2, 6, 34-35, 37-39
Spinoza, Benedict, 3

•T-U-V•

Triglandius, Jacobus, 6, 38-39
Voetius, Gisbertus, 11

•W-X-Y-Z•

Walæus, Antonius, 38
Walt, B. J. vander
    evaluation of the *Synopsis Purioris*, 10
William the Silent, 28-31
Wtenbogaert, Ioannis 3, 29, 31-35, 37,
   39-40, 101